Governance of Public Health Response to HIV/AIDS in India

Governance of Public Health Response to HIV/AIDS in India

(Ed.)

Prof. Manoj Kar

KALPAZ

First Published, 2020

Published by

Kalpaz Publications
C-30, Satyawati Nagar,
Delhi – 110052
Ph.: 011-47034999, 9811692060
www.kalpazpublications.com
E-mail: kalpaz@hotmail.com

Printed at: G. Print Process, Delhi

Cataloging in Publication Data—DK
Courtesy: D.K. Agencies (P) Ltd. <docinfo@dkagencies.com>

Kar, Manoj, author.
Governance of public health response to HIV/AIDS in India / Prof. Manoj Kar.
pages cm
Includes bibliographical references and index.
ISBN 9789353240813

1. HIV infections—Government policy—India. 2. AIDS (Disease)—Government policy—India. I. Title.

LCC RA643.86.I4K37 2020 | DDC 362.196979200954 23

If We Fail to Plan – We are Planning to Fail
— Benjamin Franklin

Dedicated to the Voiceless Silent Majority of People Living with HIV/AIDS who all depend on Effective governance AND planning of public health responses - On their Empowerment with Community Based HIV/AIDS support services in ending AIDS And also by using Health Systems Strengthening approaches For achieving Universal Health Coverage by 2030

HIV/AIDS is a crisis of poverty, enormous spiritual, social, economic, political determinants and proportions. And, increasingly, it is a problem of the young. Overcoming HIV/AIDS and attached stigma that fuels its spread is one of the most serious challenges of present day around the world. It requires tremendous amount of courage, commitment and leadership at all levels, especially among Government and Non-Government Leaders in partnerships who can use the trust and authority they have in their countries, especially in their respective communities to change the course of the pandemic.

An important point to consider when taking action in prevention, care, support & treatment for HIV/AIDS, is that there are many organizations and individuals also responding to HIV/AIDS who want to be availing of health care services. Find ways to team up with local non-governmental organizations or PLWHAS network/groups and government involving others who may be specialists in various fields. In many cases, this will mean providing the compassion for comprehensive care, support and treatment with moral support that can break through the judgement, shame and fear so often associated with HIV/AIDS. This will further contribute to address and reduce "Stigma and Discrimination" attached to HIV/AIDS and Health Care support systems including general population who all depend upon the effective governance of Equitable, Accountable and Stronger Health Systems for Universal Health Coverage.

Preface

The HIV/AIDS epidemic in India is now about twenty five years old; however, the incidence of HIV continues to give cause for alarm, as the virus continues to spread into new areas as well as new low-risk population groups. India has seen commendable responses to combat the epidemic, from the government, non-government as well as international development organizations.

Funding availability for HIV/AIDS programmes in low-income and middle-income countries rose from US$300 million in 1996 to $10 billion in 2007. However, a combination of worldwide economic uncertainty, a global food crisis, and research publications that indicate discontent with progress in fighting the HIV/AIDS pandemic will not only threaten to restrict increases in the overall availability of both donor and national funds, but will also increase the competition for resources during the move towards universal access to treatment and prevention services. The emerging challenges for good governance in generating effective in Public Health Response to HIV/AIDS management is worth sharing for a global public health community, academia, researchers and policy makers who all are struggling to draw lessons from recently convened assessment of country specific health MDGs and strategising necessary policy inputs and reforms for addressing Health and Wellbeing under SDGs (Sustainable Development Goals).

What roles have government, donors and other organisations played during this successful phase of NACP as public health response? How effective has this collective health sector response been? How can government leadership, accountability and partnerships make a greater difference to controlling the magnitude and impact of the epidemic? This book addresses these issues by focusing first on the most important aspect of the epidemic: its developmental nature. The book begins by arguing that underdevelopment and poverty are the main reasons why a significant proportion of the population is vulnerable to the epidemic in the first place. In turn, the epidemic widens and deepens poverty by its serious economic impact on individuals, households and different sectors of the economy. Finally, ill-health and poverty are the inter-twined reasons why messages of prevention and control do not make an impact on a vast majority of the vulnerable population. Thus, understanding and incorporating these linkages and mainstreaming responses are the cornerstone of management of health sector response to HIV intervention. The analysis then goes on to look at the current epidemiological scenario and at the ongoing responses of the government, donors and NGOs.

Epidemiologically, despite commendable efforts, the number of people living with HIV in South and South-East Asia is dominated by India; in 2001, 63 percent of the Asia-Pacific total estimates of 6.1 million People Living with HIV (PLWH) were in India alone. HIV prevalence among the adult population aged 15–49, 0.3% in 2015, has remained low and stable across the region. With 2.1 million (1.7 million–2.6 million) PLHIV, India has the largest number of PLHIV in the region. Surveillance data indicate that risk practices are getting diffused and infection rates continue to rise among low-risk groups like pregnant mothers.

Epidemiological Situation in India in 2017:

- 2 100 000 people were living with HIV.
- HIV incidence—the number of new HIV infections among a susceptible population during a certain time—among all people of all ages was 0.1%.
- HIV prevalence—the percentage of people living with HIV—among adults (15–49 years) was 0.2%.
- 88 000 people were newly infected with HIV.
- 69 000 people died from an AIDS-related illness.

There has been progress in the number of AIDS-related deaths since 2010, with a 56% decrease, from 160 00 deaths to 69 000 deaths. The number of new HIV infections has decreased, from 120 000 to 88 000 in the same period.

The 90–90–90 targets envision that, by 2020, 90% of people living with HIV will know their HIV status, 90% of people who know their HIV-positive status will be accessing treatment and 90% of people on treatment will have suppressed viral loads. In terms of all people living with HIV, reaching the 90–90–90 targets means that 81% of all people living with HIV are on treatment and 73% of all people living with HIV are virally suppressed.

In 2017 in India:

- 79% of people living with HIV knew their status.
- 56% of people living with HIV were on treatment.
- Of all adults aged 15 years and over living with HIV, 56% were on treatment.

Sixty per cent of pregnant women living with HIV accessed antiretroviral medicine to prevent transmission of the virus to their baby, preventing 3500 new HIV infections among newborns. Early infant diagnosis¯the percentage of HIV-exposed infants tested for HIV before eight weeks of age¯stood at 23% in 2017.

Of the 2 100 000 adults living with HIV, 880 000 (41.9%) were women. HIV treatment was higher among women than men, with 63% of adult women living with HIV on treatment, compared to 50% of adult men. Same-sex sexual relations are legal in India.

Only 26.17% of women and men 15–24 years old correctly identified ways of preventing the sexual transmission of HIV.

In 2017, the percentage of people living with HIV and tuberculosis who were being treated for both diseases was 33.4%, down from 36.3% in 2015.

Research shows, considerable under-reporting of AIDS cases hide the fact that management and care of infected and affected individuals will pose a grave challenge to the resources and capacity of the country in generating effective management of Health Sector response to HIV/AIDS. Studies on economic impact of the epidemic in India indicate that individuals and households will increasingly find it difficult to cope with the economic hardships associated with increased treatment costs and reduced income due to illness and loss in productivity. Impact would also be felt severely by the health sector and the government, with government health subsidies rising rapidly as a result of a rapidly spreading epidemic. Finally, with antiretroviral therapy becoming more accessible due to price reductions especially by Indian firms, there will be increasing pressure on central and state governments and other agencies to look at the possibility of subsidizing these drugs, though questions of equity as well financial feasibility will continue to remain important issues despite price reductions.

Some of the gaps identified in the strategic management response are in the following areas: (a) inadequate understanding of barriers to scaling up, including lack of documentation and of evidence on what works; (b) prevention priorities yet to effectively include low risk population, bridge population, paediatric population, female sex workers, adolescents and youth; (c) operational research in issues of care and support for a better understanding of the epidemic, as well as innovative ways of involving and building capacity among PLWHA in research as well as interventions; (d) operational research on links between poverty, development, governance and HIV/AIDS; (e) focus on areas that have hitherto received less attention, especially states that see a lot of in- as well as out-migration; (f) greater emphasis on monitoring, evaluation and effectiveness in Governance.

India's commitment to Health MDGs and keeping in view this overall goal of NACP Planning during Phase III was to halt and reverse the epidemic in India over the next 5 years by integrating programmes for prevention, care, support and treatment. This has been successfully achieved through four strategic objectives namely:

1. Prevention of new infections in high risk groups and general population through:
    a. Saturation of coverage of high risk groups with targeted interventions (TIs)
    b. Scaled up interventions in the general population
2. Increasing the proportion of people living with HIV/AIDS who receive care, support and treatment.
3. Strengthening the infrastructure, systems and human resources in prevention, care, support and treatment programmes at the district, state and national levels.
4. Strengthening a nation-wide strategic information management system.

Governance of NACP- III is acclaimed globally as a participative and successful programme, and it is to the credit of the policy makers that to halt and reverse the epidemic, that they, along with strengthening of the existing health systems and structures, also adopted innovative strategies and reached out to the unreached. Some of the innovative strategies include - (i) Separate TG interventions; (ii) Link Worker Schemes; and (iii) Innovations in communication strategies for prevention focus. Lessons learnt as documented for future HIV response requires that governments function as suggested National Framework of implementation using health systems strengthening and development in close collaboration with PLHA communities, address stigma and discrimination, and efficiently invest domestic resources in evidence-based HIV testing and treatment interventions for populations in locations that need them most.

Scaling up of NACP III Planning - NACP IV Strategic Components

Component 1: Intensifying and Consolidating Prevention services with a focus on HRG and vulnerable populations

This component will support the scaling up of TIs with the aim of reaching out to the hard to reach population groups who do not yet access and use the prevention services of the program, and saturate coverage among the HRGs. In addition, this component will support the bridge population, i.e. migrants and truckers. Component 1 includes the following two subcomponents:

1.1 Scaling up coverage of TIs among HRG

The interventions under this sub-component will include: (i) the provision of behaviour change interventions to increase safe practices, testing and counselling, and adherence to treatment, and demand for other services;(ii) the promotion and provision of condoms to HRG to promote their use in each sexual encounter; (iii) provision or referral for STI services including counselling at service provision canters to increase compliance of patients with treatment, risk reduction counselling with focus on partner referral and management; (iv) needle and syringe exchange for IDUs as well as scaling up of Opioid Substitution Therapy (OST) provision. This sub-component also includes the financing of operating costs for about 25 State Training Resource Canters as well as participant training costs over a period of 5 years.

1.2 Scaling up of interventions among other vulnerable populations

The activities under this subcomponent will include: (i) risk assessment and size estimation of migrant population groups and truckers at transit points and at workplaces; (ii) behavior change communications (BCC) for creating awareness about risk and vulnerability, prevention methods, availability and location of services, increase safe behavior and demand for services as well as reduce stigma;(iii) promotion and provisioning of condoms through different channels including social marketing; (iv) development of linkages with local institutions, both public and NGO owned, for testing, counseling and STI treatment services;(v) creation of "peer support groups" and "safe spaces" for migrants at destination; (vi) establishment of need-based and gender-sensitive services for partners of IDUs; and(vii) strengthening networks of vulnerable populations with enhanced linkages to service centers and risk reduction interventions, specifically condom use.

Component 2: Expanding IEC services for (a) general population and (b) high risk groups with a focus on behavior change and demand generation

IEC has been an important component of the NACP. With the expansion of services for counseling and testing, ART, STI treatment and condom promotion, the demand generation campaigns will continue to be the focus of the NACP-IV communication strategy. IEC will remain an important component of all prevention efforts and will include:

- *Behaviour change communication strategies for HRGs, vulnerable groups and hard to reach populations.*
- *Increasing awareness among general population, particularly women and youth.*

Component 3: Comprehensive Care, Support and Treatment

NACP IV will implement comprehensive HIV care for all those who are in need of such services and facilitate additional support systems for women and children affected and infected with HIV / AIDS. It is envisaged that greater adherence and compliance would be possible with wide network of treatment facilities and collaborative support from PLHIV and civil society groups. Additional Centres of Excellence (CoEs) and upgraded ART Plus centres will be established to provide high-quality treatment and follow-up services, positive prevention and better linkages with health care providers in the periphery.

With increasing maturity of the epidemic, it is very likely that there will be greater demand for 2nd line ART, OI management. NACP IV will address these needs adequately. It is proposed that the comprehensive care, support and treatment of HIV/AIDS will inter alia include: (i) anti-retroviral treatment (ART) including second line (ii) management of opportunistic infections and (iii) facilitating social protection through linkages with concerned Departments/Ministries. The program will explore avenues of public-private partnerships. The program will enhance activities to reduce stigma and discrimination at all levels particularly at health care settings.

Component 4: Strengthening institutional capacities

The objective of NACP IV will be to consolidate the trend of reversal of the epidemic seen at the national level to all the key districts in India. The planning processes and systems will be further strengthened to ensure that the annual action plans are based on evidence, local priorities and in alignment with NACP IV objectives. Sustaining the epidemic response through increased collaboration and convergence, where feasible, with other departments will be given a high priority during NACP IV. This will involve phased integration of the HIV services with the routine public sector health delivery systems, streamlining the supply chain mechanisms and quality control mechanisms and building capacities of governmental and non-governmental institutions and networks using Health Systems Strengthening mechanisms.

Component 5: Strategic Information Management Systems (SIMS)

The roll-out of SIMS is ongoing since its implementation during NACP III and will be firmly established at all levels to support evidence based planning, program monitoring and measuring of programmatic impacts. The surveillance system will be further strengthened with focus on tracking the epidemic, incidence analysis, identifying pockets of infection and estimating the burden of infection. Research priorities will also be customized to the emerging needs of the program. The relevant, measurable and verifiable indicators will be identified and used appropriately for using HSS mechanisms and effectiveness in governance of health systems.

In this edited volume of experience on NACP Planning and Strategies, we discuss the evolution of goals of public health and health systems responses in combating HIV/AIDS in India. Also, the basic structure and approaches of public health sector as it exists in response to addressing HIV/AIDS care, support and treatment is elaborated through a set of programme strategies as per the planning and designing framework. In particular the book discusses the fundamental design challenges of the crisis of human resources, capacity building, financial accountability, procurement planning, institutional arrangements, communitization process involved through network of PLHAS and HIV/AIDS care, support and prevention strategies which effect the implementation of NACP through the framework of Health Systems Strengthening and suggestions for overcoming the constraints. Decentralized planning and management is emphasized through strengthening of District AIDS Prevention & Control Units within the existing Health Systems mechanism in the concerned district.

The purpose of sharing of the planning process achievements and successful outcomes are to encourage new generation health care providers, programme managers, policy makers, young public health professionals, NGOs/CBOs/PLHAS and researchers to understand the convergence challenges of health systems strengthening efforts with NACP implementation strategies for sustaining the capacities and technical assistance needs in generating a decentralised and participatory governance of public health responses with multisectoral partnerships in reversing the direction of HIV/AIDS epidemic. This version expecting to receive the lessons learning and experience gained in the form of feedback, observations and comments which will enable the creation of future editions of NACP planning and implementation challenges in India, especially within the national framework of SDGs and Universal Health Coverage by 2030 and preparations for revised strategies in New India.

Prof. Manoj Kar
Indian Institute of Education, Pune

Acknowledgments

The following individuals served as peer reviewers and provided valuable inputs to the planning process and also for this edited volume under the Phase III of NACP:

Sir. R.K. Mishra (IAS), Team Leader, NACP III; Dr. Bhagbanprakash, Lead Member-HRD, NACP III, Dr. K. Sudhakar, Lead Member, NACP III Planning, Dr. Kurien Thomas, Lead Member-Epidemiology and Public Health, Prof. Ramesh Bhatt, Lead Member-Health Financing, Dr. Sadhana Rout (IIS)-Lead Member – IEC-BCC & Communications, NACP III Planning, Dr. S.Y. Qureshi, AS & DG, NACO, Dr. Sunil Mehra, Dr. Ravi Verma, Population Council, Dr. C.K. George, Institute of Health Systems, Hyderabad, Dr. Pramod Kumar, Institute of Development Communications, Chandigarh, Dr. Ashis Panigrahi, ORG-New Delhi, Dr.Muna Ali, PWC, Mumbai, Dr. Ruma Tavaroth, World Bank, Dr. Meera Chatterjee, World Bank, Dr. Suneeta Singh, World Bank, Dr. Kees Kosterman, World Bank, Dr. Billey Stewart, DFID, New Delhi, Ms.Alka Narang, UNDP, Dr. B.B. Rewari, NACO, Dr. Ajay Khera, Dr. Md.Shauqat, Dr. Mayank Agarwal, NACO, Ms. Annadi Yuvraj, HIV/AIDS Alliance, Ms. Nandini Kapoor, UNAIDS, Dr. DCS Reddy, Independent Experts, Dr. Jai P. Narain, Regional Adviser, HIV/TB & Communicable Diseases, WHO-SEARO, Mr. Manoj Pardeshi, General Secretary, NCPI+/NMP+, Ms. Divya Verma, ILO, New Delhi, Dr. Sunil Mehra, Mamata Institute of Mother and Child Health Care, Dr. S.D. Gupta, IIHMR-Jaipur, Dr. Sheela Godbole, NARI-Pune, Dr. A. Elangovan, NIE, Chennai, Prof. Shalini Bharat, School of Health Science, TISS, Mumbai, Prof. M. Bhattacharya, NIHFW, New Delhi, Prof. Arvind Pandey, ICMR, New Delhi and Dr. Samiran Panda, Director, National AIDS Research Institute, Dr. Rajeev Sadanandan, UNAIDS India.

Glossary of Terms[1]

Accountability: Accountability is the obligation of people and organisations to live up to what is expected of them and to report on the use of resources; it also is the assumption of responsibility for one's actions and the consequences of such actions.

Acquired – in the context of AIDS, it means an illness that can be caught from another person.

AIDS – acquired immune deficiency syndrome, the dis- ease caused by HIV.

Antiretroviral medicines/antiretroviral (ARVs)/antiretroviral therapy (ART)/ HIV treatment: These are medicines that are used for treating HIV infection. They are highly effective in suppressing HIV virus and slowing the progress of HIV disease. ART has three or more drug combination such as tenofovir + Lamivudine and Efavirenz/Nevirapine or Zidovudine +Lamivudine and Efavirenz/Nevirapine.

Antiretroviral treatment – treatment with medicines that suppress the growth of HIV in the human body.

Behaviour Change Communication (May now be referred as Social Change Communication): Targeted and tailored messages that are provided to groups or individuals and are expected to bring about a transformational change in person's behaviour as well as society.

Bisexual: A person who is attracted to as well as has sexual relation with both men and women. This is a cultural identity and is usually self-identified.

Blood screening test – a special blood test that shows the presence of antibodies – proteins produced by the body to fight off foreign substances – to HIV in the blood of a person, indicating infection with HIV.

1. Adopted from UNAIDS Terminology Guidelines, 2015. Available at http://www.unaids.org/en/resources/ documents/2015/2015 terminology guidelines. Accessed on 10 Dec 2016.

Catalytic Funding: Catalytic funding is a term introduced by the Global Fund to define a separate reserve of funding that rewards high-impact, well-performing programmes and encourages ambitious but feasible requests that cularly strong case for investment.

Combination HIV prevention: The combination prevention approach seeks to achieve maximum impact on HIV prevention by combining behavioural, biomedical and structural strategies that are human rights-based and evidence-informed, in the context of a well-researched and understood local epidemic.

Comprehensive sexuality education: Sexuality education is defined as "an age-appropriate, culturally relevant approach to teaching about sex and relationships by providing scientifically accurate, realistic and non-judgmental information". "Sexuality education provides opportunities to explore one's own values and attitudes and to build decision-making, communication and risk reduction skills about many aspects of sexuality" (United Nations Educational, Scientific and Cultural Organisation (UNESCO)).

Concurrent sexual partnerships/ concurrency: People with multiple sexual relationships where intercourse with one partner occurs between two acts of intercourse with another partner. Usual time is within past six months for any surveillance purposes.

Condom less sex: In condom less sex, the sex act is not protected by male or female condoms. Previously known as unprotected sex, this is now increasingly referred to as condom less sex; this is done to avoid confusion with the protection from pregnancy that is provided by other means of contraception.

Confidential – private or anonymous; in the context of HIV testing, confidential results are only revealed to the person being tested, not to their families, employers or other community members without the person's informed and express permission

Country Coordinating Mechanism: The coordinating body in any country set up by the Global fund to fulfil its commitment towards local ownership and participatory decision making.

Coverage rate: Coverage rate is the proportion of individuals accessing and receiving a service or commodity at a point in time. The numerator is the number of people who receive the service and the denominator is the number of individuals who are eligible to receive the service at the same point in time. This is typically measured in surveys, but it also may be measured using service data (e.g. receiving basic service package for MSM or FSW or antiretroviral therapy).

Deficiency – having a shortage of something. People living with AIDS have a shortage of the blood cells that fight disease.

Discriminate – to treat people differently (unfavourably or badly) because, for instance, of their race, sex, sex- ual orientation or religion, or because of their health status, for example, living with HIV or AIDS.

Enabling environment: There are different kinds of enabling environment in the context of HIV. For instance, an enabling legal environment would not only have laws and policies against discrimination based on sex, health status (including HIV status), age, disability, social status, sexual orientation, gender identity and other relevant grounds, but they would be enforced. In such an environment, people would also have access to justice—that is, a process and remedy if they are aggrieved. An enabling social environment is one in which social protection strategies (e.g. economic empowerment) are in place, and where social norms support knowledge, awareness and healthy behaviour choices.

Gender equality: Gender equality—or equality between men and women—is a recognised human right, and it reflects the idea that all human beings, both men and women, are free to develop their personal abilities and make choices without any limitations set by stereotypes, rigid gender roles or prejudices. Gender equality means that the different behaviours, aspirations and needs of women and men are considered, valued and favoured equally. It also signifies that there is no discrimination on the grounds of a person's gender in the allocation of resources or benefits, or in access to services. Gender equality may be measured in terms of whether there is equality of opportunity or equality of results.

Global AIDS Response Progress Reporting (GARPR): Global AIDS Response Progress Reporting (GARPR) is a process whereby countries report progress annually on an established set of GARPR indicators (previously, UNGASS indicators). The indicators are designed to assist countries assess the current state of their national HIV response and progress in achieving their national HIV targets. They will contribute to a better understanding of the global HIV response to the AIDS epidemic, including progress towards the global targets set in the 2011 United Nations Political Declaration on HIV and AIDS and the Millennium Development Goals.

HIV – human immunodeficiency virus, the virus that causes AIDS.

HIV Testing Services (HTS): HIV testing is the gateway to HIV treatment and care, and it is critical in the scale-up of universal access to HIV prevention, including in the context of male circumcision, elimination of new infections among children and antiretroviral medicine based prevention approaches (including pre-exposure prophylaxis or post-exposure prophylaxis). The term HIV testing services (HTS) is used to embrace the full range of services that should be provided together with HIV testing. HIV testing should be undertaken within the framework of the 5Cs: consent, confidentiality, counselling, correct test results and connection/linkage to prevention, care and treatment.

HIV Treatment Cascade: The term HIV treatment cascade is used to refer to the chain of events that are involved in an HIV -positive person receiving treatment until his or her viral load is suppressed to undetectable levels. Each step in the cascade is marked by an assessment of the number of people who have reached that stage, making it possible to determine where gaps might exist in the treatment of people living with HIV. It emphasizes the need to focus on all the required steps to suppress the virus in the cohort of people living with HIV. The stages of the HIV treatment cascade are as follows: the number of people living with HIV; the number who are linked to medical care; the number who start HIV treatment; the number who adhere to their treatment regimen; and, finally, the number who suppress HIV to undetectable levels in their blood.

Immune – to have a high degree of resistance to disease (in contrast, humans with 'immunodeficiency' have a shortage of the blood cells that resist disease).

Incidence: HIV incidence is expressed as the number of new HIV infections over the number of people susceptible to infection in a specified time. Cumulative incidence may be expressed as the number of new cases arising in each period in a specified population. UNAIDS reports the estimated number of incident cases that occurred in the past year among people aged 15–49 years and 0–14 years.

Intimate partner transmission: The term intimate partner transmission (also known by its full name, HIV transmission in intimate partner relationships) describes the transmission of HIV to individuals from their regular partners who inject drugs, who have sex with other people, including with sex workers, people who inject drugs, or gay men and other men who have sex with men.

Intimate partner violence: Intimate partner violence is "behaviour within an intimate relationship that causes physical, sexual or psychological harm, including acts of physical aggression, sexual coercion, psychological abuse and controlling behaviours" (WHO and UNAIDS, 2013).

Investment approach: An investment approach maximizes the returns on investment in the HIV response. It allocates resources towards combinations of interventions that will achieve the greatest impact, and it enhances equity and impact by focusing efforts on key locations and populations with the greatest needs. An investment approach also improves the efficiency of HIV prevention, treatment, care and support programmes. It does this by using empirical evidence and modelling to identify priorities and gaps, as well as enabling countries to secure sustainable funding for HIV programmes. Finally, an investment approach provides the framework to align government domestic funding strategies for the medium and long term with donor-supported efforts.

Investment case: An investment case is a document that makes the case for optimized HIV investments. At its core, it is a description of returns on investment in a country's optimized HIV response over the long term (typically more than 10 years). It summarises the state of the epidemic and the response, describing the prioritised interventions to be implemented and the populations and geographic areas that should be focused on—in order to achieve the greatest impact, indicating the resources required. It also outlines the main access, delivery, quality and efficiency issues to be addressed in order to improve HIV services, and it describes what will be done to address these issues. Finally, it includes an analysis of (and plan for) realistic and more sustainable financing of the HIV response, incorporating increases in domestic financing where relevant.

An investment case is a means of demonstrating national leadership in the response. It has the capacity to unite diverse stakeholders, including the ministries of finance, health, development and planning, civil society, people living with HIV and international partners. It articulates a common effort to identify programmatic gaps and bottlenecks, and to create a road map for action. An investment case can be different from a national strategic plan, which often includes an extensive and aspirational articulation of needs and is constrained by set time frames.

Key population: UNAIDS considers gay men and other men who have sex with men, sex workers and their clients, transgender people, people who inject drugs and prisoners and other incarcerated people as the main key population groups. These populations often suffer from punitive laws or stigmatising policies, and they are among the most likely to be exposed to HIV. Their engagement is critical to a successful HIV response everywhere—they are key to the epidemic and key to the response. Countries should define the specific populations that are key to their epidemic and response based on the epidemiological and social context. In India, in addition to the expressed group, the single male migrants and long distance truckers are also considered as a high-risk population.

Living positively – a mental attitude and physical plan that helps people with HIV or AIDS live longer, better lives.

Multipurpose technologies: Multipurpose technologies are devices or approaches that protect against both HIV and other sexual-related consequences (such as other sexually transmitted infection or pregnancy). Male and female condoms are two examples, but others are in development, including intravaginal rings containing both contraceptives and antiretroviral medicines to prevent HIV infection. In India, male and female condoms are available for use.

National AIDS spending assessment (NASA): NASA describes the flow of resources spent in the HIV response from their origin to the beneficiary populations. It provides decision-makers with strategic information that allow countries to mobilise resources, and have a stronger accountability and a more efficient and effective programme implementation. NASA is a tool within the national monitoring and evaluation framework and is a recommended measurement tool to track HIV spending at the country level.

Orphan – a child who has lost one or both parents.

Parent (Mother) to child transmission: MTCT is the abbreviation for mother-to-child transmission. PPTCT, the abbreviation for prevention of mother-to-child transmission, refers to a four-pronged strategy for stopping new HIV infections among children and keeping their mothers alive and families healthy. The four prongs are: helping reproductive-age women avoid HIV (prong. 1); reducing unmet need for family planning (prong. 2); providing antiretroviral medicine prophylaxis to prevent HIV transmission during pregnancy, labour and delivery, and breastfeeding (prong. 3); and providing care, treatment and support for mothers and their families (prong. 4). India is classified as 'Concentrated Epidemic' for HIV/AIDS. PPTCT often is mistakenly used to refer to only prong. 3— the provision of antiretroviral medicine prophylaxis. India prefers to use the terms parent-to-child transmission or vertical transmission as more inclusive terms to avoid stigmatising pregnant women, to acknowledge the role of the father/male sexual partner in transmitting HIV to the woman and to encourage male involvement in HIV prevention. Still other countries and organisations use the term elimination of mother-to-child transmission (eMTCT). The UNAIDS preferred terminology for the four programmatic prongs is eliminating (or stopping/ending) new HIV infections among children and keeping their mothers alive. It has no abbreviation.

Post exposure prophylaxis (PEP): Post-exposure prophylaxis refers to antiretroviral medicines that are taken after exposure (or possible exposure) to HIV. The exposure may be occupational (e.g. a needle stick injury) or non-occupational (e.g. condom less sex with a seropositive partner). The latter is sometimes referred to as non-occupational post-exposure prophylaxis (N-PEP).

Pre-exposure prophylaxis (PrEP): Pre-exposure prophylaxis (PrEP) refers to antiretroviral medicines prescribed before exposure (or possible exposure) to HIV. Several studies have demonstrated that a daily oral dose of appropriate antiretroviral medicines is effective in both men and women for reducing the risk of acquiring HIV infection through sexual or injection transmission.

Prejudice – to 'pre-judge'; to have negative feelings or ideas about an individual or group of people before knowing or trying to find out the truth about them.

Prison and other closed settings: Prisons and other closed settings refers to places of detention that hold people who are awaiting trial, who have been convicted or who are subject to other conditions of security. These settings may differ in some jurisdictions, and they can include jails, prisons, police detention, juvenile detention, remand/pretrial detention, forced labor camps and penitentiaries. There is a need to be inclusive in the language used to describe prisoners and other incarcerated people. Universal access to HIV prevention, treatment, care and support ideally should extend to these settings.

Second generation surveillance: Second generation surveillance for HIV is the regular and systematic collection, analysis, interpretation, reporting and use of information to track and describe changes in the HIV epidemic over time. In addition to HIV surveillance and AIDS case reporting, second generation surveillance includes behavioural surveillance to track trends in risk behaviours over time to identify or explain changes in levels of infection and the monitoring of sexually transmissible infections in populations at risk of acquiring HIV. These different components achieve greater or lesser significance depending on the surveillance needs of a country, as determined by the nature of the epidemic it is facing.

Sex: The term sex refers to biologically determined differences that are used to label individuals as males or females. The bases for this classification are reproductive organs and functions.

Sexual and reproductive health package: This term refers to programmes, supplies and multi-integrated services to ensure that people can have not only a responsible, satisfying and safer sex life, but also the capability to reproduce and the freedom to decide if, when and how often to do so. It is particularly important that this decision be free of any inequality based on socioeconomic status, education level, age, ethnicity, religion or resources available in their environment.

A sexual and reproductive health package aims to guarantee that men and women are informed of (and to have access to) the following resources: safe, effective, affordable and voluntary acceptable methods of birth control; access to appropriate health-care services for sexual and reproductive care, treatment and support; and access to comprehensive sexuality education. A package also includes (but is not limited to): pregnancy related services (and skilled attendance and delivery), as well as emergency obstetric and post-abortion care; STI and HIV prevention, diagnosis and treatment; prevention and early diagnosis of breast and cervical cancers; and prevention of gender-based violence and care for survivors of gender-based violence.

Sexual health: Sexual health is "not merely the absence of disease, dysfunction or infirmity—it is a state of physical, emotional, mental and social well-being in relation to sexuality. Sexual health requires a positive and respectful approach to sexuality and sexual relationships, as well as the possibility of having pleasurable and safe sexual experiences that are free of coercion, discrimination, and violence. For sexual health to be attained and maintained, the sexual rights of all persons must be respected, protected and fulfilled" (WHO Geneva, 2002)

Sexual orientation: The term sexual orientation refers to each person's capacity for profound emotional, affectional and sexual attraction to (and intimate and sexual relations with) individuals of any sex. SOGI, an often-used abbreviation, stands for sexual orientation, gender identity.

Sexual rights: Sexual rights embrace a "human right that already are recognised in many national laws, international human rights documents and other consensus statements: the right of all persons to the highest attainable standard of sexual health, free of coercion, discrimination and violence. This includes the following: accessing sexual and reproductive health-care services; seeking, receiving and imparting information related to sexuality; obtaining sexuality education; enjoying respect for bodily integrity; choosing a partner; deciding to be sexually active or not; participating in consensual sexual relations; engaging in consensual marriage; determining whether (and when) to have children; and pursuing a satisfying, safe and pleasurable sexual life" (WHO Geneva, 2002).

Social change communication: Social change communication is the strategic use of advocacy, communication and social mobilisation to systematically facilitate and accelerate change in the underlying determinants of HIV risk, vulnerability and impact. It enables communities and national AIDS programmes to tackle structural barriers to effective AIDS responses, such as gender inequality, violation of human rights and HIV-related stigma. Social change communication programmes act as catalysts for action at the individual, community and policy levels.

Stigma – an accusation or label that disgraces or hurts a person. People with HIV and AIDS often suffer emotionally because of prejudice and a lack of compassion from others.

Stigma and discrimination: Stigma is derived from a Greek word meaning a mark or stain, and it refers to beliefs and/or attitudes. Stigma can be described as a dynamic process of devaluation that significantly discredits an individual in the eyes of others, such as when certain attributes are seized upon within cultures or settings and defined as discreditable or unworthy. When stigma is acted upon, the result is discrimination. Discrimination refers to any form of arbitrary distinction, exclusion or restriction affecting a person, usually (but not only) because of an inherent personal characteristic or perceived membership of a group. It is a human rights violation. In the case of HIV, this can be a person's confirmed or suspected HIV-positive status, irrespective of whether there is any justification for these measures. The terms stigmatisation and discrimination have been accepted in everyday speech and writing, and they may be treated as plural.

Stigmatize – to describe or identify in unfavourable terms. People who are ignorant of the facts about HIV/AIDS may stigmatize those with the disease

Structural interventions: Structural interventions are those that seek to alter the physical, legal and social environment in which individual behaviour takes place. They also can aim to remove barriers to protective action or to create constraints to risk-taking.

Sustainable Development Goals: The agreement of Member States to launch a process to develop a set of sustainable development goals (SDGs) was one of the main outcomes of the Rio+20 Conference. The SDGs will build upon the MDGs and provide a framework for the post-2015 development agenda. The outcome document of the Open Working Group (OWG) on the SDGs proposes 17 goals, of which the third is: "Ensure healthy lives and promote well-being at all ages". Specifically, target 3.3 states: "by 2030, end the epidemics of AIDS, tuberculosis, malaria, and neglected tropical diseases and combat hepatitis, water-borne diseases, and other communicable diseases".

Syndrome – a group of signs and symptoms of a sickness that, when they appear, indicate that the illness is present.

Test and treat: Test and treat is sometimes used as a way of referring to voluntary HIV testing and the offer of antiretroviral therapy after diagnosis, irrespective of WHO clinical stage or CD4 cell count. The voluntary nature of both testing and treatment should be emphasized to ensure that individual autonomy is respected. Where test and treat is offered, it is necessary to establish strong support for adherence to keep people on lifelong treatment. In addition, test and treat strategies always should be supplemented by strong combination HIV prevention, including risk reduction counselling, condom provision and/or PrEP. In settings where it is recommended, test and treat also can include referral to male circumcision services for men who test negative for HIV.

Three 'I's for HIV/TB: The three 'I's for HIV/TB—ionized preventive treatment, intensified case finding for active tuberculosis and tuberculosis infection control and early antiretroviral therapy (per national guidelines) and for active TB (irrespective of CD4 count)—are key public health strategies to decrease the impact of tuberculosis on people living with HIV, their partners and family, and the community.

Trafficking – the illegal transport of human beings, in particular women and children, for the purpose of selling them or exploiting their labour.

UNAIDS – Joint United Nations Programme on HIV/AIDS. UNAIDS supports and strengthens the HIV/AIDS-related work of its nine co-sponsoring United Nations agencies.

Unfunded quality demand: Unfunded quality demand is a term introduced by the Global Fund to define funding requested through a concept note that is considered by the Technical Review Panel to be technically sound but beyond the funding amount available (indicative funding and any additional incentive funding awarded). An unfunded quality demand is registered for up to three years for possible funding by the Global Fund or other donors when (and if) new resources become available.

Voluntary – in the context of HIV testing, being tested out of free and informed choice (not being forced to by employers, health-care workers or family).

Vulnerable – because of structural factors, such as poverty, discrimination or hostile laws, to be in a weak- ened position to defend oneself against the risks of contracting HIV.

Acronyms

AEP	: Adolescents Education Programme
AIDS	: Acquired Immuno Deficiency Syndrome
AITD	: Asian Institute of Transport Development
ANC	: Ante Natal Clinic
ANM	: Auxiliary Nurse Midwife
APAC	: AIDS Prevention Control Project
ART	: Antiretroviral Therapy
ARV	: Anti Retro Viral
ASHA	: Accredited Social Health Activities
AWW	: Aaganwadi Worker
BMGF	: Bill & Melinda Gates Foundation
BCC	: Behaviour Change Communication
BSS	: Behavioural Surveillance Survey
BCSU	: Blood Component Separation Unit
CAAA	: Controller of Aid, Accounts and Audit
CAU	: Communication and Advocacy Unit
CBO	: Community Based Organisation
CIDA	: Canadian International Development Agency
CCC	: Community Care Centres
CGHS	: Central Government Health Services
CHC	: Community Health Centres
CII	: Confederation of Indian Industries
CMIS	: Computerized Management Information System
CMU	: Corridor Management Unit
CPFMS	: Computerized Project Financial Management System
CST	: Care, Support and Treatment
CSW	: Commercial Sex Worker
DAPCU	: District AIDS Prevention and Control Unit

DFID	: Department For International Development
DoSHE	: Department of School Health Education
DMU	: District Management Unit
DSA	: District Strategic Assessment
EQAS	: External Quality Assessment System
ESRM	: Experience Sharing and Review Meeting
FMCG	: Fast Moving Consumers Goods
FSW	: Female Sex Worker
GFATM	: Global Fund for AIDS, TB & Malaria
GIPA	: Greater Involvement of People living with AIDS
HIV	: Human Immuno-deficiency Virus
HLFPPT	: Hindustan Latex Family Planning Promotion Trust
HRD	: Human Resources Development
HRG	: High Risk Group
ICDS	: Integrated Child Development Services
ICHAP	: India Canada HIV/AIDS Prevention
ICMR	: Indian Council of Medical Research
ICT	: Integrated Counseling & Testing
ICTC	: Integrated Counseling & Testing Center
IC WM	: Infection Control and Waste Management
IDA	: International Development Assistance
IDSP	: Integrated Disease Surveillance Programme
IDU	: Intravenous Drug User
INP+	: Indian Network of Positive People
IEC	: Information, Education and Communication
IFD	: Integrated Financial Division
IHMR	: Institute of Health Management Research
MCI	: Medical Council of India
IPC	: Inter Personal Communication
ITDP	: Integrated Tribal Development Project
ITDA	: Integrated Tribal Development Agency
ITPA	: Immoral Trafficking Prevention Act
IVRS	: Interactive Voice Response System
JAT	: Joint Appraisal Team
KP	: Key Population

MDGs : Millennium Development Goals
M&E : Monitoring & Evaluation
MEA : Ministry of External Affairs
MHRD : Ministry of Human Resource Development
MOYA : Ministry of Youth Affairs
MSJE : Ministry of Social Justice & Empowerment
MSM : Men having Sex with Men
MSW : Male Sex Worker
MTP : Medium Term Plan
NAC : National AIDS Committee
NACB : National AIDS Control Board
NACO : National AIDS Control Organisation
NACP : National AIDS Control Programme
NARI : National AIDS Research Institute
NCA : National Council on AIDS
NCC : National Cadet Corps
NCERT : National Council on Education, Research and Training
NDPS Act : Narcotic Drugs and Psychotropic Substances Act
NE : North East
NFHS : National Family Health Survey
NGO : Non-Governmental Organisation
NHAI : National Highway Authority of India
NHP : National Health Policy
NRHM : National Rural Health Mission
NSS : National Service Scheme
NYKS : Nehru Yuva Kendra Sangathan
OI : Opportunistic Infection
OYV : Organisations for Youth Volunteers
OVC : Orphans and Vulnerable Children
PD : Project Director
PHC : Primary Health Centre
PIP : Programme Implementation Plan
PIU : Project Implementation Units
PLHA : People Living with HIV/AIDS
PMU : Project Management Unit

PPTCT	:	Prevention of Parent to Child Transmission
PRA	:	Participatory Rural Appraisal
PSV	:	Participatory Site Visits
PWN	:	Positive Women's Network
RACU	:	Regional AIDS Control Unit
RBA	:	Right-Based Approach
RCH	:	Reproductive & Child Health
RCSHA	:	Resource Center for Sexual Health and HIV/AIDS
RIMP	:	Rural Indigenous Medical Practitioner
RMP	:	Registered Medical Practitioner
RNTCP	:	Revised National TB Control Programme
RRC	:	Red Ribbon Club
RTI	:	Reproductive Tract Infection
SACS	:	State AIDS Control Society
SARDI	:	South Asia Regional Development Initiative
SCERT	:	State Council of Educational Research and Training
SHG	:	Self Help Group
SIMS	:	Strategic Information Management Systems
SIMU	:	Strategic Information Management Unit
SM	:	Social Marketing
SMO	:	Social Marketing Organisation
STD	:	Sexually Transmitted Disease
STI	:	Sexually Transmitted Infection
STRI	:	State Tribal Research Institute
SW	:	Sex Worker
TAC	:	Technical Advisory Committee
TCIF-BMGF	:	Transport Corporation of India Foundation-Bill & Melinda Gates Foundation
TG	:	Trans-Gender
TI	:	Targeted Intervention
TOR	:	Terms of Reference
TRC	:	Tuberculosis Research Centre
TRG	:	Technical Resource Group
TSG	:	Technical Support Group
TSU	:	Technical Support Unit

UNHCR	: United Nations High Commission for Refugees
USAID	: United States Agency for International Development
USD	: US Dollar
UTA	: University Talk AIDS
UT	: Union Territories
VCT	: Voluntary Counseling & Testing
VCTC	: Voluntary Counseling & Testing Center
WB	: World Bank
W&CD	: Women & Child Development
WHR	: World Health Report
YFIC	: Youth Friendly Information Centre

Introduction

The changing face of the epidemic has induced concurrent change in the strategies of "National AIDS Control Programmes and Policies". Over the years focus has shifted from awareness raising to behaviour change, from a national response to a decentralized response implemented by Indian states and a growing recognition of the importance of engaging Non-Governmental Organisations, Community based organisations (CBOs) and networks of people living with HIV/AIDS. The National AIDS Prevention and Control Policy (NACP) and the National Council on AIDS (NCA) chaired by India's Prime Minister provide policy guidelines and political leadership to the response.

Since 1986, the Government of India has been responding to the challenge through preventive awareness, targeted interventions and care and support programmes under the leadership of Ministry of Health. Its planned initiatives so far include the Medium Term Plan (1990-92), the first five-year strategic plan (NACP – I, 1992-99), the second five-year strategic plan (NACP – II, 1999-2006) and the third five-year strategic plan (NACP –III, 2007-2012). The present publication is an edited version of effective "Public Health Governance Response to HIV/AIDS" control in India. Strategically, this richness of multiple speciality of Interdisciplinary experience in planning phase of HIV/AIDS management led to a consensus about the goals, objectives and overall framework for shaping up of "HIV/AIDS Planning and Execution Strategies" which helped in reversing the direction of epidemic in India.

Governance issues are increasingly recognized as important dimensions in health systems performance in different health systems settings.

- Public health governance that focuses on principal–agent relationships among health system actors can provide useful insights into the dynamics of health system performance that can lead to the identification of underlying institutional incentives problems.

- The impact of HIV/AIDS on public health governance consequences in terms of the ability of government health systems to respond to the crisis of HIV/AIDS. Social sectors involving, health, education and women & child development, social mobilization, rural and urban development, public administration systems connects interdisciplinary sectors with multisectoral strategies while addressing principles and practices of gender equality, human rights and greater involvement of people with AIDS.
- The book demonstrates how governance analysis can be applied at different levels within the public health system, from national, to sub-national, and to the decentralized health facility. The findings describes India's Public Health Systems responses throughout its strategic planning, designing of implementation strategies ensures effectiveness in governance of NACP in its operationalizations through different phases of National AIDS Control Strategies. This is discussed through designing of strategic implementation and importance of public health issues to understanding the behaviors of multisectoral stakeholders and health system actors and their contributions in shaping up of NACP Phase III.
- Effective interventions to improve health governance in ways that contribute to sustainable and country-owned health system performance avoid 'one-size' good governance prescriptions, adapt reforms to existing capacities, recognize that governance has both formal and informal dimensions and pay attention to socio-political power differentials and dynamics. In other words effective governance of public health system becoming indispensible in reversing the direction of HIV/AIDS epidemic as was the goals set under Millennium Development Goals by 2015 and so also the strategic objectives under the planning process put in place for the Phase III of NACP.

Public Health Governance is widely acknowledged as an effective contributor and importance for functional health system and its performance has been increasingly recognized in public health discourse. Despite this recognition, what constitutes health systems governance and how to improve it, and how it contributes to better health systems, remain questions that policymakers continue to wrestle with. Lack of clarity, competing frameworks and normative biases in different health systems settings have variously contributed to conceptual misinterpretation and policy confusion.

With today's renewed emphasis on health systems strengthening (HSS), better governance or good governance frequently surfaces as an element of strategies and action plans (Shakarishvili *et al.* 2010). Thus, clarifying health governance is a necessary contribution to effective approaches to HSS and its approaches to various disease control programmes including HIV/AIDS and TB.

Practically, in the health sector, governance has been treated mostly as a set of tasks that are, more or less explicitly, assumed to be carried out by, or under the direction of, health ministries. World Health Organization's (WHO) health system building blocks model embodies this assumed role of health ministries, labeling one of the building blocks 'leadership and governance' (WHO 2007). WHO's concept of 'stewardship' constitutes a set of six task domains: generating intelligence (information and evidence), formulating strategic policy direction, ensuring tools for implementation through incentives and sanctions, building coalitions and partnerships, developing a fit between policy objectives and organizational structures and cultures and ensuring accountability (Saltman and Ferroussier-Davis 2000; Travis *et al.* 2002).

In theory, community/citizens can convey their needs and demands for services—and their level of satisfaction—directly to providers, who in turn offer a mix of quality services that satisfy those needs and demands. Yet from an institutionalist perspective, the governance links 'from community/citizens to providers' and 'from providers to clients/citizens' are fraught with principal–agent problems: power and information asymmetries, capacity gaps, accountability failures, perverse incentives and moral hazard (overconsumption of health care). As with the governance link from community/citizens to the state, connections to providers to increase the alignment of the goals of principals and agents can be strengthened through collective action. For example, civil society organizations can exercise their voice on behalf of service users, or village health associations can participate with health providers in needs assessments and community mobilization (e.g. Cornwall et *al.* 2000). Reforms that create health service markets and introduce competition among providers can enhance client power and increase provider incentives for accountability to service users, who have the ability to choose among providers, and/or whose views are incorporated into provider performance assessments that inform funding decisions, e.g. through service delivery surveys. Measures to reinforce the purchasing power of particular societal groups—such as, subsidies for the poor, elderly or HIV/AIDS affected—are another example of offsetting imbalances between providers and service users.

Health Systems Governance: A Model

There are three generally accepted health system goals: (1) improved health status through more equitable access to quality health services and preventive and promotion programmes, (2) responsiveness to legitimate patient and public expectations and (3) fair financing that protects against financial risks for those needing health care (WHO 2000; Roberts *et al.* 2004). While lead governance responsibility for these goals lies largely with state actors, achieving them requires the active engagement of other actors as well. Various analyses have specified the actors in the health system (e.g. Frenk 1994; WHO 2000). These three categories are useful and elaborate on the connections among them those establish the pathways through which health governance becomes operational.

The first is state actors, which includes politicians, policy makers and other government officials. Clearly, actors in the public sector health bureaucracy are central, such as the health ministry, health and social insurance agencies and public pharmaceutical procurement and distribution entities. However, other public sector actors beyond those usually associated with the health system have roles as well. These can include, e.g. parliamentary health committees, regulatory bodies, the ministry of finance, various oversight and account- ability entities and the judicial system (Brinkerhoff 2004). The case of Health Systems in Brazil focuses on such actors: municipal health councils, mayors and the federal comptroller-general.

The second set of actors constitutes health service providers. Depending upon the particulars of a given country's health system, this set mixes public, private and voluntary sector providers (Bennett et al. 2005; Lagomarsino et al. 2009). For example, this can include hospitals, clinics, testing laboratories and educational institutions in all three sectors. The provider category also includes organizations that support service provision: insurance agencies, health maintenance organizations, the pharmaceutical industry and equipment manufacturers and suppliers.

The third set of actors contains community/citizens: service users, the general public and organized civil society/NGOs. This set can be categorized in a variety of ways: e.g. by income (poor vs non-poor), by location (rural vs urban), by service (maternal and child health, reproductive health, geriatric care), by disease or condition (HIV/AIDS, TB, malaria, etc.). Civil society organizations may be community-based groups, advocacy organizations, professional associations, etc. (e.g. Tantivess and Walt 2008). The case of Health Systems in China incorporates members of this category of actors into the analysis of the governance of country's health reforms.

These actors are linked through the governance relationships illustrated in Figure 1, which builds on work at the World Bank on service delivery and accountability (2004, 2007). As specified here, these principal–agent relationships are both instrumental—related to how governance helps to achieve health system goals, and normative—reflecting commonly accepted principles of good governance (UNDP 1997). This is followed as discussed in public systems health governance relationships in more detail.

Linking the state, providers and community/citizens

The arrows in Figure 1 characterize the nature of the relationships among the various actors. 'From community/citizens to state actors', in which the community/citizens are the principals and the state actors are the agents, the key feature of the relationship is the exercise of voice, i.e. the expression of needs, preferences and demands to politicians, policymakers and public officials. Individuals can exercise their voice by visiting his/her local representative or vote for a parliamentarian who has promised health reform—but in terms of health systems and governance, how individuals respond in collective efforts to make their voice heard around common interests is a key issue. Formal efforts through political parties and elections are one form of interest aggregation and expression of voice; and advocacy and public information campaigns are another, less formal avenue. The health systems in Brazil, illustrates the salience of elections as expressions of citizen voice; a higher degree of competitiveness in mayoral contests mattered in reducing corruption in health spending. For example, also, in the case of China, popular discontent with health services contributed to putting health reform on the agenda of politicians and technocrats.

Community efforts to exercise voice and hold public officials accountable can be pursued through community initiatives to lobby local officials, specialized civil society organizations/NGOs that develop expertise in budget monitoring and service delivery report cards to expand voice both nationally and internationally. All these measures seek to align the goals and interests of community, as principals, with public health officials, as their agents.

'From state actors to community/citizens', the overriding health governance relationship is responsiveness to community/citizen needs, preferences and demands. This relationship varies in quality and degree. In countries with authoritarian governments, political leaders and health officials may not see themselves as agents acting on behalf of community-leaders. As a result, they may not be very responsive to the health needs of their community and/or they may respond through patronage networks to some community, but not to all. However, in democratic systems, health care is an issue that is often of interest to politicians, as it touches the lives of almost all of their constituents. However, it can be difficult to mobilize voters, whose attention to health concerns may be sporadic, and powerful interest groups often resist changes.

Established health interests may be better able to deliver campaign support and votes than the general public. So democracies are not immune from the patronage and community that characterize politics in authoritarian regimes. While health as a public good is not so easy for political patrons to employ as a reward to community, the health resources they control or influence can be amenable to exploitation. Rewards can take the form of, e.g. the allocation of disproportionately generous funding to particular localities, the siting of specific facilities or channeling services to certain groups (e.g. urban elites and ethnic compatriots) over others (e.g. the poor, disadvantaged and politically powerless). The examples from health systems in Brazil demonstrate that the presence of effective monitoring institutions, in this case municipal health councils, can serve as checks on community and corruption.

The governance interactions between 'state actors and providers' constitute the functional expression of principal-agent relationships. Public policymakers, as principals, specify objectives, procedures and standards; provide resources and support; and exercise control and oversight relative to providers, who function as their agents. In exchange, providers carry out the agreed-upon desires and instructions of health policymakers. Principal–agent relations are subject to well-recognized problems—information asymmetries, moral hazard and conflicts of interest—that health system principals seek to address in crafting the directives aimed at providers. These directives determine various providers' roles and responsibilities, set parameters for accountability and influence incentives for compliance. Examples include health regulatory policies and procedures, auditing programmes (as in the Brazil case), financing mechanisms and provider payment systems, quality assurance, human resources policies, etc. Pay-for- performance is a tool that a number of countries are experimenting with to align accountability with health outcomes (Ridde 2005; Eichler et al. 2007; Eldridge and Palmer 2009). Accountability is not the only health governance relationship that connects the health ministry and related agencies to health services providers. There are linkages that provide knowledge and technical information, e.g. through medical education and in-service training. These linkages can also serve as transmission vectors for shared professional and medical norms and values, which can serve to promote goal convergence between provider-agents and their principals, in line with the leadership or stewardship model mentioned earlier (Saltman and Ferroussier- Davis 2000; Van Slyke 2007).

'From providers to state actors', key governance relationships revolve around reporting the provision of information for purposes of monitoring and accountability. In theory, such reporting reduces the information asymmetry problem, enables effective and informed oversight and increases the probability that agents will pursue principals' goals. Besides accountability and motivation, another important function of the governance link between providers and state actors is to furnish data for policy making. If health policymakers are to set direction based on evidence-based policy, then providers have a critical role as an important source of evidence.

Numerous analysts have noted, dealing with information asymmetries is an important piece of making health governance effective (Lagomarsino et al. 2009). Providers' privileged position also makes the provider–state linkage a political one. Providers are not neutral sources of information; they have interests and they exercise voice and lobbying to influence state health policy and practices. Another problem affecting the state health actor–provider governance link is that of attribution. In the complex, multi-actor realm of the health system, it is difficult to assess whose contributions made a difference, or whose efforts fell short. Health outcomes are the result of numerous factors, many of which are outside of the control or influence of health & HIV care service providers or health ministries.

Public Health Governance: Challenges for Reform

An ongoing debate among governance experts is the extent to which the normative principles of good governance constitute practical and realistic guide to reform in poor and developing countries. This debate is relevant for health system reforms as well. Critics cite three key 'disconnects'. First is the gap between the requisite capacities needed to act upon the good governance principles and the available capacities in many countries, especially fragile states (e.g. Berry and Igboemeka 2004). Health governance requires sufficient state capacity, power and legitimacy to manage the policy-making process effectively, to plan and design programmatic interventions, to enforce and implement health systems. A critical issue is the extent to which such interventions can lead to broader and sustained health system changes.

Second is the frequent disparity between formal governance, i.e. what exists in laws, regulations, and procedures and so on, and the extent to which these are actually put into practice. This gap can stem from capacity problems, i.e. weak organizations, insufficient resources, non-existent and/or under skilled staff and poorly performing health systems. Thus, the governance relationships in the health system illustrated in Figure 1 may operate in two different institutional spheres: the formal and the informal domain. Donor-supported health systems strengthening (HSS) interventions tend to be situated largely within the formal governance system, and focus on idealized notions of good governance (Grindle 2007). However, a focus on de facto governance can reveal a very different reality, where, service delivery and accountability are governed by principles of communitization rather than of good governance (Brinkerhoff and Goldsmith 2004). This provides an example from India of the distortions that arise when actual practices related to health worker supervision bypass and subvert official practices, resulting in formalized lip service to accountability and creation of space for corruption and domination of health workers by political actors.

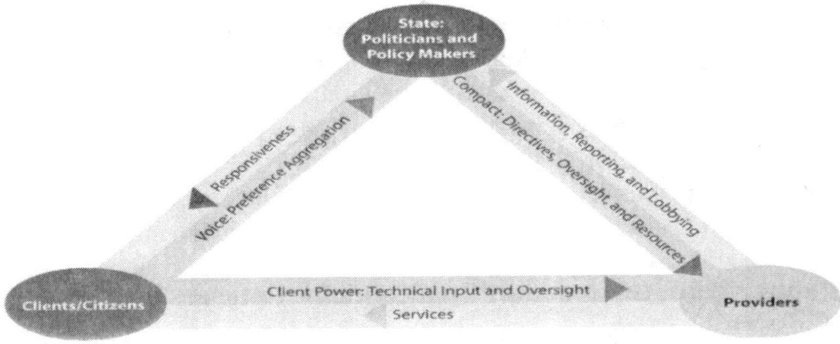

Figure 1 Health Governance Framework. **Source:** ***Brinkerhoff and Bossert (2008) adapted from World Bank (2004, 2007)***

The third lacuna, related to the other two, is the neglect of power and political economy when considering health governance (e.g. Gonza´lez-Rossetti and Bossert 2000; Fox and Reich 2011). Governance is fundamentally about power. Although Figure 1 could be interpreted as portraying each category of actors as having equal influence and power, this is not the case. The degree of power and authority among these three disconnects differs substantially (Reich 2002). The state and providers for the most part hold more power (based on institutional and legal authority, information and expertise) than community/citizens. The case exemplifies a Chinese health system where state actors and providers have dominant power. Where communitization and corruption are prevalent, the less powerful who want access to services have strong incentives to do whatever the more powerful require of them. As Lewis (2007, p. 985) observes, 'informal payments allow patients to jump the queue, receive better or more care, obtain drugs, or simply any care at all'. Community participation may exist as well between state actors and providers, where politicians and/ or health ministry officials channel resources and favours to selected providers in exchange for political support. For example, the health systems in Brazil highlight the risks of such community interactions at the municipal level for increased corruption.

While the governance dialogue is moving beyond 'best practice' to 'best fit', gaps remain in identifying both the socio-technical content and the political processes involved that will inform effective, context-specific interventions (Booth 2011). Filling these gaps is a major challenge for Health Systems Strengthening. These suggestions on health system governance, enables future research and aim to contribute to confronting this challenge while addressing HIV/AIDS control and prevention strategies.

Addressing prevention, care & support for controlling human immunodeficiency virus (HIV) infection has a comprehensive public health approach that has stopped and reverses the direction of AIDS epidemics worldwide. When HIV infection first emerged among stigmatized populations (homosexual men, injection-drug users, and immigrants from developing countries), the discriminatory responses ranged from descriptions of AIDS as "retribution" to violence and proposals for quarantine, universal mandatory testing, and even tattooing of infected persons This response led to HIV exceptionalism, an approach that advocated both for special resources and increased funding and against the application of standard methods of disease control. The need for extra resources remains essential, but the failure to apply standard disease-control methods undermines society's ability and responsibility to control the epidemic.

Now, given the availability of drugs that can effectively treat HIV infection and progress on antidiscrimination initiatives, perhaps society is ready to adopt traditional disease-control principles and proven interventions that can identify infected persons, interrupt transmission, ensure treatment and case management, and monitor infection and control efforts throughout the population (Table 1). Doing so will have political and economic costs. The political costs include offending both sides of the political establishment: conservatives who oppose the implementation of effective prevention programs, including syringe exchange and the widespread availability of condoms, and some HIV activists who oppose expansion of testing,

Table 1. Comparison of Public Health Approach to HIV Infection and Other Infectious Diseases.		
Intervention	**Other Infectious Diseases**	**HIV Infection**
Case finding and surveillance		
Named reporting of all with condition	Standard for all other reportable infectious diseases	Only recently implemented in many areas; still not implemented in some
Availability of routine testing in health care settings	Standard for all other reportable infectious diseases	Widely recommended and cost-effective but often not available
Notification and testing of partners by public health programs	Standard (e.g., testing and treatment of contacts exposed to *Neisseria meningitidis*, acute hepatitis B, syphilis, tuberculosis)	Wide variation in proportion of contacts identified, contacted, and tested among jurisdictions
Interruption of transmission		
Specific to mode of transmission	Prevention of many transfusion-transmitted and perinatally transmitted pathogens possible; vaccines widely used; condoms underused in prevention of other sexually transmitted infections	Transfusion-related and perinatal transmission largely controlled in the United States; vaccines not available; condoms neither widely available nor use strongly promoted; use of nonsterile needles by most injection-drug users
Systematic treatment and case management		
Monitoring by public health agencies to determine whether infected contacts are receiving appropriate care and treatment	Standard (outbreak-control method used for *N. meningitidis* cases in schools or day care settings, for influenza in other community settings, and for all tuberculosis-infected contacts)	Generally not done
Case management by public health departments to ensure effective linkage of affected patients to care	Standard; case manager accountable for patient outcome (e.g., in pregnant women with hepatitis B or patients with tuberculosis)	Rarely done; duplication of services between community-based and government case management
Provision of social services to patients	Done as incentive to ensure effective treatment; was essential to control multidrug-resistant tuberculosis	Linkage of social services to care and treatment in few areas
Population-based monitoring		
Contact of treating physicians by public health agencies if patients have inadequate response to treatment	Standard for some diseases	Not done; treatment complex and lifelong
Monitoring of trends in drug resistance among previously untreated patients	Standard for sexually transmitted diseases, tuberculosis, some bacterial infections	Not routine except on a research basis (mandated recently in New York State)

Comparison of Public Health Approach to HIV Infection and Other Infectious Diseases

notification of the partners of infected persons (also known as partner counselling and referral services), and what some see as inappropriate "medicalization" of the response to the epidemic. The economic costs, particularly to improve population-wide case management and notification of partners, would be substantial. But the human and economic costs of failing to adopt a comprehensive public health approach are much higher.

At the national level, from the perspective AIDS responses, critical elements of effective governance are linked to a number of requirements, including: (a) political leadership and commitment; (b) adequate capacities of relevant state institutions; (c) adequate domestic spending on HIV prevention, treatment and care in the context of the national budget (such as the commitment made by African countries at the Abuja AIDS Summit in 2001 to spend at least 15% of their total budget on health, including AIDS, which they failed to do) (UNDP, 2006); (d) efficient delivery of primary healthcare and other basic social services; (e) decentralization of authority, decision-making and resources to the local level; (f) genuine involvement of civil society in budget formulation, monitoring and tracking of public expenditure on AIDS, to ensure transparency and accountability; (g) involvement of the private sector as a partner; respect for human rights and promotion of gender equality; and (h) the incorporation of AIDS concerns into broad social and economic policies as development priorities, including linking to poverty reduction. These requirements need to be supported by an enabling environment, which necessitates a clearly defined National AIDS Strategy: a legal and policy framework that provides guidelines for implementation, identifies specific roles and responsibilities of key actors, fosters active participation of the broad spectrum of stakeholders at all levels, and facilitates the effective coordination of development efforts involving the state, civil society, and the private sector making it multisectoral in its approach.

HIV/AIDS today is an epidemic of exclusion, discrimination and vulnerability. The science of epidemic and its evidence are becoming clearer, and there are tools to end HIV/AIDS as a public health threat is an accepted challenge worldwide. However, many populations across many countries continue to face human rights barriers in exercising their right to development and to accessing the best available public health responses.

The 2030 Agenda for UN Sustainable Development Goals has put equality and non-discrimination at the core of its shared framework for action. To combat HIV/AIDS and achieve healthy lives for all as mandated by SDG 3, we need to work together to tackle the human rights barriers in order to ensure rights-based approaches that Fast-Track the responses of effective health system. In its preamble, the 2016 Political Declaration on Ending AIDS explicitly states the importance of the "promotion, protection and fulfillment of all human rights and the dignity of all people living with, at risk of, and affected by HIV" as an objective and means of ending the AIDS epidemic. The Political Declaration on Ending AIDS has also mainstreamed human rights approaches: two out of the 10 Fast-Track commitments to end AIDS by 2030 include a dedicated focus to advancing human rights, empowerment, access to justice and the elimination of all forms of discrimination and violence. In order to assess progress towards these commitments, it is important to study and understand for national monitoring and evaluation systems to be rights-sensitive and to capture progress towards removing human rights barriers to effective AIDS responses as well as governance of health systems effectively.

The book is an articulation of national level efforts on public systems governance mechanisms and processes involved in shaping up of health sector responses and strategies; it aims to support national stakeholders to assess health systems responses and strategies involving human rights approaches and barriers. Most importantly depicts the strategic planning and operational input in developing, monitor and evaluate rights-based responses to progress effective governance of health systems. The edited version advocates for "time to act is now". The SDG monitoring framework places firm emphasis on leaving no one behind and on capturing progress towards eliminating discrimination. There are certain opportunities for health, health care and Universal Health Coverage as central to human rights-based and rights-sensitive monitoring and evaluation as used in strengthening of health systems. With the global call for goal of UHC through SDGs by 2030, the world has committed to end AIDS, and it is working towards the vision of zero new HIV infections, zero discrimination and zero AIDS-related deaths. In making this global vision to become a reality, monitoring efforts need to support the commitment that no one will be left behind by the response with the availability of a stronger, equitable and accountable health system at all levels of functioning of HI/AIDS prevention, care and support strategies.

This book brings out the achievements and concerns of Health Systems' struggle in generating India's health sector responses to HIV/AIDS control programmes starting from NACP – I to NACP-IV – a journey through most successfully planned and strategized in shaping NACP III. This was envisaged with the goal of MDG 3 in reversing direction of epidemic by 2015. This effort continuing to contribute in the era of SDG 3 goal of sustaining ongoing national efforts of attaining Zero new Infection through declaration of Universal Health Coverage by 2030. The planned processes involved in NACP III and its expected outcomes strengthened India's national and state level efforts in contributing to reverse the direction of epidemic. This was discussed how effective governance of public health and health systems responses were successfully strategized throughout the implementation, monitoring, evaluation and reporting of accountable public systems responses to HIV/AIDS control in India. NACP phase III as is considered to be one of the most successfully designed strategically planned processes as useful in combating HIV/AIDS in India.

This edited volume consists of twenty chapters consisting of historic designing background of NACP strategies in its phase three including goals, objectives, epidemiological situation, programme strategies and programme targets set. The volume will be a reference document for the M.Phil. and Ph.D. research scholars in Public Health, social science researchers, masters in public health, MBA –Health Care Strategies and practitioners of public health and policy makers in the field of public health and HIV/AIDS care management in the country and in the region in South Asia. In other words this book can be useful as an academic reference for MBAs in Health Care Management, Health Care Administration and MPH and Ph.D. in Public Health researchers in Indian universities and academic institutions actively engaged in providing Health Management, Public Health and Research Programmes involving MPH and Ph.D. in Public Health and Interdisciplinary Schools of Health Sciences.

Successful strategies and governance of Public Health management of HIV/AIDS control in India is a success in case worth sharing in the form of an edited Book. As a reference book for practitioners, public health policy makers, researchers and Civil Society Organisations, PLHA network agencies and research institutions actively engaged in HIV/AIDS Planning, control and research in India and in the region in South Asia. Successive governance tools, techniques and strategies are key to mobilise research support and resource linkages as discussed through NACP planning development phase III is the central theme of the present edition in the form of a users as well as learners guide is worth referring for future research in the context of public health response to governance of HIV/AIDS.

Chapter - 1

National Strategic Planning & Objectives

Demographically, the second largest country in the world, India has also the second largest number of people living with HIV/AIDS. More than 70% Indians live in rural areas and about 28% in urban locations, including 60 million in urban slums. About 26% of the population comprising mostly of agricultural labour, rural artisan and urban casual household workers live below poverty line.

At the time of NACP Planning, India has a federal structure with 35 States and Union Territories and 611 administrative districts. It has a large three-tier health care infrastructure comprising Sub-Centres, Primary Health Centres (PHCs) and Community Health Centres (CHCs). Yet, public expenditure on health, as a percentage of total government expenditure, is quite low and, in fact, declining in many states (IDR 2004-05). Of the total amount spent on health in general, government expenditure accounts for 21.3% while private spending amounts to 78.7% (WHR 2004). There are only 48 physicians and 45 nurses per 100,000 population (WHR 2002). The country's expenditure on HIV/AIDS prevention and control is approximately USD 120 million per annum (until 2005-06).

National Health Policy (NHP 2002) and India Vision 2020 commit the country to fight all communicable and preventable diseases. With increasing life expectancy, contemporary public health scenario in India reflects two dominant trends:

(i) an epidemiological transition towards greater incidence of non-communicable / life style diseases, and

(ii) the growing challenge of communicable and preventable diseases being accentuated by HIV/AIDS. Millennium Development Goals (MDGs) as committed all countries to reverse the spread of HIV/AIDS by 2015. As a signatory nation, India stands committed to achieve this goal through its National AIDS Control Programme.

1.1 Response to the Challenge

India's initial response to the HIV/AIDS challenge was in the form of setting up an AIDS Task Force by the Indian Council of Medical Research (ICMR) and a National AIDS Committee (NAC) headed by the Secretary, Ministry of Health. In 1990, a Medium Term Plan (MTP 1990-1992) was launched in four States, namely, Tamil Nadu, Maharashtra, West Bengal and Manipur and four metropolitan cities, namely, Chennai, Kolkata, Mumbai and Delhi. The MTP facilitated targeted IEC campaigns, establishment of surveillance system and safe blood supply.

In 1992, the Government launched the first National AIDS Control Programme (NACP-I) with an IDA Credit of USD 84 million and demonstrated its commitment to combat the disease. NACP-I was implemented during 1992-1999 with an objective to slow down the spread of HIV infections so as to reduce morbidity, mortality and impact of AIDS in the country. To strengthen the management capacity, a National AIDS Control Board (NACB) was constituted and an autonomous National AIDS Control Organisation (NACO) was set up to implement the project.

The key outcomes of the project included: capacity development at the state level in the form of setting up State AIDS Cells (SACs) in 25 States and 7 UTs; a well functioning blood safety programme aimed at reducing HIV transmission through blood; expansion of HIV sentinel surveillance system; collaboration with non-government organizations on prevention interventions; and intensified communication campaigns. During this period, bilateral partners like USAID (Tamil Nadu), DFID (Andhra Pradesh, Gujarat, Kerala, Orissa and West Bengal) and CIDA (Karnataka and Rajasthan) also implemented focused programmes successfully and contributed to the state and national level efforts.

In November 1999, the second National AIDS Control Project (NACP-II) was launched with World Bank credit support of USD 191 million. Based on the experience gained in Tamil Nadu and a few other states along with the evolving trends of the HIV/AIDS epidemic, the focus shifted from raising awareness to changing behaviour, decentralization of programme implementation at the state level and greater involvement of NGOs. The policy and strategic shift was reflected in the two key objectives of NACP-II:

- to reduce the spread of HIV infection in India.
- to increase India's capacity to respond to HIV/AIDS on a long-term basis.

The aim was to keep HIV sero-prevalence: i. below 5% of the adult population in high prevalence States, ii. below 3% in States where the prevalence was moderate, and iii. below 1 and 2 per cent in the remaining States where the epidemic was at a nascent stage.

Policy initiatives taken during NACP-II include: adoption of National AIDS Prevention and Control Policy (2002); National Blood Policy; a strategy for Greater Involvement of People with HIV/AIDS (GIPA); launching of the National Rural Health Mission; launching of National Adolescent Education Programme; provision of anti-retroviral treatment (ART); formation of an inter-ministerial group for mainstreaming; and setting up of the National Council on AIDS, chaired by the Prime Minister.

1.2 Key Achievements

At the operational level, NGOs were involved in the implementation of 1033 Targeted Interventions (TIs) among HRGs and setting up 875 Voluntary Counselling and Testing Centres (VCTCs) and 679 STD clinics at the district level. Nation-wide, state level Behaviour Sentinel Surveillance (BSS) surveys were conducted. Prevention of Parent to Child Transmission (PPTCT) programme was expanded across the states. Introduction of a Computerized Management Information System (CMIS) and a Computerized Project Financial Management System (CPFMS) were the other highlights of NACP-II. In addition, a number of organizations and networks were also strengthened; support from bilateral, multilateral and other partner agencies also increased substantially. As a result of all these efforts, the HIV prevalence as indicated by recent studies and analyses seems to be stabilizing, while states like Tamil Nadu, Andhra Pradesh, Karnataka, Maharashtra and Nagaland have started showing declining trends (Rajesh Kumar et al 2006). The sentinel surveillance results of 2005 also reinforce the stabilization trends indicating that the expected outcomes of NACP-II have broadly been accomplished.

1.3 Lessons Learnt

While there has been a systematic improvement in the response, there are areas that still require greater attention and stronger focus. The lessons that have emerged from the implementation of NACP-II include the following:

- Complexities of the epidemic and its exact dimensions are yet to be understood especially in the Northern and North Eastern states of the country.

- Frequent changes of Project Directors (PDs) of State AIDS Control Societies (SACS) and other senior programme managers at the state level weakened the thrust and focus of interventions. In some highly vulnerable States, PDs were either saddled with additional non-HIV responsibilities or given SACS charge as additional responsibility. A large number of functional positions in the SACS remained vacant. These factors contributed to an uneven implementation of the programme. It is necessary to have policy safeguard against this trend.
- Decentralisation and devolution of decision-making powers to the SACS was a right step, but without commensurate capacity development and technical support, it did not produce desired results.
- Focused attention on the HRGs through TIs proved to be an effective strategy for preventing the spread of infection. However, this was not appreciated and implemented in all states, partly due to attitudes towards high risk behaviours and partly due to weak systems for partnership with civil society. Consequently saturation of coverage of HRGs nationwide is yet to be accomplished. In some States, targeted interventions were not accorded the priority they deserved. Interventions on MSM and IDU remained low. Out-of-school as well as unschooled youth, married adolescents and rural population did not get due attention.
- Condom promotion and procurement registered an improvement in 2005 but remained below the targets, emphasizing the need for more aggressive Social Marketing.
- Barring some exceptions, participation of the private sector and mainstream civil society organizations was limited.
- Potential of 21 million youth volunteers in NSS, NCC, Scouts and Guides, NYKS, Youth Clubs, Youth Red Cross and Red Crescent remained underutilised both in prevention as well as building an enabling environment.
- Convergence between RCH and NACP remained a difficult challenge.
- AIDS mortality and under reporting are issues that deserve more attention as these have a bearing on the interpretation of sero-surveillance data. This requires careful examination of available methodologies and choice of the best available method suited for India. Similarly, about 86% of transmission being sexual, it would

be necessary to find out how much of this is caused by limited access to services to women. Simultaneously, it would be necessary to ascertain to what extent this is accounted for by men having sex with men (MSM). Under NACP-III, sentinel surveillance will cover all districts for making the results more representative.

- During NACP-II, a number of regional and national level studies, assessments, surveys and laboratory research were conducted. Operational and biomedical data compiled by UNAIDS and other agencies account for as many as 500 research documents/papers, in addition to the BSS 2001. Management and utilization of such a large storehouse of knowledge for improving programme strategy, planning and monitoring remains a challenge. The existing research wing within NACO needs to be strengthened to deal with the emerging need for knowledge management.
- Notwithstanding a significant step-up of the overall resource availability for HIV/AIDS programme, India's per capita financial investment on HIV prevention, control, care and support remains one of the lowest in the world. To scale up activities and interventions in prevention, care and treatment, a much higher level of investment is required.

Strategies of NACP-II that yielded significant positive results have been strengthened in NACP-III and the gaps addressed based on the lessons learnt.

1.4 NACP-III Preparatory Process

Against this background and keeping the prevalent social context, concerns and the emerging HIV/AIDS scenario as well as drawing from the experience of the earlier two phases, NACO initiated the preparatory process for NACP-III (2006-2011). A retreat was organized in March, 2005, to reflect in depth the lessons learnt during NACP-II and chart out the future road map. In April, 2005, the Government of India constituted a national planning team to begin the preparatory work. A conscious decision was taken to make this process consultative, participatory, inclusive and transparent.

The team developed a framework document for NACP-III, discussed it with NACO and placed it before a newly constituted National Steering Committee. Soon after, the framework was field tested in one highly vulnerable state (Uttar Pradesh), one high prevalent state (Andhra Pradesh) and in the north-east (Nagaland). With inputs from these states, components of the framework were further fine-tuned and placed before the national conference of Project Directors of SACS and the development partners.

In order to enlarge the consultative process, 14 thematic working groups representing experts and practitioners deliberated on HIV/AIDS issues and concerns and submitted their recommendations. Areas covered included: programme management; implementation and organizational restructuring; financial management; mainstreaming and partnerships; gender, youth, adolescents and children; condom programming; service delivery, STI/RTI treatment and convergence with RCH; targeted interventions; communication, advocacy and social mobilization; GIPA; human rights, legal and ethical issues; care, support and treatment; research, development & knowledge management; M & E and surveillance.

For citizen participation in the planning process, UNAIDS and NACO set up an e-Consultation. This was followed by a series of handholding consultations with stakeholders at the state level for preparation of state and district level programme implementation plans (PIP). A national consultation with the civil society organisations was also organized to validate the draft strategic frame work and obtain further inputs to the planning process. The Planning Team also had deliberations with the INP+ and PWN for their inputs. A series of dialogue with the development partners was also undertaken along with a number of interactions within the Health Ministry including RCH and NRHM authorities. The National Steering Committee met six times during the preparatory phase to exchange views and review the progress in the planning process.

In October 2005, a Joint Pre-Appraisal Mission led by the World Bank assessed the status of programme preparation and critically appraised the strategic framework document. While endorsing the same, the mission provided additional inputs to improve it further. Between November and December 2005, a series of State PIP Workshops were held for developing state plans. Simultaneously, to augment the planning exercise further, the Planning Team also initiated six studies focusing on the rural dynamics of the epidemic, MSM issues, attitudes of health care providers, HIV situation among police and paramilitary forces, social marketing issues, and effectiveness of the existing communication strategies. Similarly, five assessments viz. social, financial, environmental, institutional and procurement were also undertaken.

The experience of NACP-I and NACP-II, consultations, studies and assessments led to a consensus on the goal, objectives and strategies for NACP-III adhering to the larger MDG goal.

Finally, the PIPs formulated by the States and some districts contributed to the formulation of the PIP for NACP-III.

1.5 Goal and Objectives

The overall goal of NACP-III is to halt and reverse the epidemic in India over the next 5 years by integrating programmes for prevention, care, support and treatment. This will be achieved through a four-pronged strategy:

1. Prevention of new infections in high risk groups and general population through:
   (a) Saturation of coverage of high risk groups with targeted interventions (TIs).
   (b) Scaled up interventions in the general population.
2. Providing greater care, support and treatment to larger number of PLHA.
3. Strengthening the infrastructure, systems and human resources in prevention, care, support and treatment programmes at the district, state and national level.
4. Strengthening the nationwide Strategic Information Management System.

The specific objective is to reduce new infection as estimated in the first year of the programme by:

- Sixty per cent (60%) in high prevalence states so as to obtain the reversal of the epidemic; and
- Forty per cent (40%) in the vulnerable states so as to stabilize the epidemic.

1.6 Guiding Principles

The goal, objectives and strategies of NACP-III will be informed by the following guiding principles:

- The unifying credo of Three Ones, i.e., one Agreed Action Framework, one National HIV/AIDS Coordinating Authority and one Agreed National M&E System.
- Equity as monitored by relevant indicators in both prevention and impact mitigation strategies i.e. percentage of people accessing services disaggregated by age and gender.
- Respect for the rights of the PLHA, as it contributes most positively to prevention and control efforts. NACP-III would evolve mechanisms to be put in place at all levels to address issues

related to human rights and ethics. Particular focus would be on the fundamental rights of PLHA and their active involvement as important partners in prevention, care, support and treatment initiatives.

- Civil society representation and participation in planning and implementation of NACP-III would receive priority since it is essential for promoting social ownership and community involvement.
- Creation of an enabling environment wherein those infected and affected by HIV could lead a life of dignity. This will be the corner-stone of all interventions. Stigma and discrimination associated with HIV/AIDS, which continues to pose a big challenge to policy planners and programme implementers in prevention, care and treatment efforts will be aggressively addressed.
- Having regard to the spirit behind "universal access", NACP-III will scale up efforts and activities for providing HIV prevention, care, support, and treatment services.
- For making the implementation mechanism more responsive, proactive and dynamic, the HRD strategy of NACO and SACS will be based on qualification, competence, commitment and continuity.
- Strategic and programme interventions will be evidence-based and result-oriented with scope for innovations and flexibility. Priority will be accorded to specific local contexts.

1.7 Programme Priorities and Thrust Areas

NACP-III seeks to learn from the lessons of the previous two phases of programme implementation and build on the strengths thereof. Its priorities and thrust areas have been drawn up accordingly and include the following:

- Considering that more than 99% of the population in the country is free from infection, NACP-III will place the highest priority on preventive efforts while, at the same time, seeking to integrate prevention with care, support and treatment.
- Sub-populations that have the highest risk of exposure to HIV will receive the highest priority for intervention. These would include sex workers, men who have sex with men, and injecting drug users. Of lower priority will be those groups which have high levels of exposure to HIV infection such as long distance truckers, prisoners, migrants (including refugees) and street children.

- Those in the general population who have greater need for accessing prevention services such as treatment of STIs, voluntary counselling and testing and condoms will be next in the line of priority.
- NACP-III will ensure that all persons who need treatment would have access to prophylaxis and management of opportunistic infections. Persons who need access to ART will also be assured first line ARV drugs.
- Prevention needs of children will be addressed through universal provision of PPTCT services. Children who are infected will be assured access to paediatric ART.
- NACP-III will also make efforts to address the needs of persons infected and affected by HIV, especially children. This will be done through the sectors and agencies involved in child protection and welfare. Impact of HIV on others will also be mitigated through other welfare agencies providing nutritional support, opportunities for income generation and other welfare services.
- NACP-III will invest in community care centres to provide psycho-social support, outreach services, referrals and palliative care.
- Socio-economic determinants that make a person vulnerable also increase the risk of exposure to HIV. NACP-III will work with other agencies involved in vulnerability reduction such as women's groups, youth groups, trade unions etc. to integrate HIV prevention into their activities.
- Mainstreaming and partnerships will be the key approach to facilitate multi-sectoral response engaging a wide range of stakeholders. Private sector, civil society organizations, PLHA networks and government departments would all play crucial role in prevention, care, support, treatment and service delivery. Technical and financial resources of the development partners will be leveraged to achieve the objectives of the programme.

Chapter - 2

National Situation-Epidemiological Assessments and Projections

The HIV epidemic has been evolving in the country since the first case was detected in Tamil Nadu in 1986. Based on the sentinel surveillance data, the estimated number of HIV- infected persons has gone up from 3.5 million in 1998 to over 5.206 million in 2005 accounting for one eighth of all infections in the world. These estimates indicate that there has been no dramatic upsurge in the spread of HIV infection across the country since 1998. However, state specific variations in the profile of the epidemic have been observed. Several states in southern India and north-eastern part of the country have shown higher HIV prevalence within states and diversity in predominant patterns of HIV transmission. Even low HIV prevalence states are also characterized by the presence of high risk pockets with potential for increased spread of epidemic in these states. HIV infection during the 80's and 90's reflects an increase in the number of AIDS patients and consequent medical, economic and social implications.

2.1 Categories of States based on Prevalence and Vulnerability

Based on antenatal prevalence (ANC), six states in India have been identified as high prevalence states (having more than 1.0 per cent HIV prevalence in general population), three states as moderate prevalence states (concentrated epidemic with more than 5% HIV prevalence in high risk population) and the rest as low prevalence states. However, on the basis of vulnerability factors such as migration, size of the population and weak health infrastructure, the low prevalence states/UTs have been further classified as "Highly Vulnerable" and "Vulnerable" states (see **Table 2.1**).

Table 2.1: Categories of States

High Prevalence	*Moderate Prevalence*	*Low Prevalence*	
		Highly Vulnerable	*Vulnerable*
Tamil Nadu	Gujarat	Assam	Arunachal Pradesh
Andhra Pradesh	Goa	Bihar	Haryana
Maharashtra	Pondicherry	Delhi	J & K
Karnataka		Himachal Pradesh	Meghalaya
Nagaland		Kerala	Mizoram
Manipur		Madhya Pradesh	Sikkim
		Punjab	Tripura
		Rajasthan	A & N Islands
		Uttar Pradesh	Chandigarh
		West Bengal	D & N Haveli
		Chhattisgarh	Daman & Diu
		Jharkhand	Lakshadweep
		Orissa	
		Uttaranchal	

2.2 Heterogeneity of HIV Epidemic

The epidemic in India is very heterogeneous with diverse modes of infection, particularly in southern and western states, namely, Tamil Nadu, Karnataka, Andhra Pradesh, Maharashtra and two north eastern states, namely, Nagaland and Manipur. Even within states, there is a wide variance in HIV prevalence between districts and intra districts as evidenced by data from HIV sentinel surveillance centres and Voluntary Counselling and Testing Centres (VCTCs).

2.3 Categories of Districts

Based on the HIV surveillance data, epidemiological profile, risk and vulnerability, NACO has classified the 611 districts in the country into 4 categories viz. A, B, C and D (**Table 2.2** & **Figure 2.1**) many of them located within the so called low prevalence states. For further details on categories of districts and state-wise break-up please see **Annex 1**.

Table 2.2: Categories of Districts

	Category of Districts	
1.	More than 1% ANC/PPTCT prevalence in district in any time in any of the sites in the last 3 years	A
2.	Less than 1% ANC/PPTCT prevalence in all the sites during last 3 years associated with More than 5% prevalence in any HRG group (STD/CSW/MSM/IDU)	B
3.	Less than 1% in ANC prevalence in all sites during last 3 years with Less than 5% in all STD clinic attendees or any HRG with known hot spots (Migrants, truckers, large aggregation of factory workers, tourist etc)	C
4.	Less than 1% in ANC prevalence in all sites during last 3 years with less than 5% in all STD clinic attendees or any HRG OR No or poor HIV data With no known hot spots/unknown	D

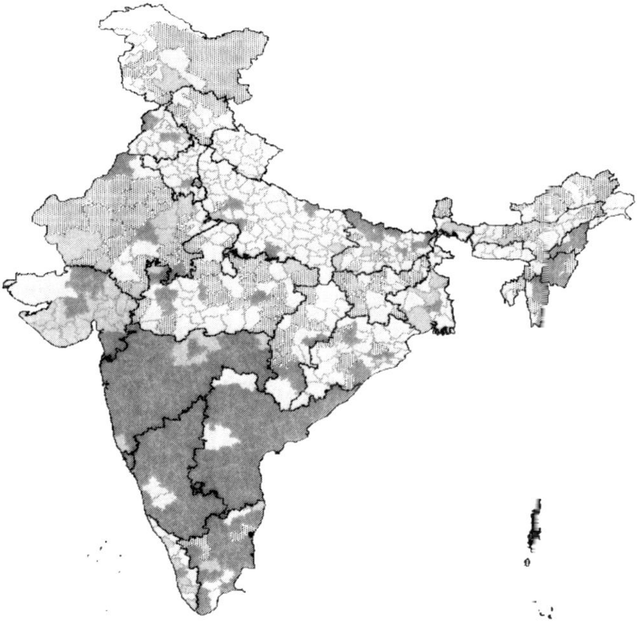

Figure 2.1: showing 611 districts and their classification based on epidemiology, risk and vulnerability

2.4 Routes of Transmission

Information from AIDS case reporting indicates that sex continues to be the main route (86%) of transmission in most parts of the country. Blood products, intravenous drug use and perinatal transmission are the other routes (see **Figure 2.2**). Intravenous drug use is the predominant route of transmission in the north eastern states of India.

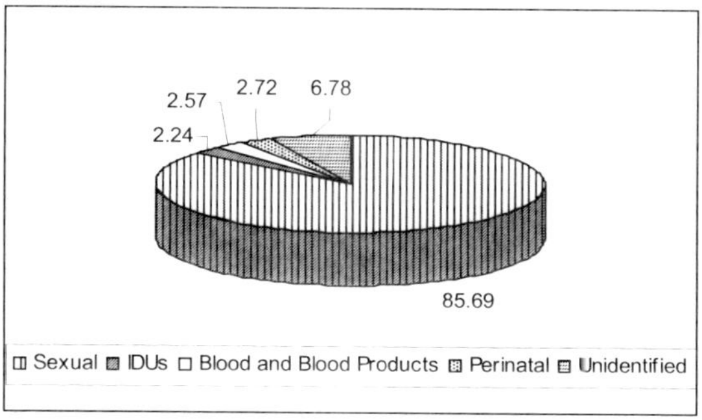

Figure 2.2: Routes of HIV Transmission

2.5 Demographic Pattern of Vulnerable Population in India

Since 2001, more than two million clients have been tested in VCTC units which provided services to nearly 800,000 people in 2005 alone. Of these, nearly 13% tested HIV +ve in 2005 (see **Table 2.3**).

Table 2.3: Testing Results Data from VCTC - All India

	2003	***2004***	***2005***
People tested for HIV/AIDS at VCTC	673,698	784,040	807,109
Number of HIV positives receiving test results	82,848	105,840	105,118
% of HIV positives receiving test results	12.3	13.5	13.0

Source: CMIS Data 2003-2005 NACO

VCTC data (CMIS 2005) show that 16% and 26% of those who access VCTC are below 25 years and 30 years respectively. These two groups represent 9% and 20% respectively of those who are identified as positive. It is also to be noted that in the age group of 15-19 and 20 -24 years, the majority were women: 60% and 63% respectively (see **Figure 2.3**).

Figure 2.3: Age and sex wise distribution of Testing and positivity at VCTC

Less than 14 years		15 – 19 years		20 – 24 years		25 – 29 years		30 – 39 years		40 – 49 years		>50 years		Age not Specified	
Male	Female	Male	Female	Male	Female	Male	Female	Male	Female	Male	Female	Male	Female	Male	Female
16962	12971	12461	19005	39717	67852	52283	54221	82421	56320	43388	22601	32365	13181	1839	1197
2142	1577	302	670	2623	4806	7876	7417	18817	9321	7663	2883	2698	855	158	91

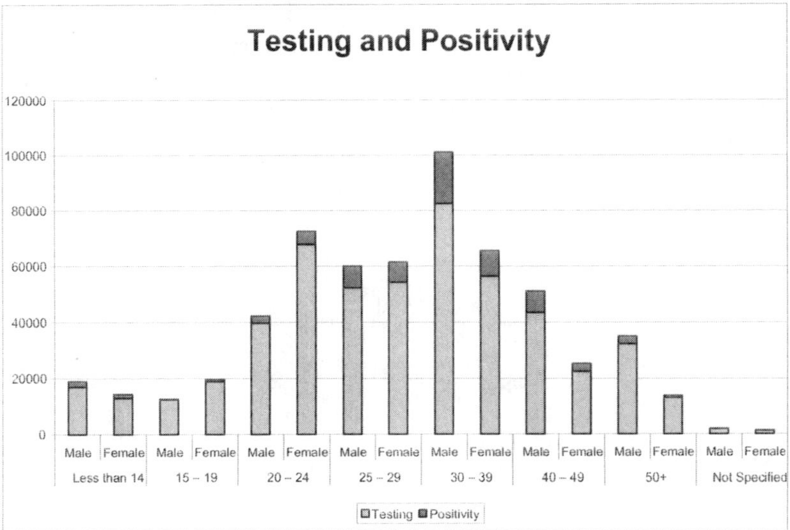

2.6 Increasing Feminization of Indian Epidemic

In the general population, women and young people are becoming increasingly more vulnerable to the infection. According to the 2005 sentinel surveillance findings, 38.4% of the infected persons in the country were women. In many states, more and more monogamous women are getting infected from their husbands. The male - female ratio of infected persons also shifted from 55/100 males in 2001 to 60/100 males in 2005, indicating increasing feminization of the epidemic (see **Figure 2.4**).

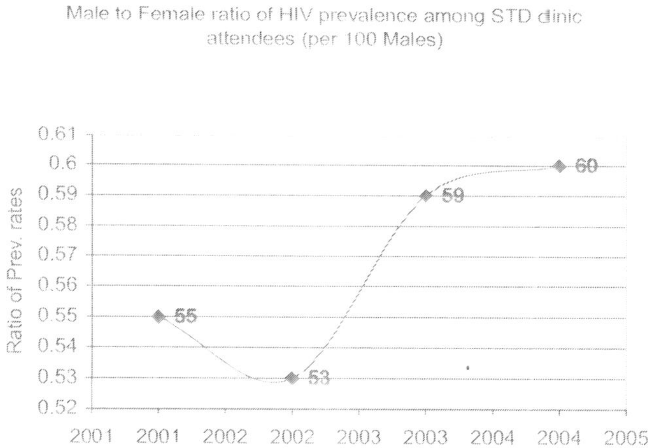

Figure 2.4: Male to Female Ratio of HIV Prevalence among STD Clinic Attendees

2.7 Knowledge and Behaviour

In 2001, a nationwide behavioural sentinel surveillance survey (BSS) was conducted to provide baseline information on risky behaviour patterns in the country, both for the general population and high risk groups like female sex workers and their clients, men who have sex with men (MSM) and injecting drug users (IDUs). The BSS revealed wide variations in knowledge of HIV/AIDS between different states and between rural and urban populations. While 76.1% of the Indian population had heard of HIV/AIDS, the figure was 93.2% for urban males and 65.2% for rural women. The values ranged from 99.5% for urban males in Kerala to 21.5% for rural females in Bihar. Only 46.8% of the respondents were aware of the two important methods for prevention of transmission i.e. consistent condom use and sex with uninfected partner. This, however, masked regional and gender based variations. For example, the lowest awareness rates were recorded among rural women in Gujarat, Bihar and UP (21.5% - 27.6%). The BSS study indicated that 50% of the people at the national level used condoms with non-regular sex partners. This figure, too, varies considerably between different geographical regions and states of India.

2.8 Prevalence of Sexually Transmitted Diseases (STDs)

STI prevalence is a good marker for HIV as both share common modes of transmission; STI also multiplies the probability of exposure to HIV infection. Over 5% of adult population in India suffers from STDs and most regions of the country show relatively high levels of STDs. HIV prevalence rates among STD patients also remains high: 22.8% in Andhra Pradesh, 15.2% in Maharashtra, 12.2% in Manipur and 7.47% in Delhi. Among women, 14% of those attending STD clinics were found to be HIV positive in some states.

Community based prevalence study conducted by NACO substantiated the findings of regional studies undertaken in some southern states of India. Vulnerability of rural and urban regions of the country to HIV is evident from the community level data (see **Table 2.4**).

Table 2.4: Summary Results of STD/RTI Community Prevalence Study (NACO 2003)

Diseases	*Low-Moderate*		*High*	
	Urban	*Rural*	*Urban*	*Rural*
No STD/RTI	83.9	86.0	84.8	82.0
Normal excluding candidiasis & B.Vaginosis	94.2	95.3	94.0	88.3
Trichomonisis	2.7	1.8	1.5	0.3
Candidiasis	6.6	5.5	6.6	8.1
Bacterial Vaginosis	7.2	6.4	4.0	6.5
Chancroid	0	0.1	0	0.1
Herpes-2	0.6	0.7	1.6	1.9
Syphilis	0.4	1.0	0.8	1.2
HPV	1.6	0.8	0.4	0.3
HIV	0.1	0.3	1.4	1.1
Gonorrhea	0.2	0.1	0.2	0.6
Chlamydia	0.1	0	0.4	0.2
Multiple Infection excluding candiasis	0.4	0.2	0.2	0.3
STI Prevalence	5.8	4.7	6.0	6.2

2.9 Risk and Vulnerability to HIV Infection

The risk of and vulnerability to HIV infection differs between sub-populations. Sex workers, IDUs, MSM including transgender sub-populations are at the highest risk. However, these groups are not isolated communities but often mixed up with other sub-populations. For instance, many drug users are also sellers and buyers of sex. Men who have sex with men may also be married and have sexual relations with spouses and sometimes with female sex workers.

2.10 High Risk Groups (HRGs)

Most of the states in India have a concentrated epidemic, focused in sub-populations, which are relatively more at risk of acquiring HIV due to their occupation (sex workers), sexual preferences (men who have sex with men) or for recreation (injecting drug users).

In 2005, prevalence of HIV in HRGs showed relatively high levels of sex workers: Maharashtra 23.62%, Karnataka 18.39%, Andhra Pradesh 12.97%; MSM: Delhi 20.4%, Karnataka 11.6%, Gujarat 10.67%; IDUs: Manipur 24.10%, Delhi 22.80, Tamil Nadu 18%, Tripura 10.9%. An expert group which carried out size estimations of the core groups at risk in 2006 (see **Table 2.5**), is of the opinion that the future of India's HIV epidemic depends on the scope and effectiveness of programmes for these groups.

Table 2.5: Estimate of High Risk Groups in India

HRG		*Estimated Numbers*
Female Sex Workers		831,677 to 1,242,819
MSM > 5 partners		2,352,133
Male Sex Workers		235,213
IDU	Male	96,463 to 189,729
	Female	10,055 to 33,392

2.11 Coverage of HRG Populations

The State AIDS Control Societies (SACS) in collaboration with NGOs in different locations in the country are currently implementing 1033 targeted intervention projects across the country (see **Figure 2.5**). Thematic distribution of these interventions undertaken by SACS, is discussed in the section on prevention and TI. More than half of these projects are located in the high prevalence states of Andhra Pradesh, Maharashtra, Tamil Nadu, Karnataka, Manipur and Nagaland. Overall, TIs are estimated to have covered about 45% to 50% of the HRG population in the country.

Though not at the same level of risk as the three groups mentioned in para 2.9 above, other groups like long distance truckers, prison inmates, migrant and mobile population and street children are also at a higher level of risk in comparison to the general population. Of the estimated 5-6 million

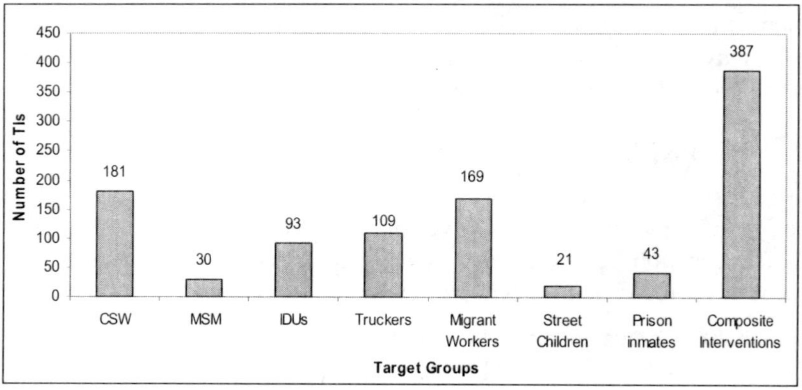

Figure 2.5: Coverage of HRG through TIs

truckers, about 3-3.5 million long distance truckers are reported to be relatively more vulnerable.

Other groups which are vulnerable include: tribals, women, youth and adolescents. Of the total number of AIDS cases reported in India in 2004, 35.5% were in the age group of 15-29 yrs – the most productive section of the society. The median age at first sex is about 21 years for males and 18 years for females. However, there are wide inter-state variations in the country, ranging from as low as 16 years in AP, Bihar, MP, Rajasthan and UP to as high as 20 years in Kerala and Goa (rural female) and a low of 18 years in MP to a high of 25 years in Kerala (rural males).

2.12 Projections for NACP-III

Mathematical and statistical models of the HIV epidemic help to understand the future course of the epidemic. Current projections are based on a dynamic mathematical modelling founded on the principles in AIDS modelling developed by Anderson and May (1988, 1991). The technique has been widely accepted as one of the key strategies to understand the progress and impact of the epidemic in different settings.

Two models were constructed as a part of the planning process of NACP-III. Statistical modelling using Spectrum software (Dr. DCS Reddy) was used for estimating NACP-II level of interventions in care, support and treatment and a mathematical model constructed by Dr. Arni Srinivasa Rao took into account planned expansion of activities under prevention, in addition to care, support and treatment during NACP-III. The basic assumptions of the models are provided in **Annex 2**.

Statistical Model: Based on the sero-surveillance data from different sentinel sites in India in ANC clinics and in other HRGs, an expert group in India has estimated the number of PLHA in India to be 5.134 million in 2004 which has been set as the baseline for the model. Using spectrum software, a group of experts has projected the PLHA population for the duration of the project (2006 to 2011) at the current level of intervention. (see **Figure 2.6**).

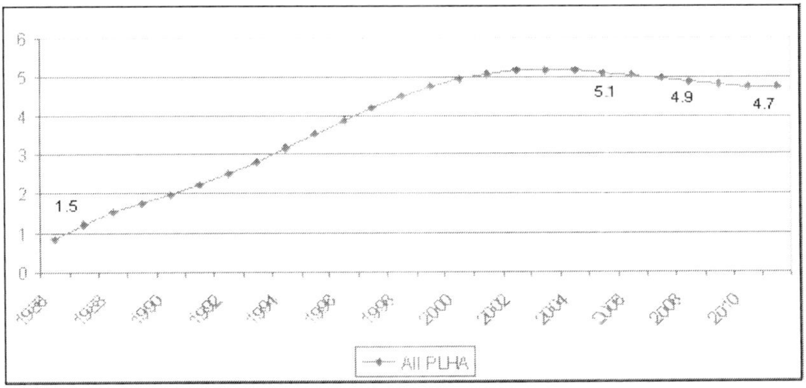

Figure 2.6: Projections on Number of PLHA (all age groups)

Data extrapolated from projections at the state level covers: i. All PLHA, ii. Adult cases with HIV/AIDS, iii. New cases of HIV/AIDS, iv. Children below 14 years with HIV/AIDS, v. Children requiring Rx with ART, and vi. Deaths of PLHA.

Mathematical Model: The following scenarios were used in the mathematical model:

- Continuation of NACP-II level of interventions;
- ART scale-up + NACP-II interventions;
- NACP-III interventions achieving 50% of target;
- NACP-III interventions achieving 75% of target; and
- NACP-III interventions achieving 100% of target.

Summary of Mathematical Modelling Results (see **Figure 2.7**)

2.13 Scenario Analysis

- Interventions of NACP-II maintained with same level of coverage

  If NACP-II level of interventions are continued during the project

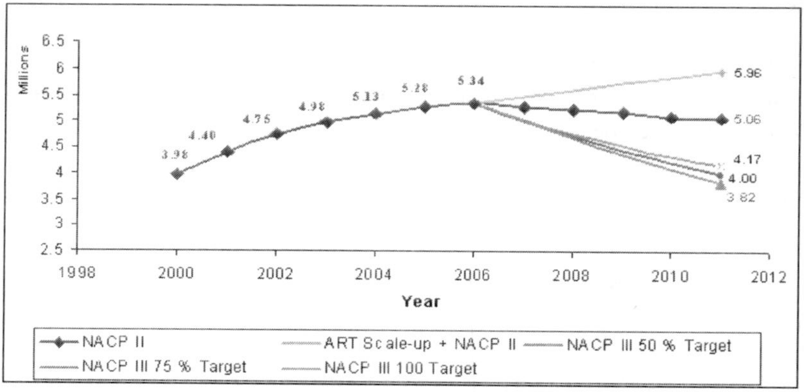

Figure 2.7: NACP-III Projection for PLHA

period of 2006 to 2011 (in terms of current levels of coverage of targeted interventions among HRG, condom use in non-regular partners (50%), ART (10%), treatment of STDs (50%), transmission through blood 0.34%,) then from 2004 estimate of 5.134 million, the projected number of PLHA is expected to come down to 5.06 million.

- **NACP-II level of Interventions**

  There is a commitment by the government to provide ART to all those who need it. However, unless care, support and treatment services are integrated with prevention, particularly positive prevention, the number of PLHA will continue to rise as predicted in the model. In such a scenario, the total number of persons living with HIV will go up from 5.134 to 5.96 million over the next 5 years.

- **NACP-III level of Interventions**

  NACP-III envisages expanding the coverage of HRGs to 80% during the programme period. The programme will target CSWs, MSM and IDU sub-populations. The ART scale-up will be associated with integration of care, support and treatment with prevention. During this period, all eligible PLHA will receive ART. They would also be targeted specifically to participate in positive prevention activities. Transmission through blood will be reduced to 0.5%, while 80% of the 27 million estimated deliveries will be covered by PPTCT programme. With NACP-III targets being achieved, the total number of PLHA will come down to 3.82 million by 2011.

2.14 Policy Implications and Future Directions (2006-2011)

If the investment on prevention activities among high risk populations is scaled up with particular attention to ART coverage and positive prevention measures, NACP-III will be able to halt and reverse the epidemic. This will involve:

- Saturation of the coverage of high risk groups through greater involvement of community based organizations and extensive network of institutions both in public and private sectors;
- Greater focus on changing attitudes and behaviour of vulnerable sections of general population to prevent transmission;
- Comprehensive care, support and treatment with adequate follow up measures;
- Providing high quality HIV related services to those who need at various levels; and
- Creation of appropriate mechanisms and capacities at national, state and district levels to implement and monitor the interventions.

NACP-III envisages a substantial increase in budgetary allocation to the programme activities with increased emphasis on prevention. Of the total programme costs, 60-70 per cent should be on prevention and 15-20 per cent on care, support and treatment. Additionally, capacity building and strategic information management will require an investment of around 10 per cent and 5 per cent of the NACP-III budget respectively to achieve the HIV related Millennium Development Goals (MDGs).

Chapter - 3

Programme Strategies - Prevention

Prevention has been and will continue to be the mainstay of the strategic response to HIV/AIDS. With 99 per cent of the adult population of the country uninfected, India has a window of opportunity to reverse the progression of this infection and reduce the overall levels of prevalence. There is increasing evidence to suggest that India's HIV epidemic is being driven by sex worker - client interactions (except in the North East where injecting drug use is clearly the major mode of spread although sexual transmission is increasing. There is evidence of increasing injecting drug use from some other regions too). MSM activity in India is not well described but the majority of men with MSM behaviour are married so the risk of spread to general population women exists.

The strategy to achieve the objective of reducing the overall level of the epidemic will consist of a three-pronged approach (also see **Table 3.1**):

- According the highest priority to the saturation of the three high risk groups (HRG) - commercial sex workers (CSWs), injecting drug users (IDUs) and men having sex with men (MSM) - with a comprehensive package of preventive services SACS will be expected to concentrate on this group before moving on to cover other groups;
- Addressing clients of SW through SW interventions, through condoms, social marketing campaigns and through addressing men in occupation settings. Truckers and migrants, categorised as bridge populations and prioritised after the three high risk groups, are key occupation groups who will be addressed. Groups with a mix of different risk levels i.e. Composite Interventions which covered populations of varying risk levels under NACP-II, will be re-designed to focus on HRGs or the bridge populations; coverage of low or negligible risk will be scaled down and funding withdrawn from year 2 of NACP-III; and

Table 3.1: Framework for Prevention

Sl. No.	Target groups and principles	Key actors/partners
1.	Saturating the coverage of three High Risk Groups: Sex Workers and their clients, Injecting Drug Users and partners, and Men having Sex with Men. Following principles will guide the implementation: - District level mapping and planning - Focus on coverage of clients of sex workers and partners of MSM as well as IDUs. - Linkages between TI and continuum of care - Focus on enabling environment (including equitable access to services) - Forming CBOs to represent the community - Setting up of TSUs at the state level to enhance capacity of partners and quality of interventions.	SACS, in partnership with NGOs/ CBOs as well as other Ministries (MWCW, MSJE) and support from bilateral and UN agencies along with PLHA networks.
2.	Expanding the coverage of two bridge populations - truckers and migrant workers: Following principles will guide the implementation: - Mapping of major halt points of truckers and hot spots of migrants. - Focus on labour related migrants between source and destinations. - Greater involvement/ownership of truckers associations, federations, unions, and relevant corporate companies. - Improved access to condoms, STI and HIV testing, treatment and care services. - Special focus on gender dimensions in sectors/areas which employ more women like agriculture and construction. - Special attention to socio economic vulnerabilities and gender inequity.	National Highway Authority of India, Ministry of Surface Transport, SACS/ NGOs, Truckers associations and unions, companies having a stake in truckers like truck/tyre manufactures and those using truckers to transport their products. For migrants, construction companies, SACS/ NGOs, relevant unions/institutions.
3.	**HIV Prevention among the general population: highly vulnerable populations, women, youth and children** Women in 15-49 years of age group (with a particular focus on spouses of truckers and migrants, survivors of trafficking and violence, women engaged in informal sector employment like agriculture, construction). Young people in the age group of 15-29 (in schools, colleges, universities, uniformed forces, out of school/college, youth in community). Youth in high and vulnerable districts, adolescents in sex work, young IDUs, working children and street children. Refugees and displaced populations. Tribals and other socially disadvantaged groups such as dalits. Special attention to socio economic vulnerabilities and gender inequity. Programmatic integration with the RCH II Programme. Rural strategy for prevention.	Ministry of Women and Child Welfare, MOHFW, and other relevant Ministries/government departments, UN/ bilateral agencies. SACS/NGOs/CBOs/PHLA networks. Ministry of Youth, Educational Institutions/Ministry of Labour and Employment. Women's empowerment Programmes and ITDP.

(Contd...)

4.	**HIV Prevention among general population: a multi sectoral response through mainstreaming** Following principles will guide the implementation: - Mainstreaming HIV/AIDS in schemes/ Programmes of different ministries (e.g. Ministry of Social Justice & Empowerment for Injecting Drug Users). - Strengthening HIV/AIDS interventions in the world of work – workplace policy and Programmes in both formal and informal sectors - Mainstreaming HIV/AIDS in Civil Society Organizations, religious organizations, and media.	NCA, NACO/ UN/bilateral agencies, different ministries/ PLHA networks. Employers' organizations, chambers/ trade unions and enterprises in public and private sector. SACS, and partners at the state level. NGOs/CBOs working in non-health sector, religious organizations media and Women's organizations.

- Reaching out to the high risk groups who are in scattered numbers in rural areas, other highly vulnerable population groups in the community, and three vulnerable groups, namely HIV affected children, youth in the age group 15-29 years and women.

Given the variations in risk among districts, Category A, B and C will receive high priority in scaling up. In category D districts and parts of category C districts, focus will be on awareness raising strategies for vulnerability reduction, risk reduction, promotion of protective behaviours and data gathering on the extent of the HRGs for initiation of TIs.

An analysis of the TI implementation under NACP-II brought out that in A districts which are high prevalent, 13.6 per cent of the districts did not receive TI and in 12.3 per cent there was no core group activity either. The situation in B and C districts was 20.3 per cent and 6 per cent and 50.7 per cent and 5.1 per cent respectively, bringing to the fore the need to ensure prioritization in the implementation of this most significant segment of the NACP strategy.

The following section analyses the current situation, the key concerns, the approach and strategic interventions proposed to be undertaken.

3.1 Targeted/Preventive Interventions among High Risk Groups

Prevalence Level among HRGs

An analysis of the Annual Sentinel Surveillance data during the years 2003-2005 showed that the three HRGs had a disproportionately higher level of prevalence of HIV infection as compared to other population groups including attendees of STD clinics (see **Table 3.2**). Read with the large body of behavioural surveillance data, it is clear that arresting the epidemic will need to be anchored on an intensive, focussed and well coordinated set of interventions among the HRGs.

Table 3.2: HIV Prevalence among High Risk Groups

Site type	*Number of Sites 2003-2005*	*per cent +ve 2003*	*per cent +ve 2004*	*per cent +ve 2005*
Female Sex Workers	32 - 83	10.30	9.43	8.44
Injecting Drug Users	18 – 30	13.30	11.20	10.16
Men having Sex with Men	9 – 18	12.10	7.50	8.74
ANC population	266 - 267	0.87	0.89	0.88
STD population	163-175	5.61	5.55	5.66

3.2 Size Estimations

An overall estimate of HRGs in the country was done through triangulation and validation of the existing mapping data from various sources by an expert group constituted for this purpose (January 2006)[1]. The estimated figures of the three high risk groups for the country show the following ranges:

- Female sex workers: 831,177 - 1,250,115
- MSM: 2,352,133; Male Sex Workers (MSW): 235,213
- Male IDUs: 96,463 - 1,89,729; Female IDUs: 10,055 - 33,392

3.3 Level of Response during NACP-II

During NACP-II, technical, financial and managerial systems to support targeted interventions were set up and mapping of HRGs completed in all states. As shown in **Figure 3.1**, the number of interventions increased five fold, from 199 during 1999 to 1088 in 2006, of which 700 were related to HRGs; 330 of these interventions covered 55 per cent of CSWs, 53 per cent of IDUs and 6 per cent of MSM.

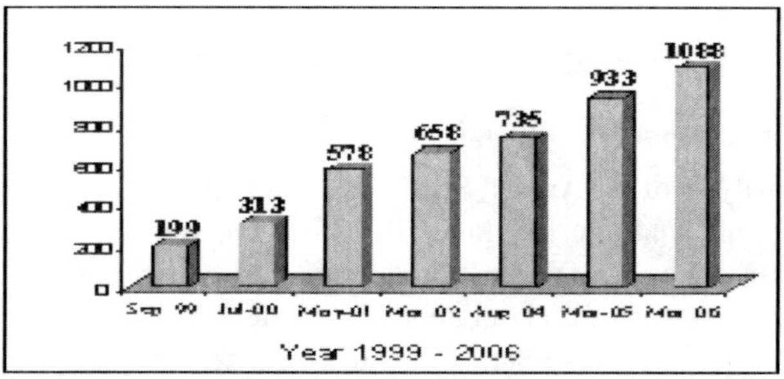

Figure 3.1: Year-wise Progress in Implementation of TIs (1999-2006)

3.4 Mid-course Corrections

Some of the initiatives and mid-course corrective action undertaken to improve the quality of implementation were as under:

- Revision of TI costing guidelines.
- Training of State level NGO advisors and Finance Managers of SACS.
- Organizing site, visits of SACS officers and NGO representatives in 9 batches to the demonstration sites developed by the APAC project in Tamil Nadu.
- Identifying 7 Regional Research and Training Centres (RRTCs) of the Ministry of Social Justice and Empowerment (MSJE) for capacity building of NGOs and establishing a Resource Centre for Sexual Health and HIV/AIDS (RCSHA) with DFID assistance in New Delhi.
- Revising the Computerized Management Information System on TIs and monitoring.

3.5 Impact of TIs

The Targeted Intervention (TI) approach has brought down prevalence level among specific groups such as sex workers in Mumbai, and IDUs in Manipur. Annual Behavioural Surveys conducted by APAC in Tamil Nadu has shown a steadily increasing rate of condom use. Repeat rounds of behavioural surveys conducted in some of the states show a significant increase in condom use by clients of female sex workers (WB[2] - 52 per cent in 2001 to 88 per cent in 2004; AP[3] - 62 per cent in 2002 to 97 per cent in 2005) and a significant reduction in STI cases - from 23 per cent in 2001 to 14 per cent in 2004- APAC[4]. Two systematic STI and HIV prevalence surveys among sex workers of Ahmedabad showed a dramatic reduction in STIs (gonococcal infections) from 19 per cent in 2000 to 6 per cent in 2003[5].

An evaluation of the TI Programmes in five states and two external evaluations undertaken in 22 states during 2002-03[6] observed that:

- TIs have a critical role in reducing spread of the epidemic and therefore, interventions must focus on groups at highest risk (CSW, MSM, IDU) and saturate their coverage.
- Capacity building of NGOs and SACS should be further strengthened as the number of trainings (2.67 / intervention / year) is inadequate and number of training days (6.63/ intervention / year) is low.

- Issues related to financial flows to the NGOs should be addressed to reduce delays (91 days) and low volume of funds (Rs. 5.44 lakhs).
- Quality of implementation should be improved.

3.6 Lessons Learnt

Implementation of TI Programme during NACP-II has 4 clear lessons which form the basis for the strategy proposed for NACP-III:

(i) More focussed approach on HRGs: With several NGOs implementing composite TIs involving a disparate group of populations at varied levels of risk and vulnerabilities such as street children, FSW, MSM etc. there has been a serious dilution in the quality and the depth of interventions. There is need to steer NGO effort to focus on HRGs only as their needs are specialized and require a multifaceted approach.

(ii) Need for establishing linkages between TI and the continuum of services: At present, TIs are not programmatically linked to the care, support and treatment services. This gap needs to be addressed in order to enhance the participation of the TIs in assessing the risk status by adopting safe practices.

(iii) Weak supervision: Given the difficult nature of the work involved, there is a great need to establish a system of supportive supervision and constant capacity building of SACS as well as NGOs so as to improve quality of implementation and stricter adherence to behaviour change, particularly in matters related to condom use.

(iv) Need to shift strategy from assistance to empowerment through the process of forming Community Based Organizations: A major failing during NACP-II was the relatively low priority accorded to replicating the Sonagachi model implemented successfully during NACP-I. The Sonagachi model demonstrated the value of involving members of the community in decision making and management of the projects. In fact, recognizing the importance of this need, TIs in a few states have been working along these lines. HRG networks such as, for example, the Indian Network of Sex Workers and the Indian Network for Sexual Minorities etc. have demonstrated how community based organisations are able to deal with vital issues such as police harassment and street violence.

3.7 Approach and Strategy under NACP-III

The approach and the strategy to be adopted under NACP-III will be guided by the experiences gained during NACP-II. Targeted Interventions will continue to emphasize and focus on the five elements that are the core activities of a TI:

(i) Behaviour change,

(ii) Access to STI services to be provided by the NGO itself or by arrangement with a public / private facility,

(iii) Monitoring access and utilization of condoms,

(iv) Ownership building, and

(v) An enabling environment.

The issues related to enabling environment will merit greater attention than has so far been the case. Besides the traditional but necessary approach of training police officers, specific projects will be designed to empower the communities to provide crisis intervention services that will consist of mobile helplines, services of a lawyer and field supervisors. This model implemented by Sangama, a MSM and transgender network in Bangalore, has been able to demonstrate its efficacy by ensuring that the response time to a crisis situation never exceeds half an hour.

Taking into account the experiences gained in the best practices, the TIs will be suitably redesigned to be more comprehensive and a clear direction given to ensure that even while upscaling the interventions to achieve saturation, all the older and more mature TIs be assisted to adopt a rights-based approach and become CBOs so as to ensure the empowerment process of the communities. Accordingly, developing leadership skills and management capacity among such NGOs will be the first priority of NACP-III.

Linking HIV related care, support and treatment with other services will be an important addition to the TI set of services Close collaboration with general health care facilities will be ensured in a manner that will enable HRGs access them without stigma or discrimination. All NGOs/ CBOs engaged in TIs will be linked to Community Care Centres, community outreach and service providers for ICTC, PPTCT centres, OI management, TB control Programme and ART. TI personnel and peer educators will be trained on treatment preparedness, adherence and psycho-social support issues. Linkages with community development Programmes and social entitlement schemes for addressing perceived needs of HRGs (like micro credit group formation, vocational training skills etc.) will also be encouraged.

3.8 Prioritization and Assuring Sustainability

The good experience of the PMU structures provided to the 8 DFID states, is proposed to be replicated by establishing similar Technical Support Units at SACS for enhancing their capacity to undertake various interventions and activities. TSUs will, however, not only assist in NGO identification and their capacity building along with creating an enabling environment and supportive supervision but also assist SACS in supervision of the care and support Programmes, logistics management, monitoring and evaluation etc.

District based planning for achieving saturated coverage, undertaking district based exercises to classify population groups based on differential risk status and geographic mapping will be the first steps. For deciding the type of intervention to be introduced, the district will be divided into four broad zones:

(i) large urban centres of economic activity, which are already covered by a TI, will be further assisted to establish CBOs with each TI having 1200 members;

(ii) peri-and semi-urban areas where concentration of HRGs may be lower, will be covered by NGOs through TIs covering atleast 800 members;

(iii) the outer periphery consisting of villages with more than 5000 population and accounting for 25 per cent of the district population will be covered by Link Workers; and

(iv) the remaining outlying part of the district will be saturated by mass media and government functionaries.

Given the variations in the levels and perceptions of risk, differential strategies, sequencing of events and pacing of the interventions will be adopted. States that have already covered major cities and towns will extend their Programme to the semi and peri urban areas, while states without data will rapidly map and implement Programmes in parallel (e.g. while Programming in big cities is rolled out, mapping in district headquarters can precede). Thus, resource allocation to specific states and districts for implementing TIs will depend on mapping of HRG to both identify state/ district specific population numbers as well as to plan the mix of service delivery models in accordance with the recommended phasing of geographic areas as described above.

Rapid scaling-up to saturate coverage to the extent of 80 per cent is proposed to be achieved through 2100 TIs covering a target of one million female sex workers and their regular partners; 1.15 million men having sex with men; and 0.19 million IDUs and their partners over a period of 5 years (2006-2011). As the HRGs are not a homogenous group, though they do share some of the vulnerabilities, differential approaches to planning and implementation will need to be undertaken at the design stage itself.

The estimates of TIs needed in each state to achieve 80 per cent coverage are detailed in the **Annex 3**. Two states will need > 250 interventions (333-Uttar Pradesh, 271-Maharashtra), while 8 states will need interventions ranging between 100-200 (Bihar, Andhra Pradesh, Tamil Nadu, West Bengal, Madhya Pradesh, Karnataka, Rajasthan and Orissa). The remaining 23 states will need up to 100 interventions.

The roll out plan for the rapid scale up of TIs among HRGs will be evolved through a series of consultative processes and workshops and developed jointly by the SACS, NGOs and CBOs. By the end of Phase III, 1000 TIs will be operating as CBO led interventions.

Table 3.3 shows the year-wise and phase-wise scale up and consolidation plan for TIs under NACP-III.

Table 3.3: Year-wise Scale-up Plan for TIs under NACP-III

	2005-06	*2006-07*	*2007-08*	*2008-09*	*2009-10*	*2010-11*
Existing Interventions	700	700	1300	1800	2100	2100
New Interventions		600	500	300	-	-
Total Interventions	700	1300	1800	2100	2100	2100
NGO Interventions	667	1127	1417	1437	1260	1050
CBO Interventions – cumulative	33	173	383	663	840	1050
% CBO Interventions	4.70	>10	>20	>30	40	50

Sustainability to TIs by upscaling the process of integrating the concepts of CBO led interventions, as opposed to NGO led, are based on the principle of community ownership and the approach is rights-based providing emphasis on the fundamental rights of the communities to dignity and self respect. It is clear from the experience gained so far that the social marginalization and disempowerment that characterise HRGs are the key vulnerabilities that need to be addressed before any interventions related to HIV/AIDS can be successfully adopted by them. By involving the communities, empowering them to handle responsibility, think and analyze the issues based on data collected by them and work out strategies to reduce their health risks in a non judgemental way, will lead to greater and more sustainable compliance to adoption of healthy behaviour practices.

All elements of a CBO led process – community selected peer educators, promotion of group dynamics, community monitoring of services, participation of community members in all management committees, involving them in the framing of byelaws, registering the organisation, designing the financial and administrative systems and agreeing on resource mobilisation and expenditure etc. – will be inbuilt as part of the design and protocol of the CBO TIs. The implication of following such a strategy means a strategic withdrawal of NGOs from being the key drivers. For achieving this goal, NACO will initiate action to build the requisite capacity among the NGOs, document lessons from best practice sites, help them prepare exit strategies and hand hold in the implementation of the CBO strategy.

Differential Strategies among HRGs

3.9 Commercial Sex Workers

The mapping exercise referred to earlier has been immensely useful in helping to plan focussed strategies. It has helped in the understanding of the concentration and dispersion points of sex workers. For example, in Karnataka, mapping has shown that the towns have a high concentration of sex workers (Bangalore city itself has over 27 such points), the larger villages / small towns have a smaller concentration, while small villages have one or two sex workers. In Karnataka, another sample study of 146 villages from 7 districts showed that 47 per cent of the villages had more than 10 FSWs while 25 per cent did not have any FSWs. Based on a regression of this data, it is estimated that a village with 5000 or higher population will probably have atleast 10 FSWs.

The mapping exercise has more importantly provided critical insights into the operational aspects of commercial sex trade. Over the years, the female sex trade has undergone dynamic shifts from being a brothel-based activity to more fluid formations such as street- based and home-based. For example, in Andhra Pradesh, it is estimated that 75 per cent of the sex workers are street-based, 22.5 per cent are home-based and 2.1 per cent are brothel- based.[7] Such operational shifts have added to the complexity of the epidemic due to the enhancement of the probabilities of the infection going unnoticed and unattended.

Analysis of the socio economic profile of the female sex workers has brought out four important factors that need to be taken note of while designing any strategy:

(i) All sex work is not forced or trafficked, but poverty is certainly a strong motivation to get inducted into this trade. This also explains the alarming increase in the number of sex workers coming to urban areas from villages;

(ii) Highly competitive nature of the market explains for the increasingly fragmented nature of the trade and the relatively low earnings. With an average of three clients per day and average number of 17 working days per month, the average earnings do not exceeding Rs.100 per day;

(iii) Due to the illegal nature of the profession, routine violence is faced at the hands of a multiple set of people – police, goons, middlemen – increasing their overall vulnerability; and

(iv) The overwhelmingly oppressive environment which denies them understanding, empathy and acceptance resulting in their marginalization and social exclusion, making a comeback difficult if not impossible.

The mapping exercise undertaken in Karnataka and an analysis of state Census data, suggest that, in that state, about 25 per cent of the villages do not have any sex workers, villages with 5000 population have less than 10 sex workers, and smaller villages account for a few scattered ones. The census 2001 shows that there are about 18,000 villages having 5000 population accounting for about 20 per cent of the population.

Given this nature of the geographical spread and certain vulnerabilities particular to the commercial sex trade, the underlying approach will be rights-based and proactive for ensuring safe spaces for CSWs. The following four components of the strategy will be undertaken in all A & B category districts, while the first two and the fourth component in C and D districts so as to saturate the coverage of all high risk groups.

(i) Formation of Community Based Organisations & Peer led Interventions for saturating coverage of all HRGs in urban areas: All towns and cities (defined as per Census 2001) will be covered with high-intensity target intervention with outreach and service provisions for sex workers (female, male and Hijra populations) and their clients.

(ii) NGO led Interventions in rural areas with 5000+ population: Given the large spread of the villages, and the probability of there being more than 10 FSWs or more practising in the villages, an outreach and service delivery plan to access these FSWs in line with the TI approach will be designed i.e., capacity building among smaller NGOs and subsequently linking them to larger networks for long term sustainability.

(iii) **Mainstreaming Interventions in rural areas with <5000 population**: In these villages, focus will be on creating general awareness about HIV/AIDS and STIs, and also providing referral services for STI treatment, VCTC/PPTCT, care and support. Such interventions will be done through a link worker model. This model implies having, for every 5000 population, 2 link workers (male and female), who will be trained in communication on HIV/AIDS and accessing referral services. The cost of the LW strategy would include monthly remuneration to LWs, travel, supervision, training etc. In large districts, an estimated 200 link workers would be required. The actual numbers required will be based on the detailed risk assessment that will be undertaken in all districts (For more details on Link Worker strategy please see Chapter 5 page 44).

(iv) **Small, scattered villages**: Focus will be on environment building and integrating vulnerable persons with economic activities to provide livelihood opportunities and reduce the intensity of the circumstances that provide grounds for resorting to sex trade. The enabling environment will be through the government machinery by mainstreaming HIV/AIDS in all departments.

3.10 MSM and Trans-Gender (TG)

As per the Report of the Expert Group on Size Estimation of Population with High Risk Behaviour for NACP-III, RCSHA- 2006, the number of MSM estimated for the whole country is 23,52,133 and Male sex workers (MSW) are estimated to be 2,35,213.

MSM denotes "men who have sex with other men" regardless of the presence or absence of any specific sexual identity. MSM are a heterogeneous group. There are many nomenclatures and categories of MSM in the country, on the basis of their sexual preferences. In terms of Programme implementation, all face a similar set of vulnerabilities and require a similar set of interventions. Programmatically, however, it is necessary to underscore the difference between male sex workers whose vulnerabilities are more akin to the female sex workers, and the MSMs who indulge in sex more for pleasure and in accordance with their sexual orientation. This difference becomes important in the approaches to be adopted for bringing in behaviour change towards adopting safe practices. The critical point of this category of the HRG is their identification as many could be bisexual, and most may be indulging in same sex casually and for pleasure without necessarily realizing their vulnerability to risk.

For reasons indicated above, due to gaps in understanding, the behaviour of certain sub-populations (such as – male sex workers, trans-genders, bi-sexual men etc.) and lack of expertise in designing appropriate interventions for them,[8] the coverage of MSM population has remained low. MSM interventions operate in an environment in which it is considered not only illegal and thus 'hidden' but also socially abhorrent. TIs for MSM are mostly operated in NGO mode with comparatively few networks.

The highly successful models of the few networks, however, are encouraging signs to undertake a strategy aimed at supporting and nurturing formation of MSM CBOs. This will require extensive capacity building among the NGOs as well as the existing networks to organize and assume ownership. Apart from the issues related to empowerment and networking, TIs for MSM will also address specific needs of the community such as ensuring access to thicker condoms and lubricants and treatment of anal STIs. Special efforts will be undertaken to bring about behaviour change through innovative communication strategies and materials. Operation research will be carried out to understand the sexual practices of bisexual men, and provide them access to preventive care, support and treatment.

3.11 IDUs

Injecting drug use has indicated an increase, covering even small towns in a majority of states[9]. The estimated range of male IDUs across the country is between 96,463 - 1,89,729 and female IDUs between 10,055 - 33,392. As many as 50,800 of these IDUs are located in the north eastern states of Manipur, Nagaland, Mizoram, Assam and Meghalaya.

IDU-driven HIV can quickly escalate from a core group to the general population, necessitating a comprehensive response based on robust epidemiological networks. Addressing HIV infections in bridge populations such as sex workers and sexual partners can be a long drawn effort and not as effective as aggressive interventions around early IDU outbreaks addressing sexual as well as drug-using risks. Clearly, innovative IDU surveillance and IDU responses need higher attention than has so far been the case.

As on December 2005, 93 IDU interventions were undertaken in 8 states - 4 states in the north east (78 TIs) and 4 states (15 TIs) elsewhere in India. Surveillance data from 30 IDU sentinel sites (2005) indicated that approximately 10.16 per cent of IDUs were infected with HIV, the highest increase among all high risk groups, though a marginal decline from earlier years - 13.3 per cent in 2003 to 11.2 per cent in 2004. Comparative year wise and state wise break-up of HIV prevalence among IDU population indicates higher prevalence in Maharashtra, Manipur, Mizoram, Nagaland, Tamil Nadu, Delhi, Assam, Chandigarh, Kerala, Tripura and West Bengal with Nagaland and Manipur showing an increased interface between IDU and heterosexual behaviour.

3.12 Inclusion of Oral Substitution – Need for Policy

Diffusion of injecting drug use across India is a cause of concern as, apart from HIV due to non-sterile injecting practices, this causes significant morbidity and mortality such as abscesses, hepatitis C etc. Drug use and particularly injecting drug use often requires long-term treatment and care. Adequate access to a range of treatment options to respond to the varying needs of opioid dependent, therefore, need to be undertaken.

Scientific evidence suggests that substitution treatment can help reduce criminality, infectious diseases and drug related deaths as well as improve the physical, psychological and social well being of dependent users.

Therefore, while globally, methadone is the most widely used agent in substitution treatment, buprenorphine is another alternative. Several countries such as USA, China, Holland, Germany, France, Thailand, Nepal and Queensland in Australia currently operate large-scale methadone Programmes. India has yet to formulate a national policy on the issue related to substitution treatment. Guidelines for quality assurance and best practice have yet to be developed and need to be laid down before a scaled up national plan is put in place. More rigorous studies using differential doses of oral substitutes in different settings need to be undertaken and documented.

At present, NACO is supporting the salary of a counsellor employed in each of the 200 MSJE–supported NGOs running Counselling, De-addiction and Rehab centres. These will need to be continued but more closely monitored.

3.13 Approach to be adopted during NACP-III

During NACP-III, IDUs and their sexual partners will be reached in diverse settings (street, community, addiction treatment centres, prisons etc.)

The Harm Reduction package would consist of a comprehensive package of services: primary health care including abscess management, needle / syringe exchange, substitution, condom provision, and residential care services to be implemented within an enabling environment which will imply active mobilization of social support for the IDUs. The high morbidity experienced by this sub-population in terms of TB, HIV, Hep B and C and psychiatric co-morbidity draws the need to leverage services that include nutrition, shelter, TB services and medical referrals. This approach will also call for closer collaborative work with the Ministry of Social Justice & Empowerment for providing support for de-addiction and rehabilitation Programmes.

A crucial component will be to build an enabling environment through adoption of state AIDS policies endorsing harm reduction approaches including the sensitization of law enforcement agencies. This will be developed though the inclusion of senior police officials who are already supportive of these approaches, efforts for stigma reduction, collaboration with vocational training centres of various government departments and employment in the corporate sector. Apart from addressing the IDU, the NACP-III will also address their regular sex partners and spouses for reduction of transmission and vulnerability to HIV.

3.14 Linking HIV related Care, Support and Treatment with other services

Close collaboration with general health care facilities and HIV related care, support and treatment services will be ensured so that the HRGs access them without stigma or discrimination. All NGOs/CBOs engaged in TIs will be linked to Community Care Centres, community outreach Programmes and service providers for ICTC, PPTCT centres, OI management, TB control Programme and ART. Joint sensitization sessions of NGOs/CBOs and PLHA networks engaged in TIs along with service providers will be organized. TI personnel and peer educators will be trained on treatment preparedness, adherence and psycho-social support issues. Linkages with community development Programmes and social entitlement schemes to address perceived needs of HRGs (like micro credit group formation, vocational training skills etc.) will be encouraged. Linkages will be established between CBOs and anti- trafficking units to prevent trafficking of women and minors and to provide support to victims of trafficking.

3.15 Implementation of the Strategy: Strengthening Programme Management Capacity

Based on lessons learnt, efforts will be made towards strengthening capacity of personnel and existing structures for optimal outcomes. These are detailed below:

- **Structural Arrangements:** The present structure for TI at NACO will be strengthened with professionals having skills in planning, managing and monitoring of the TI programmes. It will be separated from IEC and social mobilization programme and trained professionals inducted to lead the process. A Technical Support Unit will be set up in each SACS to strengthen the programme management capacity.
- **Management Capacity:** All the key players of the TI implementation viz. NACO, SACS, Technical Support Units, DAPCU, NGOs, Key CBOs of HRG will be provided training in evidence based planning and management capacity for TI, developing systems, appraisal processes, contract and grant making. Management institutions will be identified for providing such training.
- **Technical Capacity:** Among all the implementing agencies and programme managers (from the frontlines to the highest level of supervision) technical capacity will be built/ strengthened. This will range from peer educator skills in outreach to quality service provision among the key providers with training in rights, laws, ethics, gender & sexuality and rights-based approaches (RBA) for empowerment of key population (KP) etc. Capacity strengthening will include:

  learning through exposure visits to model programmes; on-site hand holding support through an identified pool of mentors (i.e. experienced programme implementers) and development of self learning modules and tools for self assessment

3.16 Selection and Monitoring of Implementing Organisations

- Selection of NGOs/CBOs will be through a transparent process as already established under NACP-II. The system of selections through Technical Advisory Committees (TAC), Joint Appraisal Team (JAT) and Executive Committee (Refer to NACO Costing Guidelines, November 2004), will be suitably modified if required and followed in NACP-III.

- Under the Monitoring & Evaluation systems, qualitative methods will also be used in project monitoring and evaluations. Periodic monitoring & review systems will be in the form of Experience Sharing and Review Meeting (ESRM), Participatory Site Visit (PSV), Cluster Meeting; other innovative participatory systems could be evolved for effective and efficient monitoring.
- Tools will also be developed for social audit, accreditation and evaluation grading of NGOs with a view to strengthen those during good work and having the potential to do better, while at the same time, weeding out the non-serious players.

All TIs will be evaluated on half-yearly basis by the group of technical experts to review the progress made. Three meetings of NGOs and SACS officials at regional level will be arranged on annual basis to share the experiences and best practices. TI supervisors will be adequately placed for sustained capacity building, facilitative monitoring & supervision at state level.

The total amount that will be spent on 2100 Targeted Interventions and 40,000 Link Workers in 200 districts for saturating the core populations is estimated to cost Rs. 2288 crore. Of this, an amount of Rs 1088 crore will be spent on CBOs, Rs. 655 crore on NGOs and Rs. 545 crore on the Link Workers scheme.

Notes

1. Report of the Expert Group on Size Estimation of Population with High Risk Behaviour for NACP-III, RCSHA, 2006.
2. BSS Wave III, 2004 WBSAP&CS (IMRB).
3. BSS Wave II, 2004 APSACS (TNS).
4. BSS Wave IX, 2004 Tamilnadu APAC (IMRB)
5. STI Prevalence among FSWs in Ahmedabad 2003 AMCACS & Jyoti Sangh
6. DFID Evaluation of Targeted Intervention in reduction of HIV Transmission in Five states in India, September, 2003–National Report.
7. Rakhi Dandona et al: High risk of HIV in Non-brothel based female sex workers in India, ASCI (mimeo).
8. HIV/AIDS and men who have sex with men in India: A desk review by Population Council for NACP-III, February, 2006.
9. Injecting Drug Use and HIV/AIDS in India, An Emerging Concern, MSJE, UNODC ROSA and UNAIDS, 2004.

Chapter - 4

Programme Strategies – Targeted Interventions among Bridge Populations

Bridge populations comprise such people, who, through close proximity to high risk groups, are at higher risk of contracting HIV. Quite often they are clients/partners of male and female sex workers. They will be addressed through different strategies such as mainstreaming (e.g. prisoners, uniformed services) and as part of targeted interventions (e.g. spouses of injecting drug users). States may also decide to address bridge populations specific to their state, e.g. riverine transport workers in Brahmaputra, through appropriate strategies. Two major bridge populations who need specific and nation wide interventions are transport and migrant workers.

4.1 Truckers and Transport Sector Groups

Of an estimated 3.3 million km. of road network, about 61,359 km., constituting 2 per cent of the total road network accounts for 40 per cent of the total road traffic. The Asian Institute of Transport Development (AITD) and IHMR have estimated that there are around 5 million truck drivers in the country. Of them, about 50 per cent (about 2.5-3 million) ply on long-distance routes. They are more vulnerable compared to short-distance truckers to sexually transmitted diseases. Given 11-16 per cent expected HIV prevalence level amongst long-distance truckers in India, there could be an estimated 0.6-0.7 million truckers who might be HIV positive out of a total of 2.5 - 3 million long-distance truckers (2005).

4.2 Truckers and Vulnerability to HIV

Truckers have been a critical group because of the link of their 'mobility with HIV' having multiple interactions with local populations as they travel. The living and working conditions, sexually active age group and separation from regular partners for extended periods of time; availability of cash being carried to meet their travel needs make them attractive customers to the sex industry; and inadequate access to treatment for sexually transmitted infections are the major factors that put truckers at risk of contracting and transmitting the virus.

4.3 Sex Workers and Highways

It has been observed that there are diverse settings where sex takes place between the mobile population and the sex workers e.g.

(i) on the highways – 'dhabas' or unorganised house-based brothels located nearby halt points (HPs) and, therefore, more accessible and approachable to truckers' community; and

(ii) in small towns and cities – lodges, rented houses etc. It has also been recognised that sex workers operating in one location easily move to other locations and have greater degree of mobility.

Sex workers catering to the mobile population are normally either from the neighbouring villages coming to halt points during the day time or local tribeswomen, slum dwellers from the industrial towns located near the halt points, migrants or daily wage labourers from the construction sites, vegetable or fruit vendors at the halt points etc.

4.4 Current Truckers Interventions in the Country

Truckers interventions are being carried out by NGOs at locations where truck drivers halt for sufficient duration for carrying out BCC activities. The interventions are mainly along highway stretches, business activity areas, check posts or port areas. These are major transhipment centres, where trucks halt for loading or unloading. These interventions are supported with funds from several partners: 122 by NACO; 17 by TCIF-BMGF and now NHAI, covering 3100 km. stretch of national highway, with support from 27 NGOs at the truckers halt points on the highway.

4.5 Programme Strategies in Trucker Interventions

The intervention package through the NGO led intervention comprises basically of the following three core components-:

(i) BCC-activities through individual or group interaction with the target community for creating awareness by organizing camps among target groups, usage of IEC materials to convey messages on HIV/AIDS, condoms and STI, and through peer educational activities;

(ii) Condom promotional activity through both social marketing and free distribution of condoms; and

(iii) STI treatment through referrals for STI, VCTC services to nearby government/ private hospitals or clinics or through project owned clinics for STI treatment.

4.6 Impact of the Intervention

The APAC-BSS (wave VIII-2003) showed encouraging trends as indicated in **Table 4.1**.

Table 4.1: Behaviour Sentinel Survey Trends in Tamil Nadu

Indicators	*1996 (%)*	*2003 (%)*
Truckers reporting having sex with non-regular partners-Reduction	48	26.1
Truckers reporting having paid sex – reduction	38	22.1
Truckers reporting having casual sex–reduction	16.4	7.61
Condom usage with non-regular partner–increase	44	83.3
Condom usage with paid non-regular partners–increase	55	90.9
Condom usage with casual partner–increase	19	68.8
Perception of risk among non-users of condom–increase	38	66

Source: BSS-APAC (Wave VIII-2003 data), Tamil Nadu

4.7 Lessons Learnt

Key lessons learnt after working for over a decade on this intervention are:

(i) Local community's involvement is critical, as peer educators, participation in local events, sponsoring some events for truckers etc. ;

(ii) Selection of "peer" educators from the locally stationed trucking industry members (dhaba owners, paan and tea shop owners, petrol pump attendants, brokers staff) is more sustainable and useful than from the mobile population. These peer educators (though not strictly peers in the truest sense) have been able to provide services to the truckers / helpers with a measure of success.

(iii) Need for equal focus on sex workers in the intervention programmes at sites: dhabas, line hotels etc. along the highway, as sex work activity at commercial business halt points is minimal.

(iv) Need for focus on providing access to STI treatment, an issue that continues to be a challenge. Truckers either self medicate, or go to local RMPs and private practitioners. The BMGF is trying to brand the Khushi Clinics on the highways for greater visibility, enhancing the recall factor of the name/services, better access and availability of services. The impact of the strategy needs to be evaluated. VCTC services are generally referred from the halt points to the nearby government clinics, but the number of truckers seeking free services at public facilities is low because the travel distance and the time required act as disincentives.

4.8 Strategies under NACP-III

Under NACP-III, a mix of strategies are proposed to address the trucker related issues. These include:

- Mapping of truckers, their partners and identification of the larger congregation points of truckers;
- Greater involvement of trucker associations, federations, unions and related organizations in Trucker Intervention programmes;
- Improved access to condoms all along the highways, halt points etc. through professional social marketing organizations;
- Mapping the preferred providers and points convenient to the truckers for establishing facilities that will provide free access to counselling, testing, treatment and health education services;
- Linking the primary health facilities to care, support and treatment centres; and
- Facilitating increased ownership of the HIV/AIDS control programmes by the community based organizations.

For implementing the above and contrary to the existing model of one NGO being provided a stretch of the National Highway to provide the intervention, the strategy to cover the truckers under NACP-III will consist of a partnership between five major players led by the NHAI:

(i) The National Highway Authority of India (NHAI) will take primary responsibility to cover the 2 per cent of the national highways that carries 40 per cent of the traffic in the country. NHAI will identify major halt points and negotiate with the local vendors, oil companies etc. to provide free space for putting up IEC materials such as hoardings, condom vending machines in male toilets etc. Major points of focus will be the comprehensive wayside amenities – situated every 50 km, providing eating place with snack bar & restaurant, drinking water and toilet facilities, dormitories for short duration rest, fuelling and servicing facilities, repair shops, trauma care centre for victims of accidents and truck parking facilities. As of now, 228 small wayside amenities that provide drinking water, toilet and telephone facilities, 100 toll plazas and 80 construction management units located at major towns or cities have been identified;

(ii) Social Marketing Organizations which will identify and establish sale points for condoms;

(iii) Truckers Associations at state and district levels which will harness the local trucking community, associations, brokers and others and gradually hand over ownership of the interventions to them;

(iv) NGOs in areas where the Association presence is weak and in the states such as Punjab, Haryana, Rajasthan and TN for specific intervention targeting spouses of truckers as well as the sex workers along the highways; and

(v) NACO in collaboration with NHAI and State Transport Authorities for identifying the treatment centres and the preferred providers and provide training and funds to establish ICTC, STD treatment facility and condom availability.

4.9 Migrants & Populations in Cross-border Areas

There are over 200 million migrants in India (NSS). A recent analysis of the Census 2001 data indicates that during 1991-2001, about 61 per cent migrants moved within the districts, 24 per cent within the states and 13 per cent inter-state. Additionally, 3 million Indian migrants live in Gulf countries, most of them from Tamil Nadu, Kerala, Andhra Pradesh and Punjab. However, not all migrants are at equal risk. The 8.64 million temporary, short duration migrants (NSS survey 1999-00) are of special significance to the epidemic because of their frequent movement between source and destination areas.

In the existing pattern of concentrated epidemics with pockets of high prevalence, movement of people in the absence of migrant friendly services can result in the rapid spread of the infection.

Migrants can be classified into 3 broad categories:

- In-country rural to urban migrants (e.g. Ganjam to Surat) or rural to rural (Bihar to Punjab);
- Trans-border migrants (those who move between India and the neighbouring countries); and
- Overseas migrants (mostly those who move to Middle East and East Asia).

4.10 Issues Relevant to NACP-III

- Inter-state labour migration is an importatnt feature of the Indian economy, mostly being from the most populous and poorest states. Therefore, HIV/AIDS interventions need to be mainstreamed with the poverty alleviation schemes;
- Assessing the vulnerability of migrant population for identifying the stages which make the workers most vulnerable and the key actors / influencers who can play a vital role in HIV/AIDS programmes;
- HIV/AIDS interventions have mostly concentrated on migrant workers at destination locations. Interventions at the source points could be equally productive. Based on careful mapping of source and destination states and in order to upsacle the coverage, partnerships with NGOs and other organisations will be formed to reach out to migrants and their families for providing them information and education services;
- Along with the educational programmes for prevention, attempts should be made to create an enabling environment for reducing the prevailing stigma and discrimination associated with HIV/AIDS;
- Companies that employ migrant/contracutal workers in their projects must integrate HIV/AIDs in their welfare programmes and must be encouraged to include a clause to this effect in their contracts. While prevention programme costs can be covered by the companies, workers can be linked to the public sector care, support & treatment programmes;
- Women impacted by migration include those who migrate and those whose partners migrate; they are vulnerable to sexual abuse and exposure to HIV. Additionally, India currently hosts around 200,000 refugees (UNHCR). Global experiences demonstrate that refugees/asylum seekers, especially women and children are often highly vulnerable to HIV, calling for designing special interventions by the respective Ministries and working in collaboration with NACO; and
- Successful examples of source-destination pilot initiatives (ICHAP, SARDI) demonstrate the importance of promoting volunteerism, working through peers and engaging a range of partners at source and destination sites to reach out to migrants and their families. Under NACP-III, a large segment of the migrant population will be reached through these best practices.

4.11 Activities under NACP-III

Under NACP-III, NACO will focus on the short term migrants accounting for 8.9 million. These migrants typically live in large cluster formations, around industries or cities in unauthorised slums. Factory owners, construction companies and other employers engaging the services of these migrants will be motivated to undertake preventive education activities among them. The model of volunteerism as implemented by CARE in their migrant worker projects will be replicated. Under this model, active volunteers among migrants will be identified, trained and encouraged to disseminate preventive messages among their fellow workers.

It is estimated that one such peer educator will be able to cover 250 workers as most tend to live in clusters. 25 peer educators can be supervised by one out-reach worker. Thus, under this model, the NGOs/owner companies etc. will be provided assistance, on a sharing or full cost basis, for paying an honorarium of Rs. 4000 per out-reach worker along with IEC materials. The out-reach workers can later also become depot holders and incentivized to earn more on social marketing of products such as condoms etc. This will ensure sustainability to this activity even after the cessation of this project. The companies/surrounding industry owners will also be encouraged to establish ICTCs and condom sale outlets at their cost. It is estimated that, to cover 8.9 million workers, 35,600 peer educators and 1424 out-reach workers will be required.

For achieving the above objectives, following activities will be undertaken:

- Map clusters of migrants, both within and inter-country, in key source and destination sites to identify geographic areas for focused interventions;
- Develop database on number, routes and types of migration and prioritize risk groups among them;
- Partner with NGOs in identified source areas to facilitate safe migration and reduced vulnerability to HIV;
- Establish "safe spaces" for migrants in destination areas where they are provided access to services and information on HIV/AIDS;
- Establish peer support groups in destination areas for in-migrants and trans-border migrants; and
- Introduce HIV/AIDS modules in the Ministry of Labour's pre-departure training programmes for overseas migrants and MEA's orientation programme for Embassy staff.

It is estimated that this activity will involve an expenditure of Rs. 132 crore be spent on 3 million truckers (Rs. 87 crore) and 8.9 million migrant workers (Rs. 45 crore) during the project period.

Chapter - 5

Programme Strategies - Targeted Interventions among General Population

5.1 The Problem

Women seemed to be on the periphery of the epidemic a decade ago; today they are at the epicentre. Presently, almost 40 per cent of India's population living with HIV/AIDS comprises women. Among women, the peak age for HIV prevalence tends to be around age 25, which is 10 to 15 years lower than the peak age for men[1]. In 2004, it was estimated that 22 per cent of HIV cases in India comprised housewives with a single partner[2].

HIV and AIDS affect young people disproportionately. Nearly 33 per cent of the reported AIDS cases till June 2005 were in the 15 to 29 years age group. Very young adolescents or children (10-14 years) or youth (10-24 years), because of their lack of correct information and life skills, behaviour of experimentation and above all their biological predispositions, are especially vulnerable to risks of HIV infection.

In 2002, an estimated 4 million children lived on the street[3] and approximately 9 per cent of all children[4] under the age of 18 had lost one or both parents. It is estimated that 170,000 children below the age of 15 years are infected with HIV/AIDS in India[5] and 57,000 children infected every year through mother to child transmission[6]. The cumulative number of HIV infected children (0-15 years) was estimated to be about 220,000 by 2004.

5.2 Rationale

It is expected that women have a two-fold higher incidence than men (2005), due to female sex work, as well as a higher biological susceptibility of high- and low-risk women to HIV infection. The higher incidence among women is likely to be maintained till 2015, and a larger number of low-risk women (mainly wives of men who visit sex workers sometimes or often) will be infected.[7]

Physiologically, young people are more vulnerable to STIs than adults; girls more than boys. Gender imbalances, societal norms, poverty and economic dependence all contribute to young people's risk of STIs. Many young people lack control over the choice of their marital and sexual partners, information, access to condoms or risks involved in unprotected sex. Almost 73 per cent of young people have misconceptions related to modes of transmission of HIV/AIDS[8]. Few know where to access contraceptive supplies or other services. 'Other' young people like street children, adolescent sex workers, orphans and migrants, are 'marginalized' and are hence even more vulnerable. Their poverty forces them to endure situations that put them at risk of unprotected sex and substance abuse.

5.3 Response under NACP-II

Under NACP-II, responses to these three vulnerable groups were fragmented and patchy. Under the composite targeted interventions, street children were "included" in high risk groups. There are no evaluations on the impact of the interventions with street children on arresting the epidemic. Regarding youth, substantial work has been done under the Adolescent Education Programme by training teachers and students of all 1.4 lakh high schools but there were limited interventions for either the out of school or university youth. Whatever was done for youth and young women groups was on account of the initiatives of some SACS and development partners – be it the AASHA programme in AP that focussed on harnessing the energies of the SHGs in the state, the RRC in Tamil Nadu which sought to mobilize college youth into committing themselves to promoting healthy living among their peers, and the behaviour change education programme for most at risk young people in high prevalence districts of AP, Maharashtra, and Tamil Nadu. Lessons drawn from these initiatives will form the basis for a more coherent response to these population segments under the social mobilization and mainstreaming efforts.

5.4 Vulnerability of Women, Youth and Children: Approach and Strategy under NACP-III

5.4.1 Vulnerability can be defined as the degree to which an individual or a section of population has control over their risk of acquiring HIV, or the degree to which those people who are infected and affected by HIV are able to access appropriate care and support[9]. Various contextual and structural factors prevailing in India are generally favourable to an increased incidence of HIV/STIs across the country. Increasing pace of urbanization, high internal population mobility, unbalanced male-female ratio (leading to an excess of men in cities), geographical and economic disparities, illiteracy, lack of preventive knowledge and skills, rural-urban differentials in knowledge, poverty, gender roles, spectrum of high-risk sexual behaviour (initiation of sexual activity at younger ages, engaging in sexual intercourse without using a condom) are the documented risk factors. Thus, the risk perception and behaviour of the young people are likely to determine the future direction of HIV/AIDS in the country. Under NACP-III, women, youth and children in special settings viz., young people in high prevalence districts, school drop-outs, especially girls, working children, children of sex workers, orphans of HIV/AIDS infected and affected shall be focused targets for specific interventions.

5.4.2 Women

Definition: All women in the reproductive age group of 15-49 are the target group.

Outcome: The overall outcomes envisaged are i. reduction in the rate of growth of HIV infection among women and girls and mitigating its impact among the infected and the affected, and ii. increased access of women and girls (including widows of positive men, survivors of trafficking and violence, partners/spouses of migrant and mobile population/long distance truckers, single women etc.) to accurate and comprehensive information related to HIV/AIDS prevention.

5.4.3 Youth

Definition: Consistent with the earlier policy of NACO, youth are defined as persons in the age group of 15-29 years.

Outcome: Youth are not a homogeneous group and different sub-populations of young people are exposed to different risk settings. For effective HIV prevention programming, NACP-III will categorize young people into three groups based on the level of their risk and vulnerability to HIV infection. These are a. young people in general population (in schools, colleges, universities, uniformed services and out of school/non-student youth in community), b. especially vulnerable young people in high and low vulnerable districts (with large concentration of CSWs, IDUs, MSM, significant out-migration, high HIV prevalence etc.) and c. young people most at risk of infection (adolescents in sex work, young IDUs, street children, working children etc.). While the high risk young people under 'c' category will be mostly dealt by TIs and the community based efforts through dedicated workers and CBOs, the 'a' category will be covered through curricular and the mainstreaming efforts initiated by respective ministries. The 'b' category of especially vulnerable young people will be addressed through behaviour change education efforts of dedicated workers (link workers and volunteers) explained later.

The overall outcomes envisaged under NACP-III for young people are reduction of risk behaviour, especially among young people, and reduction in rate of HIV infection among young people.

5.4.4 Children

Definition: The Convention on the Rights of the Child has defined children as persons up to the age of 18 years.[10]

Outcome: The two basic principles to guide prevention among children are i. increasing the coverage of most vulnerable children and strengthening child protection systems, and ii. mainstreaming HIV/AIDS in the existing schemes and programmes for children. NACP-III will seek to achieve reduction in risks of HIV/AIDS infection among extremely vulnerable children and mitigate impact on children infected and affected by collaborating with the Ministry of Women & Child Welfare.

5.5 Strategic Vision for these Sub-populations under NACP-III

Children, Youth (including adolescents) and Women who are identified as highly vulnerable will be addressed through specific human resources put in place upto the village level. General population will be covered through inter-ministerial mainstreaming process. As vulnerability and accessibility of these sub-groups have many overlaps, these will be addressed through a common operational plan but with specific outcomes among each sub-population i.e. Children (mitigation of impact of HIV), Youth (reduction in risk behaviours) and Women (reduced risks and vulnerabilities and increased access to treatment through PPTCT and paediatric AIDS in the treatment rollout).

5.6 Operational Plan

5.6.1 National Level

- Inter-ministerial coordination for developing synergy of actions between different line ministries up to district levels; and

- Establishing a task force of MOYAS, MOHFW, MHRD, MSJE, UN agencies, national level NGOs and Positive Network of Women for overall facilitatory role to develop national guidelines and standards for wider implementation across the country. It would be important to develop sub-taskforces for each sub-section to formalize the M&E, National Standards, consistent & correct IEC/BCC tools for different levels and any other specific areas of concerns.

Involvement of CBOs and NGOs: Identification of State and District level NGOs working in development sectors will be undertaken. It is also proposed that, in each state, a State Technical Resource Institute will be identified and capacity to provide technical support for training, BCC tools and other backup needs of these target groups, built up within the first year. These institutions will work in close participation with SACS (somewhat like the RCHSA).

5.6.2 State Level

Geographical Outreach: It is proposed that A and B districts would be taken up for coverage in a phased manner. Prioritization would, however, be done for highly vulnerable populations through different sets of interventions in these districts.

It is being envisaged that in NACP-III, NACO will strengthen the technical capacity of SACS. At the same time, it will also introduce at the district level, units consisting of four key personnel - coordinator, technical expert, M&E expert and an account staff. The coordinator will be designated as the nodal officer for Children, Youth and Women intervention.

5.6.3 District Level

At the district level, the following key activities are being proposed (see **Table 5.1**).

District Situation Mapping will be undertaken to plot the spread of the vulnerable populations at village level. Assessments will be conducted using standardized DSA tools and PRA mapping techniques, namely, the standardized snowball techniques. This information will enable preparing the district vulnerability maps. This will be the first step to identify designing the most epidemiologically appropriate and cost effective interventions.

Table: 5.1 District Level Intervention Plan

Activities	*Implementation Agency*	*Timeline*	*Deliverable*	*Monitoring Agency*
District Situation Assessment	DMU/Research Unit Inst	2-3 months	District mapping of highly vulnerable communities/groups	SACS/ State Technical Resource Institution (STRI)
Programme Planning	DMU/ DNGO	1 month	District Action Plan and Selection of District Resource Teams	SACS/ STRI
Selection of Link workers	DMU/ DNGO	1 month	200 Link workers and 10 Supervisor Link workers	DMU/SACS
Training of Link workers	District Resource Team, DMU and NGOs	6 months (15 days training in batches of 30)	Trained work force (Pre- Post Test assessing BCC and monitoring abilities available)	DMU and NGOs
Advocacy	DMU/DNGO at District level; Link workers at cluster/village level	1 month and ongoing	Government functionaries, Community and government leaders, media partners supportive of the District Intervention plan	DMU/DNGOs (District level) and Link supervisors (cluster level)
Development of web-based application for MIS	National Task Force (Sub Group)	6 months	Web based MIS available	National Task Force
Identification of youth volunteers	DMU/DNGO and Supervisor Link workers	6 months and ongoing	5-10 Youth Volunteers at village level (2, male and female/village, for the 5 assigned villages) for each link workers	DMU
Establish Red Ribbon Clubs (Youth Friendly Information Centres at the Cluster level)	Link worker and Volunteers	10 months and ongoing	RRC/YFIC with information, games, condoms, at a cluster/village level	Link supervisor and DMU
Develop specific communication campaigns (state level mass media and district level IPC activities) that reinforce the BCC activities conducted by link workers and volunteers	State Task Force/DMU	Referenced in the IEC social mobilisation and mainstreaming section		

Note: Programme outreach begins around 6 months onwards.

Link Workers: A cadre of Village Level Link Workers is proposed to be set up in a phased manner in A and B category districts. Link workers (both male and female) are motivated community level paid youth workers with minimum level of education to work in each cluster of villages around a 5000+ population village which will be the node for this sub-group intervention.

A district has about 1000 villages on an average. Of these, an estimated 25% will be covered by CBO/NGO TI; 25% will be at the periphery and covered by Government Departments. For the remaining 500 villages, it is proposed to establish a cadre of 200 link workers in each district, each link worker covering 2-5 villages. Each link worker, in turn, will identify preferably 10 volunteers representing youth, women, locally elected bodies and SC/ST from each of these villages and train them. Village level volunteers will be trained by the link workers to spread prevention message, conduct continuous BCC activities among target groups practicing high risk behaviours and act as an information post for services (accurate information, condoms etc), linkages and referrals. These village level volunteers will also act as backups for concerned link worker. These volunteers can be rewarded for their work by a certification/citation from respective SACS.

Supervisor Link Workers: For every 10 link workers, one worker would be elevated to the status of supervisor with prime role of being a link worker with the additional responsibility of reporting, monitoring and assuring a minimum standard of output expected out of link workers.

Role of Link workers: Link workers will work under the district management unit for addressing the following key issues through life skills-based participatory learning process rather than information delivery mode.

- Mobilizing especially the vulnerable women and young people;
- Strengthening accurate knowledge on sexuality, gender & HIV/AIDS in especially vulnerable youth and women:
- Train community volunteers to provide basic information on HIV/AIDS (reducing barriers to access)
    - Train community volunteers to motivate and increase the intention to try out safer behaviours among especially vulnerable young people and women
    - Reduce stigma and assist communities and affected households to cope with the epidemic, provide psycho social support for the affected and infected families, in particular children

- Sensitize school children to adopt healthy living habits and pass on the same to their parents and out of school children
- Help the community to fight alcoholism and other forms of substance abuse

- Increasing access to condoms and coordinating linkage between communities and service institutions (esp. VCTC/ICTC);
- Encouraging communities to avail of the free testing services available and early treatment for STDs etc;
- Developing functional linkage between CBOs and the national scheme and programme; and
- STD management, partner notification and linking the clients to health institutions and qualified practitioners.

Training and Capacity Building: District level resource persons and link workers will be trained and their capacity built through a cascade training mechanism – based on state, district & village level training protocols.

(i) 200 out of A&B districts will be covered in a phased manner in NACP-III. It is proposed to develop a training resource team consisting of 2 persons in each district;

(ii) These resource persons should have a reasonable understanding of issues relating to HIV/AIDS, gender, children and youth and, above all, a public health and development background;

(iii) Training for these district level resource persons will be conducted by State Training & Resource Institutions in partnership with SACS and other training institutions/ academicians etc;

(iv) District resource persons will be trained for 15 days in batches of 30;

(v) These trained resource persons, in coordination with district level SACS unit, will conduct a two-week residential training programme for link workers at the PHC level. These training programmes will then be followed by two follow-up training/ problem addressing/ handholding and reinforcement programmes of two-day duration;

(vi) A training module along with a Ready Reckoner is proposed to be developed at the central level with local vernacular translations for training of district resource persons. At the same time, state Training and Resource Institutions along with SACS and local experts will develop training modules along with Hand Book for link workers following the guidelines developed for developing central level resource materials. It is imperative that an information guide is prepared for training community volunteers; and

(vii)BCC tools and materials for RRCs/YFICs will be provided.

5.7 Development of Training Module at Central Level

Contents for different modules and support materials will be developed through existing materials while filling up the gaps identified. The focus will be to move beyond awareness to behaviour change communication activities. For district level resource persons training, a central level module will be prepared; and for link workers and community volunteers, state level modules will be put in place (see **Table 5.2**).

Table 5.2: Training Matrix

Category	*Total Number*	*Number of Training (in batches of 25)*	*Number of days*	*Resources (other than financial)*
District Resource Persons Training	400 (approx.) (national level)	16	15 days/ batch	3 Resource persons Training Module Ready Beckoner
Link worker and Supervisor	200 / district / 200 Districts	8 / District x 200	15 days/batch	2 district level Resource persons Training Module Hand Book Condoms demonstration models Condom boxes
Community Volunteers (max.10/ village)	2000 / District	On the Job training	3-4 days/ month	Link worker and Supervisor Information Leaflet Give away materials

It is essential that the operational plan results in a national level workforce of around 600 middle to senior level trainers, 40,000 trained youth working as link members and nearly 4 lakh volunteers at the community level engaged in BCC activities on HIV prevention. It is important that such a workforce reaches out to the larger rural populations that have multiple vulnerabilities and exposure to risk of HIV infection. This workforce will, not only, be trained and capacitated for HIV/AIDS but also for issues of gender sexuality, STIs, communication and above all on mobilization for difficult-to-reach, especially vulnerable sub-populations. This sub-population is usually marginalized and on the periphery of health services. Linking them to these services/ICTC and then their follow-up back to communities is one of the key gap areas that is expected to be addressed by these link workers and community volunteers, besides achieving reduction of stigma.

All this shall result in enhanced information and knowledge, motivation to practice safer behaviours, increased access to condoms and services, better skills to use condoms, better life skills in adolescent youth and women to handle peer and social pressure and above all negotiate safe sex, delay sexual debut or practice abstinence. Above all, the rural emphasis shall address the epidemiological evidence for the shift of the virus from urban to rural population.

Having dealt with the highest vulnerable populations which address the children, youth and women outside the institutional mechanism, there is also a felt need to work through existing institutions of children and youth who are part of the mainstream i.e. the organised sector.

Organizations of youth volunteers (OYV), namely, Volunteers of the National Service Scheme and Nehru Yuva Kendra Sangathan (NYKS) have done good work in the past on preventive education through University Talk AIDS and Village Talk AIDS programmes although their full potential as peer leaders and educators on HIV and youth health remain under-utilized. The country has 21 million student and non-student youth volunteers working in different organizations: 2.6 million student youth volunteers of NSS; 8 million rural volunteers in 200,000 youth clubs of NYKS; 3.5 million adolescents volunteers of the Scouts & Guides; 6 million volunteers of the Youth Red Cross/Junior Red Cross and 1.5 million volunteers of NCC. Every year, these organizations hold about 17,000 camps in community/village settings.

During NACP-II, a National Adolescents Education Programme (AEP) was developed in collaboration with the MHRD. It has already covered 93,000 secondary and senior secondary schools out of the proposed 1,44,409 schools in the country which will be covered by March 2007. In 5 states, peer education clubs have been established at school level and in 16 States, content on HIV prevention education has been integrated into the school curriculum. It is proposed to consolidate and scale-up ongoing Adolescence Education Programme that is being implemented by MHRD-DoSHE through co-curricular coverage; curricular integration; in-service and pre-service teachers' training curriculum; integration into alternate innovative education schemes and integration in the education policy of measures to prevent discrimination and ensure accurate content in the curriculum. This programme will then be phased out over a period of two years from NACO programme and mainstreamed into MHRD-DoSHE for its ongoing effort.

Under NACP-III, AEP peer educator clubs /Red Ribbon Clubs in high schools will be strengthened and Red Ribbon Clubs will be established in villages to provide youth oriented counselling, life skill education, recreation and guidance in a confidential and enabling environment through teachers and peer educators/link workers/community volunteers. The recent NACP-III study on Health Care Providers' attitude corroborates the assumption that the health sector lacks a youth orientation as much as the youth sector lacks a health orientation. In view of this, it is essential that the health and youth sector join hands together to empower the young people to avoid exposure to risk situations, HIV and STI infection and lead a responsible and productive life. In this context, the RRC approach will be to adapt and orient the existing health centres/ structures to increase access to youth friendly life skill services to the young people, both married and unmarried, in an understanding and supportive environment. This approach will also cover the non-health youth sector in universities, colleges, youth clubs, NGOs/CBOs and organizations of youth volunteers.

Red Ribbon Clubs/Groups will be formed/promoted to cover young people at greater risk to HIV both in-campus and in-community. The programme will address the knowledge, attitude and behaviour of youth in the areas of HIV/AIDS and sexuality. Thus, Red Ribbon Clubs (RRC) will serve as a complementary and comprehensive prevention intervention to support and reinforce the youth initiatives conducted by community volunteers and link workers. It is estimated that, to initiate student-based activities centered around HIV in the 1.44 lakh high schools and 16,000 colleges, through Red Ribbon Clubs as well as in coordination with the NYKS, NSS, NCC etc. an amount of Rs. 160 crore would be required over a five year period (details in **Annex 4**).

5.8 Key Activities

- Support establishment of RRCs in colleges and high schools in partnership with MHRD and Min. of Youth Affairs & Sports. Improve/establish youth friendly linkages for referrals and follow-ups between health services and ICTCs, STI services etc.
- Promote social marketing of condoms through RRCs/youth clubs/ youth development centres (more than 200,000 youth clubs are affiliated to the NYKS-20,000 selected youth clubs to be involved).

5.9 Protecting Tribals from HIV

Tribal population is estimated to be 8.2 per cent of nation's total population. Seven states account for more than 75 per cent of the tribal population: main concentration of tribals is in the central tribal belt and in the north-eastern States, namely, Arunachal Pradesh, Meghalaya, Mizoram and Nagaland. Prominent tribal areas constitute about 15 per cent of the total geographical area of the country and correspond largely to underdeveloped areas of the country (IDSP 2003).

A social assessment conducted during NACP–III preparatory phase has identified factors of their vulnerability to sexual networking patterns, migratory status and exposure to tourists and external influences. The study has referred to a number of states where tribal women/girls are now being increasingly lured into commercial sex and trafficking.

As regards knowledge and awareness about HIV/AIDS/STI, the study found it to be low among tribals. In the matter of treatment seeking behaviour, gender differences exist among these groups across all states except Manipur. Overall, however, non-availability and/or lack of access to health care facilities were the main factors inhibiting health seeking on the part of tribals. Trust in faith healers and an unqualified private practitioner was identified as another area of challenge. During NACP-III, the capacity building of such providers and their role in referrals will be accorded due importance while implementing the programme. Inter-sectoral collaboration with the Ministries of Tribal Affairs, Social Justice & Empowerment and Tourism will be the main vehicles for reducing the vulnerability of tribal people to HIV/AIDS.

5.10 Current Interventions by SACS, District Health Programmes and NGOs

Under NACP-II, there was no specific interventions among tribals except in NE. In Andhra Pradesh and Rajasthan, these populations were covered under the interventions designed for the high-risk (CSW and migrants) and other groups. Very few NGOs were reported to have been working specifically with tribal population on HIV/AIDS. Except in places where TI programmes for tribals were being undertaken, there was a dearth of IEC material communicating in local dialect of tribal community.

5.11 Approach and Strategies during NACP-III

- Special needs of tribals to be reflected in strategic plans in accordance with their special needs and vulnerabilities to external forces of change, and also to HIV/AIDS epidemic.
- Establish linkages with the Departments of Tribal Welfare and the Department of Health and Family Welfare at the state levels and

mainstream HIV AIDS prevention education and access to services through their ongoing district health plans, being prepared to strengthen the health delivery system in these areas which are known to be weak. Accordingly, NACO activities will be fully converged with RCH-II and NRHM.

- In North East, establish a sub-office of NACO to coordinate, supervise and monitor the implementation of State plans in the NE states.
- Develop specific plans for implementation under Tribal Sub-Plans and utilization of 10 per cent funds earmarked for NE.
- Increase awareness, IEC and BCC activities in tune with the tribal vocabulary, beliefs and practices.
- Sensitize and involve traditional healers and PPs practicing in tribal areas in the management of STIs and CIs and encourage referrals to ICTCs.

Barring the NE, there are 194 districts, which have a large population of tribals. In such districts, HIV education will be taken up in coordination with the Integrated Tribal Development Projects (ITDP) of the Ministry of Tribal Affairs, especially through tribal facilitators who carry out IEC activities of the projects. ITDAs in these areas will be provided technical support to analyse vulnerabilities of the settlements especially in areas which have a tradition of interaction with non-tribal populations. They will also be supported to integrate prevention strategies based on their analysis into the Tribal Sub Plans and other specially funded programmes. The Tribal Welfare ministry supports NGOs for running hospitals, dispensaries and mobile clinics. The ministry will integrate HIV into all the activities of these partner organisations.

Steps are being taken under NRHM and RCH programmes to strengthen weak health care delivery system in tribal areas. NACO will integrate NACP activities with these efforts. Traditional healers and non-qualified private practitioners will be recognised as partners in this effort. They will be trained on syndromic management of STIs and referrals to ICTCs. All ICTCs will honour such referrals and reimburse cost of travel and incidental expenses to the attendee and a companion. Such reimbursements will also be made for every visit for CD4 tests and ART. Cost of CD4 tests will be waived for tribal patients.

Ministry of Tribal Development will be requested to map the source, transit route, destination and seasonal patterns of migration of tribals. Priority areas, which have the largest in or out migration, will be studied to ascertain their vulnerability. Based on this assessment, appropriate source-to-destination projects will be designed to address vulnerabilities of migrant tribal population.

An adhoc amount of Rs. 5 lakh per ITDP has been allocated for IEC activities in tribal dialects and training of grass root health functionaries. Tribal Strategy through the implementation of Tribal Action Plan is expected to provide indigenous (tribal) people with benefits within its ambit to expand HIV/AIDS prevention, treatment, care and support to vulnerable rural and tribal areas (**Annex 5**).

5.12 Mainstreaming HIV into Sectoral Programmes

HIV is impacted by activities and policies of many sectors and hence impacts the efficiency of those sectors. For instance, the structural rigidities in the road transport system that enforces timing restrictions on truckers force them to idle their time at makeshift resting places, thereby exposing them to the risk of HIV. In turn, the morbidity and mortality of transport employees caused by high prevalence of HIV could lead to loss of morale and lower profitability in the transport sector. Therefore, mainstreaming HIV into core activities of concerned sector is a necessary condition for achieving the objectives of NACP-III. It will also help the sector achieve revenue and efficiency targets.

5.13 Categories of Mainstreaming

An organisation/sector can mainstream HIV prevention internally and externally. Internal mainstreaming is the process of reducing susceptibility of the organisation to the impact of HIV/AIDS. Most of the activities relate to HR, including providing the staff access to knowledge and services and developing alternate strategies if the core staff is infected or affected by HIV. External mainstreaming seeks to influence the spread of HIV in the domain in which the organisation operates, e.g. agriculture department may incorporate HIV related messages in its outreach work and support HIV affected households to adopt labour saving agricultural practices. It may also seek to improve its own business practices so as to make structural changes that positively impact HIV prevention and mitigation of impact, e.g. drug enforcement authorities may shift their focus from prosecution to harm reduction within the leeway allowed by law.

5.14 Mainstreaming in NACP-II

Since NACP is located in the Health Ministry and awareness on HIV was low, the first phase of NACP had very little of mainstreaming. The notable exceptions were HRD, where NCERT linked up HIV prevention to its population education programme; Ministry of Youth Affairs, which designed the University Talk AIDS programme, and implemented it through National Service Scheme; and Ministry of Defence which took active measures to protect members of the armed forces. In addition, Ministries of Labour, Railways and Steel developed active programmes. Organisations such as National Highway Authority, Border Security Force, and Central Board of Workers' Education set up their own prevention and/or treatment services. Private sector also started integrating HIV in their workplace and outreach practices and as focus areas of corporate social responsibility. The highpoint of mainstreaming was when the National Council on AIDS accepted it as a core activity of the ministries represented on the NCA.

5.15 Challenges and Constraints to Mainstreaming

Due to its positioning in the health sector, HIV is perceived to be the concern of health department. Funding of mainstreaming activities out of NACO budget has helped in reinforcing this activity. It was perceived to be an external activity, added as an extra charge to an official tasked with core departmental functions. There was also lack of conceptual clarity on the need for, and modalities of, mainstreaming; and no technical support was made available to departments. There were structural constraints in addressing the most vulnerable sub-populations managed by the departments, e.g. unorganised labour, out-of-school children and the youth.

With the AIDS control programme in India slated to move beyond addressing risks to addressing vulnerabilities and mitigating impact of AIDS on the community, NACP-III will see a broadening of the national response through more sectors and organisations developing ownership of AIDS prevention and control programmes in their sphere of influence. The leadership provided by National Council on AIDS and technical assistance from the NACO will drive this initiative.

5.16 Objectives of Mainstreaming

The strategy of NACP-III on mainstreaming will work towards having:

- HIV mainstreamed into the work plan of major government/ private (for profit and not-for-profit) organisations and modify their core practices to respond to the challenges of HIV/AIDS; and
- Partner organisations demonstrate ownership of the HIV/AIDS prevention and control strategies by allocating internal resources to the programme.

5.17 Key Strategies for Mainstreaming

For the National Commission on AIDS, NACO analysed the potential and reach of different departments to assist in HIV/AIDS prevention and control. All 31 ministries represented on the National Commission on AIDS are committed to mainstreaming. But, given the nature of the core business of many of the ministries, mainstreaming may extend to only internal mainstreaming for its employees and carrying information through their outlets for information. Based on the analysis, NACO has identified 11 priority departments for mainstreaming. While providing general support to all 31 ministries in the activities they have planned, NACO will focus the advocacy and technical support on these ministries. These are: Education, Home Affairs, Labour, Panchayat Raj, Ports and Surface Transport, Railways, Rural Development, Tourism, Women and Child Department, Tribal Affairs, Youth Affairs and Sports. NACO will also collaborate with the Ministries of Defence, Industry, Labour and Railways to use their medical infrastructure for prevention and treatment, including treatment of STIs, promotion of condoms, ICTC, PPTCT, treatment of OIs and ART.

NACO will follow the following strategies with each of the identified department to achieve specific outputs expected from that department.

- Advocate with ministries directly and through other platforms, e.g. NCA, to constitute a focal unit and to allocate time and resources for mainstreaming HIV in their core strategies.
- Work with the focal unit to analyse the relationship between HIV and the sector managed by the ministry (how activities in the sector affect spread of HIV and how HIV could impact the core businesses of the sector). Based on the analysis, NACO will support developing/modifying action plans for integration of HIV in their core work. It shall be NACO's responsibility to arrange for technical support to the ministry.
- Work with the faculty of the training institutions under the ministry to add HIV/AIDS related information to their training curriculum. One or more training institutions identified by the ministry will be supported to become the nodal resource centre for the sector, e.g. V. V. Giri National Labour Institute. NACO will map available resources (persons, tools, institutions) for mainstreaming and help in building additional resources through training institutions, inside and outside the ministry.
- Work with the ministry in developing workplace policies for institutions under their management.

- Support SACS to manage mainstreaming with state ministries and departments.
- Advocate with Planning Commission to prevail upon ministries/ departments for earmarking specific outlays for HIV/AIDS.
- Document and disseminate good practices, and create a forum for ministries to share information and learn from each other.

5.18 Implementation Arrangements

In NACP-III, the emphasis will shift from direct implementation and funding to advocacy and providing technical support. To facilitate this, NACO and SACS will have a focal point on mainstreaming. The focal point and supervisors will work with the ministry concerned to identify a focal person/unit in each ministry. They will be given an induction orientation. NACO will work with focal point to analyse the situation in the ministry and to develop an action plan in the ministry by providing technical support. In time, each ministry will have dedicated technical experts seconded to them.

As secretariat to the National Commission on AIDS, NACO will receive progress reports from each ministry. These would be analysed and submitted to the Prime Minister's Office for scrutiny. Copies would also be provided to the committee of Secretaries of the Ministries represented on NCA. NACO will also constitute a theme group of focal points for sharing of experience and mutual learning.

5.20 Key Indicators

- Number of ministries/ depts./ organisations with plans of action and allocating dedicated human and financial resources to HIV/ AIDS.
- Percentage increase in number of people from the ministry and organisations under the ministry accessing HIV/AIDS information and services.
- Number of organizations implementing workplace policy.
- Number of training programmes which have course material dealing with HIV/AIDS.

5.21 Activities proposed for different Ministries

The components of action plan will flow from the situational analysis of the sector to be conducted in year one of NACP-III. However, based on the deliberations of the National Council on AIDS, NACO has prepared a recommended list of activities for most of the ministries represented on the NCA. The activities for the focus ministries are given in **Table 5.3**.

5.22 Expanding HIV/AIDS Interventions in the world of work

As the epidemic spreads to the general population, workers are likely to be increasingly affected by HIV. India has a working population of 398.41 million (28.07 million in the formal and 370.34 in the informal sector). Most of the workers (93%) are in the informal sector – mainly engaged in agriculture, manufacturing, trade, hotels and restaurants, construction, transport, storage and communications. These sectors also attract huge number of migrant workers, who stay away from families for long periods, have low access to health care facilities and low health seeking behaviour. They have either no or low social protection benefits. Hence, they are even more vulnerable to STIs/HIV/AIDS.

Increasing HIV prevalence in the workforce can have a negative impact on economic growth - absenteeism, loss of skilled workforce, loss of morale, low turnover, increased recruitment costs. Workplaces offer a structured entry point for HIV related activities into other sectors. It is, therefore, necessary to strengthen HIV/AIDS programmes in the world of work covering both formal and informal sectors. Relevant ministries, employers and workers organizations are the best places to do this. Some good workplace initiatives have started in NACP-III. NACO and ILO have facilitated signing of an Indian Employers' Statement of Commitment on AIDS signed by key national level employers' organizations. NACO has also issued guidelines to SACS for strengthening the HIV/AIDS policy and programmes in the world of work. The National Council on AIDS in India has recognized workforce as one of the three priority groups.

5.23 Key Activities

Formal sector:

- Undertake advocacy with, and provide technical support to, public and private sector enterprises and government ministries/ departments to develop and implement workplace policy.
- Ensure private sector mobilization through employers' organizations/chambers/ unions/PLHA networks to start/upscale enterprise-based interventions.
- Advocate with private sector for up-scaling HIV prevention and treatment services.

- Mobilize private sector insurance companies and pharmaceutical companies to define their role and contribution in the National AIDS Control Programme.

Informal sector:

- Mainstream HIV/AIDS in the programmes/projects of civil society organizations/NGOs, engaged in adult education, health, income generation, poverty alleviation, youth etc. covering large number of people.
- Engage trade unions, particularly in the areas where they have their sectoral unions like the mining workers unions, agriculture workers unions, postal workers unions, plantation workers unions, transport workers union, construction workers union etc.
- Encourage corporate sector to cover their contractual workers as well as workers in their supply chains.
- Develop projects for workers engaged in small and micro enterprises by carefully mapping them and building partnerships with local associations and civil society organizations.
- Up-scale coverage of mobile and migrant workers through SACS and other development partners' programmes with a focus on construction workers and seasonal agriculture workers.

5.24 Key Outputs

- 40,000 link workers and 4 lakh volunteers put in place.
- 300 Youth Friendly Centres/Red Ribbon Clubs established in all the 300 Universities/150,000 schools.
- Networks of HRG formed in each state and districts with linkages to mentoring groups.
- Tribal plan for HIV/AIDS operationalized.

For the activities indicated above, a total amount of Rs. 724.7 crore is proposed to be incurred over the five years as under:

1. Support for State Level Resource Centre, one in each of the 20 large states: Rs. 10 crore.
2. Link Worker Program: Rs. 545 crore.
3. Other activities among schools and colleges with NYKS, RRC: Rs.160 crore.
4. Assistance to 194 ITDPs: Rs. 9.7 crore.

Table 5.3: Proposed Activities for Focus Ministries

1	Education	a. Integrate HIV/AIDS into curriculum and curricular activities of schools, adult education schemes, distance education and open schooling programmes. b. Train nodal teachers to function as mentors and lay counsellors. c. Train children to be ambassadors to reduce stigma and discrimination in the community. d. Ensure that children infected and affected by HIV are retained in the school system and supported to complete their education. e. Train Mahila Samakhyas to address vulnerabilities of rural women especially infected and affected ones. f. Constitute Red Ribbon clubs in all educational institutions.
2	Home Affairs	a. Amend police procedures to deal with HRGs which enhance their vulnerability to HIV. b. Amend jail rules so as to reduce the risk of HIV to prisoners. c. Include protecting self and others from HIV in all training and field briefing manuals and ensure that all policemen of all ranks receive training on HIV. d. Create an enabling environment for policemen to access HIV prevention and treatment services and increase access to services. e. Train policemen to respond to the vulnerabilities of trafficked and migrant women.
3	Labour	a. Amend labour laws to make work place policy on HIV mandatory and have the inspection wing verify them. b. Provide the package of services including prevention and treatment services in all major ESI hospitals. c. Advocate with and facilitate trade unions to manage provision of services to migrant labour and workers in the informal sector and to lead on reducing stigma of infected workers and their families. d. Integrate HIV prevention in all training programmes undertaken in labour department.
4	Panchayat Raj	a. Revise for income generation and welfare schemes to support HIV infected and affected persons especially widows and orphans. b. Change rules to have assets given to families under joint ownership of husband and wife. c. Issue instructions to panchayats to protect infected persons and affected households from discrimination and protect the inheritance of widows and orphans. d. Issue guidelines to Panchayats to discuss HIV related issues relevant to the village in Gram Sabhas and other meetings. e. Request Panchayats with their own budget to allocate resources to supplement HIV prevention and control programme. f. Develop guidelines on how panchayats can take up work with high risk and marginalized populations. g. Train all elected representatives and executive officials by integrating HIV in training institutions.

(*Contd...*)

5	Ports and Surface Transport	a. Create halting centres in all places where large numbers of truckers have to wait for more than two hours, including facilities for rest, toilets, bathroom and recreation. b. Support transport associations and truckers unions to manage HIV prevention services at truckers halting points. c. Provide HIV prevention messages and condoms at wayside amenities. d. Port authorities/dock labour board to provide comprehensive package of service to shipping and port labour and support NGOs to work with SWs in the region.
6	Railways	a. Replicate the peer education model from Vijayawada. b. Provide a comprehensive package of prevention and treatment services in major railway hospitals. c. Install condom vending machines at railway stations. d. Identify trains used by migrant workers and arrange for HIV related messaging on these trains and stations of (dis)embarkation. e. Display HIV related messages in stations and trains. f. Integrate HIV modules in all training institutions, build in-house capacity and train all personnel on HIV.
7	Rural Development	a. Integrate programmes into SHGs to reduce vulnerabilities of women and prevent trafficking of girls. b. Expand the mandate of SHGs to enable them to work with high-risk groups in their area and to become facilitators for accessing HIV prevention and treatment services. Train them to work with Red Ribbon clubs and provide treatment, literacy and psycho social support to women. c. Amend guidelines of welfare and income generating schemes to give preference to HIV infected and affected populations and to make marginalized populations, such as sex workers, eligible for them. d. Integrate HIV into all training programmes and train all personnel especially field staff.
8	Tourism	a. Advocate with hotel and tour operators to modify their operating practices to integrate HIV prevention. b. Engage with NGOs working with high risk populations in tourist destinations to reduce vulnerabilities. c. Train staff of partner institutions.
9	Women and Child Department	a. Modify ICDS guidelines to integrate nutritional support to women and children on ARVs. b. Train Anganwadi workers to detect and report HIV related discrimination in villages. c. Establish Red Ribbon clubs among adolescent girls and provide them access to holistic development - life skills, distance education, nutrition and messages on HIV/AIDS prevention. d. Integrate HIV into all departmental training programmes.

(*Contd...*)

10	Youth Affairs and Sports	a. Conduct special campaigns/programmes by the NSS on youth health and HIV for rural youth b. Expand Universities Talk AIDS (UTA) to cover students as well as non-student young populations. c. Train all NSS Programme Officers and NYK coordinators. d. Undertake social marketing of condoms through 25,000 Youth Clubs, Youth Development Centres. e. Reorient 2,600 Youth Development centres at university/college level youth centres to provide Young People Friendly Information Services.
11	Tribal Affairs	a. Integrate HIV into all tribal affairs activities being conducted by the tribal welfare and forest department. b. Provide technical support to ITDAs to analyse the vulnerabilities of specific tribes, especially migrants and in areas which have close contact with outsiders. c. Train traditional healers and unqualified doctors with influence in the community on management of STIs and referrals to ICTC centres.

Notes

1. UNAIDS and WHO. 2001. AIDS Epidemic Update: December 2001 (UNAIDS/ 01.74E–WHO/CDS/CSR/NCS/2001.2). Geneva: UNAIDS/WHO.
2. Hefferman G 2004 Housewives account for one fifth of India's HIV cases, experts says, India Post and NCM, April, 16.
3. Silent Cries and Hidden Tears, Veena Johari, 2002, Lawyers Collective.
4. Children on the Brink 2004: A joint report of new orphan estimates and a framework for action. UNAIDS, UNICEF, USAID. 2004: www.unicef.org/ publications/index 22212.html.
5. Mother R Emerging initiatives to decrease the HIV vulnerability of marginalized children in India: The example of children of sex workers and street children Sexual Health Exchange 2005-1 http://www.kit.nl/frameset.asp?/ils/exchange content/html/2005-1 emerging initiatives to.asp&frnr=1&.
6. Task Force on Children and HIV coordinated by the Department of Women and Child Welfare.
7. Gray RH, Wawer MJ, Brookmeyer R, Sewankambo NK, Serwadda D, Wabwire-manager F, et al. Probability of HIV-1 transmission per coital act in monogamous, heterosexual, HIV-1 discordant couples in Rakai, Uganda. Lancet 2001; 357:1149-53.
8. NACO, 2001, Disaggregated data from National Behavioural Surveillance Survey: KAP of Young Adults (15-24 years).
9. http://www.aidsvancouver.org/basics/risk/index.html
10. http://www.unicef.org/crc/index 30229.html.

Chapter - 6

Programme Strategies-Communication and Social Mobilisation

6.1 Introduction to the Communication & Social Mobilisation Strategy

The key principle that drives the NACP-III programme is the scaled-up synergy between communication response and service delivery at all levels. Therefore, Communication Strategy and Implementation is a cross-cutting and integral strategic intervention in all components of HIV/AIDS prevention, care and support and treatment programmes under NACP-III.

Chapter 6 presents specific communication strategies that primarily address the high risk, vulnerable and general population segments. At the secondary level, advocacy, social mobilisation and mainstreaming strategies are focused on all segments and the larger programme goals. Communication Strategy and Implementation Plan supplements the communication efforts embedded in other sections and programme components:

- Chapters 3-5: Targeted Interventions and Targeted/Preventive Interventions with high risk, bridge and highly vulnerable populations
- Chapter 7: Programme Strategies on Prevention through a Package of Services, including Convergence with RCH/RNTCP/STD Services, Condom Supply, Blood Safety and PPTCT
- Chapter 8: Care and Support
- Chapter 9: ART and Treatment-related Issues
- Chapter 11: Public – Private Partnerships to Improve Service Delivery

- Chapter 12: Human Resource Development and Capacity Building
- Chapter 13: Enabling Environment – GIPA and Stigma Reduction
- Chapter 14: Programme Management – Institutional Framework
- Chapter 15: Monitoring and Evaluation
- Chapter 18: Financial Requirement

NACP-III proposes a Communication Strategy which will i. motivate Behaviour Change in a cross-section of identified populations at risk, including the High Risk Groups (CSW, IDU and MSM) and Bridge Population Groups (Clients of Sex Workers, Migrants and Truck Drivers); ii. raise awareness levels about Risk and the Need for Behaviour Change and the Use of Condoms among Youth and Women in the General Population; iii. generate a demand for health services; and iv. create an enabling environment for prevention as well as institutional and community care and support.

This Strategy aims to contribute to the achievement of the programme objectives to achieve the Goal: **Halt and Reverse the Epidemic in India over the Next Five Years.**

6.2 Situational Analysis: Overview of NACP-II Communication

Different states and different districts in India present different levels of prevalence and the situation and response needs are highly varied. The Communication Strategy, therefore, needs to be innovative and flexible in order to be adopted and adapted according to different audience needs. Equally, it has been designed to build and reinforce the gains of NACP-II according to the evidence base, while developing a strategic response to the emerging communication challenges in the new programme.

NACP-II was marked by some of the following communication interventions:

- Institutionalization of evidence-based planning and review mechanisms for IEC collaborative media products (TV, Radio and Print).
- Initiatives with national and international partners.
- Media campaigns in partnership with media units of the Ministry of Information and Broadcasting.

- Capacity building of State AIDS Control Societies
- Advocacy initiatives from Parliament to Panchayats
- Youth parliament at the national level
- Legislature sessions at state levels
- National media summit

6.3 Evidence - based Impact Assessment of NACP-II Communication

The evolving communication response in the past 15 years (NACP-I & NACP-II) has contributed to raising the level of awareness and concern on HIV prevention, care and support across the broad spectrum of the nation. The national BSS I (2001) placed the general awareness level at 76 per cent. A recent study by BBC-WST (2005) has shown that the general awareness on two important methods of protection against HIV, namely, condom and single (faithful) partner sex was in the range of 64-94 per cent across rural and urban segments.

Several States also conducted their state level BSS and Communication Needs Assessment studies at periodic intervals. Tamil Nadu, Maharashtra, West Bengal and Andhra Pradesh (2004, 2005), in particular, tracked the behaviour patterns of different segments of audiences. These studies have shown that the strategies for condom promotion and demand generation for services as well efforts in reducing stigma have yielded good results, but much more is still required to be done to control the epidemic. Studies have also brought out the association between perceptions and beliefs as well as communication gaps and vulnerability factors. Further evidence which could serve as a baseline would be available through NFHS III and the BSS II which are under progress now.

Overall Conclusion: There was a significant increase in awareness about the infection but it did not match a corresponding behaviour change towards safe sexual practices and optimal utilization of services. There were initiation towards creation of a non-stigmatized and enabling environment for PLHAs at the institutional level or in the community but again they need to be made at more significant levels.

6.4 NACP-III: Communication Strategy

NACP-III Communication Strategy is based on the available and current evidence, but as it progresses through the programme, it will need to be re-vitalized and strengthened by:

1. A system of further research and evidence-gathering built into the programme itself and undertaken by different levels of programme functionaries for the various sections of the target audience, and
2. Supported by professional research agencies and Capacity building institutions.

Key areas of focus for the research will be:

Communication needs assessment –

- Are new messages required
- Is new positioning required
- Are audience segment specific messages required
- What kind of form/content is preferred

Communication impact –

- Are the messages relevant, remembered, and acted upon
- Are they felt to be appropriate, sensitive and motivating

Media reach and relevance –

- Is the communication available where the target audience can access it most effectively
- Is it timely
- What further delivery mechanisms are required

Behaviour change –

- Through the regular system of the BSS, analysis of uptake of services and sales of condoms, et al
- Through repeated studies, interactions, group discussions, inter-personal communication by outreach workers/peer educators in the Targeted Interventions

Institutional changes (service delivery levels, political will and commitment) and social change –

- Is there an enabling environment for discussions on sexuality and safe sex
- Are work environments truly non-stigmatized
- Is GIPA in practice
- Is the social space accepting PLHAs
- Is there an attitude change among healthcare service delivery providers

6.4.1 Strategic Programme Objectives of NACP-III

NACP-III Communication Strategy defines a set of Priority Objectives based on the Programme Objectives, at various levels and components (see **Figure 6.1**).

6.5 Communication Objectives

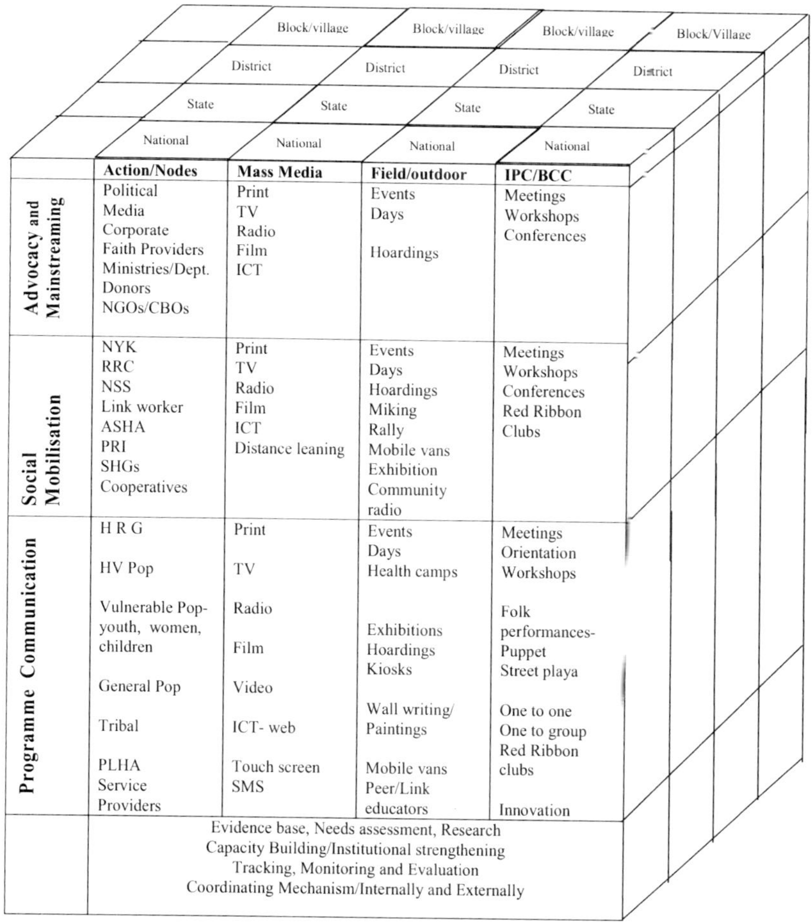

Figure 6.1: Communication Strategy Framework

Priority One:

Motivate Behaviour Change in a cross-section of identified populations at risk, including the High Risk Groups (CSW, IDU and MSM) and Bridge Population Groups (Clients of Sex Workers: Truck Drivers and Migrants).

P1| High Risk Groups - Objectives

CSW:

- Create awareness about the imperatives of using condoms with clients
- Create awareness about the need for advocacy with madams, pimps and police about the imperatives of using condoms and empowering the community to make this possible
- Make clients aware that protected sex with condoms is necessary for their health as it protects them from HIV/STD
- Create awareness about utilising the services available – ICTC/STD/PPTCT/ART

IDU:

- Create awareness that HIV spreads through infected needles and thus it is necessary to use clean needles, accept needle exchange and drug substitution.
- Increased and consistent use of condoms with CSW and regular partners.
- Reduction in number of casual partners.
- Create awareness about utilising the services available – ICTC/STD/ PPTCT/ ART

MSM:

- Create awareness generation that protected sex is necessary because of the risk of STD/HIV
- Increased and consistent use of condoms with casual and regular partners
- Reduction in number of casual partners
- Create awareness about utilising the services available – ICTC/STD/ PPTCT/ ART

P1| Bridge Populations - Objectives

Clients of CSW: Truck Drivers and Migrants

- Create awareness that every unprotected act of sex can put them at risk of STD/HIV
- Increased and consistent use of condoms with casual and regular partners

- Reduction in number of casual partners, being faithful to partner/ wife
- Create awareness about utilizing the services available - ICTC/ STD/PPTCT/ ART

Expected outcomes from implementing the key objectives of P1 – HRG and Bridge Populations

- Sustained awareness about HIV, routes of transmission and personal risk perception in the target audience
- Behaviour change - understanding and ownership of the fact that the risk applies to them because of their behaviour; hence behaviour change through reduction of multiple partners and consistent use of condoms is necessary
- Enabling environment to make behaviour change possible
- Increased awareness that a range of services is on offer in a non-stigmatized environment and therefore, they should avail of them

Priorities Two - Four:

The secondary focus and apportioned resources will be divided between the following three priorities [P2 – P4] with the key objectives as under:

P2] Vulnerable/General Populations/ Children/ Tribal Populations and PLHA - Objectives

Youth:

- Raise awareness levels about the risk of HIV
- Raise awareness about the need to abstain, being faithful, delay sexual debut and avoid experimentation/casual and commercial sex
- Use condoms in all sexual encounters
- Create awareness about utilising the range of services available - ICTC/STD/ PPTCT/ART

Women:

- Raise awareness about the need for husbands/partners to use condoms.
- Raise awareness that condoms are a protection against STD/HIV and not only unplanned births.
- Enable them through social advocacy and community mobilization to be able to discuss safe sex with husbands/partners and negotiate

the use of condoms.

- Create awareness about utilizing the range of services available - ICTC/STD/ PPTCT/ART.

PLHA:

- Raise awareness about social mobilization efforts to reduce stigma towards them and the need to utilize the services available - ICTC/ PPTCT/ART/STD
- Raise awareness about the need to use condoms to protect partners
- Impress upon them the need for greater networking and advocacy within their own community for strength and empowerment
- Motivate them to take advantage of the fact that NACP-III is creating economic and social empowerment for them

Expected outcomes from implementing the key objectives of P2 (Youth and Women)

Youth

- Sustained awareness about HIV, routes of transmission and personal risk perception that casual, unplanned sexual encounters can put them at risk, whether with CSW or other partners
- Must use condoms and preferably, follow the "A" of ABC

Women

- Sustained awareness about HIV, routes of transmission and personal risk perception
- must negotiate the use of condoms with husbands and partners

For both Youth & Women

- Increased awareness that a range of services is on offer in a non-stigmatized environment and therefore, they should avail of them

Children

- Make society and civil society aware that children who are homeless or in exploitative labour situations are at constant risk of sexual abuse and that this puts them at risk of HIV Infection
- Reassure children about the availability of safe houses, night shelters and counselling services
- Reassure children that they can be checked for STD/HIV without fear or discrimination

- Raise awareness levels in children about sexual abuse

Expected outcomes from implementing the key objectives of P2 (Children)

- Increased awareness about STD/HIV and that sexual abuse can lead to this infection
- Increased awareness about using condoms (where applicable)
- More support infrastructure for such children
- Increased uptake of all services - ICTC/STD/PPTCT/ART

Tribal Populations:

- Raise awareness about STD/HIV and that unprotected sex is the cause of this infection
- Raise awareness about necessity of using condoms in casual sexual encounters
- Inculcate behaviour change to avoid multiple partners
- Raise awareness that young girls are vulnerable to exploitation, sexual abuse and trafficking
- Raise awareness that a range of services is on offer in a non-stigmatized environment and therefore, they should avail of them

Expected outcomes from implementing the key objectives of P2 (Tribal Populations):

- Increased awareness levels about HIV and the need for safe sex through consistent use of condoms
- Increase in community and community-based organizations becoming involved in maintaining the continuum of awareness levels, reducing the vulnerability of young girls and encouraging the uptake of services (ICTC/PPTCT/ART/STD)

Expected outcomes from implementing the key objectives of P2 (PLHA)

- Increased workplace HIV policies and programmes which allow PLHA involvement
- Enhanced networking within PLHA groups for greater security and social acceptance
- Greater Community care and support/and care centres
- Increased uptake of all services - ICTC/STD/PPTCT/ART

P3] Services + Service Delivery - Objectives

Services + Service Delivery: Healthcare Staff in PHCs and Hospitals

- Improve quality of services and service delivery leading to better uptake across all Institutional Care and Support Systems (ICTC/ART/PPTCT/STD etc).
- Improve quality standards and infrastructure and communicate the change to the "customers" of such services
- Give intensive training and build capacities of the relevant service providers
- Sensitize healthcare personnel to the requirement of attending to general information and service seekers and specifically, to the various target audience segments and PLHA without stigmatization or discrimination
- Training on universal precautions will lessen fear of infection on contact with a person who is HIV+.

NRHM Staff RCH and RNTCP Staff

- This group of service providers will be trained to recognize the linkages between HIV and their area of work
- They will also be trained on the basis of this understanding to add HIV-related messages to their target audience and motivate them to avail of the services

Blood Banks

- Improve blood safety through improved screening, storage and maintaining quality standards
- Encourage voluntary blood donation drives
- Improve staff training and communication skills for rational use of blood products

Expected outcomes from implementing the key objectives of P3 (Service+ Service Delivery):

- Quality care and service delivery for better uptake of services
- Better synergy between different programmes
- Motivation of staff leading to upgraded knowledge and better efficiency

P4] Mainstreaming and Multi-sectoral Partners, Social and Community Organizations, Community Leaders, Influencers and the Media - Objectives

Mainstreaming & Multi-sectoral (Govt. Ministries/ Departments, PSUs, Corporate Sector)

- Motivate the target audience to include HIV/AIDS as a normal part of communication initiatives, Human Resource policies and practices
- Pursue the media to publicise programmes regarding integration of HIV-positive employees in work place
- Start public dialogue on HIV/AIDS prevention
- Start community outreach as part of corporate social responsibility (CSR) to reduce vulnerability and encourage safe health-seeking behaviour
- Work with NACO to start programmes about awareness generation and Behaviour Change within their sphere of activities

Expected outcomes from implementing the key objectives of P4 (Mainstreaming and Multi-sectoral Partners):

- Coordinated multi-sectoral communication response supporting HIV/AIDS initiatives at all levels
- Avowed and visible declaration of political will to help the national effort to fight HIV/AIDS

Social & Community Organisations, Community Leaders, Influencers and the Media

- Attempt to leverage wider social mobilization of people through events, activities and discussions about sex and sexuality, HIV prevention and behaviour change in public
- Attempt to reduce stigma and discrimination towards PLHA by sensitization of PRIs, SHGs and women's groups, religious organizations, social clubs, NGOs, CBOs and the Media
- Motivation of influencers, professionals, community leaders to inculcate behaviour change, and sustain the momentum of NACP-III as a programme, and themselves as stakeholders with a role to play

Expected outcomes from implementing the key objectives of P4 (Social &Community Organizations, Community Leaders and Influencers, and the Media):

- "Normalization" of the topic of Sexuality

- Greater acceptability for the word "Condom" in various forms of communication and discussion
- Greater public engagement in HIV/AIDS dialogue to create an enabling environment for behaviour change among different Target Audience
- Greater integration for PLHA within social framework

6.6 Target Audience and Communication Messages

NACP-II "**First Generation**" Messages had a medical orientation and fear approach to raise awareness levels, encourage use of condoms and motivate behaviour change.

NACP-III "**Second Generation Messages**" will position the benefits of behaviour change through Mass Media and other forms of communication such as Interpersonal Communication, Group Meetings, Role Models, Community Leaders, Grassroots Involvement through Link Workers and the functionaries of the ASHA and RCH programmes, a broad spectrum of Advocacy Programmes and Social Mobilization (these will be supported by a specific genre of communication materials) (see **Table 6.1**). The objective will be:

- To help the process of understanding and accepting the need for behaviour change
- To believe in and adopt behaviour change
- To sustain behaviour change
- To become a change agent for behaviour change in turn

Table 6.1: Matrix showing Second Generation Messages

Target Audience	***Segment***	***Objective***	***Message***	***Outcome***
Priority One				
HRG	CSW IDU MSM	Behaviour Change from casual, multiple partner, unprotected sex Reassurance through enabling environment	Use condoms Opt for STD Treatment and ICT services Supportive Environment	Awareness about HIV/AIDS Behaviour Change to use Condoms Increased STD check-ups Increased off-take of ICT services Environment – empathetic and non-abusive
Bridge Populations	Clients of CSW Truckers Migrants	Behaviour Change from casual, multiple partner, unprotected sex, Being faithful to partner/wife	Use Condoms Opt for STD Treatment and ICT services	Same as above

(*Contd...*)

Priority Two				
General Population	Youth Women	Awareness Generation of about Personal Risks and Safe Behaviour	Youth – Abstinence / Be faithful Delay Sexual Debut, Use Condoms Women – Be aware of need for husbands to use condoms, about STD/ICT and PPTCT	Same as above
	PLHA	Networking and Utilization of services	Non-Stigmatization and social Acceptance Friendly environment to live and work	Better environment for networking, care and support Motivating more HIV-infected and affected people to opt for ICT, ART Better environment for Jobs
	Children (Street Children Runaways Child Labour)	Awareness of HIV/AIDs and danger of sexual abuse Acceptance of NGOs working for their health/STD check-ups, etc	Friendly environment Safe houses Freedom from harassment	More protection from sexual abuse and hence, STD/HIV infection More awareness about need to seek check-ups if abused Awareness about condoms
	Tribal Populations (Different ethnic groups and in different areas)	Awareness of Safe sex and need to use condoms Behaviour Change	Use condoms Opt for STD Treatment and ICT services	Awareness about HIV/AIDS and Behaviour Change Awareness of STD/ICT
Priority Three				
Service Providers and Healthcare Workers	Hospital Staff NRHM/RCH/ RNTCP STD/VCT	Sensitize/ Improve Attitude to PLHA Offer Better Quality Service	Training and Capacity Building	Better quality care and service delivery which creates better off-take Better synergy between different programmes Higher motivation levels among staff Upgraded knowledge and efficiency levels
Blood Banks	All Staff	Sensitize to Blood Safety Issues and Need to Improve Quality Promote Voluntary Blood Donation	Training and Capacity Building	Same as above

(Contd...)

Priority 4				
Mainstreaming & Multi-sectoral Partners	Govt, Ministries, Departments. Other Govt Services, Corporate Sector, PSU	Include HIV/AIDS into their communication efforts, programmes, HR policies, community welfare programmes	Sensitization through top level Govt/NACO Meetings, Workshops, etc	Wider scope to tackle Awareness generation about HIV/AIDS, promote Behaviour Change, Create policies which support programmes and initiatives around HIV/AIDS
Social Mobilization and Advocacy Community Involvement – Leaders and Influencers	All sections of society Organizations, Clubs and Media	Create an environment to discuss HIV/AIDS and Safe Sex	Sensitization Through Media, Local Influencers, Youth	"Normalization" of the topic of Sexuality and Behaviour Change and the word "Condom" More public involvement in spreading awareness about HIV/AIDS No stigma for PLHA

For details please see **Annex 6.1**

6.7 Extensions of Communication Channel

Link Worker as a Communicator

The Link Worker is an important part of the NACP-III Programme Strategy and Implementation Plan in that he/she will support the communication initiative right to the grass-roots levels and especially in 'media dark areas.' (Please refer to chapter on Targeted / Preventive Interventions among General Population: Women, Youth and Children)

Advocacy and Social Mobilization

Suggested activities:

- Media Workshops for better media understanding of the issues relating to HIV/AIDS for correct and sensitive reporting.
- Collaborative Workshops with Mainstreaming Partners so that their interest levels are sustained for the continuum of the Advocacy and to give them inputs for their media campaigns. Political constituencies like Parliament, Legislatures and PRIs can contribute to policy reform, and help raise a collective voice to reduce stigma and sustain the momentum of NACP-III. This collective pressure will sensitize the Administrative Machinery for enforcement of laws, policies and entitlements, while facilitating procurement, service delivery, etc.

- Meetings and Workshops with Faith-based Organisations to gain support for reducing stigma, discrimination and care & support initiatives.
- Meetings and workshops with Business and Industry for mainstreaming and adoption of HIV policies and services. Greater involvement of bodies like the Confederation of Indian Industry etc.
- Broad-based Civil Society involvement as partners in programme design and implementation and to catalyze social ownership.

Constituents, Organizations and Stakeholders

- Civil society networks and organisations like SHGs, NYKS, NSS, PRIs, Youth Clubs, Sporting Clubs, Schools, Colleges, Mahila Mandals, Cooperatives, etc.
- RCH, Rural Development, and workers like ANMs, AWWs, ASHA will be a part of the communication effort.
- HIV positive networks will also play a key role as communicators to help their empowerment and acceptance into society, while reducing stigma and discrimination.
- Red Ribbon Clubs could be branded communication outlets at various levels and a part of community-led initiatives that offer a physical space for congregation and meetings and a link to services.

Communication through Events Inspired by the Mass Media Campaign

The Mass Media Campaign will include events around HIV/AIDS, and help localization and customization at the State and District levels. Local activities can be in the form of exhibitions, parades, rallies, street theatre, dance, mime, etc. Identification of these activities would be done at the State and District levels.

Communication through Service Delivery Points

Over 10,000 service delivery points including blood banks, ART centres, PPTCT centres, ICTC, STD clinics, district nodal offices, community care centres, District Information Centres, and condom outlets will be developed as communication hubs to i. train functionaries in communication skills, and ii. Become stock-point of IEC material

6.8 Communication Activities at National, State, District and Community Levels (see Table 6.2)

Table 6.2: Communication Activities at different levels

	Level	*Activity*
1.	National	Strategic framework; PIP; guidelines; executive instructions/circulars; budget/funding; advisory support; training and capacity building; organizing events; advocacy at the highest level; facilitating the mainstreaming process in Government sector & corporate/ private sector; pooling of resources - financial, technical and managerial; conducting communication needs assessment survey; BSS; Monitoring and Evaluation.
2.	State	Communication needs assessment; special research studies to assess micro level requirements; State-specific strategic framework; PIP; guidelines; designing the IEC/BCC material, with involvement of NGO/CBO/PLHA; advocacy initiatives; customized media plans to cover border areas; mainstreaming plans with Government departments/ sectors/ units; devolution of powers/decision making processes to Districts (micro level plan for community mobilization); organizing events; implementing communication activities (AIR, TV programmes); reporting to NACO; Monitoring and Evaluation.
3.	District	Micro-planning exercises; PIP; media plan; advocacy plan; mainstreaming with existing departments; training and capacity building of IEC teams; social and community mobilization strategies; interpersonal communication strategies; distribution of IEC material printed at State/National level, tapping the potential of local systems; linking to local cultural events - fairs/festivals, gatherings; linkages with service delivery mechanisms; partnerships with civil society organizations; faith based organizations; PLHA; empowerment of NGOs; reporting to SACS; Monitoring and Evaluation.
4.	Community	Red Ribbon Clubs; Panchayat forum; Youth forum may be made as voluntary wings of the DAPCUS to facilitate the community conversation processes; linkages with SHGs, literacy clubs; Linkages with folk art performing troupes and training them. Keeping the DAPCUS informed and helping with information gathering for Monitoring and Evaluation.

Please see Annex 6.2, 6.3, 6.4 and 6.5 for details.

6.9 Institutional Mechanisms to Implement Communication Strategy

Role of NACO and SACS

NACO

- Will manage and coordinate the NACP-III Communication Strategy and Implementation Plan – ensuring that the Key Objectives are being met through the activities of the SACS, DAPCUS and Partners.

- Will support the States with Technical Assistance for communication requirements which support the Targeted Interventions, Reach out to Bridge Populations and identify priority elements for the General Population.
- Will provide those SACS which have the requisite capacity - assistance in developing materials, customizing the main Communication Strategy for Specific Target Audiences and Region/ Location.
- Will support those SACS whose Capacity is weak – by developing resources/databank of materials and offering Training and Capacity Building Programmes.
- Will strengthen its own Capacity by accessing international experience, commissioning behavioural and operations research, compiling experiential learning and sharing best practices with international partners, the SACS and District partners and all NGOs working in the programme.
- Will maintain a Central Management of Information Services (CMIS) for maintaining records and documentation and for supporting all Monitoring and Evaluation activities.

Communication and Advocacy Unit (CAU) in NACO

For NACO to play its role effectively, it is proposed that a Communication and Advocacy Unit (CAU) is set up to meet the requirement of its expanded role. CAU would be NACO's dedicated communication resource staffed by professionals, whose contracts for the duration of NACP-III would be subject to annual performance review. This unit:

- Will assist in implementing the NACP-III Communication Strategy to deliver the outcomes according to the Objectives.
- Will coordinate the support provided by different partners of NACO to foster synergy between the collective resources going into the programme.
- Will be a centre for "knowledge management" accessed by NACO and SACS/DAPCUS IEC Team and communication managers.
- Will coordinate, evaluate and monitor the contracting and performance of different "vendors" appointed by NACO such as advertising agencies, printers, designers, film-makers, et al – according to specific Terms of Reference.

- Will be responsible for the development of all Training and Capacity Building Initiatives as well as information gathering through Communication Needs Assessment, Operations Research, et al.

Technical Support Groups

A Technical Support Group for communication would be developed for active support to the IEC Division at NACO. This would include eminent persons from the industry and programme sectors. Its job would be to provide basic TORs, facilitate and review strategies and media plans, provide data sources and resources and be part of the review, capacity building and advocacy efforts.

Similar Technical Support Groups would be established at the regional level for Communication and Advocacy initiatives under NACO and CAU. These are recommended as a consortium of institutions and agencies with the same professional expertise at the regional level which has been identified at the national level.

Customization of national level communication through Mass Media Campaigns and the development of IEC support materials by CAU and the TSG at NACO will be a shared and consultative process. The development of Training and Capacity Building programmes would also be done with the help of CAU. IEC officers at the SACS will be trained by CAU to meet the needs of NACP-III Communication Strategy and Implementation Plan and the State PIP.

SACS

- Will manage and coordinate the NACP-III Communication Strategy and Implementation Plan – ensuring that the Key Objectives are being met through the activities of DAPCUS and NGO Partners.
- Will support the Districts with Technical Assistance for communication requirements which support the Targeted Interventions, Reach out to Bridge Populations and identify priority elements in the General Population.
- Will provide those DAPCUS assistance in developing materials, customizing the main Communication Strategy for Specific Target Audiences as well as for different Regions and Location.
- Will support DAPCUS with resources/databank of materials and by offering Training and Capacity Building Programmes.

- Will strengthen its own Capacity by accessing NACO support through CAU and Technical Support Groups, while constituting Technical Support Groups of its own.
- Will build the capacities of its NGO Partners and CBOs working within its operational framework.
- Will feed information into the Central Management of Information Services (CMIS) for maintaining records and documentation and for supporting all Monitoring and Evaluation activities.

6.10 Training and Capacity Building

National, State and District Levels

Training and capacity building for communication, advocacy and social mobilization is a critical component of the overall strategy in NACP-III. Both routine and needs-based technical support plans will be developed at the National and State levels for building capacity and conducting training. These will cover IEC - development of communication materials, strategy implementation through media planning and buying; IPC – various forms of Interpersonal Communication, Meetings and Groups Discussions.

The scope of Advocacy and Social Mobilization will fall under IPC and the personnel involved will be all IEC officers/ staff at NACO/ SACS/ Districts along with Partners.

National and state level institutions and resource persons will be identified for conducting training programmes. Appropriate IEC/BCC/IPC training modules will also be developed. Advocacy workshops for media persons, CBOs, PRIs, political leaders, administrative machinery, corporate and business houses, opinion leaders, youth and faith based organizations will be organized at the national and state levels.

Objectives of Training and Capacity Building Programmes

- Develop technical, creative and managerial competence in planning, implementing mass media and non mass media campaigns including community and social mobilisation and advocacy.
- Develop in-depth knowledge and understanding of the issues related to HIV/AIDS prevention and control programme and the communication sensitivities related to gender, PLHA and culture.
- Develop liaison and networking competencies with government departments, private sector, development partners, NGOs, CBOs,

Media and the specifics of Convergence with RCH/RNTCP/NHRM.

- Undertake communication research and analysis for designing strategies and media plan for effective and efficient use.
- Upgrade administrative and financial skills for managing people, district teams and consultants engaged for communication purposes.
- Develop knowledge management – a resource pool of documented case studies, media stories, research, newsletter, press briefing and conferences, advocacy-led events, public meetings, et al.
- Provide customised training to the Link Workers, at the District level, and to put in place coordination mechanisms for a smooth working relationship between the SACS and DAPCUS and the SACS and DAPCUS together with NACO.

6.11 Monitoring and Evaluation of Communication

6.11.1 All Assessment /Evaluation will be done through NACO

- A periodic Monitoring and Evaluation process will be initiated through mechanisms such as field visits by officers, surprise visits and review meetings for evaluating the process and progress of communication initiatives.
- External evaluations of the communication initiatives would be undertaken every year.
- Monitoring and Evaluation will conform to input process, output and outcome/impact indicators. Formats of IEC in CMIS will be revised accordingly.
- A simplified and regular feedback mechanism will be developed to improve or correct design and implementation of the communication strategy.
- The BSS, conducted periodically, will provide information regarding impact of communication initiatives.
- They will be the reference point for constant Monitoring which feeds into the more complex data gathering of BSS or HIV Sentinel Surveillance, at a later stage.
- The Communication Impact Assessment will be done through the NGO Partners at State and District Levels, Healthcare workers, Link Workers, ANMs, ICDS and Anganwadi Workers, Rural Health Practitioners, School Teachers, Women's Self Help Groups.

- Overall, there will be inputs, guidance and supervision by professional research agencies.

6.11.2 Impact Assessment

The Outcome of the NACP-III Communication Strategy and Implementation Plan is Behaviour Change in individuals, communities and institutions through risk reduction, vulnerability reduction, stigma reduction, increased awareness levels and an increased demand for services and its utilization over the five years.

The Outcomes broadly defined are:

- Increased consistent condom use
- Increased ICTC / PPTCT/ STD services uptake
- Increased PLHA off-take of ART
- Increased Social acceptance/understanding of HIV
- Increased Social acceptance/empathy towards PLHA

Component-wise Impact Assessment

- **Communication** – Number of communication campaigns developed and implemented (Mass Media, Local Media, IPC) and its impact in awareness generation and behaviour change and increase in use of health services;
- **Advocacy** – Number of advocacy events held with (and by) key stakeholders and positive change in laws, policies, programmes, funds, partnerships, sponsorship, and representation in media; and
- **Social Mobilization** – Number of social mobilization activities organized and increased participation and ownership by communities, institutions and civil society.

6.11.3 Indicators for Behaviour Change

- Increase in percentage of people who recall correctly the modes of transmission and the modes of prevention;
- Evidence and observation of changing social norms about discussion and dialogue on sex and sexuality;
- Increased acceptance of the dialogue and discussion on sex and sexuality in public domain;
- Increase in the number of people who have no myth/misconception about transmission and prevention;

- Self-reported increased abstinence/Self-reported increased faithfulness;
- Decrease in number of sexual partners; and
- More requests for information about STDs/HIV/AIDS.

6.11.4 Indicators for Advocacy

- Increased discussion of HIV/AIDS policy issues in legislative bodies;
- Increased press coverage of ethical and legal issues dealing with HIV/AIDS issues;
- Increased openness about sexual issues in the media;
- Fewer complaints (e.g. letters to the editor) about media references;
- Increased religious / business leaders speaking in a positive way about HIV/AIDS;
- Increased business policies developed to protect HIV + workers from discrimination;
- Increased business policies initiated to promote HIV prevention education activities;
- Emergence of new coalitions and alliances among community organisations to address HIV issues;
- Improved inclusion of those most affected by HIV/AIDS and their views in policy-making forums and increased leadership roles for PLHA.

6.11.5 Indicators for Social/Community Mobilisation

- Widespread interest and participation in special AIDS observations
- Grassroots participation (e.g. Panchayat, SHG, youth clubs/PLHA) in HIV/AIDS campaign activities
- Participation of more women, girls and adolescent in community meetings.

6.11.6 Links between Communication-linked Indicators and Other Programme Components

Condom Promotion

- Increased condom availability at discos, hotels, bars, pubs, health service providers, healthcare centres;
- Self-reported evidence of more open conversation about use of condoms; and

- Self-reported increased consistent use of condoms with non commercial partners.

STI/STD

- Self-reported ability to recognize STD symptoms;
- Decreased time between recognizing an STD symptom & seeking treatment;
- Self-reported STD treatment-seeking and preventive behaviour; and
- More first-time attendees at STD clinics/fewer repeat attendees.

Ictc, Pptct, Art, Oi, Hiv-tb

- Information about and availability of services with materials developed and disseminated;
- Increased voluntary testing and counselling; and
- ART Adherence materials developed and disseminated.

6.11.7 Mechanism of collecting Feedback

The District and Panchayat Administrative Machinery will be a key resource in collecting feedback on Impact Assessment of Communication – SDO/BDO/DMO. This will be fed to the SACS and then passed on to NACO.

The abovementioned objectives will be achieved through a synergy of inputs under various sub activities of the program. A total outlay of Rs. 1018 crore is proposed for covering both the needs of IEC.

Chapter - 7

Programme Strategies – Prevention

Major focus of NACP-II was prevention. Gradually, care, support and treatment got added attention as new activities got introduced into the programme. A major shortcoming of NACP-II was, however, the inability to link services with prevention, and supply of services with demand. Condom supplies were not necessarily linked to STD services and access to these services were not linked with the Targeted Intervention programmes in a coherent way. Hence, to operationalize the concept of continuum of care at every level, it is proposed to provide a package of services, by defining clearly what will be available where and also ensure linkages between components.

7.1 Package of Services

Efficient delivery of HIV related services in prevention, care, support and treatment is crucial to the success of the HIV/AIDS control programme. During NACP-II focus was on service delivery through tertiary and district level health care institutions. Significant scale-up was achieved through substantial increase in the number of VCTCs, STD clinics and PPTCT centres. However, it is observed that HIV services provided at the tertiary and district levels are not easily accessible to vulnerable and high risk populations like the CSWs, MSM, IDUs, truckers and migrants. The low demand for services from the general population in VCTCs and STD clinics (on an average 3-4 per day in each centre/clinic) is also a matter of concern. Under NACP-III, it is therefore proposed to integrate and scale-up service delivery to sub-district and community levels through existing infrastructure in the public and private sectors. The type of services delivered at different levels will be based on HIV prevalence, capacity and need (see **Table 7.1**).

The nature of the heterogeneous epidemic in India requires rationalization of service delivery based on categorization of 611 districts in the country into 4 epidemiological categories as described in sub-section 2.3. As services are scaled up under NACP-III to sub-district levels, special attention will be given to demand generation along with capacity building and quality assurance. The total cost of a preventive service package proposed under the NACP-III will be Rs. 1,255 crore over the 5-year period.

Table 7.1: Services provided under NACP-III for different components

Preventive Services	***Care, Support and Treatment Services***
i. Creating awareness about symptoms, spread, prevention and services available ii. Management of STI and RTI iii. Condom promotion iv. Promotion of voluntary blood donation and access to safe blood v. Integrated Counselling and Testing (ICT) vi. PPTCT vii. PEP viii. Promotion of safe practices and infection control	i. Management of Opportunistic Infections ii. Control of TB in PLHA (RNTCP) iii. Anti-retroviral Therapy and related services iv. Outreach community/home based care v. Reducing stigma and discrimination
Specific Services for HRGs linking Prevention, Care and Support	
i. STI services - programme owned, programme linked and referral ii. Condoms – free and social marketing iii. BCC through peer and outreach iv. Building enabling environment v. Community organizing and ownership building vi. Linking HIV related care and support services	IDU (Additional components) i. Detoxification, de-addiction and rehabilitation ii. Needle exchange iii. Substitution therapy iv. Abscess management and other health services MSM (Additional components) i. Lubricants and appropriate condoms

7.2 District Level – Expanding Access to Package of Services

Packaging of services will help to target services based on need at different levels of health care. It will also improve the efficiency of services delivered and avoid duplication. At the district level, the full complement of preventive, supportive and curative services will be made available in all medical colleges / district hospitals. These hospitals/clinics will provide the whole spectrum of HIV related 'core and integrated services': psycho-social counselling and support, ART, OI management as out- and in-patient, positive prevention services, TB, STI, specialized paediatric HIV care and treatment, palliative care and pain management as well as referral for specialist needs such as surgery, ENT and ophthalmology etc.

Linkages of NGOs/CBOs with the hospitals will help provide the additional components of continuum of care and support with outreach, peer support services and home-based care. Additional testing facility for

PPTCT services will be provided in medical colleges and in district hospitals in the antenatal clinics so that rapid screening of pregnant women is made possible. Community linkages will also provide means to follow-up with children born to HIV-positive women, support at the community level and outreach.

At sub-district hospitals and CHCs, the package will be tailored to more basic needs as specified in **Table 7.2**. The table also describes the differential services at district, sub-district and community levels which will be delivered through existing public and private health care facilities. Specific list of components at different levels will ensure uniformity of HIV services obtained through private and public sector health providers.

Table 7.2: Differential Package based on Epidemiological Profile of the District

Category A Districts (High Prevalence)		
Level	Target Groups	Services Provided
Medical colleges /District, block and sub-divisional hospitals village/community	General population, HRGs & PLHA	All HIV related services will be made available under one roof. This will include: ICT, PPTCT, STD, OI and ART with necessary linkages CHC / not–for–profit private health institutions will provide: ICT, PPTCT, STD and OI with necessary linkages to prevention and care and treatment services PHC /identified private providers will be responsible for STD control, OI and condom promotion Mobile ICTC to reach hard to reach areas
Category B Districts (Concentrated Epidemic)		
District, block and sub divisional hospitals village/community	HRGs, general population, PLHA (services curtailed at the periphery)	all HIV related services will be made available similar to category 'A' districts Similar to category 'A' districts, supplies to be adjusted as per reduced load of patients 24 Hr PHCs will function as in category 'A' districts
Category C Districts (Low prevalence with increased presence of vulnerable populations)		
District, block and sub-divisional hospitals village/community	Vulnerable populations and HRG	As above - ART provision clinic will be added only for large districts and if not available within 6 hours travel by road. ICTC will be established in CHCs where the case load for testing is high (averaging more than 15/day including PPTCT). Where case load is less existing staff will be trained to provide counselling services. Drugs and supplies will be adjusted as per reduced case load in category 'C' districts PLHA related services – community care centres to be established only if there is a minimum of 50 PLHA identified in the district.
Category D Districts (Low Prevalence and low/unknown Vulnerability)		
District, block and sub divisional hospitals village/community	Basic service package	ART Services limited to medical colleges if available. CHC will provide STD and OI management but not ICTC Services limited to syndromic management of STD, IEC and condom promotion

7.3 Service Delivery and the Personnel required at different levels of Service Delivery

Various components of the package of services (25 preventive and 12 CST) as listed in the **Table 7.3** targeting the vulnerable population and PLHA will be delivered through existing public and private health care facilities. The list of persons to have primary responsibility of service delivery at different levels of health care is given in the table below:

Table 7.3: Personnel Responsible for Service Delivery at different levels

	Levels of Service	*Personnel delivering Services*	*Type of Services*
i.	Community	i. ASHA (NRHM states) ii. RMP	Referring pregnant women for test and follow up of PPTCT prophylaxis treatment Treatment of STDs, minor ailments and OIs such as diarrhoea and condom supply
ii.	PHC/private provider /30,000 population	i. PHC doctor/ private practitioner ii. Nurse iii. Lab Technician iv. Pharmacist/Dispenser v. Record Keeper	STD control and condom promotion Testing and counselling for HIV Treatment and prophylaxis of OI Antenatal care and counselling for prophylaxis
iii.	CHC/Trust Hospitals/ 100,000 population	i. CHC doctor/ Trust hospital doctor ii. Counsellor iii. Nurse iv. Lab Technician v. Pharmacist/Dispenser vi. Record Keeper vii. Out reach workers	STD control and condom promotion Integrated health counselling/testing PPTCT services, delivery, abortion and sterilization services for women including those who are HIV positive Diagnosis and treatment of common OIs ART follow up and referral Maintaining computerized patient records
iv.	District level/ Teaching hospitals	i. Specialists ii. Doctors iii. Nurse iv. Counsellors v. Lab Technician vi. Manager Drugs and Supply Chain vii. Treatment supporter (NGO/ PLHA/CBO etc.) viii. Out-reach worker	Management of complications ART Support care Integrated counselling/testing Management of STD and OI PPTCT Ensuring drug supply at district level Facilitating access to care and support for PLHA
v.	NGO/CBO/FBO/	i. NGO/CBO in administering CCC and family support centres ii. NGO/FBO/other managing TI iii. Outreach worker	Palliative care, treatment of minor OI, STD treatment Counselling, social service Adherence monitoring

7.4 Convergence with RCH, TB and other MOHFW Programmes

Since many components of the National AIDS Control programme will be delivered through the health system, integration with the national disease control programmes is crucial. Government of India has launched the National Rural Health Mission (NRHM) to coordinate the delivery of services under different disease control programmes. NACP will synergise all its services with the NRHM, especially with the Reproductive and Child Health (RCH) programme and the Revised National TB Control Programme (RNTCP) in the light of the recommendations of the Tasks Forces constituted for the purpose. Action Plans prepared by the State Health Society set up under NRHM and the State AIDS Control Society and their M&E systems will be dovetailed into each other for more effective implementation.

The impact of TB and HIV is interlinked and it will be difficult to control one of them without managing the other. Both programmes can share implementation arrangements such as ICTC and sputum microscopy centres, collaborating with civil society organisations, demand generation, training programmes, surveillance and logistics. The components of RTI/STI, blood safety, condom promotion, sentinel surveillance and PPTCT have close links with RCH and NACP. This will be reflected in the training and implementation arrangements including procurement and logistics. Collaboration is also feasible with such other programmes as CGHS, Drug De-addiction, Hospital Waste Management and Integrated Disease Surveillance Programme. NACP-III will utilise the expertise available in research institutions under the ICMR and Health Ministry.

A detailed operational plan with key activities will be developed jointly by NACO/SACS and the programme managers of the MOHFW after initial consensus is achieved on modalities of convergence.

7.5 Provisioning of Services

Service provisioning is categorized into three activities: preventive services; care and support; and treatment. The approach will be to ensure that access is not to a service but to a package of services either directly or as referral. This is based on the fact that condom use and counselling could be as relevant and necessary for the person at the ICTC as the AIDS patient at the ART centre. The services proposed to be provided under the three categories of services are detailed below:

7.6 Preventive Services

Preventive services will be provided in tandem with the IEC and demand generation programmes such as awareness generation. Crucial services under this head, all along the system right up to the community level to the extent feasible, include: (i) STD services; (ii) Access to Condoms; (iii) Safe Blood; (iv) Integrated Counselling and Testing Services; and (v) Prevention of Parent to Child Transmission.

7.6.1 STD Services

STD is one of the determinants of HIV transmission. Community studies on prevalence in India have shown that 4-6 per cent of the adult population suffer from STDs. Under NACP-II, 922 STD clinics in medical colleges and district hospitals were provided financial assistance. With 2-3 STD patients per day being treated at these centres, the utilization has been sub-optimal, making it clear that most of the vulnerable population access STD care from private service providers. The centres are also not linked with TIs in a manner that would provide access to the high risk groups. Syndromic guidelines are being validated and revised to reflect high levels of antimicrobial resistance to major STDs. Anal and oral STDs are also not covered under the existing syndromic guidelines. There are also limited diagnostic facilities to manage difficult STDs even in referral centres.

Under NACP-III, STD services will be expanded through effective integration with the RCH-II programme, which will provide training to the medical and paramedical personnel and drugs and equipment at all PHCs and CHCs. The health budgets will need to provide the required funds for drugs to the district and sub-district facilities, while NACO will provide training to the providers or supplement funding if required. This arrangement will then enable NACO to focus on developing capacity for treatment among the private sector providers at the community level (RMPs), GPs and private hospitals which are providing STD services. NACO will also support identified NGOs and not-for-profit private providers in STD management, drugs and diagnosis for treating persons of High Risk Groups.

Routine screening of the HRG population for STD by a designated NGO administering TI and referring them for treatment will be one of the important STD strategies under NACP-III. This will be facilitated through project owned or project linked or referral networks as described in the TI section. It is expected that 2 per cent of the subjects who are not responding and a random sample of subjects referred from TIs will have laboratory surveillance of STD.

Regional centres for monitoring drug resistance to gonococci will be established during the programme period. Cervical smears collected from random sample of HRGs coming for check - ups will be transported for monitoring drug resistance and deciding on syndromic management guidelines. This will be done in collaboration with the ICMR STD network as specified.

It is estimated that 5% of adult populations in India has STD symptoms. The programme will cover 50% of those with the symptoms i.e. about

15 million persons. These persons will be progressively provided access to treatment through the large network of public health facilities as well as an estimated 25,000 accredited private providers who will be trained and assisted to deliver services to key populations. It is estimated that an amount of Rs. 150 crore will be spent over the five year period on drugs, equipments, training and research.

Key Activities

- Put in place standard operating procedures and training modules and provide training to public & private service providers with focus on revised protocols;
- Modify syndromic management protocol to introduce oral/anal STIs;
- Establish EQAS for STI services;
- Establish convergence with State health system and RCH-II in STD control at district and sub-district levels for uniform protocol for RTI/STI across programmes;
- Identify preferred private service providers and franchise them after training to provide quality services on payment through a voucher system;
- Supply appropriate equipments and consumables to identified private providers of STD care;
- Initiate regular surveillance of STI in HRGs in collaboration with STD network laboratories;
- Generate demand for services through BCC;
- Establish regional centres to monitor antimicrobial resistance of bacterial agents causing STI; and
- Commission two national STI prevalence studies.

7.6.2 Condom Supply

Condoms have been promoted under the National Family Planning Programme since 1960s. Under the National Programme, condoms were provided free through the public health channels and at subsidized prices through retail channels. Condoms at subsidized prices were initially marketed through the private sector companies like Hindustan Lever Ltd, ITC etc. Subsequently leading NGOs were enlisted as the social marketing organizations. Condom promotions for NACP-I and NACP-II have been done through linkages with the National Family Planning Programme. Procurement, subsidy administering, programme management and supply chain management up to the state level were the responsibilities of MOHFW. The supply chain at state level has been managed through State Family Welfare Departments. NGOs implementing Targeted Interventions developed linkages at the district level for getting condoms. The social marketing programme operated through SMOs linked with SACS of some states and implemented focused social marketing programmes (see exhibit 1). NACO has focused on the generic promotion of condoms.

Condom promotion in NACP-II has led to an increase in the awareness levels about consistent condom use for preventing HIV, estimated to be above 80 per cent in high risk groups and 59 per cent in general population (73 per cent urban and 54 per cent rural). Despite high awareness and increase in condom availability, its use remains at less than satisfactory levels. Condom use for family planning was as low as 3 per cent (NFHS 2) and 49 per cent among general population with non-regular partners. Among the sex workers condom use presented a diverse picture among the paying and non paying clients at 50 per cent and 20 per cent respectively. Lack of self-risk perception continues to be the reason for the low condom use. Condom use for family planning presented a diverse picture across the country. The high prevalence southern states were having the lowest condom use for family planning where as some of the high vulnerable states like UP presented a relatively better picture of condom use.

Major gaps identified in condom promotion are summarized in **Table 7.4**. The ongoing social marketing programmes are mapped in **Figure 7.1**. The mapping of the ongoing programmes indicates very low focus on the highly vulnerable states.

Table 7.4: Condom Promotion Gaps

1	NGOs implementing Targeted Interventions were dependent on the linkages with District Health Authorities for condom supply. Quite often this led to stock-outs;
2	Promotional initiatives were quite often limited to mass media which has a limited potential in reaching high risk, bridge and rural population;
3	SACS did not have a supply chain for condoms leading to disruptions in supply;
4	Social marketing initiatives were limited to states where bilaterals and private foundations supported social marketing programmes. This led to effective programmes in some states whereas in some states no programmes were supported;
5	Due to the diffused ownership of condom promotion, critical issues such as brand management, product management, monitoring and impact assessment was not given priority attention; and
6	The ongoing social marketing programmes are very condom focused and does not focus on other services like VCT, STI Care, and PPTCT etc.

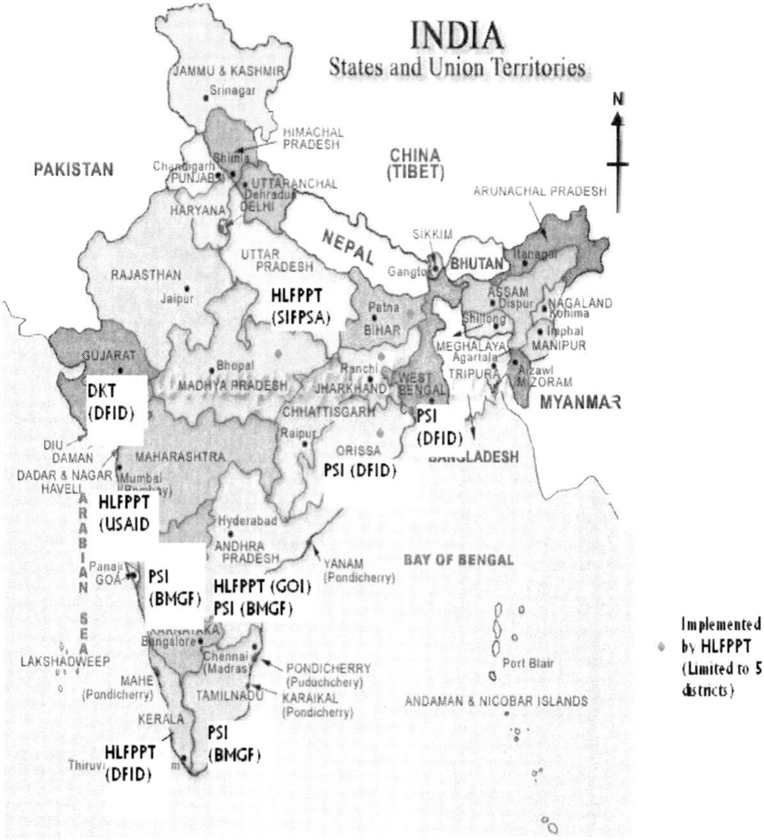

Figure 7.1: Social Marketing Programme

Strategic Framework

Social marketing has increased the use of condoms and other HIV prevention services in various countries. A strategic framework has been evolved for the effective use of social marketing and increased use of condoms and other HIV prevention services like STI care, VCT, PPTCT etc. Following is the audience segmentation:

- High risk population comprising CSWs, MSM and IDUs;
- Bridge population comprising clients of sex workers, truckers, migrants etc.;
- General population; and
- People living with HIV.

Audience-specific strategies are summarized in **Table 7.5**.

Table 7.5: Audience Specific Strategies and Milestone Activities

Audience	*Strategies*	*Milestone Activities*
High Risk Population	i. Integrating free and social marketing in Targeted Interventions for promoting condoms and other HIV prevention services like STI, VCT, PPTCT ii. Building effective supply chain iii. Condom promotion and negotiation skill building iv. Introducing new prevention technologies	i. Social marketing approaches will be integrated in Targeted Interventions for promoting condoms, VCT, PPTCT and STI services. ii. Social marketing organizations will be contracted to work along with NGOs so that the scale activities like communication programming can be managed by SMOs whereas NGOs focus on the execution. iii. Free condoms distributed with minimal wastage iv. Supply chain interventions for ensuring easy access to free condoms from SACS and social marketing condoms from SMOs v. Social franchising of STI, VCT and PPTCT involving private providers accessed by High Risk Population for heath care vi. Capacity building of peer workers for condom promotion vii. Evidence based programming of Female Condoms and extra thick & extra lubricated condoms for MSM
Bridge Population	i. Targeted social marketing programmes ii. Brands at varied level of subsidy and new value propositions iii. Social franchising of prevention services through private providers	i. Social marketing approaches focused on bridge population to be managed as targeted social marketing programmes ii. Access creation in non traditional outlets in high risk areas for condoms iii. Behaviour Change Communication using mass and mid media by SMOs. NGOs to complement IPC. iv. Innovative brand marketing approaches to promote condoms at varying price points v. Social franchising of STI, VCT and PPTCT services
General Population	i. General social marketing focused on dual protection message for condoms ii. Rural marketing through private sector partnerships iii. Social franchising of VCT and PPTCT services iv. Mainstreaming v. Linkage with NRHM	vi. Social marketing programmes implemented by SMOs focused on unreached urban pockets and rural areas with dual protection message vii. Contracting private sector marketing companies with good rural reach for promoting condoms viii. Provisioning of free condoms for BPL families ix. Social franchising of VCT and PPTCT services to leverage the reach of private solo practitioner with lab facility x. Condom promotion through Link Workers, Volunteers, ASHA Workers, ICDS workers, ANMs focused on building condom negotiation skills for women xi. Mainstreaming through linkages with Ministry of Youth, Surface Transport, Railways, Women and Child Department etc. xii. Mainstreaming with other health and community based programmes
People Living with HIV	i. PLHA Networking	ii. Condom promotion through district PLWA networks iii. Condom promotion at ARV centres i. Provisioning of free condoms at ART centres

Implementation of this strategic framework will indeed require a paradigm shift in the current programming approach. The responsibility matrix for various milestone activities are summarized in **Table 7.6**.

Table 7.6. Responsibility Matrix for Strategy Execution

Strategy	*Planning*	*Execution*	*Monitoring*
Integrating social marketing with TI for high risk population	NACO	TI NGOs and SMOs	SACS
Building effective supply chain	SACS based on guidelines from NACO	SACS and their PSUs	NACO
Condom promotion and negotiation skills for high risk population	NACO	SACS and their PSUs	NACO
Social franchising or accreditation of STI prevention services	NACO	SACS and their PSUs	NACO
Targeted social marketing for bridge population	SACS and their PSUs	SMOs	NACO
Branding and expanding the choices for bridge population	NACO	SMOs	NACO
Social franchising or accreditation of STI prevention services	NACO	SACS PSU and SMOs	NACO
Condom promotion for general population	NACO-MOHFW	SMO	NACO - MOHFW
Rural marketing through private sector contracts	NACO	Private sector FMCG companies	SACS
Social franchising for general population	SACS	NGOs or SMOs	NACO
Mainstreaming	NACO	Departments with technical support from NACO-SACS	SACS
Linkage with NRHM	NACO	District Project Management Unit	SACS
Condom promotion for PLHA	NACO-INP+	PLHA groups at district level	SACS

The objective is to increase condom use to 3.5 billion pieces per annum by the year 2009 from the present level of about 1.6 billion per annum, through intensive demand generation and supply efforts with support from an outsourced agency.

The growth trajectory for condoms under NACP-III is depicted in **Figure 7.2**.

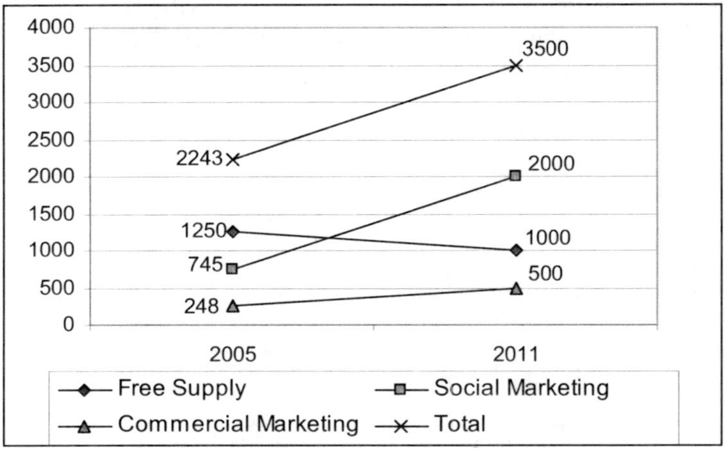

Figure 7.2: Growth Trajectory Condom Supply

All the three channels of condom supply – free, social marketing and commercial sales – will work in a complementary manner, each providing products to different target groups. The consumer base for socially marketed condoms will be increased by switching the current users of free supply condoms with appropriate behaviour change strategies and motivating the non users to use condoms in all non spousal sex acts. Free supply of condoms will be limited to those who can not afford to buy socially marketed condoms.

Key Activities

Expanding Social Marketing Programmes

- Social marketing organizations, NGOs with marketing competence, private sector marketing companies and institutions like agricultural co-operatives, milk co-operatives etc. will be contracted to design and implement social marketing programmes on a large scale to create perceptible impact. It is felt that the numbers of social marketing organizations need to be increased from the present five active SMOs to at least twenty five;
- Access will be expanded by opening non-conventional outlets in priority areas. An estimated three million outlets for consumer goods will be explored for sale of condoms from the present 6,00,000 outlets. Care will be taken to ensure that increase in the number of outlets does not result in a drop in condom off-take levels in existing outlets;

- Installation of condom vending machines in priority areas in close coordination with SMOs will also help increase the access. For preventing any potential cannibalisation between the retail sale and vending machines, a new brand of condoms with very low subsidy will be introduced. This will ensure that the convenience created by vending machines is priced higher than the price of social marketing condoms available in retail outlets;
- Behaviour change interventions will be at the core of social marketing programmes with focus on sexually active men, clients of male and female sex workers and MSM. A BCC strategy will be designed to enhance the risk perception in various population segments – general population, commercial sex workers and MSM – and to promote knowledge and use of condoms;
- Current system of contracting will be replaced with a dynamic performance based mechanism. Funding will be changed from the uniform Rs.0.10 per condom to a performance based funding;
- In order to suitably design condom programming and up-scaling in NACP-III, a district focus will be adopted; and
- Differential packages for condom programming for districts will be implemented with prioritized intensity based on risk, vulnerability and needs. For this, following four categories of districts have been proposed (see **Figure 7.3**):

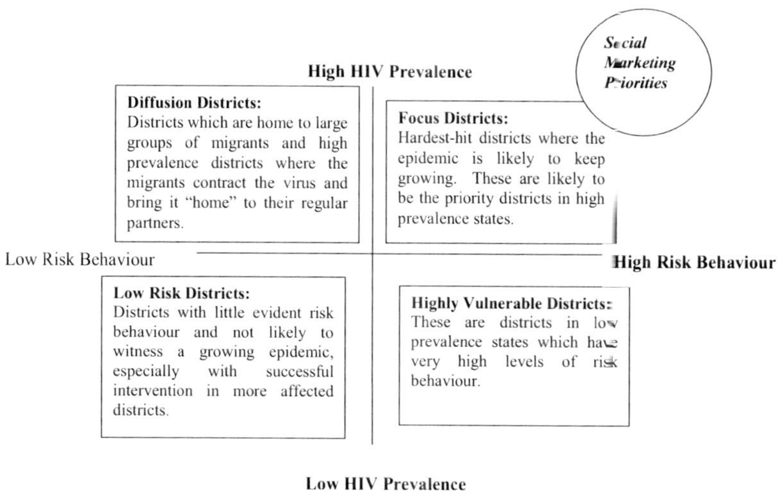

Figure 7.3: District Level Packages for Condom Programming

Based on the district level segmentation as outlined above, the condom programming typology recommended for NACP-III will be as follows (see **Figure 7.4**):

District	Social Marketing Typology
Focus Districts	- Promotional activities in high risk areas - sex sites, entertainment establishments, liquor shops etc. - Focus on clients of male, female and transgender sex workers - Social marketing in rural areas - Normalisation initiatives focused on youth, migrant and other marginalized population in towns
Highly Vulnerable Districts	- Normalisation initiatives - Social marketing in towns focused on clients of sex workers - Promotional activities in rural areas through SMOs
Diffusion Districts	- Focus on migrant population - Social marketing focused on male population - Promotional activities in rural areas through integration with NRHM
Low Risk Districts	- Generalised social marketing programme - Promotional activities in rural areas through NRHM

Figure 7.4: Condom Social Marketing Typologies

Normalizing Condoms and making Enhanced Efforts in Rural Areas

- Condoms will be re-positioned as a device of triple protection (i.e. against unwanted pregnancy, STI and HIV), and will focus on low income groups and on the youth population. High visibility drives and communication campaigns (both for generic and brand promotion) will be undertaken at all levels for reaching out to various audience segments; and
- For creating better access in underserved rural areas, public - private partnership will be promoted with leading FMCG brands by motivating them to distribute condoms through their distribution network. Besides, village level interface will be developed by networking with community level organizations and community led initiatives (e.g. SHGs, milk cooperatives, post offices, rural banks, youth cubs/NSS/NYK/ NCC, health workers) and skill building of link / health workers.

For achieving this, inter-sectoral collaboration will be necessary. NACO, through its mainstreaming initiatives, will work with various ministries as detailed below to ensure condom promotion:

(a) Ministry of Youth and Sports: Ministry of Youth and Sports will undertake condom promotion through various youth groups – youth clubs under NYKS, NSS and NCC units. The youth based promotion will be taken up in campus, community and for peers. All sporting events especially cricket will be used for normalizing condoms among the young;

(b) Ministry of Tourism: The practice of tourists accessing commercial sex has been observed in various settings and the tourist circuit depends on indirect sex workers who are not reached through TIs. A select group of cab drivers, hotel boys, tourist guides etc. will be sensitized for condom promotion and provisioning;

(c) Ministry of Labour: Through work place interventions in the industries located in high risk areas, workers will be sensitized for behaviour change and condom access will be ensured;

(d) Ministry of Information and Broadcasting: Full use of electronic media will be made for condom normalization campaigns. Advocacy with the I & B Ministry will help remove any self imposed restrictions on print/electronic media for condom advertising;

(e) Ministry of Information Technology and Telecommunications: Technology platforms created for communications (mobile phone, internet etc.) would be used for transmitting condom promotion messages to match the changing nature of sex industry (from brothel based to indirect networks);

(f) Ministry of Law: In view of the present legal environment, outreach workers/peer educators of TIs face police harassment for doing condom promotion with sex workers. Advocacy with law enforcement agencies will be undertaken and appropriate policies will be adopted to facilitate display and vending of condoms in entertainment establishments, liquor shops etc; and

(g) Ministry of Petroleum: The large network of petrol pumps will be used for installation of condom vending machines.

Minimizing Wastage in Free Supply (in public health system and NGO channel)

Free supply of condoms will be strengthened through appropriate IT enabled logistics and supply chain management (see Report on the Impact of TNMSC in Tamil Nadu for strengthening drug procurement and logistics). This will ensure flow of condoms from the procurement point to the consumption point and also track the supply to sub-district levels.

A study has indicated that wastage of condoms that occurs both at the provider and client level, could be minimized through appropriate training of peripheral level health workers. A passbook system could be introduced for drawing condoms from the supply points at district level. This system has been effectively implemented in the state of Tamil Nadu for drugs.

Periodic studies for assessing fate of condoms provided through the public health system and NGO channels will be undertaken for constantly assessing the areas where wastage is reported and appropriate management action initiated. (Report on the periodic condom fate studies in South Africa indicates that wastage could be minimized to the extent of 3-5 per cent with periodic fate studies).

The present supply led free distribution of condoms has often pushed more condoms than what the client may need. The demand led interventions will be pursued by motivating the clients to make sustained use.

Promoting Special Condoms

Female condoms, thicker condoms with additional lubricants, condoms lubricated with benzocaine and pleasure enhancing variants will be introduced and promoted in general populations and among various sub-populations.

Operations research for introducing female condoms and special condoms for groups like MSM will be done through NGOs and SMOs. This research will help evolve scalable programming approaches based on price sensitivity and acceptance studies.

Institutional Mechanism for Condom Programming

As recommended by the Working Group for NACP-III, NACO will provide strategic direction, policy framework and procurement support. Free condoms and subsidized condoms for the social marketing programme will be provisioned to the supply nodes of SACS and SMOs/private marketing companies respectively. NACO will constitute a Technical Resource Group through the Hindustan Latex Family Planning Promotion Trust (HLFPPT). The TRG will provide the needed technical assistance to NACO and SACS in implementing the social marketing and franchising of condoms and other HIV prevention services. It will have a team of seven specialists in marketing, contracting, research and communication and 20 managers to be posted in various states. It will draw up operational plans for attaining the target of 3.5 billion condoms in NACP-III. Under the supervision of NACO, the Team will work in close coordination with states in the implementation of social marketing programmes. It will also provide product and brand management inputs besides designing marketing communication.

The amount required for condoms, sale points and other operational costs comes to Rs. 2000 crore spread over five years.

Key Indicators

- Increase in number of condoms sold under social marketing programmes implemented by SMOs;
- Increase in number of non-traditional retail outlets stocking condoms;
- Increase in the consistent use of condoms by populations with high risk behaviour to near 100 per cent;
- Increase in condom off-take in focussed and highly vulnerable districts;
- Increase in access of condoms within 15 minutes walking distance to 95 per cent in urban and 80 per cent in rural areas from the existing levels of 78 per cent and 41 per cent respectively;
- Consistent condom use among men reported having sex with non-regular partners from the present level of 32 per cent to 80 per cent by 2011; and
- Increasing the number of female condoms socially marketed and distributed free.

7.6.3 Access to Safe Blood

Access to safe blood is mandated by law and is the primary responsibility of NACO. Currently, it is supported by a network of 1230 blood banks including 82 blood component separation centres. During NACP-II, NACO supported the installation of blood component separation units and also funded modernization of all major blood banks at state and district levels. In addition to constantly enhancing awareness about the need to access safe blood and blood products, NACO has supported the procurement of equipments, test kits and reagents as well as the recurring expenditure of government blood banks and those run by charitable organizations that were modernized. Notwithstanding these achievements, there are still 39 districts in the country with no facilities for supply of safe blood. Based on population standards, the requirement of blood for the country is estimated to be 8.5 million units/year, whereas the available supply is only 4.4 million units/year. Moreover, in public sector blood banks, currently only 52 per cent of blood is obtained from voluntary donations.

Broad objective of the blood safety programme under NACP-III is to ensure provision of safe and quality blood within one hour of requirement in a health facility through a well-coordinated national blood transfusion service. The specific objective is to ensure reduction in the transfusion associated HIV transmission to 0.5 per cent. This is sought to be achieved by:

- Ensuring that regular (repeat) voluntary non-remunerated blood donors constitute the main source of blood supply through phased increase in donor recruitment and retention;
- Establishing blood storage centres in the primary health care system for availability of blood in far-flung remote areas;
- Vigorously promoting appropriate use of blood, blood components and blood products among the clinicians; and
- Developing long term policy for capacity building to achieve efficient and self sufficient blood transfusion services.

NACP-III is also committed to introducing new activities and strengthening existing ones i.e. accreditation of blood banks, External Quality Assessment Scheme (EQAS) for HIV testing, organizing trainings on appropriate clinical use of blood for clinicians, quality management programme in blood transfusion services and promotion of voluntary non-remunerated blood donation.

National and State Blood Transfusion Councils were registered as societies in 1996, and supported by NACO. At state levels, these councils oversee the voluntary blood donation and appropriate clinical use of blood, training and manpower development, and supervision of blood transfusion services in the State. The councils will receive continued support for their assigned tasks.

Voluntary Blood Donation

As stated earlier, there is a serious mismatch between demand and supply of blood in the country. Another issue of concern is that the proportion of voluntary blood donation is to the tune of 52 per cent only which is grossly inadequate. Several activities to promote public awareness of the need for voluntary blood donation have been undertaken in collaboration with NGOs. These will be strengthened. In addition, through collaboration with the Indian Red Cross Society, voluntary blood donation camps and other activities will be regularly undertaken to increase blood collection in the country. The target is to raise voluntary blood donation to 90 per cent by end of the programme. NACO will also enhance quality assurance programme for blood banks and improve systems for transportation and storage of blood and blood products.

Key Activities

- Set up district level blood banks in 39 districts, having no blood transfusion facility as of now;
- Establish blood storage centres in 3222 CHCs. (Equipment grant by RCH-II & annual recurrent grant by NACO);
- Make available refrigerated vans in 500 districts for networking with blood storage centres;
- Establish additional model blood banks in 22 States;
- Set up additional Blood Component Separation Units (BCSU) in 80 tertiary care hospitals and separate at least 50 per cent of the collection at all BCSUs (162) into components;
- Expand EQAS for blood services to cater to expansion of blood storage facilities in CHC;
- Sensitize clinicians on optimum use of blood. blood components and products;
- Promote autologous blood donation;
- Liaise with Indian Red Cross Society and Ministry of Youth Affairs and Sports to promote voluntary blood donation among the youth;
- Make available the services of one social worker for district level blood banks and two social workers for blood banks in teaching hospitals;
- Sensitize and train medical, surgical and OBGY staff of district hospitals and CHCs on rational use of blood;
- Set up 32 blood mobiles in various states;
- Liaise with the Indian Medical Council (IMC) to mandate the requirement of a department of transfusion medicine in all medical colleges;

- Liaise with MCI and DNB to include appropriate transfusion practices in the syllabus of MD/MS clinical subjects;
- Establish one additional plasma fractionation facility in the country regulated by NBTC and DCG (I); and
- Establish four Centres of Excellence in blood transfusion services in the four metros on a 50:50 share basis with IRCS.

Plan for supervision

With a large network of blood banks and Blood Component Separation Facilities in the country, it is essential to supervise various activities undertaken both among blood bank techniques as well as voluntary blood donation at different levels. The suggested levels of supervision are as follows:

(i) At the District Level

There is at least one NACO supported blood bank in most of the districts in the country. This blood bank in collaboration with district branch of Indian Red Cross Society, Nehru Yuva Kendra (NYK) and NSS will organise minimum one voluntary blood donation camp in each of the district. This number can be more than one. The existing District Nodal Officer (DNO) in charge of AIDS Control Programme in the district, will visit each and every camp organised in his jurisdiction to ensure proper coordination. He will also visit the existing blood bank once in a month and review the implementation of blood bank technique as per the laid down check-list.

(ii) At the State Level

State AIDS Control Societies (SACS) have state level officials like Joint Director (Blood Safety); Dy. Director (Blood Safety) and Drug Inspector (FDA). In addition to these staff, the State Blood Transfusion Council is also established in each of the state. Both SACS and SBTC will work out a joint supervisory plan by including some technical experts from outside and ensure that each of the blood bank in the state is supervised once in three months as per the designed check-list. On a random basis the team will also visit voluntary blood donation camps in the state.

(iii) At the National Level

The institutional framework available at the national level for supervision purpose is three fold. The blood safety division in NACO, National Blood Transfusion Council (NBTC) and Technical Resource

Group (TRG) on Blood Safety. Based on the performance of the States in Blood Transfusion Services, the states will be divided into (a) Poor performing; (b) Average performing; and (c) Better performing states as per laid down indicators. The poor performing states will be visited by the Consultant (Blood Safety) once in a quarter, while other states will be randomly selected for supervisory visit. Members of NBTC as well as members of TRG on Blood Safety will be assigned one state to give feedback to NACO on the overview of Blood Transfusion Services twice a year.

This institutional arrangement for supervision will be in place during the entire project period of NACP–III. A total amount of Rs. 955 crore will be spent during the project period to achieve the stated objectives.

7.6.4 Integrated Counselling and Testing Services

Services relating to voluntary counselling and testing have expanded over the years with only 79 VCTCs in 1998 to 445 in 2002. By March 2006, 2815 Integrated Counselling and Testing Centres (ICTCs) were functioning in the country. Distribution of ICTCs is given in **Table 7.4**.

Table 7.4: Distribution of ICTCs

General ICTCs without PPTCT facility	*General ICTCs with PPTCT facility*	*ICTCs with exclusive PPTCT facility*	*ICTCs under HIV-TB co-ordination*	*Total ICTCs*
777	1,378	502	158	2,815

Notwithstanding this expansion, access to services for vulnerable groups has been poor under NACP-II. It is estimated that the percentage of people in the country who know their HIV status is only about 5-7 per cent of the people who are infected. Under NACP-III, existing VCTCs and PPTCT centres will be re-modelled as a hub to integrate all HIV related services (see **Figure 7.5**) and called Integrated Counselling and Testing Centres (ICTCs) with the district, sub-district hospitals, CHCs and RNTCP microscopic centres. Accordingly, with a view to provide universal access to ICTCs, additional 2140 centres will be established during the project period, taking the total number of ICTCs in the public sector to 4955.

ICTCs will provide entry points for both men and women requiring different services. For instance, pregnant women will be referred to PPTCT centres, those with STI symptoms to STD clinics and those with TB symptoms to RNTCP centres. Additional counselling services will be

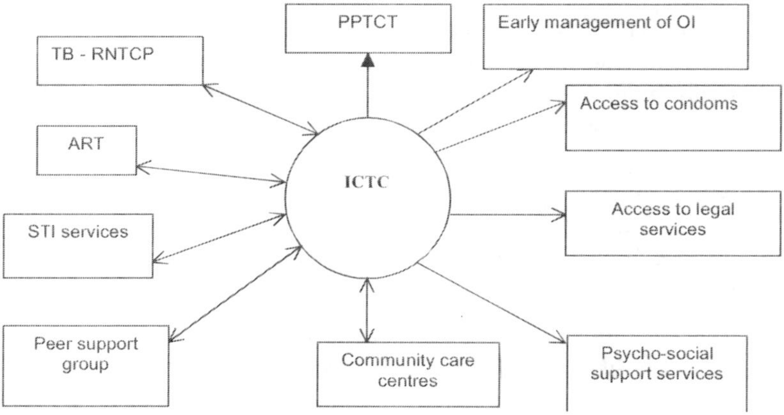

Figure 7.5: Integrated Counselling and Testing Centre (ICTC) and its linkages

provided in PPTC centres for counselling and testing of pregnant women attending ANC clinics. All clients who access services from the ICTCs will be provided advice on prevention also. Further, counsellors at these centres will ensure access to the following services through linkages:

- IEC/BCC;
- Condom promotion;
- STI treatment linkages;
- Prophylaxis and early management of OI;
- DOTS for TB; and
- ART Services.

As ICT services are scaled up to sub-district and CHC levels, IEC activities will focus on demand generation by vulnerable populations so that each ICTC performs at least 15 tests per day by the end of NACP-III. The scale up plan for testing will be as follows (see **Table 7.5**):

Table 7.5: Scale up plan for testing at ICTCs

Year	*Year 1*	*Year 2*	*Year 3*	*Year 4*	*Year 5*
Average number of tests / day / ICTC	5	8	10	12	15
No. of people tested per year	6.5 million	12 million	15 million	18 million	22 million
No. of existing ICTCs	2,815	4,333	4,955	4,955	4,955
No of new ICTCs	1,518	622	0	0	0

Integration of counselling services under all HIV related services will also be accomplished through the centres. In hard-to-access areas and tribal areas, mobile ICTCs will be made available to provide counselling and testing services. The quality of tests will be assured by internal and external quality assurance mechanisms. Private sector institutions desirous of setting up ICTCs will be provided with access to training and EQAS.

In addition to the above, private providers at the primary level who have a good client load of STI cases will be identified and encouraged to do provider-initiated testing and counselling of patients who access their services. These private providers will be provided access to training and EQAS as well as accreditation by the National AIDS Control Organization as an incentive to take up provider-initiated testing and counselling of patients. It is expected that the accredited private providers will provide an additional 12 million tests per year to clients who access their services, charging them at an actual cost basis.

Training of available manpower for expanding counselling services will be accomplished in addition to recruiting additional counsellors for the services. The programme will establish linkages with RNTCP, PPTCT, ART and STD services.

Supervisory Plan

All category A and B districts will have a co-ordinator who will oversee the functioning of ICTCs and PPTCT centres in a district. This co-ordinator will be appointed on a contractual basis and will not only supervise the functioning of ICTCs and PPTCTs in a district but will also work out strategies to enhance the client load in all ICTCs so as to achieve the target of 15 tests per day by year 5. The co-ordinator will also oversee the functioning of accredited private providers who will do provider-initiated testing and counselling of clients. In addition to the co-ordinator, the counsellors working in Medical Colleges will be identified as master counsellors who will support and supervise the functioning of counsellors at ICTCs in district hospitals as well as CHCs.

The total outlay proposed for this component is Rs. 836 crore for five years.

Key Activities

(i) National Level

- Set up integrated counselling and testing facilities in all districts of the country and make district ICTCs as model training and referral centres for other such centres;

- Set up EQAS for testing and quality assurance systems for counselling;
- Ensure availability of quality test kits;
- Ensure availability of master counsellors to support and supervise other counsellors;
- Provide special books on youth and sexuality free for all those who attend ICTCs;
- Make available appropriate and age specific IEC material, particularly for youth at the ICTCs; and
- Integrate routine voluntary free health check up for high risk population at the testing facility.

(ii) State Level

- Establish ICT services upto the level of CHCs subject to need assessed by epidemiological profile of the district;
- Ensure provider-initiated testing and counselling of clients by selected private providers after undergoing a process of accreditation;
- Establish ICT services in non-health sector and make such services more accessible for the youth and other vulnerable groups;
- Build a pool of counsellors to provide quality service during rapid up-scaling of ICTCs at district and sub-district levels;
- Set up mobile ICTCs to access hard-to-reach and tribal areas;
- States with poor testing load need to ascertain reasons for poor use and take remedial measures;
- Generate demand to seek ICT services through district ICTC co-ordinator;
- Oversee the functioning of all ICTCs through district ICTC co-ordinator;
- Build capacity of preferred providers identified by the community; and
- Develop systems for referral up to medical colleges.

(iii) District and Community Level

- Monitor quality of ICT services provided by the units; and
- Mobilize demand generation.

7.6.5 Prevention of Parent to Child Transmission (PPTCT)

It has been estimated that out of 27 million pregnancies in India nearly, 189,000 occur in HIV + mothers leading to an estimated cohort of 56,700 infected babies (Joint Technical Mission on PPTCT). PPTCT programme using Nevirapine was initiated in the country in 2001. However, by 2004, only 3.94% of all pregnant women received HIV counselling and testing and only 2.35% of the HIV-positive pregnant women received the antiretroviral drug prophylaxis. Currently, a total of 1882 PPTCT centres are functioning in the country which includes 502 stand alone PPTCT centres as well as 1380 ICTCs which offer PPTCT services. While the majority of these centres are in the public sector, a few are also in the private sector. Of these centres, 1600 are in the six high prevalence states of Andhra Pradesh, Karnataka, Tamil Nadu, Maharashtra, Nagaland and Manipur which account for 73% of all the people living with HIV in the country. It is estimated that, to provide universal access to these services throughout the country, additional 2140 centres will need to be put into place. There will be no additional costs, however, as these will be part of the ICTCs discussed above, to the extent that they cover the CHCs and sub district hospitals. Medical Colleges and District Hospitals will, however, have a separate PPTCT.

In March 2000, NACO initiated a 2-year PPTCT feasibility study aimed at designing an implementation model of PPTCT for the public health sector. The study supported by the Government of India and UNICEF involved 11 major hospitals of the 5 most affected states in India. Besides demonstrating that it was possible to implement PPTCT in the public sector, these studies also found that the programme provided opportunities for HIV prevention counselling, STI diagnosis and treatment of 98-99% of the women who were uninfected.

Based on the results of this study, PPTCT programme was scaled up in the country with Nevirapine as the regimen of choice. Although, the regimen is simple to deliver and has an efficacy rate of 48% in prevention of HIV transmission in the mother baby pair, data suggests that there is increased drug resistance to ART on mothers who were treated with prophylactic single dose Nevirapine. Hence a feasibility study will be conducted to assess the feasibility of the offer of new revised regimen. Based on the results of this study, NACP-III will plan a shift in the prophylactic antiretroviral regimen for HIV positive mothers and their infants.

In keeping with the recommendation of the Expert Committee on PPTCT, NACP-III will scale up PPTCT services through public-private partnerships. Also, PPTCT services will be extended upto the level of CHCs as part of ICT centres to be established there. The aim is to prevent vertical transmission of HIV in an annual cohort of 189,000 HIV positive pregnant women throughout the country. In addition, NACP-III will strengthen referrals and linkages. Till now CD4 counts were performed only for a small percentage of HIV positive pregnant women. NACP-III will have an institutional mechanism to know the CD4 count of all pregnant positive women. Blood sample of all pregnant positive women will be sent to the nearest ART centre and proper referral of all eligible HIV positive women to the nearest ART centres will be ensured.

Of the 27 million deliveries which take place annually in the country, about 60% are institutional while the remaining is non-institutional. Of the institutional deliveries, 50% occur in the public sector while the remaining 50% occur in the private sector health care system.

Targets for PPTCT have been calculated on the basis of the proportion of deliveries that occur in public and private sector and their coverage and anticipated proportion of pregnant women receiving ARVs. In high prevalence states, current proportion of deliveries in public sector for year 1 is 30% which is assumed to increase by 5% every year. The proportion of pregnant women receiving ARVs in public sector in year 1 is 70% with an increase of 10% each in year 2 and 3 and is assumed to reach 98% from year 4 onwards.

The proportion of deliveries in private sector is assumed to remain at 40% throughout, and their coverage for year 1 is assumed to be 5% which is assumed to increase by 5% each year.

The epidemiologically critical states contribute to PPTCT coverage from year 2 onwards. Their coverage for public sector in year 2 is assumed to be 10% with an increase of 5% each year. The proportion of HIV + pregnant women receiving ARVs is assumed to be 50% in year 2, 70% in year 3, 80% in year 4 and 90% in year 5. A significant contribution from remaining states is assumed to begin from year 4 where 10% deliveries in public sector may have 50% women taking these medicines. The coverage would also increase by 5% in year 5.

It is assumed that the outreach efforts envisaged in PPTCT strategy proposed in NACP-III and integrated efforts through RCH-II will enhance capacity to achieve these targets.

The scale up plan for PPTCT services is as follows (see **Table 7.6**):

Table 7.6: Scale up plan for PPTCT services

Year	*Year 1*	*Year 2*	*Year 3*	*Year 4*	*Year 5*
Number of pregnant women to be covered	2,025,000	3,782,000	4,900,000	6,500,000	7,500,600
Number of HIV positive women to be covered	20,000	36,700	55,000	71,000	75,600

PLHA would be employed as outreach workers to ensure adherence and compliance of medication by HIV positive women. An outlay of Rs. 250 crore is proposed for this component.

In addition to the above, private maternity homes with a good load of antenatal cases will be identified and encouraged to do provider-initiated testing and counselling of pregnant women who access their services as well as provide positive women with prophylactic antiretroviral therapy. These private providers will be provided access to training and EQAS as well as accreditation by NACO as an incentive to take up provider-initiated testing and counselling of patients. Public private partnership would be established to expand delivery of PPTCT services including DNA PCR testing. Partnership with obstetrics association (FOGSY) Federation of Obstetrics and Gynaecologists would be established to facilitate implementation. It is expected that these accredited private providers will cover an additional 10 million pregnant women who access their services charging them at an actual cost basis.

Key Activities

- Develop and implement a costed population-based PPTCT scale up plan upto the level of CHC so as to ensure that at least 80% of the annual cohorts of 189,000 HIV positive women receive prophylactic antiretroviral therapy;
- Define a minimum package of services to be provided at different levels of care, including development of standard operating procedures for strengthening linkages between PPTCT and ART services for infected parents and children;
- Phase implementation of the revised PPTCT guidelines to ensure smooth operationalization and transition;
- Strengthen follow-up services for HIV positive mothers and their HIV-exposed children to ensure a continuum of prevention and care by employing PLHAs as outreach workers;

- Intensify HIV/STI preventive interventions that can feasibly be provided in health facilities within the context of PPTCT;
- Strengthen infant feeding counselling skills to reinforce mother's decision and support infant feeding method of their choice;
- Include the definition of a minimum PPTCT package of care, including specific primary prevention services for HIV negative women, for different service delivery points in the ongoing development process of PPTCT guidelines;
- Request for technical assistance from partners to develop standard operating procedures (SOPs) to strengthen linkages within and between health facilities by the level of health system and type of facility including referral mechanisms, information sharing and monitoring procedures and tools;
- Plan and conduct pilot testing of SOPs and tools;
- Implement effective communication strategy especially for people in high risk groups and symptomatic persons;
- Adopt long term follow up of mother and child for OI and ART and integrate with RCH services;
- Facilitate participation of private sector in PPTCT programme by sensitization and training; and
- Operationalise research to identify barriers in implementation of PPTCT and identify remedial measures.

7.7 Safety Issues: Infection Control, Waste Management and Construction Aspects

The IC-WM Plan and Environmental Management for Construction activities details various steps for waste management as required under Government of India's Biomedical Waste (Management and Handling) Rules, including waste segregation, treatment and disposal. The Plan also highlights infection control measures to be practiced by healthcare workers involved in testing and treatment activities. The success of managing IC-WM programs is depending on the collective leadership of the MOHFW and partners. The plan will be implemented in coordination with the department of health in particular RCH, Tuberculosis Control and NRHM programmes.

The IC-WM Plan and Environmental Management for Construction activities, provides a consolidated guidelines on IC-WM good practices that may be further tailored to suit the facility's needs. The Plan is based on the following framework:

- Infection Control and Waste Management
- Institutional Framework and Capacity Building
- Monitoring & Evaluation and Implementation Schedule
- Environmental impacts related to civil works and construction aspects

The broad objective of IC-WM Plan, is to ensure the efficient and sustainable management of potentially harmful waste generated from healthcare facilities, which cater to the prevention, care and treatment of HIV/AIDS. Mainstreaming of HIV/AIDS activities in the health service delivery mechanisms will certainly provide appropriate foundation for an integrated approach to IC-WM.

Specific objectives of IC & WM Plan which will include generic guidance and protocols for healthcare waste management in accordance with size of healthcare facilities, alternative technologies for treatment, transportation and disposal. This is sought to be achieved by:

- Ensuring implementation of guidelines for Training, establishment of Institutional framework and Monitoring and reporting systems
- Establishment and operation of broad time-schedule, cost estimate and recommendations for private sector participation
- Developing implementation strategies to provide appropriate guidance to the States reparation of long-term policy support for capacity building to achieve effectiveness in the implementation of IC & WM plan

An implementation schedule is suggested for the first year of the NACP – III with components of accountability, training of paramedical staff, WM facilitators, Medical Colleges personnel, allied health workers, minor civil works at facility level, treatment and disposal, monitoring and evaluation (Please see **Annex 7.1**).

NACO will ensure effective implementation of IC-WM plan by engaging multiple stakeholders which will enhance;

- Extensive capacity building using multi-sectoral approach as beneficiaries of IC & WM intervention strategies;
- Wider outreach to local communities involving CBOs/NGOs/ Civil Society Organizations and representative of urban local bodies and local self institutions. SACS will increase the scope of

their interventions to include as many persons from the local communities as possible, either directly or through CBOs/NGOs.

- High degree of alignment between SACS and Medical Colleges & Health Bodies which will further strengthen IC & WM strategies during NACP III implementation phase

Similarly, Construction Management Guidelines will be useful for the purpose of any upgradation/renovation of a building with potential environmental impacts, which can be minimized through good construction management practices during the implementation of NACP III. NACO and SACS will ensure that the requirements defined in the Addendum are included into the bid documents with civil works contractors. Additionally, experts in environmental planning and designing will review and approve all designs before construction. NACO and SACS will undertake periodic reviews of construction practices and ensure these guidelines are being adhered to (Please see **Annex 7.2)**.

Under the National Plan, there is a provision of Rs. 75 crore for contingency and innovation, which will be accessed for improving Infection Control, Waste Management and site environmental conditions. An additional amount of Rs. 25 crore is available for community and social mobilization.

Chapter - 8

Programme Strategies - Care and Support

The care, support and treatment needs of people infected with HIV vary with the stage of the disease. In the initial 3-4 years after infection, people infected with HIV remain asymptomatic. However, after 6-8 years of infection the condition of most AIDS patients deteriorates further, necessitating palliative care for relief of symptoms and psycho-social support without treatment. Major problems that arise relate to labelling and associated stigma and discrimination in the society. As immunity falls the threat to life is heightened by related infectious diseases and disorders that accompany it. Access to prompt diagnosis and treatment of such opportunistic infections (OIs), including TB, will ensure that a larger number of PLHA are enabled to live longer and healthier than would have been possible otherwise. As the immunity falls further, AIDS patients develop infections with organisms which are not normally pathogenic to healthy people. Provision of appropriate chemo-prophylaxis is essential to avoid serious infections. ART delays the onset of AIDS and further deterioration of the immunity. It also prolongs and improves the quality of life of infected people.

Under NACP-II, focus was given on low cost care, support and treatment of common OIs. ART programme was launched in 2004 in 8 institutions in 6 high prevalence states and Delhi. Since then, it is being gradually up-scaled and, as on 31st May 2006, a total of 54 ART centres were functional with 33,638 patients (including 1352 children) receiving free Anti Retroviral Therapy at these centres. However, this constitutes only 10 per cent of the estimated eligible patients needing treatment.

NACP-III will adopt a comprehensive strategy to strengthen family and community care, provide psycho-social support to individuals, more particularly to marginalized women and children affected by the epidemic and ensure accessible, affordable and sustainable treatment services.

Expanding care, support and treatment (CST) and linking them with prevention will not only help reduce AIDS related mortality but also positively impact on reduction in poverty, stigma and discrimination, and help achieve the primary objective of controlling the spread of the epidemic. The strategy would include identification of institutions, strengthening referral linkages for CD4 testing, capacity building of ART teams and procurement of ARV drugs. It is expected that about 100,000 patients will be put on free ART by March 2007 in about 100 ART centres and 300,000 patients on ART by the end of 2011 through approximately 250 ART centres (see **Table 8.1**). The total cost of care, support and treatment under NACP-III is estimated to be Rs. 1460 crore over 5 years.

Biological, social and cultural factors make women highly vulnerable to HIV infection. Feminization of the epidemic would lead to more children being infected and affected. NACP-III will focus on women and children as special targets and address their special needs. Besides, synergies of existing programmes under RCH and ICDS will be strengthened. CSOs working on women's and children's issues will be sensitized and supported to provide care and support to women and children infected and affected by the epidemic.

Table 8.1: Overall Targets for Care and Support Activities

Number of PLHA with AIDS	0.38 million
Number of people needing care with access to OI treatment	0.33 million OI episodes under public sector
Number of PLHA needing TB referral	2.8 million
Number of PLHA provided ART in the programme	0.3 million under public sector
Number of children to receive ART	40,000

8.1 Expected Outcome

- Reduction in HIV associated morbidity and mortality with comprehensive HIV management;
- Increasing number of PLHA accessing care, support and treatment services, including ART, with priority being accorded to women & children referred from TIs and those below poverty line;
- Adherence and compliance to the prescribed ART regimen increasing to more than 95 per cent;
- Participation of those who access care and support services in positive prevention and other programme activities leading to greater reduction in the spread of HIV;

- Reduction in stigma and discrimination to PLHA in the community; and
- Greater involvement of PLHA in the care, support and treatment activities.

8.2 Linking Care and Support with Prevention

Nearly 5.21 million PLHA can be a potential source of spreading infection in the country, unless provision of ART is accompanied by behavioural change in PLHA. Under NACP-III, all care centres (Community Care Centres, TB Clinics and ART Centres) will also focus on preventive strategies, thus ensuring that HIV spread is reduced from the affected individuals. At the same time, linking prevention strategies (ICTC, PPTCT, STD Clinics and TIs on high risk groups) to care centres will ensure that stigma and discrimination is reduced and substantially more PLHA are targeted for communication interventions designed to change high risk behaviour. A total of Rs. 37 crore has been allocated for activities linking care, prevention and positive living.

8.3 Key Activities

- Develop risk reduction strategies for PLHA and their partners and integrate risk reduction counselling into OI and ART care;
- Build capacity of PLHA networks to participate in prevention programmes (IEC, advocacy, workplace interventions, school and college AIDS programme);
- Establish linkages of TIs, ICTCs, PPTCT Centres, STD clinics with ART centres and TB clinic so that PLHA can access care, support and treatment services and behavioural communication;
- Partner referrals through counselling; and
- Screen TB/STI of PLHA.

8.4 Opportunistic Infections (OIs)

Improved access to prophylaxis and management of opportunistic infections and continuum of care will be an important activity. HIV accounts for the highest number of deaths caused by any single infection. The threat to life is not so much due to the virus, but by opportunistic infections and related disorders that accompany it. Early recognition of the HIV status, with access to chemo-prophylaxis, prompt diagnosis and treatment of OIs will ensure that morbidity and mortality of those infected is reduced and quality of life improved. Incremental requirement of drugs for treating HIV infected persons for OIs would be provided through the programme in public sector health care units and training for private sector providers for quality management of common OIs facilitated in collaboration with Indian Medical Association and other professional bodies.

Table 8.2 shows HIV-related infections and illnesses most frequently encountered in India.

Table 8.2: HIV related Infections and their frequency

Infection	***Frequency per year***
Bacterial	
Tuberculosis	# 10 per cent of HIV with 15 per cent chance of TB/year
Bacterial respiratory infections	# 10 per cent of HIV with 2 episodes/year
Bacterial enteric	# 10 per cent of HIV with 1 episode/year
Atypical mycobacteriosis	# 1 per cent of HIV with 1 episode/year
Viral	
Herpes simplex virus diseases	# 2 per cent of PLHA with 1 episode/year
Varicella Zoster	# 5 per cent of PLHA with 1 episode/year
Cytomegalovirus disease	# 1 per cent of PLHA with 1 episode/year
Human Herpes virus type 8 infection	# 1 per cent of PLHA with 1 episode/year
Fungal	
Candidiasis	# 5 per cent of PLHA with 3 episodes/year
Cryptococcosis	# 5 per cent of PLHA with 1 episode/year
Pneumocystis jiroveci pneumonia	# 5 per cent of PLHA with 1 episode/year
Parasitic	
Toxoplasmosis	# 2 per cent of PLHA with 1 episode/year
Cryptosporidiosis	
Microsporidiosis	
Isosporiasis	Diarrhea caused in 40 per cent of PLHA with an average of 3 episodes/year = 120
Giardia	
Stongyloides	

Opportunistic infections cause an increased burden on the health system and the family. At the macro level, these lead to filling up of essential bed capacity in district and teaching hospitals and, at the micro level, an increase in household expenditure and impoverishment of the family. Making treatment for OIs available locally, at lower cost with effective referral system will reduce the burden on the society. Some OIs (Pneumocystis jiroveci pneumonia and toxoplasmosis) have a proven preventive strategy and these will be given importance in the programme.

Tuberculosis is the most common infection among HIV infected individuals and is also the leading cause of death in PLHA. The programme will therefore strengthen the synergy between HIV and TB programmes in the country by developing standard HIV/TB protocols and setting up ICT services in microscopic centres of RNTCP, so that patients with HIV/TB co-infection are identified, offered preventive services and treatment for HIV infection. Similarly, referral of all HIV positive subjects identified through ICT and having pulmonary or extra pulmonary symptoms suggesting TB to RNTCP will be made mandatory. It is expected that nearly 30 lakh referrals of suspected patients from ICT to RNTCP will be required to initiate TB treatment in a majority of PLHA having active TB infection also. Treatment of TB will follow RNTCP guidelines.

Majority of common opportunistic infections like skin infections, candidiasis, diarrhea, respiratory tract infections including TB can be treated at the community level at PHC, CHC and Community Care Centres. It is expected that private providers would continue to provide treatment for 40 per cent to 50 per cent of all OIs. Standard guidelines and protocols would be made available at all sites for management of OIs and training provided in collaboration with IMA and other professional bodies

Serious infections including severe pneumonia and central nervous system infections would be identified and referred to district hospitals or medical colleges for management. Referral linkages and guidelines will be established. Smart card system will be integrated and up-scaled to cover the entire country to see if it is feasible to track infections in individual patients. **Table 8.3** refers to the levels of care for different opportunistic infections proposed under NACP-III.

Table 8.3: Levels of Care for Prophylaxis and Management of OIs

Levels of Care for OI	*Types of OI*	*Diagnosis, Prophylaxis and Management of OIs*
Tertiary Level Institutions	All common OIs including Severe bacterial, fungal or parasitic pneumonia, Enteric bacterial infections, Toxoplasmosis, Cryptococcal meningitis and Cytomegalovirus infections.	Syndromic and prophylactic management of OI; Etiological, where indicated.
District Hospitals/Trust hospitals	Bacterial, fungal or parasitic pneumonia, Enteric bacterial infections, Fungal infections of the skin and Viral hepatitis.	Essential syndromic and prophylactic management of OI. Basic diagnostic services as specified in the guidelines
CHCs	Prophylaxis of toxoplasmosis and pneumocistis and Herpes Zoster, Tuberculosis, other respiratory infections, Oral candidiasis, Skin infections, Enteric bacterial infections and Chronic diarrhea.	Syndromic and prophylactic management of OI. Etiological management for TB.

(Contd...)

PHC/Mission hospitals	Prophylaxis of toxoplasmosis, Herpes Zoster, Tuberculosis, other respiratory infections, Oral candidiasis, diarrhoea and skin infections.	Syndromic and prophylactic management of OI. Etiological management for TB.
Community Care Centres	Diarrhoea, fevers, Oral candidiasis and Skin infections.	Syndromic management and referral as per protocol.

Provision of essential laboratory tests are required based on disease conditions and their treatment protocol at different levels as defined in the OI guideline. Capacity exists for routine diagnosis of common OIs. For minor ailments that can be addressed at home, local village medical practitioners will be provided training in treatment and referrals. This single intervention will provide access to treatment and more importantly save substantial expenditure incurred on travelling long distances to access the formal health system. Further, the staff at PHCs and CHCs will be trained through NRHM, while in district and tertiary hospitals, through the state health system.

Table 8.3 provides the minimum requirement of laboratory services and their levels. Quality of laboratory tests would be assured through establishment of EQAS for laboratory needs. Currently the skills and human resources for providing laboratory support is poor and this will be enhanced through training.

The total allocation for OIs excluding HIV/TB co-infection under NACP-III is proposed at Rs 159.65 crore (OI drugs 129.35 + 30.3 crore).

Key Activities

National Level

- Disseminate guidelines on OI management for different levels of service delivery and referral linkages and train as well as retrain;
- Develop guidelines and capacities for establishing standards of care; and
- Further strengthen linkages with DOTS programme for HIV/TB co-infection.

State Level

- Supply essential drugs to government hospitals for treatment and prophylaxis of OI and establish monitoring systems;
- Establish referral system for appropriate management;

- Ensure that all cases of HIV showing symptoms of pulmonary or extra-pulmonary TB are screened for tuberculosis;
- Ensure that all AIDS patients are protected by initiation of cotrimoxazole prophylaxis;
- Provide sensitization and training to all CHC and PHC doctors on management of TB as per RNTCP guidelines;
- Sensitize doctors in private sector through Indian Medical Association and their access to referral linkages; and
- Establish sentinel surveillance of OI in each state and monitor hospital records on OIs to detect any discernible trends in prevalence of different infections.

District Level

- Ensure OI drug supply chain in PHC and CHC through effective monitoring based on patient load and targets;
- Ensure compliance to DOTS; and
- Ensure transport subsidy for PLHA who are below poverty line; and children have access to treatment facilities.
- Ensure that women.

8.5 Community Care Centres

Under NACP-II, 122 Community Care Centres were set up to provide treatment for minor OIs, but more importantly psycho-social support. These were envisaged more as short stay homes for those who were thrown out of their homes and needed care, rest and even decent burials. They were, therefore, not linked to other activities or programmes.

With the introduction of treatment into the programme, CCCs have now a critical role in helping PLHAs gain easy access to ART treatment and counselling on primary prevention, nutrition, drug adherence etc. Acting as a bridge between PLHA and the ART centre, CCCs will be attached to an ART centre and ensure that all patients are provided counselling at CCC either prior to initiation of ART and/or through outreach worker at community level as part of follow up. The outreach worker will be trained in home based care and ensure drug adherence.

Under NACP-III, it is proposed to set up an additional 228 such centres over the next 5 years in partnership with PLHA networks in all A and B districts, and in C districts, based on PLHA load. NGOs and other civil society organizations will strengthen community care and support programmes. These centres will be established in districts based on epidemiological profile and PLHA load and linked to the closest ART centre. The phasing of the centres will therefore be in tandem with the ART facilities. These centres will focus on providing four types of services to PLHA: (a) Counselling, in particular for drug adherence; (b) Treatment support; (c) Referral and outreach for follow up; and (d) Social support services. SACS will ensure access of high risk groups who need the services of community care centres through linkages between TIs and the centres.

Table 8.4 indicates the types of services to be rendered, activities to be undertaken by these centres and the resources and supplies required by them. Community Care Centres will have a maximum capacity of 30 beds. Five hundred community care centres would cost the programme Rs. 367 crore (259 for CCC + 108 for NGO Rx support) over 5 years.

Table 8.4: Services to be rendered by Community Care Centres

Types of Services	*Activities*	*Resources Required*	*Supplies and Infrastructure*
Counselling Services	Counselling on Drug Adherence and positive living Family Counselling Nutritional Counselling Occupational Counselling Treatment literacy Psychosocial support	Counselling Services to be provided by two counsellors	Contracting out counselling services; Facilities for Integrated Counselling services
Treatment and Patient Management	Provision of compassionate care for sick patients (Hospice) Treatment of minor OIs Facilitation of home based care for terminally ill Minor surgical procedures	Services of one doctor, Four nurses, One cook and One janitor	Contracting the services of doctor for OPD services Provision of 10-30 bed care facility Basic laboratory facilities and facilities for minor surgical procedures Drugs and equipment for treatment minor OIs
Referral and outreach	Support for adherence Default retrieval Transportation of sick PLHA to district hospital	Services of two health workers for HIV affected household visits	Contractual for services of two health workers to cover 25 PLHA/ 2000 families / 50 villages
Social Service	Support for PLHA who face social rejection Link with lawyers collective for obtaining legal help against stigma and discrimination Linkage with SACS	Link Person	

Expected Outcome

- Treatment adherence to be more than 95 per cent;
- Increased participation of PLHA in preventive efforts;

- Facilitation of linkages for nutritional and other support programmes;
- Reduction in stigma and discrimination;
- Improved care for PLHA who require treatment for minor illnesses; and
- Better home based care for terminally ill patients.

Key Activities

- Develop SOPs and guidelines for CCC in tune with the increased flexibility in terms of bed strength and additional roles proposed in NACP-III;
- Identify committed NGO/CBO/FBOs who will be contracted to run the units;
- Provide training to identified providers;
- Build capacity for PLHA networks to participate in CCC activities;
- Sensitize PRIs on the roles of CCCs;
- Provide drugs for treatment of STI and minor OIs & TB;
- Establish link with RNTCP to make these as DOTS centres, where feasible; and
- Supervise and monitor activities of CCC by DAPCU.

8.6 Providing Care and Support for Children Infected and Affected with HIV/AIDS

According to UNAIDS estimates, approximately 50,000 children per year below the age of 15 years are infected with HIV/AIDS in India. The present responses on care of children infected and affected by HIV/AIDS, provide just short term benefit to these children and not to cater to their best interests in terms of their right to health, protection, education and nutrition. In addition, a long term strategy to sustain the support systems within the community is practically non-existent.

Psycho-social support[1] strategies and systems are also non-existent in the government set-up except for 'family counsellors' in health centres. These are absolutely essential for children who are infected and also for those who have lost their parents in order to cope with the sense of loss and feeling of insecurity. The health system, too, needs to be upgraded to cater to the emotional and medical support needs of families and specifically children affected by HIV/AIDS. In the short term, NACP-III will seek to:

- Provide special training to counsellors for paediatric counselling;

- Provide linkages with social sector programmes (MWCD, MSJE, MHRD) for accessing social support for infected children;
- Improve early diagnosis of HIV exposed children under 18 months as well as among symptomatic children;
- Increase the number of HIV-exposed and HIV-infected children receiving cotrimoxazole prophylaxis; and
- Improve the access to existing HIV and ART services for children living with HIV.

In the long term, the goal is to achieve the highest quality of life for HIV-infected and affected children and their families through delivery of a comprehensive package of care and support services.[2]

Key Activities

- Generate a baseline data on the number of AIDS and non-AIDS orphans, school drop-outs, homeless, their economic status and security through a situational analysis;
- Optimize early diagnosis of HIV-exposed infants and early identification of HIV infected children;
- Define comprehensive paediatric HIV care package for each level of the health system;
- Provide comprehensive package including outreach and transportation subsidy to access ART and follow up, nutritional, educational recreational and skill developmental support;
- Decentralize delivery of components of the paediatric HIV clinical care package;
- Update policies and legal documents pertaining to confidentiality, consent, and disclosure for orphans, vulnerable children and adolescents;
- Strengthen the response of NGOs/CBOs, faith based organisations and other stakeholders to support children affected by HIV/AIDS;
- Improve the quality of care and protection provided for children through community, foster care and institution-based interventions supported by the government, donors etc.;
- Establish and enforce minimum standards of care and protection in institutional, foster care and community based care systems; and
- Develop linkages between PLHA networks, ICTC, PPTCT and ART centres with community care centres, ICDS and other child

care institutions to increase access to services for children and their families.

This component of care and support will require an amount of Rs. 493 core for the five-year period.

8.7 Psycho-social and Livelihood Support

As the epidemic spreads, an emerging issue of concern is the impoverishment of PLHA and their families. In addition to the costs related to treatment, families often suffer due to the loss of income, especially if the infected person is the main bread earner. The care-givers, too, may suffer from partial or complete loss of income depending on the extent of care they are needed to provide. Since PLHA have low level of energy and immunity, nutrition becomes a key component of care and treatment. Unless these issues are addressed, ART and positive prevention strategy may not be effective.

While NACP-III will not directly fund livelihood support, which has to be obtained from other income and employment generation and social welfare schemes, the programme will support advocacy and capacity building to access them and encourage pilot projects in this direction.

8.8 Nutritional Support to PLHA receiving ART

There is evidence to suggest that micronutrient supplements in HIV infected people influence clinical outcomes. Nutritional supplements of multi-vitamins and trace elements like zinc, selenium, magnesium, iron, iodide and copper can be obtained through good diet which includes available and affordable food items. Nutritional counselling including dietary modification would be an integral part of care, support and treatment and efforts will be made for information sharing with various agencies and government departments, such as rural development, women and child development, AYUSH etc. It will also support nutritional support for PLHA admitted to community care centres.

An amount of Rs 36 crore have been provided in the project for impact mitigation and livelihood support.

Notes

1. Psychosocial support encompasses all means of supporting social & emotional needs and well being of young children, including family and community care. This enables children to develop faith in future, learn life skills, have a sense of life worth and participate in society. Some key interventions that may be taken

up include life skills, education, peer support groups, awareness building in schools and community to reduce stigma.

2. This package constitutes, nutrition, education, social security and medical support for these children and livelihood support for the families. In the long run this will be taken up by MWCD, MSJE and MHRD as their responsibility.

Chapter - 9

Programme Strategies - Treatment

9.1 Anti-retroviral Therapy for Adults and Children

Under NACP-III, first line ART drugs will be provided to all those who need it. Public health facilities will ensure that ART is provided to (a) PLHAs referred from targeted interventions; (b) sero-positive women particularly those who have participated in PPTCT programme; (c) infected children; and (d) those below poverty line. The primary aim of ART strategies is to suppress viral replication. Successful viral suppression restores the immune system, slows or halts the disease progression and improves the quality of life. Since adherence is the key to the success of the ART programme as well as to the prevention of HIV drug resistance, NACP-III will seek to achieve drug adherence rates of 95 per cent and above. Similarly, the quality of ART delivery will be enhanced by providing training to service providers, linkages to community care, adherence to monitoring systems, setting up of EQAS and a mechanism for certification and accreditation.

NACP-III recognizes the role of private sector in the provision of care and support services. Currently, a majority of PLHA are provided treatment by the private sector. Many non-governmental organizations, particularly non-profit charitable institutions have been providing excellent care, support and treatment services to PLHA. Having regard to their track record and subject to strict quality parameters, they will be identified and covered under NACP-III for supply of free drugs, capacity building and linkages (see **Table 9.1**).

NACP-III estimates that in order to meet the targets, 250 ART centres across the country will have to be set up. CD4 tests are integral to ART delivery. Presently, there are reported to be about 250 CD4 count machines, both in private and public sector in India. These machines are adequate to cover the testing load of ART patients. NACP-III envisages developing and contracting out private providers to provide this service through public-private partnership free of cost to prioritized sub-populations.

Table 9.1: Scale-up plan for ART during NACP-III (Based on Spectrum Projections)

Year	*2006*	*2007*	*2008*	*2009*	*2010*	*2011*
Total AIDS cases estimated	508,200	501,800	493,000	486000	478,000	473,500
Target for ART in the public sector not including 40,000 children	31,234	100,000	125,000	150,000	184,000	300,000
Proportion of AIDS patients covered with ART	6.1%	20%	25%	31%	38.5%	63%

All ART centres will be located in medical colleges, district hospitals and other institutions willing to collaborate with NACO and subject to the following criteria:

- Public sector or not-for-profit private sector institutions;
- Geographic distribution based on need;
- Availability of qualified personnel;
- Availability of space as prescribed in the manual;
- Number of PLHA currently on treatment in the location; and
- Willingness to abide by protocol and participate in EQAS, certification and accreditation programmes.

Minimum additional manpower norms that are proposed to be followed for an ART centre are indicated in the **Table 9.2**.

Table 9.2: Additional Manpower Requirements for ART Centres as per Patient Load

50-500 patient Load Basic Manpower	*500-1000 Patient Load*	*1000 – 2000 Patient Load*	*2000 + Patient Load*	*Qualification*
Services of paediatrician contracted based on need	Senior Medical Officer (1 post) Services of paediatrician contracted based on need	Senior Medical Officer (1 post) Services of paediatrician contracted based on need	Senior Medical Officer (1 posts) Services of paediatrician contracted based on need	Postgraduate (MD) in Internal Medicine/Paediatric or any other clinical subject
Medical Officer (1 post)	Medical Officer (1 post)	Medical Officer (1 post)	Medical Officer (2 posts)	MD or MBBS

(Contd...)

Laboratory Technician (1 post)	Laboratory Technician (1 post)	Laboratory Technician (1 post)		Trained from institutions approved by State/UT Governments in medical laboratory technology
ART Counsellor (1 post) and 1 Peer Educator	ART Counsellor (1 post) 2 Peer Educator	ART Counsellor (2 posts) and 2 Peer Educators	ART Counsellor (4 posts) and 2 Peer Educators	Preferably a post graduate degree e.g. MA in Psychology, Master's in Social Work, Master's in Human Development (M.Sc.)
	Pharmacist (1 post)	Pharmacist (1 post)	Pharmacist (1post)	Degree / diploma in Pharmacy
Data Entry Operator (1 post)	Data Entry Operator (1 post)	Data Entry Operator (1 post)	Data Entry Operator (1 post)	Graduate and computer literate

ART will be delivered through ART clinics established in the Departments of Medicine to provide integrated HIV services as specified in the section on package of services. In category A and B districts (total 228) these clinics will be strengthened to deliver ART. This will allow the integration of services of 2 counsellors and laboratory personnel under ICTC and STD services to complement the ART services. Additional infrastructure support will be provided to cater to increased needs of ART service in teaching hospitals or in district hospitals and integrate HIV services without stigmatization. A PLHA network person will be posted in all ART centres to facilitate access to care and treatment services of PLHA at these centres referred from community care centres, CHC/PHC or by self referral. Initiation of ART in adults will be determined as per the criteria for ART (see **Table 9.3**):

Table 9.3: Criteria for ART

CD4 (cell /mm^3)	***Actions***
< 200	Treat irrespective of clinical stage
200 – 350	Offer ART for symptomatic patients Initiate Rx before CD4 drop below 200 cells/mm^3 For Asymptomatic people *
>350	Defer treatment in asymptomatic persons

* If CD4 is between 200-250, this should be repeated in 4 weeks and treatment to be considered in asymptomatic patients.

Current Criteria: WHO Stage 4: treat irrespective of CD4 count; WHO Stages 3,2,1: guided by CD4 count and CD4%.

Eligible PLHA and those initiated on ART will be provided adherence counselling and support through the community care centre nearest to their residence prior to initiation of ART, and through ART clinics at the time of initiation. Those on treatment will be followed up on a weekly basis by the outreach worker and will be sensitized on drug adherence, compliance and issues related to toxicity and monitoring schedules. This will ensure 100 per cent adherence to the drug regimen prescribed by the ART centre. Follow-up at the ART centre will be once a month on a regular basis or more frequently as required.

Community care centres will have outreach workers depending on the number of PLHA. There will be one outreach worker for every 25 PLHA/ 50 villages/2000 families. Outreach workers will preferably be selected from PLHA networks.

9.2 Paediatric Care & Support

Currently, in the 54 ART centres an estimated 1352 children are being provided ART. It is proposed to upscale this to 40,000 children by 2011 (see **Table 9.4**).

Table 9.4: Plan for Paediatric ART in NACP-III

Scale up year	*2006-07*	*2008*	*2009*	*2010*	*2011*
Estimated No. of children	10,000	15,000	20,000	30,000	40,000

The goals of the Paediatric prevention, care and treatment programme are:

- Prevention, care and treatment of children infected or affected by HIV/AIDS;
- Provide ART to more than 90 per cent of children living with AIDS at the end of 5 years; and
- Prevent HIV infection to newborns through PPTCT programme scale-up.

9.2.1 Treatment Protocols for Paediatric Care

NACO has, in consultation with the Indian Academy of Paediatrics, formulated the Paediatric ART Guidelines, Formulations & Dosing Guide, Protocol for Diagnosis & operational rollout. The strategy is proposed to be implemented simultaneously with the up-scaling of PPTCT services.

For babies below 18 months, early diagnosis will be done using DNA PCR at 6 weeks of age as per protocols such as: a repeat test if positive and after six months in case of it being negative; in cases of children breastfed by positive mothers; repetition of the test after 6-8 weeks after stopping breast feeding. In case of children more than 18 months same policy as for adults will be adopted. Monitoring of ART will be done using CD4 counts for all infected children.

HIV infected mothers will be counselled on making an informed choice on infant feeding. Exclusive replacement feeding is the ideal option but in Indian conditions may be difficult to prescribe as a norm. Evidence from some African countries seems to suggest that in conditions where access to hygienic living is not guaranteed, the promotion of exclusive replacement feeding has resulted in higher levels of infant and child mortality. Given these ground realities, exclusive breastfeeding for the first six months will be promoted.

Stavudine-based FDC regimen will be used predominantly, in the initial period of the programme. For children with TB and those with Nevirapie toxicity, EFV in tablet and suspension form will be made available. Subsequently it has been recommended to use Ziduvidine-based Paediatric FDC as they become available. Entire procurement plan is based on the use of dispersible formulations & scored tablets, except for babies less than 5 kg for whom liquid formulations have been recommended. All infected children will have access to drugs to prevent and treat OIs.

9.2.2 Delivery of Paediatric Treatment Services

Paediatric ART programme will be implemented through all the existing and planned 250 ART centres in the country. This will ensure single point delivery of services both to parents and children. They will be supported by a Paediatric Referral Centre in each state. It is also envisaged to have a Paediatric "Centre of Excellence" in each region of the country. Thus, an effective referral linkage will be created from the point of first entry to the tertiary level. These centres will have varying roles and responsibilities for delivery of care and support to infected children. PPTCT centres will be linked with paediatric and adult ART centre for follow up and early diagnosis in children and mothers.

The staffing pattern of Paediatric ART Centres at the State and regional level will consist of a full time paediatrician, counsellor trained in paediatric HIV infection, a laboratory technician and a nutritionist. At ART centres having less than 100 children, services of paediatricians and nutritionists belonging to the hospital or taken on contractual basis on a fixed day clinic basis will be organized. Counsellors of the ART clinics will be provided additional training in nutrition and paediatric counselling.

9.3 Capacity Building

Faculty of the Medical Colleges where ART centre is located has already been trained. Paediatricians at ART centres with more than 10 children living with HIV, will be trained on a priority basis on the training modules developed by IAP. Module for training of counsellors on paediatric issues is being developed by NACO.

9.4 Ensuring Quality in the delivery of ART Treatment

Based on various indicators, the existing 54 ART centres were graded. Barring the 14 in Tamil Nadu, the rest were mostly in the B and C grades. Inspections revealed serious physical constraints adversely impacting on the quality of services and patient satisfaction. Based on this data, financial provision for civil works in the ART centre wherever needed is proposed to be provided for building up the required infrastructure capacity to deliver care in an acceptable manner.

Besides, improving the environmental conditions, quality will also be ensured by periodic training till all the providers gain the required level of competencies.

Finally, to ensure strict adherence to the treatment protocols and standards laid down, for every 10 ART centres, or at the state level a Consultant will be appointed to exclusively focus on the functioning of the ART centres, and monitoring the availability of supplies, drugs and consumables etc. These consultants will be directly appointed and supervised by NACO and will facilitate the delivery of the goals and objectives laid down for care, support and ART treatment services to PLHAs in a manner that is both supportive and proactive.

9.4.1 Monitoring of ART Care

A critical element of monitoring the ART treatment programme will be the computerized MIS. In the 4 High Prevalent States of TN, AP, Maharashtra and Karnataka, all patient records will be computerized and patients will be provided SMART cards. Based on the outcome of this initiative, action to upscale it further will be undertaken. In the management of HIV in children where absolute CD4 counts as well as CD4% is important, the information will be made available through public private partnership.

9.4.2 Key Activities (ART)

- Establish 250 ART clinics at district level based on need and capacity;
- Make available DNA PCR for infant diagnosis including newer technologies including dry blood spots (DBS) for all children through selected 6 national reference centres;
- Provide ART training to concerned personnel at ART centre, CHC/PHC, CCC and Link outreach workers;
- Provide SOP and manuals to all ART centres and build capacity for diagnostic testing facilities as prescribed in the manual;
- Ensure procurement and supply of ART drugs through effective supply chain management;
- Make available paediatric ART formulations by end of year one;
- Develop effective assessment and accreditation criteria for labs both in public and private sectors;
- Establish linkages of ICTC, PPTCT and DOTS centres and TIs with ART centres;
- Identify counselling centres and build capacity for counseling, specifically targeting children;
- Where CD4 count and CD4% count machines are not available, develop effective transport logistics by end of the first year to ensure capacity utilization;
- Integrate diagnostic services at the district level;
- Extend EQAS programme for CD4 and HIV testing at all government and private facilities;
- Identify and support NGOs / PLHA networks to provide community outreach, home based care and psycho social support; and
- Appoint 25 Consultants and establish a sound supervisory system and computerized monitoring.

9.5 ARV Drug Resistance, Surveillance & Monitoring

For providing life long ART, a long term view needs to be taken regarding reduction of drug resistance in the community. Rapid scaling up of services without ensuring adherence and monitoring of drug resistance is likely to make first line ART ineffective and compromise the lives of many future PLHA. Even though development of drug resistance is inevitable, there is need to slow down the process while taking into account the needs of a large number of PLHA who require drugs for survival. Global evidence suggests that resistance to first line ART is about 4-8 per cent per year. This means that nearly 25 per cent of those who are on first line ART will be resistant to these drugs by the end of fourth year. It is important that a strategy for alternate drug regimens be considered at the time when ART is being initiated and expanded to cover large number of subjects. Following activities are planned to delay the onset of drug resistance and management of PLHA acquiring during resistance:

(a) Build capacity into current monitoring systems for early warning indicators at the level of ART providers;

(b) Build capacity of referral institutions to manage complicated cases, especially management of PLHA with drug resistance; and

(c) Reinforce adherence through the continuum of care.

The expected outcome is that development of first line ART drug resistance will not be more than 4-6 per cent per year.

9.5.1 Key Activities

- Establish 10 research centres for resistance testing by end of year one;
- Negotiate with government agencies and industry regarding generic second line drugs which are affordable and finalize a policy on second line drugs for the treatment of AIDS;
- Arrange for packing and forwarding of blood samples for resistance monitoring; and
- Identify of referral centres and arrange orientation of doctors.

9.5.2 Drug Resistance Monitoring Network

National AIDS Research Institute (NARI) would be the nodal institute and reference laboratory with Tuberculosis Research Centre (TRC), Chennai and CMC, Vellore as additional reference laboratories. There will be 10 sentinel sites for collection of specimen, namely, i. JJ Hospital, Mumbai; ii. NARI, Pune; iii. NIMHANS, Bangalore; iv. AIIMS, Delhi; v. NICD, Delhi; vi. NICED, Kolkata; vii. CMC, Vellore; viii. MGR University/MMC, Chennai; ix. IIH/KEM, Mumbai; and x. Government Hospital, Tambaram (GHTM), Chennai. Institute of Research in Medical Science (IRMS), Delhi will help in designing plans for data analysis and data management.

Three years of surveillance would cost approximately Rs. 2 crore including upgradation of infrastructure in selected laboratories.

9.5.3 Key Indicators

- Initiation of at least ten regional units for resistance monitoring by the end of 2007; and
- Development of base line data on drug resistance by 2008.

9.6 Innovative Financing of ART Drugs

The natural history of HIV allows a window period of healthy life before immuno-suppression is manifested in the form of AIDS. It is expected that expansion of ICTC services will allow early diagnosis in a larger proportion of subjects with HIV allowing 4-5 years of time for savings schemes and alternate financing arrangements to be considered for eventual ART drugs, including costlier second line therapy. The programme will facilitate linking up with public sector banks and/or community financing initiatives to set up recurring, savings and other self financing schemes. NGOs and CBOs will be encouraged to administer the programme. Equity filters will be developed based on earning capacity and other socio-cultural factors.

9.6.1 Key Activities

- Facilitate linking up with public sector banks or community financing initiatives to set up recurrent, saving, or other self financing schemes to be administered with the help of NGOs/CBOs;
- Develop equity filters based on earning capacity and other socio-cultural factors; and
- Develop and implement demand side financing mechanisms such as a voucher system for which guidelines will be formulated.

The treatment component will require substantial investment as given in **Table 9.5**.

Table 9.5: Estimated Financial Requirements

Establishment of ART Centres	
Civil Works for ART Centres	Rs. 46.2 crore
10 Centres for Excellence	Rs. 4 crore
Paediatric Drugs	
10 Drug Resistance Monitoring Centres	Rs.10.5 crore
5 ART Consultants	Rs. 0.75 crore
Nutrition Support	Rs. 52.5 crore
Smart Card (Patient Monitoring)	Rs. 35 crore

Chapter - 10

Programme Strategies - Assuring Quality of Care

Institutionalized quality assurance is a weak area in India's health system. In the context of HIV/AIDS, low quality in diagnostics can lead to false positive and false negative results, with its implications on stigmatization and denial of care and poor quality in service delivery particularly ART. This is likely to have serious implications on drug resistance. Mindful of the importance of the criticality of this aspect, focus under NACP-III will be on exploring several ways in which basic minimum standards and quality of care are assured in the public and the private health care delivery system. The challenge in doing so is the absence of any regulation controlling provider behaviour. Taking this as a constraint and as experience is gained; attempts will be made to use instruments that would incentivize private providers to follow good practices.

There are clearly two very important elements that are integral to quality assurance:

(i) Continuous training and upgrading of the skills and knowledge of provider teams; and

(ii) Strict supervision to ensure adherence to standards laid down.

In view of the importance of these two aspects, these will be dealt with separately. Other issues related to quality assurances that will be given attention under NACP-III are listed below:

10.1 Developing Standard Operating Protocols

Technical committees set up by NACO for developing SOPs for HIV services in collaboration with technical partners (WHO, CDC, ICMR), will continue into the NACP-III phase also. The SOPs will be made available to all centres of service delivery so as to ensure a basic uniformity in standard of care being provided. So far, NACO has developed SOPs on management of ART, paediatric care, OIs, laboratory waste management, laboratory procedures, quality standards for HIV testing, CD4 testing and PPTCT.

10.2 Internal Quality Control Procedures

As part of the standard operating procedure, in laboratory set-ups, internal QCs will be maintained and monitored by the supervisory staff as listed in the manual of operations. All laboratories participating in the National Programme will ensure that Internal Quality Control (IQC) is practiced on a day-to-day basis and proper records of IQC procedures are maintained for review by the supervisory staff.

10.3 External Quality Assessment of Laboratory Services

External Quality Assessment System (EQAS) is an essential complement to core HIV laboratory services provided at district level. The objective is to achieve compatability among different laboratories and the methods employed by them for quality assurance. The principle is that test material will be sent from a national or regional EQAS laboratory to a large number of participating units delivering laboratory services.

EQAS system will evaluate two types of HIV related services:

(i) CD4 Testing Laboratories; and

(ii) HIV Testing Laboratories in ICTC, PPTCT and Blood Banks.

10.3.1 EQAS for CD4 Testing Laboratories

The following diagram (**Figure 10.1**) depicts the hierarchical structure of the apex, regional and participating laboratories in EQAS for CD4 Testing Laboratories. Two to three rounds of EQA have been conducted for CD4 labs. Since, the EQA panel was imported, the capacity will be developed by the apex and the national reference labs as per the organogram to prepare panels in the lab for conducting EQA as is being done for HIV testing.

10.3.2 HIV Testing Laboratories in ICTC, PPTCT and Blood Banks

An EQA programme is operational at NACO since 2001. This EQA programme is implemented through a network of laboratories as shown in **Figure 10.2**. The programme will ensure that each HIV testing facility in the public and private sector produces accurate results. All public sector

EQAS Structure for CD4 Testing Labs

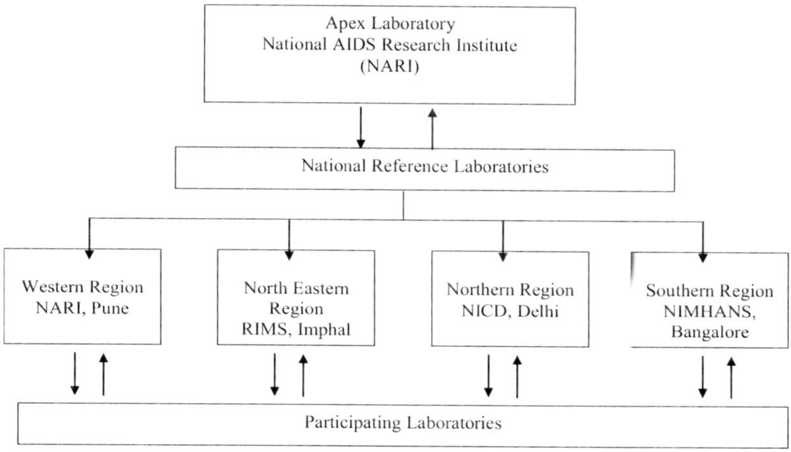

Figure 10.1: EQAS Structure for CD4 Testing Labs

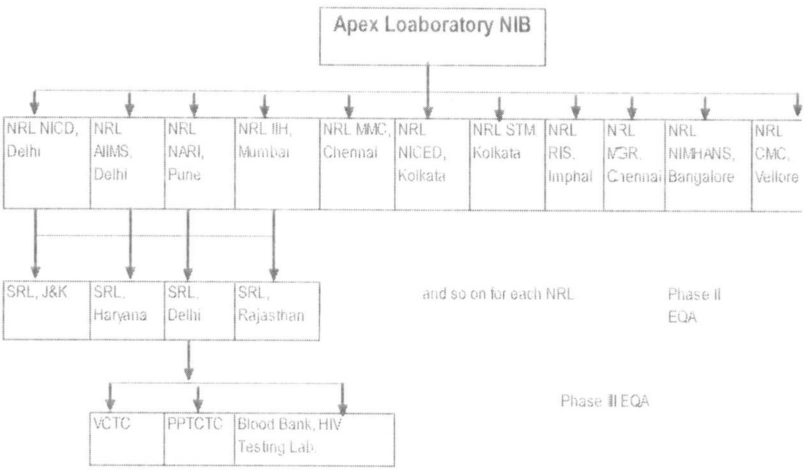

Figure 10.2: Network of HIV Testing Facilities for EQAP

labs will be requested to participate in EQAP being conducted through the national and state reference labs. All private sector laboratories providing HIV testing will be encouraged to participate. However, EQAP participation will be mandatory for private laboratories participating in the national programme prior to reimbursement.

10.4 Certification Based on Standards

Based on the new standards of care developed by WHO/NACO, method of certification and / or accreditation process will be initiated by the programme on a voluntary basis. The objective of certification process will be to lay down minimum standards of care and ensuring their compliance through a combination of strategies – advocacy, training, recognition and rewards, financial incentives, and regulation if found necessary. Under NACP-III, a system of enforcement of these standards will be formulated. A group of technical experts will be constituted in each state to evaluate service delivery and grade the facilities for issue of certificates. The process of certification will be initiated for the following important HIV services:

i. HIV testing, counselling and referral;
ii. Preventing parent to-child transmission of HIV infection;
iii. Prophylaxis and management of opportunistic infections including TB; and
iv. Provision of ART including adherence.

10.5 Licensing

Currently blood bank services require to be licensed. Expanding such a legal requirement to other laboratory services will be explored.

10.6 Accreditation

The long term objective of the programme is to get HIV services, being provided in the country, accredited by an independent agency. Currently, Diagnostic Kits (NIB) and ART drugs (WHO) manufactured and supplied, are under accreditation. NABL has also initiated a system of accreditation of laboratories. NACO will support and link with the current system to accredit all participating centres for ART, ICT and PPTCT services.

A sum of Rs. 10 crore is proposed as an adhoc amount to facilitate the process of quality assurance.

Chapter - 11

Programme Strategies – Public-Private Partnership

Private sector plays a dominant and increasing role in Indian economy. This is evident in the delivery of medical and health care services in India. It is estimated that more than 80 per cent of the people use the private sector for outpatient care and more than 50 per cent for in-patient care. NACP-III will leverage the strengths of private sector to make it an active partner in the programme. It will be encouraged to offer prevention and treatment services as part of employee welfare programmes, provide linkages to government services including capacity building, support and extend the services to the immediate community through outreach services and facilitate investment in HIV prevention and treatment as part of corporate social responsibility.

11.1 Public-Private Partnerships

NACO will set up a National Steering Committee on public-private partnership consisting of Industry associations such as CII, ASSOCHAM, NASCOM, FICCI, ILO, USAID and other relevant government departments to develop a joint operational plan and identify mechanisms for strengthening linkages between the private and government sector. All constituents will be consulted to finalise guidelines to be issued to SACS and state units of industry associations. States will also constitute a similar consultative group on public private partnerships. .

State consultative groups will map out potential thematic and geographical areas for private sector participation. These could include activities to support vulnerable and infected population, mobile VCTCs, behaviour change communication through outreach, or such innovative activities as provision of smart cards or vocational classes for children of sex workers. SACS, with the support of NACO, ILO and USAID will provide technical support to private sector agencies interested in participating in such activities. This will be funded from the technical support budget for hiring of consultants. Since the activities will be financed by private agencies from their own resources, no separate budget is earmarked for public-private partnerships.

11.2 Public–Private Partnerships in Medical Services

The strategy to provide medical services envisages the involvement of private health care providers through public-private partnerships in preventive and treatment services with appropriate safeguards to ensure quality. Contracts will list out the conditions for such collaboration, e.g. compliance with protocols related to treatment and patient management, referrals, maintenance of patient records and reporting, matters related to fees and reimbursements etc.

The services in which public-private partnerships will be forged include the following:

- **STD Treatment**: It is estimated that more than 3/4th of the STI cases go to the private sector. Therefore, cooption of the private providers in the treatment and ensuring universal access to STI services will be an important policy initiative under NACP-III. The proposed mapping exercises will also include identification of providers most frequented for STD care; the quality of the treatment being provided and their competencies evaluated for ensuring standardized quality through training. An estimated 15 million STD episodes will be treated in the private sector. Government will seek to collaborate with the private sector providers for treating an additional 7 million cases to cover persons from high risk groups and those below poverty level.
- **Gynacological Services:** Due to stigma, several HIV positive women face great difficulty in accessing services for abortion, sterilization or delivery. This is true of both the public and private sector. Besides, due to multiple factors women prefer to go to the private sector, including quacks, for these services. Given the need to ensure adherence to infection control standards and proper follow-up, private institutions, particularly where the public sector services are not forthcoming, will be identified and contracted to provide the required package of services.
- **ICTC – Fixed and Mobile:** Private sector facilities will be identified for expanding access to ICTC facilities as a routine

service. Since distance is a great barrier to access, it is proposed to identify and provide such areas with mobile services, for making a package of services available on pre-determined dates. Mobile services are envisaged to provide IEC and education about condoms, testing and counselling, treatment for minor ailments and preventive care such as ANC services etc. Such an intervention will not only expand access but will also help in reducing stigma. Schemes will be formulated under which the private sector would provide the vehicle, manpower and management, while the government would provide drugs and consumables. Almost 1000 ICTCs would be needed for this purpose.

- **ART Centres**: NACP-III estimates that, there would be atleast 75,000 to 100,000 PLHAs who will seek private care. This could either be on account of choice or as employees of the private sector organizations where they are entitled to medical benefits. Based on these assumptions, an additional 126 ART centres across the country may be required to be set up. These centres will mainly focus on providing access to treatment to an estimated 7 million workforce directly and a threefold number as contract labour employed by the private industry under the workplace intervention policy. Each centre is expected to cost about Rs. 1.70 lakh in fixed expenditure per month, while the variable cost per patient would be Rs. 522 per month. NACO will provide training and, based on feasibility, consider the supply of drugs at government rates which are far cheaper. Besides, where Government infrastructure is not functioning well, private hospitals will be contracted for providing the services for the surrounding populations.
- **Outsourcing Laboratory Services**: There are an estimated 250 CD4/8 count machines both in the private and public sector in India today. These machines are adequate to cover the testing load of existing ART patients. NACP-III envisages contracting out private providers to provide this service through a system where the private service provider will pick up the blood sample, transport to the testing site and provide the result within the specified time. Preliminary cost estimates indicate this to be cheaper than purchasing new machines.
- **Other Services:** NACP-III envisages setting up of 350 Community Care Centres to be managed by NGOs and faith based organizations through a contracting out process. Likewise,

there are a large number of blood banks working in the for-profit and not-for-profit sectors in the country. Appropriate linkages through public-private partnerships will be developed to achieve the goal of ensuring that safe blood is available within one hour from any location in the country.

- **Training:** Public-private partnership will be encouraged in planning and organizing training of different types for different categories. Private sector institutions will be involved in capacity building in technical, managerial, communication and other areas as identified in an earlier section. A Core Group at NACO will work out the modalities and approaches to forge partnership with the private sector training institutions and organizations. In addition, an Interactive Voice Response System (IVRS) which has the capability of automating a number of messages and helping a lot in IEC activities will also be developed in partnership with private service providers.

Not all the above services will be paid for by the government. The objective of public-private partnerships as listed above is to ensure that the private sector is co-opted as a responsible partner in the fight against HIV/AIDS by: i. providing a range of health care services as per national protocols that lay down minimum standards, in a fair and non-exploitative manner; and ii. directly enter into contracts for expanding access to services. For further facilitating this, appropriate demand side financing mechanisms such as the voucher system would be developed. The capacity of SACS to develop and monitor these contracts will be strengthened. NGOs, CBOs, and oversight committees will be constituted at the district level for monitoring provider behaviour as well as ensuring equity of access.

No separate budgetary allocations under the head PPP is shown as, for most of the collaborative arrangements proposed, the budgets have been indicated under each specific intervention.

11.3 Key Activities

- Identify preferred private sector providers and enhance their capacity to deliver quality services;
- Develop training manuals and standard operating protocols and make these available to all private sector service providers to standardize quality;
- Establish a system of referral between private and public sector providers;

- Ensure quality of service delivery through external quality assurance systems and/or certification process of the services provided by various partners based on minimum standards of care;
- Develop and implement demand side financing mechanisms to target people affected by HIV/AIDS, by introducing financing instruments such as voucher system; and
- Establish Oversight Committees/ Ombudsman at the district level for developing awareness about these mechanisms and developing capacity of the people to demand services in an equitable and fair manner.

Chapter - 12

Programme Strategies - Human Resource Development

National Commission on Macroeconomics and Health has clearly laid down that more than the availability of financial resources, a major barrier that will constrain India's ability to achieve the MDGs is the inadequate supply of the required skills and competencies. This is relevant to the efforts to contain the HIV epidemic as well.

NACO recognizes the importance of the need of skilled and competent human resources at all levels of programme implementation, i.e. national, state, district and community, public and private health systems, non-governmental organizations and the civil society. It recognizes that the availability of the critical mass of well trained human resources is the backbone to the elaborate organizational structures, institutional arrangements and strategies proposed under NACP-III.

In the last two phases of NACP, the focus was mainly on the technical aspects of prevention and control and a fair amount of technical knowledge and skills was imparted for diagnosis and clinical management. However, building capacity in leadership and strategic management, programme management, particularly in the areas of logistic and supply, finance, information management, collaboration and partnership development, behaviour change, community participation and NGO management remained a low priority. The challenges of capacity building have now been further compounded with the proposed expansion of the organizational structure to the district level.

The aim of NACP-III is to build capacity of the programme managers at the national, state and district levels in leadership and strategic management; technical and communication skills of the health professionals and health care providers at all levels of care and health care organizations,

CBOs and NGOs; and technical, communications and counselling skills of the grass-roots level workers and functionaries of various government departments.

NACO recognises that building capacities will need more than training. Resource persons will continue to provide on and off site technical assistance and mentoring. In order to take advantage of differentials in capacities within the country, institutions that need support, including SACS, will be attached to those with proven capacity. Impact assessment of training will be conducted annually and training methodologies suitably updated.

12.1 Training Policy and Strategies

NACO will develop a training policy which will identify priorities and training needs, types of training process and mechanism, training institutions and cadre, quality assurance, and monitoring and evaluation of effectiveness of training. The existing status of training in the health sector is well known. Currently, there is no training policy and the training infrastructure in the states is grossly inadequate. The training system is not functioning well as it receives a low priority. NACP-III will provide an opportunity to the states to develop a proper overall training system and infrastructure capacity.

NACO realizes the need to reposition training with emphasis on skill development for better performance, behaviour change for health outcomes as well performance of the organization. NACO considers the need for changing current training paradigm from knowledge and competence building to organizational transformation. This will imply balancing the needs of skill development with those related to changing attitudes and mindsets and inculcating a measure of commitment to the organization and profession.

The training policy will identify:

- Training priorities and needs in HIV/AIDS prevention and management;
- Areas of training – technical, managerial, communication, advocacy, counselling;
- Types of training – orientation, induction, on-going in-service training and experiential training;
- Target groups and levels;
- Mechanism of integration of various training activities;
- Training institutions and strengthening management of training;

- Trainers;
- System for quality assurance in training;
- Mechanism for monitoring and evaluation of training; and
- Coordination and support to health system.

12.2 Strengthening Training Systems and Infrastructure

NACP-III will emphasize on developing and strengthening the training systems and infrastructure in NACO as well as in the states. A Training Coordination Unit will be established at NACO. A senior manager will be responsible for HRD and training activities that will include: planning, monitoring, supervision and coordination. He/she will be responsible for curriculum and resource material development, standardization of the training process, coordination of collaborating training institutions and quality assurance in training. In order to develop effective and functional training system, states will be encouraged and supported to develop the processes and operational mechanisms for training in various components of competency and skill needs.

Some of the guiding principles will include:

- Decentralization of planning, monitoring, evaluation of training and decision-making at the state and district level. The states would prepare an annual training plan and schedules;
- Autonomy to all training institutions for implementation of training – planning and undertaking training programmes. However, initial strengthening of the institutions and capacity building of the faculty will be ensured;
- Accountability in terms of training effectiveness and efficient utilization of resources;
- Synergy with the state and district health system with the participation and coordination of the line departments;
- Linking the training function with HRD, especially the career system; and
- Establishing a system of concurrent evaluation to drive a process towards achieving excellence at the individual and organizational level.

12.3 Types of Training

Following types of training will be organized during this phase in a planned manner:

12.3.1 Induction Training

A short duration induction training will be organized for the project staff at the national, state and district levels. The induction training will include orientation to goals and objectives, project concepts and strategy, implementation plan, monitoring, quality assurance and participation of key stake holders. Concepts related to HIV/AIDS (magnitude, epidemiology, general preventive approaches etc.) will also be covered during the training. Similar induction training will be conducted for the CHC and PHC staff, stakeholders, functionaries of other departments (PRI, Education, WCD), ASHA, CBOs, and NGOs etc.

12.3.2 In-service Training

In-service training will be conducted for Prophylaxis treatment, treatment for STDs, ART management, infection control, blood safety, counselling, targeted interventions, surveillance, monitoring, programme management, BCC, advocacy etc. Reorientation/ refresher training will be conducted for those who had received training earlier but need further orientation.

12.3.3 Experiential Training

Programme managers at the national, state and district level will be provided opportunities to learn from successful projects aimed at HIV prevention and management within the country and abroad. Exposure visits, participation in workshops and conferences etc. will be supported under the programme. Study tours will be arranged for project teams and other stakeholders.

12.4 Areas of Training, Competency and Target Groups

Following areas of training have been identified in NACP-III

12.4.1 Managerial Skills

Programme Officers in NACO, SACS, DAPCUs and TSU will be the recipients of capacity building activities in this area are:

- Leadership and Strategic Management;
- Programme Management;
- Communication Planning and Management (Planning and Management of BCC);
- NGO Management;

- Planning and Management of Targeted Interventions;
- Monitoring and Evaluation and Impact Assessment;
- Strategic Management Information System (Including CIMS);
- Procurement, Logistics and Supply and Equipment Management;
- Finance Management and Accounting; and
- Community Mobilization, Convergence and Partnership.

12.4.2 Technical Skills

Service providers will be the main beneficiaries of these skills.

- AR Treatment and Management;
- Infection Control and Medical Waste Management;
- Blood Safety;
- Opportunistic Infections, PPTC;
- Quality Assurance in Hospitals and Laboratories (Technical Standards);
- STI RTI Management;
- Counselling Skills Development;
- Outreach skills for BCC;
- HIV/STI Surveillance;
- Behaviour Surveillance;
- Operations Research;
- Care and support for PLHA;
- Social Marketing and Condom Programme; and
- Gender and equity, stigma, discrimination, human rights and legal aspects, and workplace environment.

The project has developed a skill matrix and target groups for capacity development as presented in **Annex 8**.

12.5 Development of Training Curricula and Materials

Training curricula and training material will be developed and standardized for various training programmes referred above. To develop the training curricula, Technical Resource Groups will be constituted to review the performance and quality, curricula and resource materials already developed in the previous phase of NACP, identify gaps if any and initiate steps to have them developed, translated and disseminated. Special care will be taken to ensure that there is no duplication in this effort or replication of available materials, if found adequate.

12.6 Training Plan

A comprehensive five-year training plan has been prepared to provide various types of training to different types of personnel working in the health sector as well as outside the health sector. For making the training implementation appropriate and effective, special focus will be given to: identification of trainees, training load in each category, identification of trainers, duration of training, training sites, number of batches to be organized, and time frame on an annual basis. The training plan will be operational as soon as NACP-III is launched (see **Table 12.1**).

12.7 Training Institutions

Of the vast network of training institutions available in the country, nearly 60 institutions have been identified for being strengthened as training resource centres. Management education and training institutions in the private and public sector, will be involved in development of skills and capabilities. These Training Resource centres will be involved in reviewing the training needs, existing training curricula and resource materials, developing and designing training curriculum and resource material, organizing ToTs and standardizing pedagogy and training methods. After TOT, a representative of the Training Resource Centre will be available to mentor the second tier training institutions to ensure quality. Where the Training Resource Centres conduct the training directly, faculty will visit states to provide on-site mentoring. Under NACP-III, funds will be provided to the collaborating institutions to recruit additional faculty and strengthen training capacity on the condition that they commit themselves to NACO for the whole project period.

12.8 Training of Trainers

In order to standardize the training content and pedagogy, and building capacity of the identified training institutions, training of trainers (ToT) will be conducted. Effective trainers would be developed for imparting clinical/technical, managerial and other trainings to various categories of staff, and other categories of the target groups. The trainers will be carefully selected and positioned in the training institutions. A Core Group of trainers at the national, state and district levels will be created to provide continuous support to the training activities and monitor performance and quality.

12.9 Monitoring and Evaluation of Training

The monitoring of training will be inbuilt into the project activities and will be done right from the start of training activities. A benchmark for indicators for measuring performance of the staff will be developed to facilitate monitoring. The output of the training activities will be monitored continuously. Impact indicators such as improved quality of clinical care, reduction in mortality, reduction in new infections, reduced stigma and discrimination, enhanced utilization of services are some of the pointers which could be used for assessing the effectiveness of training. This will be carried out through periodic evaluation of the quality and impact of training programmes by external institutions/agencies.

A mid-term evaluation of training programmes will be undertaken in the middle of the third year of the project by independent agencies in order to assess the implementation and effectiveness of the training programmes conducted for various functionaries on various subjects. Major objectives of the mid-term evaluation of training are:

- Review the training institutions with regard to training capacity and loads, clinical case load (in case of clinical training) and quality of training offered;
- Assess the quality of training material and methodologies followed;
- Understand the perception of trainees/trainers on the training programme conducted;
- Assess the performance of trainees in their work situation;
- Suggest corrective actions for improving the organization and overall quality of training for future programmes; and
- Assess the contribution of capacity building programmes to the efficiency and quality of programme delivery and organisational efficiency.

The end-term evaluation of training component will be undertaken in the fifth year of the project to assess the overall impact and effectiveness of the training on the performance of NACP-III on selected output and impact indicators.

Table 12.1: Implementation Planning – Important Milestones

Activities	*Yr 1*	*Yr 2*	*Yr 3*	*Yr 4*	*Yr 5*
NACO Capacity Building Unit					
1.1 Establish Training Coordination Unit at NACO	***				
1.2 Constitute Working Groups for curriculum development for different training areas	***				
1.3 Establish systems for commissioning, contracting, and performance monitoring of Training Institutes	****				
Capacity Building Plan					

(Contd...)

2.1 Identify training institutions for various training programmes	**				
2.2 Finalize comprehensive Training Plan	***				
2.3 Develop guidelines for preparing training curricula for various categories	****				
2.4 Identify consultants for developing training curricula for various training programmes	****				
2.5 Finalise curricula and develop resource materials (modules)	****				
2.6 Training of Trainers	****				
2.7 Clinical/Technical Training	****	****	****		
2.8 Managerial Training	****	****	****		
2.9 Other trainings	**	****	****		

12.10 Building Capacities of Public/Private Agencies, NGOs, CBOs and PLHA

All persons involved in programme delivery, management and M&E including the implementing and collaborating partners and health workers in the private sector will need to be inducted into the programme and appropriately trained and re-trained. NACP-II had witnessed a rapid turnover of the staff which would necessitate a comprehensive and timely orientation package for the new entrants. NACP-III will adopt the following approaches for capacity development of the key personnel and programmers:

- Training, re-training, orientation, refresher courses and workshops;
- On-site technical support and experiential learning; and
- Mentoring, exchange visits and exposure to best practices.

12.11 Key Processes

Naco Capacity Building Unit

A senior manager at NACO and SACS will remain incharge of HRD to ensure that appropriate trainings are organized for various types of personnel in time, its impact is evaluated and corrective measures taken. It must be ensured that everybody in the organization undergoes at least one training and one refresher course during a three year tenure.

Capacity Building Plan

- Identify and develop a pool of institutions including centres of excellence, academia, health training institutions, national/regional training organizations and reputed civil society organizations including selected PLHA/GIPA networks for long term collaboration on human resource development including training.

- Outsource an expert agency as soon as NACP-III is launched to complete the initial processes like review and update of material and modules, curriculum development, designing a training guide etc.
- Training coordination units in NACO and SACS will work out the number of persons to be trained, their experience, their professional/ occupational needs, their potential (in decision making, programme development and programme management) and the role they will play after the training. They will have regular interactions with the training institutions to ensure that the quality and relevance of the training is maintained.
- It will be the responsibility of NACO to facilitate training programmes for its senior programme managers as well as those of SACS, whereas it will be the responsibility of SACS to ensure training for its own personnel and district level programme staff as well as NGOs/CBOs working in the field of HIV/AIDS.
- A training plan will be prepared as soon as NACP-III is launched. Broadly the key areas and action steps of the training plan will be:
    - Identification of the trainees' universe and their needs through TNA;
    - Review of existing training manuals, modules, and development of learning materials to meet emerging training needs;
    - Estimating the training load;
    - Identifying centres of excellence/institutions with suitable training facilities;
    - Strengthening infrastructure and faculty at such facilities;
    - Arranging for infrastructure and faculty outsourcing;
    - Networking with available training and capacities in different sectors;
    - Technical assistance and support to institutions already engaged in HIV training activities;
    - Preparation of training calendar, time-line and load;
    - Identification of resource persons, subject specialists and trainers at various levels;
    - Organisation of trainers' training programmes; and
    - Evaluation of impact of the training including concurrent evaluation.

- Special training modules for front line health care and treatment providers, special mobilisers, community based organizations engaged in targeted interventions and prevention services, private health sector personnel, peer leaders, youth volunteers, and outreach workers, will be made available.
- For supervisors, on-site, function-specific and workplace oriented training designs will be developed.
- NACO, in-collaboration with its development partners, will work out training package for Doctors and para-medics in the private health sector dealing with HIV/STI related treatment. Doctors dealing with ART will be specially trained.
- A joint task team in NACO and SACS will ensure that the training components are not repeated for the same trainee.

A detailed capacity development plan is attached at **Annex 8.**

12.12 Technical Assistance for NACP-III

Given the complexity and diversity of the skills involved, it is unlikely that entire capacity needed for programme implementation will be available or built in implementing agencies at the beginning of the programme. These would have to be sourced from external units as technical support.

Most of the technical support to programme implementation will be provided by the technical institutions. NACO will also support a state institution/consortium which will take over the technical support functions from year 3 of the programme. Technical support will be purchased by NACO and SACS from the technical support providers based on TORs developed from an analysis of technical support needs of the state. Generating demand for and facilitating provision of technical support will be done by NACO and SACS. An operational plan for technical support is at **Annex 9**.

12.13 Accountability of Implementing Partners

Progress towards delivering components of NACP-III will be monitored internally through MIS, CPFMS and internal control mechanisms. These would be analysed and made available to decision makers at all levels. Quarterly reports are to be provided to Parliamentary and state legislators' forum on AIDS, members of the National Council on AIDS, AIDS Control Board and Executive Committee and Governing Body of SACS. Civil society partners' forum at district, state and national level will also receive the performance report. In addition, every SACS will set up a web page where all information regarding procurement, financial and programme performance will be available.

An estimated 3,80,000 persons are going to be trained, sensitized, oriented over the five year period in accordance with their needs for knowledge and skills. An estimated amount of Rs. 220 crore will be spent on this activity.

Chapter - 13

Programme Strategies - Enabling Environment

Effective prevention, care and support for HIV/AIDS is possible in an environment in which human rights are respected and where those infected with or affected by HIV live a life of dignity, without stigma and discrimination. This would necessitate a review and reform of structural constraints, legal procedures and policies that impede interventions aimed at marginalised populations. Affirmative action is needed to reduce stigma and discrimination associated with the infected and affected persons and their access to prevention and quality treatment, care, insurance and legal services. The existing national guidelines for GIPA need to be reviewed with a view to engage marginalised and affected groups too. NACP-III will work in partnership with PLHA networks and other stakeholders towards creating an enabling environment by addressing issues of stigma, discrimination, legal and ethical concerns.

13.1 Greater Involvement of People Living with HIV/AIDS (GIPA)

Implementation of NACP-II has established that People Living with HIV/AIDS (PLHA) are a critical resource for appropriate and effective response to the epidemic. A significant development during NACP-II has been a shift in the role of PLHA from being beneficiaries of services to becoming important partners of NACO, SACS, civil society organizations and service providers. They will be represented on the executive committees of SACS and the National AIDS Control Board. NACO has established clear guidelines for mobilization and networking among PLHA and utilizing them as advocates for prevention as well as care, support and treatment programmes including setting up of Drop-in centres.

PLHA have now organized themselves into networks/formal and informal organizations/ groups at the national and state level and in some cases district and sub-district levels. Till December, 2005, two national level networks, 25 state networks and 65 district networks were funded under the national programme. A number of initiatives taken at the national and state levels have led to substantial capacity building amongst PLHA including positive women. Some organised groups of PLHA along with NGOs/CBOs and development organisations are now engaged in treatment education, positive living counselling, psychosocial support and positive prevention programmes. As more and more networks are established it will be necessary to accredit them and have explicit criteria for recognising networks for partnerships with government. NACO will, in partnership with PLHA networks, develop criteria for assessing and accrediting networks and modalities for representing them on decision making bodies.

Despite the steps taken to implement GIPA, there are several gaps in the desired response. Effective partnership with PLHA at all levels has not yet been achieved and there is inadequate understanding of GIPA principles and implementation. Further, there are problems in systematic referrals from the VCT, PPTCT and ART to district level PLHA support groups/structures. Necessary institutional mechanisms to support the implementation are still to be evolved. There is absence of clear organizational policies on hiring people living with or affected by HIV/AIDS.

NACP-III will build on the experience already gained by strengthening the organisations of PLHA at national/state/district level and promoting GIPA through sensitizing implementing agencies (government, private sector and civil society) and creating an enabling environment for enhanced involvement of PLHA and affected people.

Key Activities

- Facilitate establishment of PLHA networks in most districts and all states by the year 2010;
- Develop criteria for accrediting positive networks and for formalising their partnership with NACO and SACS;
- Integrate positive prevention into various training programmes;
- Strengthen capacities of PLHA/organized groups for positive prevention and care, support and treatment activities;
- Develop institutional structures within NACO, SACS and at district levels including all agencies, for planning, implementation and monitoring of GIPA;

- Establish mechanisms to facilitate linkages of PLHA, organised groups, networks with ongoing/new interventions for prevention, care, support and treatment at all levels;
- Develop a strategy for addressing the gender dimensions of stigma and discrimination;
- Advocate with and build capacities of implementing agencies (government, private sector and civil society) to facilitate GIPA; and
- Review, adapt and develop advocacy, social mobilisation and communication strategies and tools to promote GIPA and create an enabling environment for PLHA and vulnerable communities.

13.2 Reducing Stigma and Discrimination

Stigma and Discrimination (S&D) faced by people living with HIV/AIDS and marginalised populations such as sex workers, MSM and IDUs is one of the most serious obstacles to an effective response to HIV/AIDS. S&D often emanates from service providers - medical, non-medical, government and private sectors. It is also manifest in a variety of ways at work places and at community and family levels. Several studies have shown a high level of discrimination – nearly 70 per cent – against PLHA and marginalised groups. Nearly 18.3 per cent faced discrimination from their neighbours and 9 per cent from community/educational institutions, etc. Further, PLHA and vulnerable populations themselves are largely unaware of their rights especially in remote and rural areas. There is also evidence that S&D is in many aspects a gender phenomenon.

According to the findings of a Study (commissioned by NACO & UNDP, and conducted by NCAER) to understand the socio-economic impact of HIV/AIDS (2006), 74 per cent of the respondents from PLHA did not disclose their HIV status at the workplace. The same study also indicates that the gender difference is more noticeable in the context of HIV/AIDS. Nearly 5.5 per cent of female PLHA have been asked to leave home in comparison to only 1.9 per cent of the male PLHA. Also, more women are supportive of their HIV-positive husbands (12.4 per cent) than men are of their HIV-positive wives (8.5 per cent). Moreover, more women report problems like being "deprived of using basic amenities" than men and this gender difference is manifest irrespective of the place of residence.

Over the last decade, addressing stigma and discrimination has found a prominent place in the national agenda. A strong catalyst in this process has been the communication and social mobilisation efforts to combat S&D

at various levels. National AIDS Prevention and Control Policy also clearly enunciates that "discrimination against people living with HIV/AIDS denies their rights to access health care, information and other social and economic rights guaranteed by the Constitution to its citizens."

NACP-III proposes to address the issue of stigma and discrimination at all levels through evidence-based research and advocacy, capacity development and partnership building. This would include preventive and redressal strategies.

Key Activities

- Develop and implement guidelines for direct involvement of PLHA in service delivery;
- Undertake advocacy and media promotion for generating broad based awareness about the (proposed) HIV/AIDS Bill;
- Organise periodic training of service providers including counsellors. (training of counsellors to include trauma/grief counselling);
- Create an institutionalised interface between selected PLHA/ representatives of sexual minorities and service providers - both for capacity building as well as monitoring;
- Advocate with members of Parliament and members of legislatures, Panchayat leaders, women's group leaders, youth leaders and faith-based organisations on a rights-based approach to HIV; and
- Implement a communication plan, including sensitization of the media that directly addresses issues of stigma related to sexuality, condom use and unsafe sexual practices. This will include communication products and strategies implemented by NACO and the coverage by print and electronic media.

13.3 Human Rights, Legal and Ethical Issues

Several initiatives were undertaken as part of NACP-II to enforce the rights of people living with HIV/AIDS and people vulnerable to infection. One such initiative, in collaboration with the Lawyers' Collective, has resulted in a draft legislation on HIV/AIDS. A high level inter ministerial task force has also been set up to review existing laws that impede HIV prevention programmes. While some gains have accrued from these efforts, the issue of human rights in the context of HIV is far from resolved. Among the most common rights violations have been the denial of health care, breach of confidentiality and lack of consent/counselling before and after testing. While the National AIDS Prevention and Control policy is rights-based, necessary institutional arrangements to support the implementation are yet to be in place. As a result, speedy redressal of rights and ethical violations has not been possible. Criminal statutes such as Narcotic Drugs and Psychotropic Substances Act, Immoral Trafficking Prevention Act and section 377 of IPC continue to hamper implementation of targeted interventions with IDUs, sex workers and MSM.

NACP-III will strive to ensure that PLHA as well as vulnerable and high risk populations have access to rights and requisite services are made available to them in a non-discriminatory manner based on ethical codes and guidelines. There will also be a legal framework to facilitate speedy redressal of rights violations.

Key Activities

- Establish linkages between NACO and SACS with National and State Human Rights Commissions for speedy redressal of violations;
- Develop Model Code of Ethics through community involvement and constitution of Ethics Committees;
- Translate and disseminate HIV/AIDS legislation and advocate for speedy adoption;
- Sensitize and train law enforcement authorities, judiciary, civil servants, lawyers, service providers, community networks and PRIs;
- Constitute a Task Force to review existing laws and advocate for necessary amendments with different ministries, legislators, judiciary, civil society etc;
- Ensure that ethical standards are adhered to in research (clinical, social, surveillance);
- Strengthen legal networks and provide free legal aid to all affected by HIV; and
- Establish minimum standards for prevention, care, support and treatment services.

An estimated amount of Rs. 47 crore will be spent on activities related to strengthening PLHA networks, reducing stigma as well as discrimination and human rights issues.

Chapter - 14

Programme Strategies – Management of Institutional Systems

The institutions, systems and processes designed to implement the first two phases of the National AIDS Control Programme achieved significant results in most parts of the country. By outsourcing and contracting of services, the required management skills were mobilized at the national and state levels. During NACP-II, systems for surveillance, management and financial monitoring were developed, providing a solid foundation for scaling up the programme under NACP-III.

Notwithstanding the significance of the efforts indicated above, the rapidly evolving nature of the epidemic did entail a large amount of ad-hocism. This was inevitable. NACP-II was essentially designed for a strategy aimed at prevention. But, in the course of its implementation, a range of new services were added. The definition of primary prevention was broadened to include a set of services such as prophylactic treatment to HIV pregnant women. Likewise, ART treatment was introduced in the programme necessitating provision of competencies not available at NACO or SACS. The unplanned growth, compounded by the diversity of expertise required to manage the programme, prevented the emergence of an effective framework of governance based on the principle of integrating prevention with treatment. Since NACP-III proposes to scale up and broaden the programme components to provide for such integration, the reconfiguration of the institutional arrangements is a clear necessity for achieving programme objectives.

14.1 Institutional Frameworks

Under NACP-III it is proposed to take the programme implementation further, down to the district levels by establishing HIV Resource Units within District Health Societies. The organizational structure and the complex web of relationships that will be forged at each of these administrative levels for securing the required level of involvement and participation from all stakeholders may be seen at **Figure 14.1.** Broad functions of the institutional structures at each level of governance are outlined below:

14.1.1 National AIDS Control Organisation (NACO)

NACO provides leadership to the HIV/AIDS Control Programme in India, implementing one National Plan within one monitoring system. NACO was set up as an administrative unit within the Ministry of Health when the first National AIDS Control Programme was launched in 1992. During Phase I of the programme, NACO undertook direct implementation of many of the programmes as capacities were not available in states. With the formation of autonomous State AIDS Control Societies in NACP-II, NACO has decentralised the implementation of a large number of service delivery components, albeit, under the direct superintendence of and with financial assistance from NACO.

During NACP-III, NACO will continue to work on the decentralized model evolved during NACP-II. Under NACP-III, the capacity of NACO will be further strengthened for coordinating with the large number of partners within and outside the government, laying down and enforcing technical protocols and operational guidelines on the interventions to be undertaken, ensuring quality and assisting SACS to build its technical capacity for managing the programme implementation based on evidence. NACO will, however, undertake a more interventionist role in states that fail to deliver till such time their capacity is built.

Governance structure of NACO will consist of:

(i) National Council on AIDS: National Council on AIDS (NCA), under the chairmanship of the Prime Minister, and 31 participating ministries and civil society representatives as members, is the highest body overseeing the National AIDS Control Programme. This body will provide the political will and support to the implementation of the national framework on AIDS Control, particularly in the context of mainstreaming HIV prevention within all organs of government as well as the private sector and civil society. Accordingly, all agencies will be called upon to develop action plans and provide information on the status of implementation at periodic intervals.

(ii) National AIDS Control Board: Programme management of NACO will be overseen by the National AIDS Control Board, chaired by Secretary (Health). The Board shall meet at least once a quarter. It will approve the NACO Annual Plans and review quarterly performance reports. The Board will also have access to reports of the Development Partners' forum and will be empowered to seek clarifications from programmes being implemented by donor partners outside the national budget framework. Minutes of the meeting of the National AIDS Control Board shall be posted on the NACO website within a month of its meeting.

(iii) Technical Advisory Groups: For guiding and assuring technical oversight of the programmes, NACO will constitute Technical Advisory Groups on various thematic areas i.e. public health, clinical services, surveillance, monitoring and evaluation, IEC, Targeted Interventions and Research. These Groups will be expected to meet as per need and also visit states to review the quality of implementation of interventions and provide guidance.

14.2 Programme Management by NACO

NACO, as an integral constituent of the Ministry of Health & Family Welfare, will be responsible for the implementation of the National Policy on HIV/AIDS and directly accountable to the NCA and NACB. Due to the special vulnerabilities of north-eastern states, a sub-office of NACO, embedded in the governance structure of NRHM, will be set up to provide programme implementation support to the north-eastern states.

14.3 Staffing of NACO

In keeping with the functions and responsibilities outlined and for facilitating the growing number of players in the implementation of the HIV/AIDS strategies, the organizational structure of NACO HQ will be suitably reconfigured. The current structure, depicted at **Figure 14.2** clearly shows the wide gaps in the tasks to be performed and the skills available. Managed largely by consultants, with limited commitment to the organizational goals as evidenced with the high turn over rate, NACO has failed to establish sound foundations of oversight and close supervision for several of its important programme interventions resulting in inadequate implementation at the field level. This needs to be addressed on priority. Accordingly, under NACP-III, the organizational structure of NACO is proposed to be strengthened as depicted in **Figure 14.3.**

14.4 National Rural Health Mission

Government of India launched a flagship programme called the National Rural Health Mission with the objective of expanding access to quality care to rural populations and integrating programmes for achieving better efficiency. Under NRHM, many states have set up state and district health societies. Since one of the aims of the NRHM is to move away from narrowly defined projects and ensure integrated management of all disease control programmes, there is need for HIV /AIDS programmes also to be integrated into the public health system. However, given the fact that the core programme activities, namely targeted interventions are largely focussed on "outlawed groups", not normally addressed by the public health system, it is essential that NACO and the State AIDS Control Societies continue to function as separate entities with suitable mechanisms to ensure co-ordination with other public health programmes. However, each state will be provided the option to take a view on this matter. In both scenarios the functional responsibilities and therefore the personnel and programme management needs will be similar.

To ensure effective coordination with NRHM, a NACP-NRHM Coordination Committee (NNCC) will be set up in MoHFW to provide policy direction and functional oversight. The NNCC will be chaired by Secretary (Health) and be charged with the responsibility of ensuring coordination between the two important centrally sponsored programmes, namely RCH and RNTCP. Decisions of the NNCC will be binding at all levels of implementation.

At the state level, a Joint Planning and Monitoring Committee (JPMC) will be similarly constituted to ensure effective implementation and coordination of the centrally sponsored schemes, particularly where SACS is not merged with the State Health Society. Further, in such states, the Programme Director of SACS will be a member of the Executive Committee of the State Health Society, while the CEO of the State Health Society will be a member of the Executive Committee of SACS.

At the district level, the district HIV Unit will be a part of the District Health Society but in all A category districts, appropriate experts to assist the HIV Unit will be provided.

14.5 State AIDS Control Societies (SACS)

At the commencement of the HIV/AIDS Control Programme, State AIDS Cells were constituted as a part of the health departments. During

NACP-II, decentralised autonomous societies were set up, which provided the required level of functional independence to upscale and innovate. Even today, states that have not delegated adequate authority to SACS are the ones that are lagging in programme implementation. Experience gained so far clearly points to the advantage of having empowered and independent units to push through this programme. Therefore, the characteristics of SACS will continue to be maintained even in the event of any State seeking to merge these societies as part of the State Health Societies.

SACS will be the main implementing arm of NACO but will also have a governance structure at the state level for programme support and oversight:

14.5.1 Governing Body

Governing Body is the highest policy making structure of SACS and is headed either by the Minister in charge of health or the Chief Secretary. For the sake of uniformity and administrative convenience, it is suggested that the Governing Body should be headed by the Chief Secretary while the Executive Committee should continue to be headed by the Principal Secretary/Secretary (Health). Governing Body is required to meet at least twice a year. Represented in the Governing Body will be key government departments, representatives of the civil society (elected by the state level civil society forum), representatives of trade and industry, private health sector and representatives from PLHA Networks.

Governing Body of SACS will approve its annual action plan, annual budget, appoint statutory auditors and accept the annual audit report. It will also approve new policy initiatives, if any. For better financial and operational efficiency, the Governing Body will delegate adequate administrative and financial powers to the Executive Committee and the Programme Director. It will also exercise all other statutory powers as ordained under the Societies Registration Act.

14.5.2 Executive Committee

Executive Committee of SACS will exercise powers as delegated to it by the Governing Body. For functional efficiency it should be a small and compact body with limited representation from key departments (finance being mandatory).

14.5.3 Project Director

Project Director (PD) is a pivotal position in SACS. Frequent transfer of PDs has interfered with programme implementation in many states. In order to avoid this, as part of the MOU, states will be requested to set up a selection committee with a representative of NACO as member for selecting a suitable person as PD. All PDs will be mandated to undergo an orientation and induction training within three months of their joining. The tenure of the PD should be a minimum of 3 years.

14.5.4 Functions of SACS

With the setting up of District AIDS Prevention and Control Unit, there will be an increased emphasis on improving coordination functions at state level and in supporting programme implementation at district level. Health related interventions will continue to be delivered through the public health system. This would entail collaboration with NRHM, RCH, RNTCP and other health programmes as required.

Functions of SACS have been categorized into three groups:

- Medical and Public Health Services;
- Communication and Social Sector services; and
- Administration, Planning, Coordination, M&E, Finance and Procurement.

Since the work load in SACS is contingent on the size and population of the state and the burden of disease, states have been divided into three categories:

Category I (Large)	AP, Karnataka, Maharashtra, Tamil Nadu, U.P., M.P., Bihar, Jharkhand, West Bengal, Orissa, Chhattisgarh, Rajasthan, Punjab, Gujarat, Assam, Kerala, J&K, Nagaland, Manipur
Category II (Medium & Small)	Mizoram, Haryana, Delhi, Mumbai, Arunachal Pradesh, Goa, Himachal Pradesh, Uttaranchal, Meghalaya, Sikkim, Chennai, Ahmedabad; and
Category III	All Union Territories

While all states will receive assistance from NACO to provide for the posts indicated in the **Table 14.1**, category I states will be provided with additional support in the form of a Technical Support Unit.

Staff structure for the above mentioned States and UTs are as under:

Table 14.1: Staff Structure at different categories of States and UTs

Staff Structure	*State/UT Categories*		
	I	*II*	*III*
Project Director	1	1	1
Addl. Programme Director	2	1	0
Joint Director	6	6	1
Deputy Director	2	0	0
Asst. Director	15	10	3
GIPA Coordinator	1	0	0
NGO Coordinator	1	1	0
Statistical-cum-data Processing Officer	1	1	0
Manager (supply and logistics)	2	1	0
Accountant	3	2	1
Programme Assistant	18	12	7

(also see Figures 14.4, 14.5 & 14.6)

14.6 State Council on AIDS

Political commitment and support at the highest level is crucial for successful implementation of the HIV/AIDS programme. All States will be requested to constitute a State Council on AIDS (SCA), patterned on the National Council on AIDS, to be headed by the Chief Minister, with the Minister (Health) as the Vice Chairperson. The State Council with representation from various departments of the government and civil society will set policy guidelines, review the State's performance including mainstreaming by key departments.

14.7 Technical Support Unit

Since the emphasis of the strategic framework is on prevention of infection among high risk groups and since the Technical Support Units have been found to be successful in most states, every SACS will have the option to obtain external technical support to facilitate social mobilization in all components of the programme.

TSUs in category 'I' states will have the following additional support:

Team Leader and Social Development Specialist – one;

Manager (Finance and Administration) – one;

NGO Partnership Manager – one;

Training Officer – one;

M&E Officer – Epidemiologist – one;

Regional Officers - 5 (TI-2, Care and Support-1, Service Delivery-1, ART-1); and

Support Staff – five.

In large states, SACS will have the option to set up regional units or organise the support structures as per thematic area. In small states, the posts of NGO partnership manager + training officer and Manager (F&A) + M&E officer will be combined. TSU will not be provided in UTs.

14.8 District AIDS Prevention and Control Unit (DAPCU)

DAPCU will operate within the District Health Society, sharing the administrative and financial structures of NRHM. While the unit will report to and work through the Chief Medical Officer of the District for medical interventions, it will also be responsible for non-health related activities such as Adolescent Education Programme, supportive supervision of TIs, M&E and mainstreaming. These activities will be carried out through the office of District Collector or Zilla Panchayat. The district level staffing structure (category wise) proposed under NACP-III is given in **Table 14.2.**

Table 14.2: District Level Staffing Structure (Category-wise)

Staff	*Categories of Districts*			
	A	*B*	*C*	*D*
District Programme Officer (HIV/AIDS)	1	1	1	1
Assistant-cum-accountant	2	2	1	1
M&E Assistant	1	1	1	
Support Staff	1	1	1	1
Additional Supervisors for NGO and Care & Support Programmes	2	2	-	-

14.9 Support to States with weak Capacities

During the first two phases of NACP, states varied in scale and quality of their programme delivery, partly by political support and partly by technical assistance available in the state. However, the experience of Project Management Unit (PMUs) established with development partners assistance has been positive.

During NACP-III, NACO will ensure that all states perform at the planned level. The MoU between NACO and SACS will be revised to ensure greater accountability on the part of SACS and responsiveness on the part of NACO. It will secure the commitment of state governments for remedial action to prevent frequent changes of senior level functionaries including the PD, assignment of dual charge to the PD and a large number of posts lying vacant in these areas. If the states fail to abide by these commitments, NACO will undertake the responsibility of recruiting the personnel and appointing them in SACS. In the event of further default on any of these commitments, the MoU will have enabling provisions authorising NACO to allocate budgets earmarked for the state to agencies identified by NACO for direct execution.

The role and functions of NACO, SACS and District Units to deliver each component of the programme are listed in **Annex 10.**

14.10 Civil Society Partnership Forums

Civil society organisations have been active partners in the national response to HIV/AIDS. Their partnership in the planning and implementation process will be formalised. The task of facilitating partnership at district and state level will be entrusted to Technical Support Units where they exist or an NGO with recognised work in HIV in states where TSUs do not exist. The facilitating institution will undertake mapping of civil society organisations working in each district. The base unit of civil society partnership will be at the district, to be organised if the number of potential partners exceed ten. Any civil society organisation, including NGOs, CBOs, Red Ribbon Clubs and PLHA networks, private sector organisations and academic institutions working in the area of HIV in the district can become member of the District Forum. The Forum will be informed of the district implementation plans and will be provided data to review progress.

The State Level Forum will consist of representatives of the District Forums, not exceeding two per district, while the National Forum will have representatives from the state level fora. States which do not have district forums can constitute the same directly if the number is below 30. Where any of constituencies (e.g. primary stakeholders such as sex workers, MSM, IDUs and PLHA; secondary stakeholders such as academic institutions) is not represented at the national or state level forum, NACO or SACS will nominate a representative from that constituency. District and state fora will meet quarterly, while the National Forum annually. The civil society fora at different levels will have access to programme reports from the District, State and National AIDS Control units.

14.11 Steering Committee of Development Partners

In line with the principle of "Three Ones", all agencies working in the area of HIV/AIDS will be required to enter into an MoU with NACO with a clause to align their work to the national framework approved by the National Council on AIDS and to provide inputs into the national M&E framework.

As part of the MoU, all agencies – government, private foundations, UN agencies etc. – will be members of the Steering Committee of Partners at the national and state level. The Steering Committee will be chaired by the DG, NACO and by the PD at the state level. Following are the main objectives of this Committee:

1. Ensuring no duplication and a harmonised working relationship.
2. Sharing of information on action plans. NACO will compile these plans into a common template and make it available on the public domain. NACO will also negotiate with partners so as to avoid duplication and to move resources to underserved areas. The final decision on these issues will be taken by NACO.
3. Review of performance. All partners will make available to the forum their performance on the agreed parameters. Consolidated data on performance will be available to the public.
4. Development of and adherence to a common monitoring and evaluation framework. NACP-III has indicated common parameters that all development partners are to report on. Development partners' forum will facilitate systems, structures and skills of all partners to report into the M&E framework and to access results of the analysis of this data.

Development partners who work in the state and satisfy eligibility criteria will be invited to be members of a state forum, convened by SACS. They will carry out functions parallel to the national forum at state level. DPs will have to dovetail their action plans in line with the unified framework prepared for the state as directed by the SACS. Any dispute between SACS and DPs will be referred to NACO for resolution.

14.12 Institutional arrangements for Outsourcing

NACO and SACS will outsource services where there is comparative advantage in outsourcing. The services to be outsourced are:

- Procurement and logistics: One National Procurement Support Agency;
- Condom Programming: Five regional social marketing agencies;
- Strategic Information Management;

- Surveillance: One national agency for technical support to surveillance and another for management of the operation. In addition, one institution will be built up in every state for epidemiological support to SACS;
- Behavioural surveillance: One national agency;
- Research and Knowledge Management: Five institutions or consortia of institutions with skills in bio-medical and social sectors will serve as Research and Knowledge Management Centres;
- External Quality Assurance: One National Reference Laboratory supported by five regional laboratories in year one, going up to 12 in year 3 and thereafter;
- Development and production of communication protypes and materials;
- Migrant support: One national agency to support NACO; and
- Technical support: Technical support will be provided by national and regional institutions and development partners with expertise in the area.

The institutions/agencies to provide these services would be selected on the basis of clear terms of reference through the process laid out in the section on procurement.

A total amount of Rs. 910 crore will be spent on various programme management activities discussed above.

Chapter - 15

Programme Strategies–Monitoring and Evaluation, Surveillance and Research Outcomes

India's response to the evolving HIV epidemic is largely influenced by the available surveillance data, implementation capacities and political commitment at state level. The HIV surveillance system in India has been characterized by a growing network of sentinel and facility based HIV sero-prevalence surveys, used for measuring trends in HIV prevalence and developing state and national prevalence estimates. Behavioural surveillance surveys and research studies have also been conducted in a number of states to track HIV related risk behaviours. The Computerized Management Information System (CMIS), established nation-wide, is another source of strategic information for programme monitoring and evaluation. Similarly, NACP has also successfully established a Computerized Project Financial Management System (CPFMS). Programme implementation, however, lacks a strategic approach and the implementation units have not effectively used programme data for planning.

Of particular concern is that neither programmatic data from CMIS, nor sentinel surveillance data are sensitive enough to detect emerging "hot spots". Analytical capacities at the state level are weak and, with few exceptions, have not utilized the existing data for planning purposes. State ownership and recognition of the importance of M&E are weak and only 50 per cent of the M&E positions were filled by 2005. Andhra Pradesh and Tamil Nadu have developed state specific initiatives and showed leadership in utilizing programme data for effective programme planning and monitoring. Tamil Nadu has also brought on board all the key partners in the state and created a common platform to share the programme data and implementation plans. With further decentralization to the district level, there will be even greater need to enhance these skills in all states.

15.1 One Nationwide Monitoring and Evaluation Framework

Based on the lessons learnt from NACP-II and consultations with SACS and development partners (DPs), NACP-III will establish "one nationwide monitoring and evaluation framework" in the spirit of the "Three Ones". This framework will ensure effective use of information generated by government agencies, NGOs, civil society and development partners. An M&E Working Group involving representatives of various DPs is actively engaged in developing the strategy and implementation approaches. The group has also developed programme indicators, operational plans and initiated the development of an "Operational Manual for Strategic Information Management (SIM)". During the course of pre-appraisal and appraisal of NACP-III, DPs have given inputs on the SIM issues and recommended that they will have one M&E framework and one Joint Review mechanism by signing Partnership Agreements between themselves and the Government of India. (see **Annex 11.1**)

15.2 Computerized Management Information System

CMIS was designed to provide information on specified NACP-II components to NACO and SACS to assist in programme monitoring and planning. CMIS is a 3-tier data flow system with the capability to handle state and district data for monthly and annual reports. Major modifications of CMIS have been carried out twice based on feedback received from SACS/MACS. These modifications have led to a more comprehensive and flexible system, that allows for generation of customized reports with the provision of electronic data collection mechanism from the primary data generation units.

A number of gaps and deficiencies have, however, led to incomplete implementation of CMIS. These include: (a) low reporting by primary data generation units (in 2005, on an average, only 70 per cent units reported); (b) lack of skills to appropriately use information generated through CMIS; (c) poor quality of data due to inadequate training of the primary data collection units; (d) lack of routine feedback from NACO to SACS and from SACS to primary data collection units; and (e) lack of systems to regularly share information with key stakeholders.

NACP-III will revamp CMIS to address the existing gaps and add features to support decentralization to the district level in the first year. Manpower and infrastructure needs for operation of CMIS will be supported through contracts to professional agencies. Regular review of issues related to CMIS will be carried out through bi-annual meetings of programme managers and M&E officers. A programme to enhance the capacity of primary data reporting units and programme managers at national and state level for evidence based planning with support from partners will be developed.

This increased investment of effort in CMIS will improve monitoring of NACP-III at all levels. However, information collected in CMIS should not be considered the only source of data for programme planning and implementation; other systems, such as behavioural and facility surveys, will also need to be strengthened during NACP-III.

15.3 Strategic Information Management Unit (SIMU)

In order to maximize effective use of all available information and implement evidence based planning, NACP-III will establish a Strategic Information Management Unit (SIMU). It will be set up at national and state levels to address strategic planning, monitoring and evaluation, surveillance and research. SIMU will assist NACP-III in tracking the epidemic and the effectiveness of the response and help assess how well NACO, SACS and all partner organizations are fulfilling their commitment to meet agreed objectives.

NACP-III envisages a robust Strategic Information Management System (SIMS) which will focus on programme monitoring evaluation and surveillance, and knowledge gathering. Quality standards for all programmatic areas will be established in consultation with technical officers, and will be the basis for measuring performance, analyzing variances, identifying bottlenecks, alerting the programme managers and facilitating corrective measures.

SIMUs, established in NACO and SACS, will enhance data flow and feedback at all levels. Responsibilities of programme officers in SIMU are depicted in **Figure 15.1**.

15.4 Data Dissemination: An Important Activity of SIMU

At the national level, SIMU will be established with necessary complement of skilled staff to coordinate and provide technical oversight to State SIMU. At the State level, SIMU will provide support to SACS for programme planning, implementation and monitoring and will oversee and provide supportive supervision and capacity building for the district level monitoring and evaluation. At the district level, an M&E system will be established to monitor programme activities within the district and provide information and feedback on programme performance to SACS and

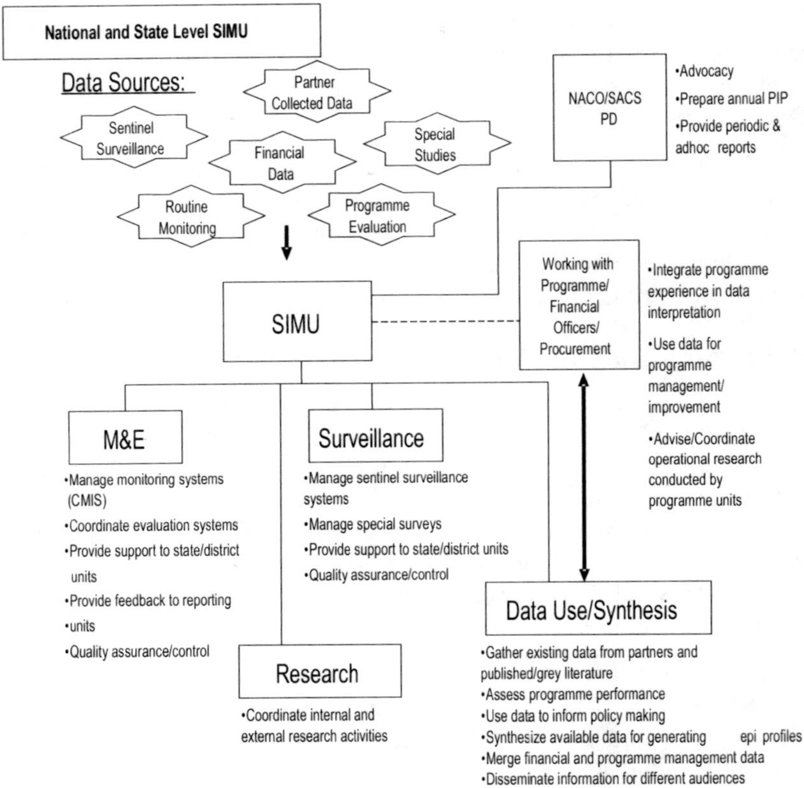

Figure 15.1: Strategic Information Management Units and Data Flows

implementation partners. Induction training of newly recruited SIM and M&E personnel, Project Directors and technical officers at district and State levels will include basic training on monitoring, evaluation and appropriate use of strategic information.

15.5 Improving Evidence Based Strategic Planning, Programme Management Capabilities

All programme officers will be trained on evidence based strategic planning methodologies, information use and programme management. A minimum of one programme officer from each SACS will receive additional training on epidemiology and evidence based planning. A training programme/syllabus for these training programmes will be clearly established before hand to ensure standardization across these training activities. Quarterly review meetings will be initiated to monitor the quality and effectiveness of the key functions. Annual plans will be reviewed against appropriate analysis of existing data to justify programmatic direction and expenditures.

Key institutions for providing technical support to strategic planning, including the development of materials, will be identified. An Operations Manual for SIMS will also be developed within the first year of the project.

15.6 Monitoring Systems

Based on the experience gained in NACP-II, several areas that require to be strengthened in NACP-III have been identified. These include:

- Review and modify indicators to be consistent with national needs and international standards and global comparison (e.g. ART). A draft list of indicators is at **Annex 11.2**;
- Upgrade CMIS software to include indicators from newly developed programmatic areas (i.e. TB/HIV, ART, and PPTCT) and to allow entry of data from all partners and newly developed programmes;
- Combine technical, logistic and financial programme monitoring;
- Create standardized reports for each programme area which can easily be generated by various implementation units; and
- Carry out regular reviews of the programme at district, state and national levels.

A detailed monitoring plan will be developed and implemented with the assistance from technical support groups and development partners.

15.7 Evaluation

Although a number of new initiatives were undertaken during NACP-II, evaluation of programme activities was not given adequate attention. Independent evaluation should, therefore, be done. Under NACP-III all intervention programmes will include evaluation plans. Tools to support such evaluation will be developed for each programme component by NACO and its designated technical partners. Ongoing evaluation of district and state programmes and midterm and terminal external evaluation of such programmes will be carried out as outlined in **Table 15.1**.

Table 15.1: Evaluation Plan

Product/Tool	*Levels*	*Purpose/Audience*	*Sources of information*
Dashboard Quarterly	National State	Management tool for NACO and partners. Used by NACB to monitor NACO & NACO to monitor SACS	CMIS State dashboards
State of the Epidemic and Response Annual	National State	Strategic management and governance tool for NCA, NACB, NACO, SACS, partners, GoI, public, International Community. • Planning • Monitoring • Accountability • Quality • Dissemination	CMIS, Surveillance, Special surveys, Research, CFMS
External Programme Evaluation Reports Mid-term, end of programme	National State and District	Measurement of progress against objectives GoI, NCA, NACB, NACO, Development partners, SACS	Annual reports, special surveys, evaluation process
Programme Reports Monthly/Quarterly	National State and District	Programme management of specific areas e.g. ART, Blood safety. Programme Managers at National, State and District level	CMIS
Published Research/ other Reports Periodic	Any	NACO, SACS, partners, wider audience	Research studies, Surveys

15.8 Programme Management, Implementation and Monitoring Tools

Five key data streams have been identified to strengthen programme management, accountability, learning and planning aspects. These include:

- Programme reports will be produced on a monthly/quarterly schedule at the national, state, and district level using information from CMIS. The report will focus on specific areas of programme management such as ART and blood safety. Programme managers at national, state and district level will be the key users of these reports;
- A "Dashboard" with information on key indicators will be prepared which will serve as a quarterly monitoring tool. It will be based on data from CMIS and state monthly programme reports. It will also help in management oversight at SACS, NACO and NACB levels;
- A report on State of the Epidemic and Response will be produced on an annual basis at the national level using data from CMIS, surveillance, special surveys, research, CPFMS and other sources;
- External programme evaluations will be undertaken at mid-term and at the end of programme. These will take place at the national,

state and district levels. These evaluations will be based on information from the field, annual reports, special surveys, and evaluation processes.

- Key research findings, surveys, special studies and other reports will be published on a regular basis to inform NACO, SACS, partners and a wider audience.

In consultation with development partners, formats for two products have been prepared – Quarterly Dashboard, and a set of annual Core Evaluation Indicators. These will form the basis of the Annual State of the Epidemic report.

15.8.1 Dashboard

This is the key tool for programme management at national and state level. It comprises a set of process indicators – inputs and outputs – which can be collected quarterly. These will inform managers on the programme implementation status and provide early warnings of weaknesses or processes which are failing. Dashboard will facilitate management oversight starting from NACB, NACO and SACS. NACO will use State Dashboards to monitor and brief NACB about indicators which are off track and overall performance of SACS (see **Table 15.2 & 15.3**).

Table 15.2: Dashboard for NACP-III

Indicator	*Target*		*Annual Core Indicator*
1. Number of TIs (by category)			
2. Percentage of TIs reporting condom stock-out in last quarter			
3. Number of ICTC clients tested and receiving result			2.2
4. Number of HIV+ pregnant women (mother and baby) receiving a complete course of ARV prophylaxis			2.4
5. Percentage of blood units provided by voluntary donors			
6. Number of ART service centers			
7. Number of eligible people with advanced HIV infection receiving ART (disaggregated by sex and age)			2.5
8. Percentage of SACS with HRG representatives included in SACS decision-making bodies			
9. Percentage of districts with at least one functioning PLHA network			2.3
10. Percentage of funds disbursed relative to targets			
11. Percentage of SACS with approved financial and administrative delegation			

(Contd...)

12. Percentage of states where partnership forum met in the last quarter			
13. Percentage of SACS' NGO Adviser positions filled			
14. Percentage of SACS with PDs in sole charge for more than one year			
15. Percentage of states with at least 80% CMIS reporting			4.1
16. Percentage of states which submit their dashboards to NACO regularly			4.2
17. Percentage of due procurement contracts awarded during the original bid validity period			
18. Percentage of ICTC centers with test kit stock-outs during quarter			
19. Percentage of ART centers with ART stock-outs during quarter			
20. Percentage of SACS where governing body met at least once during reporting quarter			
21. Number of district units established, staffed and reporting, relative to targets			

The Dashboard will be reviewed after year 1 and any adjustments required will be undertaken. Efforts will be made to enhance the use of State Dashboards not only as management tools but also for rewarding good performance, local innovations and perhaps even for performance-based financing.

15.8.2 Core Evaluation Indicators

The proposed set of core indicators is included at the end of this section. This is a subset of 130 indicators selected on the basis of their validity, utility and feasibility. The indicators cover the goal and objectives of NACP-III and UNGASS targets. Information on core indicators will provide the basis for the Annual Report on the State of the Epidemic and Response in India. This report will be widely disseminated, and will fulfil global information needs. It will also be used to track progress of the programme. It is important to recognise that these indicators will not answer all questions about programme performance or progress against targets and do not preclude special studies on particular issues or more robust evaluation processes. State level targets will also be identified and agreed between NACO and SACS.

15.9 Surveillance

One of the significant outcomes of NACP is the establishment of a well functioning and credible HIV sentinel surveillance (HSS) system. In 2005, HSS was carried out in 702 sites of which 175 were clinic based

Table 15.3: Proposed Annual Core Indicators for NACP-III

Objectives	*OVI*	*MOV / Source*	*Targets*	*Dashboard*
Goal To halt and reverse the epidemic over the next 5 years				
Outcomes/Outputs				
1. New infections in high risk groups and vulnerable populations prevented	**Behaviour Change** 1.1 Percentage of female sex workers reporting consistent use of condoms with clients in the last 12 months increased from X to 80% 1.2 Percentage of IDUs who have adopted behaviours that reduce transmission of HIV in the last 30 days from X to 80% 1.3 Percentage of men reporting use of condom the last time they had anal sex with a male partner from X to 80% 1.4 Percentage of population aged 15-49 reporting condom use in last sex with non-regular partners (disaggregated by sex and age subgroup) 1.5 Percentage of men reporting they are clients of SW 1.6 Percentage of population aged 15-49 with accurate knowledge on HIV/AIDS (recall three modes of transmission, 2 modes of prevention and who reject major misconceptions about HIV transmission) increased from X to 100% disaggregated by gender and age **Intervention Coverage** 1.7 Percentage of sex workers report being reached by TIs increases to 80% 1.8 Percentage of IDUs reporting being reached by TIs increased from X to 80% 1.9 Percentage of MSM (high as defined by NACO) reporting being reached by TIs increased from X to 80% **Intervention Planning** 1.10 Percentage of districts which have done high risk mapping increased from 10% to 100%.	1.1 – 1.6 IBBS/BSS Baseline from 2006 National BSS HRG survey. Mid-line BSS in 2009. End-line BSS in 2011. 1.7– 1.9 CMIS, reports and special studies 1.10 CMIS, Consultant reports		1.7 – 1.9 Linked to Dashboard 1

(*Contd...*)

2. Proportion of persons living with HIV/AIDS receiving care, support and treatment increased.	**Services / Coverage** 2.1 Number of ICTC (PPTCT / VCT) facilities increased from X to Y by 2011 2.2 Number of ICTC clients tested and receiving result increased from X to Y by 2011 (disaggregated by sex and age) 2.3 Percentage of districts with at least one functioning PLHA networks increased from X to Y% **Treatment and Care** 2.4 Percentage of HIV+ pregnant women (mother and baby) receiving a complete course of ARV prophylaxis increased from X% to Y% by 2011. 2.5 Number of eligible people with advanced HIV infection receiving ART (disaggregated by sex and age) increased from X to Y by 2011 2.6 Number of affected and vulnerable children receiving care and support through programmes increased from X to Y by 2011.	2.1 CMIS 2.2 CMIS 2.3 CMIS, special studies 2.4 CMIS, PPTCT records 2.5 CMIS 2.6 CMIS,		2.2 Dashboard 3 2.3 Dashboard 9 2.4 Dashboard 4 2.5 Dashboard 7
3. Infrastructure, systems and human resources in prevention and treatment programmes at the district, state and national levels strengthened.	3.1 Annual increases in budgets for HIV/AIDS in other ministries/ departments 3.2 Percentage of SACS which achieved at least 80% of planned expenditure targets 3.3 Percentage of audit reports completed and forwarded within time limits to NACO 3.4 Percentage of TIs run by CBOs	3.1 SACS records, interviews with key staff		
4. Strategic Information Monitoring and Evaluation Systems enhanced.	4.1 Percentage of states with at least 80% CMIS reporting 4.2 Percentage of states which submit their dashboards to NACO within time limit 4.3 Percentage of states whose annual plans demonstrate strategic and tactical changes in response to previous M&E data	4.1– 4.2 CMIS 4.3 State PIPs, State BSS, HSS data, programme reports, interviews with key stakeholders.		4.1 Dashboard 16 4.2 Dashboard 17

sites; 268 urban ANC and 128 rural ANC sites; 30 IDU sites; 83 FSW sites and 18 MSM sites. However, the number of surveillance sites in the northern states requires strengthening and coverage in urban and rural areas and high risk populations needs expansion. The information obtained in surveillance programmes needs to be more completely analyzed and more robust management systems need to be developed.

The National Behavioural Surveillance Survey (BSS) conducted in 2001 was a landmark effort and helped NACP to establish a baseline of risk behaviours. But, the second round of BSS was delayed and the programme will make only certain assumptions until the second round results are available. In addition, STD surveillance was very weak and community level STI surveillance and health facility surveys were conducted only once.

Under NACP-III, the surveillance system will focus on: tracking the epidemic, identifying pockets of HIV infection and estimating the burden of infection in the country. Surveillance activities will involve: BSS and HSS including measurement of HIV incidence, STI surveillance and tracking of other surrogate markers, e.g. Hepatitis B, Hepatitis C etc., AIDS case reporting, HIV associated morbidity and mortality, Anti-retroviral and STI drug resistance surveillance and other methods /sources of data (e.g. ongoing surveys). Given that the PPTCT programme successfully monitors HIV among ANC attendees, NACP-III will explore the possibilities of integrating PPTCT surveillance and ANC surveillance systems.

The possibility of integrating HSS with Integrated Biological and Behavioural Surveillance (IBBS) every 2-3 years among High Risk Populations will also be explored. In addition, following activities will be undertaken:

- Conducting two types of BSS, namely, a) annual risk assessment at the district level and b) methodologically rigorous BSS at state level, at least once in three years;
- Inclusion of key HIV service units in existing / planned health facilities surveys;
- Use of periodic surveys (NFHS-HIV) to calibrate and validate ANC estimates;
- Undertaking rapid annual district risk assessments based on simple practical guidelines (including mapping and size estimations of HRGs);
- Reporting of paediatric HIV/AIDS to be strengthened along with the adult case reporting and deaths;

- Development of guidelines to define high prevalence / vulnerability in districts;
- Initiating surveillance for STIs, HBV and HCV and other surrogate markers of HIV in the general population and high risk groups;
- Initiating sentinel surveillance of OIs;
- Enhancing the coverage, quality and use of biological markers sero-surveillance for estimation of prevalence of HIV in general and high risk populations;
- Initiating laboratory based surveillance of paediatric infections and STI infections;
- Conducting studies to estimate incidence of HIV;
- Conducting periodic studies (once in two years) to estimate mortality from AIDS to validate the results of model based estimation;
- Strengthening the overall mortality data through Registrar General of India; and
- Strengthening the capacity of SACS to carry out district-wise estimation using available models/software.

Surveillance activities will be coordinated by NACO in association with reputed institutions in the country and technical support through epidemiologists, biostatisticians and programme specialists. The existing HSS task force will also be further strengthened.

15.10 Key Indicators

- Percentage of reporting units (75 per cent) providing complete, regular and timely reports;
- Number of States with 70 per cent completion of the district data analysis sheets (to be measured every six months);
- Number of SACS producing a report every quarter which includes (i) monitoring indicators (ii) findings of the ongoing evaluation;
- Number of States conducting at least two key intervention evaluations per year;
- One participatory programmatic and one scientific/analytical evaluation by NACO every three years;
- Number of States with timely annual ANC HIV reporting according to standard protocol including PPTCT programme;
- Proportion of districts with M&E staff in place;

- Percentage of budget spent on M&E at national, State and district level; and
- Number of State PDs conducting: a) quarterly review meetings including a review of M&E information; b) engaging partners in the review meeting; and c) providing feedback on performance and reporting.

15.11 Research

Successful HIV interventions reported from various parts of the world are always based on sound knowledge and research support and are in turn scientifically evaluated and tested for efficacy and replication. Since early 90s, HIV related research in India in diverse disciplines, i.e. epidemiological, clinical, behavioural and social sciences, has contributed to a much better understanding of the dynamics of the epidemic. However, issues of quality of research, knowledge utilization, transfer and management continue to be areas of concern. Further, much research remains non-validated, scattered and underutilized because of poor documentation and dissemination practice. The potential of intervention/ action research and inter-disciplinary approach to cross cutting themes have remained underutilized.

The main objective of the research agenda is to position NACO as the leading national body, promoting and coordinating research on HIV/AIDS nationally and in the South Asia region through partnerships and networking with multiple stakeholders, supporting capacity building for research through established national academic and other research institutions, and as the central repository of all relevant resources, research documents and data base on HIV/AIDS in the country.

The overall outcome of the research in NACP–III will be: enhanced knowledge and evidence base on various aspects of the epidemic, up-scaled HIV research cross cutting, multi-disciplinary themes, improved research quality, better research capabilities and expanded partnerships; better mechanisms for effective and efficient production, utilization and management of research based knowledge on HIV/AIDS; relevant, measurable and context specific indicators for tracking the epidemic and assessing impact; and an action oriented research agenda for testing and evaluating interventions for prevention, care and support.

15.12 Key Activities

- Establish a Research Wing/ Division at NACO with strong linkages developed with research/academic institutions at regional/ state level;

- Constitute a multi-disciplinary Research Advisory Committee to guide implementation of research agenda during NACP–III;
- Identify critical gaps in existing knowledge through a commissioned comprehensive research review in relevant disciplines to develop an appropriate research agenda for filling in gaps at various levels;
- Identify key areas of research in bio-medical, clinical, epidemiological, behavioural and social fields which have a direct bearing on the HIV epidemic;
- Support ongoing applied research programmes for better understanding of the epidemic – its spread and impact and filling critical gaps in existing knowledge;
- Strengthen operations research and evaluation studies on the design, strategies, implementation and testing of HIV intervention programmes and measure their impact related to risk/vulnerability reduction, behaviour change, stigma reduction, HIV prevalence rate etc.;
- Build and improve capacity of researchers in the country for undertaking HIV research including inter-disciplinary, multi-site, action, intervention and operations research, and to increase skills in communicating research findings for impacting policy and programme;
- Build capacity for developing innovative methods to carry out studies on "hard to reach" and marginalized populations, mobile and migratory groups, stigmatized populations and other vulnerable groups like youth, adolescents, children, housewives, MSM and transgender groups;
- Build capacity for monitoring and evaluating community based interventions, school based adolescent education programmes and support groups of positive people;
- Build networks, alliances and partnerships with national, state and district level research organizations, universities, UGC, CSIR, ICMR, ICSSR, AIU, individual researchers, NGOs, PLHA networks and others, around key research themes (i.e. stigma, discrimination etc.) to produce contextualized knowledge for local initiatives; and
- Identify and promote a national research agency/ consortium to organize national conference on HIV/AIDS research once in every two years to share new developments on HIV/AIDS research

A total amount of Rs. 360 crore will be spent under this component including Rs. 195 crore for nation-wide M & E system, Rs. 80 crore for expanded 1200 Surveillance sites and Rs. 85 crore for research related activities.

Chapter – 16

Programme Strategies – Procurement Systems

16.1 Procurement of Civil works, Goods & Services

With a view to achieve the Goals and Objectives of NACP-III, it has been proposed to seek assistance of development partners for procurement of the following goods and services, civil works etc. during the project period (see Summary **Table16.2**).

16.2 Allocation for civil works, goods and services are as follows :

16.2.1 Civil Works Rs. 36500 lakh

The civil work component consists mainly of small and medium scale works scattered widely in the districts. These works relate to alteration to existing facilities, creation of adequate and well - organized storage rooms to accommodate supply of drugs/fitting the sink/providing overhead tanks/ plumbing and fitting of electrical points or making the rooms airy. This may also include providing small laboratory furniture. Average expenditure per unit would be approx. Rs. 2 lakh per year.

Approximately 10% of the proposed outlay on minor modifications etc. is likely to be spent on maintenance.

The method of contracting and the level at which decision will be taken to award such contracts for 'Civil Works' are as per **Annex 12.1**.

16.2.2 Goods

(i) Drugs

Supplies of drugs & medicines for OI, STI & PPTCT are maintained by providing financial assistance to various District Hospitals from out of the funds released to SACS. This pattern of assistance would continue during NACP-III to enable the hospitals to treat such infections. An abstract of the medicines for OI & STI that may have to be provided are indicated in **Annex 12.2 & 12.3** respectively.

(ii) Equipments

(a) 39 Districts level Blood Banks. – **Annex 12.4**.

(b) 22 Model Blood Banks, 4 Metro Blood Banks. – **Annex 12.5**.

(c) 80 new Blood Component Separation Units. – **Annex 12.6**.

(d) Equipment for I.C.T.Cs (2136 nos.) – **Annex 12.7**.

(e) Plasma Fractionation Plant – 1 No. – **Annex 12.8**.

Procurement of equipments at (a) to (c) above are proposed to be made during first three years of the project. (d) will be procured during the first two years. Procurement of Plasma Fractionation Plant will be made during year 2.

A provision of Rs.14941 Lakhs (being 10% per annum on progressive basis) has been retained for consumables for equipments.

Procurement plan including mode of tendering & method of procurement of each items/package over the project period is given at **Annex 12.9**. Requirement of equipments will also be reviewed during the implementation of the project.

(iii) Supplies

Diagnostic Test Kits

Whereas the HIV (Rapid) Test Kits "1" are procured at central level and supplied to SACS, the HIV Test Kits "2" & HIV Test Kits "3" will be procured by SACS (on an estimated basis of 10% of Test Kits "1" for Test Kits "2" and further 10% of Test Kits "2" for Test Kits "3"). Other diagnostic test kits (HIV Elisa, HCV Elisa, HCV Rapid, Hepatitis B Elisa, Hepatitis B Rapid and VDRL) will be procured on ICB basis at NACO only.

The procurement plan including mode of tendering & method of procurement of each item/package over the project period is given at **Annex 12.9**.

(iv) Vehicles

It is proposed to procure 270 diesel utility vehicles for SACS and 500 Refrigerated Vans for District and 32 Mobile Blood Banks. As for as possible, procurement of vehicles will be organized on ICB/NCB – rate contract of DGS&D. Procurement plan including mode of tendering & method of procurement of each items/package over the project period is given at **Annex 12.9**.

A provision of Rs. 73.65 crore (approx. 10 % per annum, on a progressive basis) has been made for expenditure such as operating costs (remuneration of drivers, technical Staff, POL for vehicles) and maintenance of vehicles.

Note: SACS will develop a mechanism to ensure that the equipments, vehicles etc are repaired / maintained properly by entering into AMCs. Similar arrangements have to be made for maintenance of regular supply of spares, consumables and reagents.

16.2.3 Consultancy

Procurement of goods during NACP-II was made centrally, by appointment of National PSA. In the course of review of the procurement plan for NACP-III, it was suggested that this arrangement should be substituted and a qualified procurement agency under mutual agreement of the World Bank and the Government of India would be appointed. The qualified procurement agency should either be sole sourced UN agency or an agency selected through QCBS guidelines of the World Bank. Since the selection of such an agency would take time, in order to maintain regular supply of goods and services, procurement would be made by an entity under TOR, and arrangements satisfactory to the Associations as defined in the relevant DCA. (Empowered Procurement Wing (EPW) of MoHFW would be such an entity and the above procurement could be made under the oversight of the International Consultant Organisation hired with the assistance from DFID for capacity building of EPW or another Consultant to be hired for providing oversight.

Similarly, an independent inspection agency would be appointed in case such services are not available with the qualified procurement agency being referred to above (see **Table 16.1**).

Strengthening of the procurement capacity at NACO has also been agreed upon in the GAAP for effective monitoring of procurement and supply chain management. Procurement arrangements at SACS would also be reviewed and strengthened before NCB procurement is commenced by SACS.

Table 16.1: Procurement Services

No.	*Name of the Item*	*Approx. value (Rs in lakhs)*
1.	Engagement of procurement agency @ 3% of total value of procurement through ICB	Rs. 2685
2.	Engagement of inspection agency in case such services are not offered by procurement agency @ 2% of the value of procurement through ICB	Rs. 1790
3.	Monitoring of Inventories	Rs. 400
4.	One time evaluation of the progress of procurement functions of NACP-III.	Rs. 150
5.	Supply chain management	Rs. 150
	Total	Rs. 5175

Contractual Services (including IEC services) Rs. 202750

As per Annex 12.10.

16.3 Procurement Manual

A separate document enlisting procurement procedures has been prepared. Instructions given in the document will be adhered to, for all procurements for the project.

16.4 Governance and Accountability Action Plan (GAAP)

A separate document has already been prepared, in which steps and commitments for various actions relating to procurements have been agreed upon.

16.5 Technical Specifications

A high level Technical Committee has been formed in Ministry of Health & Family Welfare in which experts from Medical Institutes, Drug Controller, BIS, and IIT are associated to finalize specifications for goods procured for NACO. Essential conditions regarding packing, warranty & after sale service have been prescribed in the bid document.

For civil works, SACS would be advised to follow the norms prescribed by Public Works Department. Similarly, for services, TOR are prepared by NACO before hiring the services of consultancy firm/individual professionals.

16.5 Inspection of Goods & Equipments

It is proposed to assign the inspection of goods & equipments procured to an independent agency during NACP-III in case such services are not offered by the qualified procurement agent.

Quality Assurance in pharmaceutical industry refers to a thorough understanding of a drug substance as a pre-requisite to product quality. It is an obligation of the manufacturer to design, test, and produce formulations that provide the consumer with products having the attributes of quality, purity, uniformity of content, stability and safety. It will be ensured that the drugs and pharmaceuticals are appropriately labeled (meeting statutory requirements) and packed with suitable packing materials. Compliance with these requirements is a statutory requirement and its enforcement is done through the Drugs & Cosmetics Act.

WHO Expert Committee on Specifications for Pharmaceutical Preparations has suggested following requirements for quality control:

(a) Licensed pharmaceutical products should be manufactured only by licensed manufacturers only, and are subject to strict quality control compliance.

(b) Pharmaceutical products are designed and developed in accordance with Good Manufacturing Practice (GMP), and other associated codes like Good Laboratory Practice (GLP), and Good Clinical Practice (GCP). This ensures safety, efficacy and quality of the product.

In the Standard Bidding Document for Drugs & Pharmaceuticals of the World Bank, specific provisions have been made for ensuring that the suppliers selected for award are capable of supplying the products of required quality.

16.6 Storage

NACO have been utilizing the services of GMSD under MSO for limited pre-dispatch inspection of drugs and storage of supplies. During NACP-III, SACS will be asked to enhance their storage capacity. Suitable proposals have accordingly been made for civil works in para 16.2a.

16.7 Procurement of good under non-pooled resources

Procurement and supply of first line Anti Retroviral Drugs have recently been commenced by NACO at various ART Centers. Global Fund for fighting AIDS, Tuberculosis and Malaria (GFATM) have been supporting this initiative of NACO in high prevalence States. It is proposed to upscale the coverage substantially during NACP-III. An abstract of ARV drugs required during the project period is at **Annex 12.11**.

The procurement and distribution of Condoms to States and Social Marketing Organizations has been envisaged in NACP-III, the procurement arrangement for condoms will be retained through EPW in Ministry of Health & Family Welfare, as hitherto being done for Department of Family Welfare. The distribution and supply of condoms is proposed to be reorganized under NACP-III. A tentative allocation of Rs. 1865 crore has been made for procurement and supply of condoms during the project period.

An abstract of procurement of supply of condoms (Male / Female) during NACP-III is at **Annex 12.12**.

Table 16.2: Procurement Plan Summary

	(Amount in lakh)
Civil Works	Rs. 36,500
Goods	
Drugs (OI drugs & STD programme)	Rs. 46500
Equipments	Rs. 45948
Consumable	Rs. 14941
Supplies	Rs. 34429
Vehicles	Rs. 15210
Operating Cost for vehicles	Rs. 7365
Office equipments	Rs. 145
Total for Goods :	Rs. 1,64,538
Consultancy	
Consultancy fee - Procurement Agent	Rs. 2685
Consultancy fee – Inspection Agent	Rs. 1790
Independent Evaluation Fee	Rs. 150
Monitoring of Inventories	Rs. 400
Supply Chain Management	Rs. 150
Total for Services:	Rs. 5,175
Contractual Services (Including IEC)	Rs. 2,02,750
Grand Total	Rs. 4,08,963
SUMMARY FOR FUNDING FROM OUTSIDE THE POOL	
Drugs (ARV Drugs)	Rs. 67500
Condoms	Rs. 186490
	Rs. 2,53,990

Chapter - 17

Programme Strategies - Financial Planning & Management

NACP-III recognises that the financial management of programme assumes critical importance. The financial management of the programme deals with the following:

- practices and arrangements for review and approval of annual work plans (AWPs) and budgets;
- funds flow mechanisms;
- financial powers and delegation;
- financial accounting system;
- internal controls to ensure funds are effectively used for programme objectives,
- financial reporting which includes management reporting and external reporting; and
- audit and accountability at Centre (NACO) and State (SACS).

NACP-III envisages implementing the programme up to district level and in an up-scaled manner. Financial management system will accordingly be modified to include the provision of reporting and accounting up to district levels. The system will also address the issues of up-scaling and challenges it poses because of financial management perspective.

During the implementation of NACP-II, implementing agencies experienced a number of financial management system delays and some constraints. These include procedure delays in releasing of funds, lack of uniformity in reporting the utilization of funds, inadequacy of reporting of performance based on resource concept in the absence of pooling of resources, issues related to financial delegation and powers, and management of funds at NGO level. This chapter discusses the financial management of the programme at various levels and addresses these issues and challenges.

17.1 NACP-III challenge of scaling-up of Programme

NACP-III recognises that scaling up will require a new modus operandi, including adjustments to its institutional framework nationally and at the state level and at district levels, and also an expanded participation of partners. In order to respond to this, it is expected that partner organisations will pool funds together in support of the national programme. Adequate efforts are already on for putting greater emphasis on building national partnerships along with the mainstream efforts for combating the epidemic, and adopting a programmatic approach in the next phase of funding to ensure coordination and synergy. It envisions changing NACO's role from implementer to a more catalytic/facilitating role, establishing strong coordination mechanisms, developing a comprehensive communication strategy for raising general awareness about HIV/AIDS to create an enabling environment (reducing stigma and increasing knowledge), strengthening monitoring and evaluation, building implementation capacity in weaker states, decentralizing the programme further, and fostering greater private sector involvement and convergence with other health programmes including Reproductive and Child Health and TB. Financial management role of implementing agencies, therefore, assumes critical importance.

17.2 Role of Financial Management

It is important that the programme focuses on further strengthening/ improving the existing financial management arrangements and practices. As discussed above, the financial management aspects such as funds flow are critical. Timely availability of funds is important and critical from programme implementation point of view. It is important that the process of preparing budget and developing annual plans must get completed on time. Financial reporting system should facilitate the monitoring of programmes effectively. NACP-III will make an attempt to move towards performance based monitoring system.

The new challenge in the programme would be linking the financial management system up to district level. This includes budgeting and annual work plans, financial accounting, internal controls, financial reporting (management reporting & external reporting), audit and accountability at centre (NACO), state (SACS) and local levels; adequacy of the finance/ accounts staff in NACO, SACS and districts in view of the increased resources and partners to be managed with specific reference to staffing norms at centre, state and district levels, and training requirements, job descriptions and required skill sets.

The role of DAPCUs would be more of monitoring the programme at the periphery level. DAPCU will be part of existing district society and will not have separate bank account. However, it will be required to keep account of expenditure incurred and resources used at the district level. These are essential to keep track of funds utilisation. The computerised financial system of NACO will be accordingly modified to include the expenditures incurred at the district level. DAPCU will also be responsible for monitoring and ensuring that programme components are implemented effectively.

NACP-III observes that there is a substantial scope for improvement in the existing financial management system in respect of certain aspects relating to budgeting, flow of funds, auditing, monitoring and reporting.

17.3 Addressing delays in Funds Disbursement

Releasing of funds has to go through processes which ensure propriety and getting appropriate approvals at various levels. Many times it has been experienced that these create delays. Financial concurrence is required from the Integrated Finance Division (IFD) before release of funds to SACS/ MACS. It has been experienced that this takes time. Even after the approval, release of funds takes time. The process of release of funds by its very nature entails these delays. NACP-III envisages resolving some of these issues to reduce the delay. The process of authorization will be looked into and the following points will be taken into account while doing this review:

- NACO handles large number of proposals and these vary in terms of size and amounts. Based on the size and amounts of proposals, appropriate system of authorization will be instituted to ensure that delays are minimized. MoHFW will develop appropriate system of authorization so that proposals below certain amount are completely delegated within NACO.
- NACO over the year has developed effective systems and all proposals go through greater scrutiny. Appropriate systems are already in place to ensure that funds are utilized for the purpose for which they have been allocated. There is, however, a scope and need for financial delegation.
- Once the funds are ready for release, these are transferred from NACO to SACS in the form of demand draft by registered post. It has been observed that this transfer may take up to two weeks. Finally the funds reach SACS/MACS towards the end of the first quarter of the financial year. These delays have implications for

programme performance as they have an impact on funds to programme implementing agencies.

- It has been observed that in many cases the first instalment is released by NACO to SACS/ MACS (generally comprising 50% of approved AWP) in the month of July i.e., in the fourth month of the financial year. This is mainly attributed to the delay in finalisation of the AWP for the financial year. Hence there is no transfer of funds from NACO to SACS in the first 3 - 4 months of the financial year and the recurring expenses of such period are met out from left over funds of the previous year. NACP-III has developed proposals and recommendations to address this problem. These are discussed in the following sections of the chapter.

17.4 Financial Authorisation – Delegation

At SACS level, the Project Director is authorized to release the funds subject to the delegation of financial power. However, it has been observed that the financial powers given to Project Directors vary significantly from state to state. Further, it was observed that in certain SACS, the financial power of Project Director is not adequate considering the volume of funds to be disbursed at SACS level. This leads to delay in the process of fund disbursement at SACS level.

The competent authority within SACS must accord approval on all matters having financial implications with the concurrence of finance division of SACS. NACO will ensure that SACS have the appropriate financial and administrative delegation powers. The administrative and approval mechanisms should ensure that delays arising because of processing of proposals at various levels are minimised. This will be incorporated in the MoU between GoI and the state governments. The authorisation power would be vested with the SACS; making PD and FC in the case of SACS, Project Manager/Accountant in the case of NGOs responsible for activities. The process would be made transparent with a system of proper financial scrutiny at every stage from administrative sanction to expenditure sanction.

In NACP-III it is suggested that adequate delegation is instituted at various levels for fast decision making. The model delegation of power will be made an integral part of Finance and Accounts Manual. The states and UTs would be required to follow the manual enlisting delegation of powers to GB/Executive Committee/PDs of SACS through executive order. This would be incorporated in the MoU likely to be entered for the new project.

17.5 Electronic Transfer of Funds

Considering the amount of funds, involvement of multiple agencies, long duration of the project, and increased volume of activities, NACO would explore the possibility of transferring the funds electronically to SACS.

Electronic payments have been endorsed by CVC as the mode of all government payments and the facilities under core banking solutions will be explored. As soon as the electronic transfer of funds becomes technically feasible, the same will be adopted.

17.6 Budget Preparation and Planning

Under NACP-III, budget processing, preparation and compilation process will be standardised and computerised in a phased manner. Computerisation of budget preparation and planning will be linked to overall IT upgradation programme. Standardisation will be done to ensure that budgets across all states are prepared in a consistent manner. Through the process of computerisation, data collation and compilation will be ensured. Also LAN/ internet connectivity would be established to make the transmission of data and reports faster. Development of software and systems will also incorporate facilities of defining the cost centres and developing costing system. There are already costing guidelines in existence and these will be made an integral part of the system. The data availability on computers and on-line system will reduce the delays.

For up-scaling the programme and implementing the components at district level, it will be ensured that budget incorporates inputs from various levels. For this purpose, a pre-budgeting conference will be organised before the next budget cycle begins wherein the relevant instructions/ guidelines would be provided to the staff of budget centres. This would ensure uniformity in the methods of estimation.

NACP-III plans training workshops for all the components officers and accounts and finance units in respect of financial management which includes budget preparation and compilation process.

Evidence based bottom-up planning approach would be followed by states. With adequate flexibility, this will form core of budgeting process. All stakeholders would be actively associated in planning and preparing state AAP. NACO should play more strategic leadership and programme catalyst role in the process.

National PIP has been prepared based on NACP-III objectives, keeping in view the epidemiology of states and strategic thrust of programme. State PIPs, therefore, form an integral part of the national PIP. However, states may envisage spending more resources or implementing new activities not part of PIP for which the appropriate approvals would be sought from NACO and then included in their annual activity plan. All such plans would be made in consultation with key stakeholders.

The multi-year plan will be revised on an annual basis and SACS will be informed of their annual financial allocation at the start of the planning process each year. The annual action plan of SACS will capture all sources of funding.

NACO, generally, organises conference of PDs to discuss the budget. During NACP-III this will be further strengthened to ensure the completion of budget process in time.

Budget preparation is a two stage process with the states developing their budgets at their level and the same being scrutinised and finalised at NACO level. Budget preparation process at the State level needs to be strengthened. NACP-III proposes to constitute an independent appraisal process of these yearly plans/PIP prepared by the states. This will be done by NACO and in-house team to ensure that all relevant information and data has been taken into account in developing the budget. Mid-term review of state performance will be incorporated in the state PIP.

When the budget goes through revision and if there are changes in financial allocations, the physical targets should also change. This would ensure that performance evaluation and comparison are logical and appropriate.

NACO will strengthen department for financial planning and analysis at the NACO level. The role of this department should include the following: (a) facilitation in the preparation, review and approval of AWP by SACS and NACO, (b) analyse the links between activities and budgets, (c) selective performance based analysis where the outputs can be measured in quantitative terms, (d) comparison of planned and actual performance and discussing the reasons.

The budget process of NACO and SACS will follow a time bound action, as mentioned in **Table 17.1**.

Table 17.1: Annual Budget Preparation Process

Date/Month	*Process and who will do it*
September/ October	SACS prepare inputs for AWP process (using standard budget formats, PIP targets)
End November	NACO indicates resource envelope to SACS. (Resource envelope will be based on number of targeting interventions in PIP, expenditure trends, overall budget forecasts etc.)
End December	AWP sent to NACO from SACS
Mid February	NACO completes appraisal of SACS budget
End March	Plans approved by NACO
Beginning April	AWP approval letter received by NACO
May	Funds released to SACS
October	Mid-Term Review

Reprogramming of budget expenditure will be allowed after taking appropriate approvals from NACO. The option to re-programme the budget would be provided during the NACO mid-term review of states performance process.

17.7 Financial Management Manual

NACO will update the financial management manual before the implementation of NACP-III. The updating will incorporate changes suggested in financial management practices and budget preparation process at the beginning of implementation and periodical updating may be ensured by way of amendments, additions, etc. to capture the changes in programme implementation and mid course corrections. State specific operational handbook (including financial management aspects) will be tailored to each state using the model developed by Tamil Nadu. NACO will provide support to SACS that have lower capacity to enable state operational manuals to be produced.

17.8 Expenditure Monitoring

The current system of CPFMS is quite well laid out and will be shifted to a web base during NACP-III and further strengthened. Web enabling and computerisation of the reporting process will be linked to the overall IT up-gradation programme. Simultaneously, reports from all SACS will be standardised and budgets will be further broken up into quarterly/six monthly targets. Quarterly budget variance report will be prepared by comparing:

(i) Budget and actual expenditure per intervention/ activity/ component per SACS; and

(ii) Budget allocation vs. release vs. expenditure.

NACO will monitor SACS expenditure on a monthly basis and adequate support will be provided (either by NACO or Project Support Units) to those SACS that are unable to report on a monthly basis and help them in strengthening their system to report on monthly basis.

CFMS will be modified to (a) facilitate multi-donor accounting and reporting and (b) also provide for capturing investment/expenditure by development partners funding the programme outside the budget. The requirement to share this information with SACS will be included in the partnership arrangements for DPs. To keep a tab over the total funds available at the SACS/implementing agency level, it is recommended that periodical reports (say, six monthly) should be submitted by various SACS/MACS providing details of funds received directly from the external funding agencies (agency-wise and activity-wise). SACS/MACS should ask for similar information from the implementing units below them and send the compiled information to NACO in respect of funds received from other sources within the state.

NACP-II had the problem of advances not being liquidated by implementing entities below the SACS on time. There are a number of good practice models that have been developed in the States to address this. For example, in West Bengal quarterly workshops are held to collect Statements of Expenditure and provide advances on a quarterly basis. The financial management manual needs to incorporate such models to address this issue.

17.9 Assessment through Internal Audit/External Audit

Presently, there is no internal/management audit in place; only a statutory audit is carried out by Chartered Accountants' firms selected out of the empanelled list. The existing audit coverage is limited and focused towards scrutiny and vouching of the expenditure statement submitted by the implementing agencies. Other important aspects such as adequacy and effectiveness of accounting system, internal control practices etc. are not covered.

17.9.1 Management Audit

NACP-III proposes to introduce the management/internal audit at NACO as well as at SACS to improve the efficiency of the financial system.

The scope of audit would cover:

- Audit of the processes followed for submitting claims to the donor agencies through CAAA;

- Certification of accuracy of the claims raised on donor agencies;
- Management structure, policies and practices followed;
- Overall budgeting and monitoring process followed;
- Overall rate of delivery – financial as well as physical;
- Fixed asset management system;
- Funds utilisation;
- Project evaluation; and
- Good governance practices followed, etc.

For this purpose, management/internal audit activity of NACO will engage internal audit team which will be integrated with Ministry of Health and Family Welfare Internal Audit Wing.

The management audit will have the following scope:

- Management processes (including governance practices, organisational structure, management policies);
- Financial processes (including expenditure, claims, budgeting, monitoring, fixed asset, fund utilisation, fixed assets, inventory management); and
- Project delivery.

The management audit will be carried out for all SACS on an annual basis and may be outsourced to selected firms or to the Internal Audit Wing of Ministry of Health and Family Welfare. NACO will play a monitoring role which would include selection of audit firms, planning the audit, review of reports, compliance with audit paras, etc.

SACS have the option of a more formal internal audit if they feel it is required. External audit will continue to be performed on the quarterly basis as at present. However, appropriate steps would be taken to ensure the quality of audit reports. NACO would also examine the fees paid to auditors for carrying out this activity and revise it suitably to ensure quality work. The appointment process of auditors will also be strengthened to ensure appropriate independence.

17.9.2 External Audit

The present system of statutory audit by Chartered Accountants on a quarterly basis would be made more effective. All concerned persons doing auditing will be made aware of new programme design and its complexities. It would be ensured that these aspects are included in their audit review. Appropriate TOR would be drawn keeping the changes in the programme. This would also be included in the finance manual.

17.10 Performance-based Reporting

NACP-III proposes to use the performance based reporting and evaluation where financial allocations and expenditures are linked to activities and output indicators of these activities. However, it may not be possible to use performance based system as all the activities cannot be linked with the directly measurable outputs and outcomes. Particularly, this may not be feasible on year to year basis. There are, however, opportunities where some of the components of the programme can be linked with performance based indicators. The budgets of components such as PPTCT, VCTCT and ART are output based and these can be used to implement performance based evaluation.

17.11 Financial Reporting

All SACS are registered bodies and are expected to prepare financial statements. Uniformity of financial reports across SACS would help in programme management. NACP-III will implement uniform system of reporting based on all resource concept. Some SACS receive funding from different sources and prepare separate financial reports to meet the requirements of funding agencies. These SACS would be required to produce the financial statements on consolidated basis. The expenses and grants received under different funds/from different funding agencies should be shown in the income and expenditure account.

NACO and SACS will be preparing the following MIS reports online for better financial management and monitoring:

- Fund flow statement;
- Statement of budget v/s actual expenditure;
- Statement of total fund release v/s utilization;
- Statement on status of claims submitted by NACO;
- Quarterly reconciliation statement of inter unit release of funds;
- Funds position of SACS;
- Statement showing time period consumed in release of funds from NACO to SACS;
- Statement showing time period consumed in release of funds from SACS to NGOs; and
- Reporting of efficiency in incurring of expenses by implementing agencies.

NACO and SACS will calculate the following key financial indicators to determine the efficiency/adequacy of budget preparation, fund disbursement, advance adjustment etc. on a half yearly basis.

- Ratio of approved budget to requested budget along with the adjustment in activities;
- Ratio of released funds to approved budget;
- Ratio of utilized funds to released funds;
- Ratio of unutilized funds to utilized funds;
- Average holding period of advances;
- Ratio of advances outstanding as on last date of the period to funds released during the period;
- Budget cycle period;
- Performance of SACS in terms of utilization of funds;
- Statement showing comparative utilization of the funds by each state; and
- Ratio of Grant-in-aid refunded over Grant-in-aid received during the period.

Web enabling and computerization of the reporting process will be linked to overall IT up-gradation. The Chart of Accounts will be updated and aligned with the NACP-III programme.

17.12 Pooling of Resources by Developing Partners

Pooling of Resources will follow principles of "Three Ones" for effectiveness in Fund Flow and Accountability in strengthening good governance. At the time of NACP-III planning, there was no system for pooling of all resources by various development partners under the programme. While a few of the bilateral agencies routed their funding through GOI, others disburse directly to SACS and NGOs e.g., UNDP assisted projects (charka project in UP), funds from Foods and Drugs Department for capacity building, state government contributions in certain states, etc. In the absence of pooling of resources of different funding agencies, it becomes difficult to get a consolidated figure of total funds received or spent in respect of a particular activity / total funds received from a particular agency during the year. This may also result in disproportionate funds availability at various SACS. Since, it may not be possible for all development agencies to pool resources, NACP-III will ensure that financial statements of SACS are based on total resource concept. This will be duly incorporated in the finance manual. Large development partners will be persuaded, based on "Three Ones" principle, to agree to revolving fund/special account funding type mechanism similar to WB.

If any funds are received by SACS/ MACS directly from external agencies, FCRA regulations are to be adhered to sustain the principles of "Three Ones".

17.13 Strengthening Financial Management Capacities

17.13.1 Staffing

The Project Financial Management Unit (PFMU) in NACO is headed by Director (Finance). Currently, the sanctioned strength of PFMU comprises eight regular posts and one contractual post. Director (Finance) is supported by an Assistant Director (Finance) and Consultant (Finance). In addition, there is one post of System Analyst/ Programmer and four supporting staff (2 Technical Assistants, 1 Assistant Accounts Officer and 1 Personal Assistant). The post of Consultant (Finance) is on a contractual basis. PFMU will be strengthened to ensure that there is sufficient resource with appropriate competencies allowing for longer term contractual appointments.

At the state level, the Accounts and Finance Unit (AFU) is headed by a Finance Controller in large states, Finance Manager in medium states, and Finance Officer in small states. The Finance officer assists the Finance controller/ Finance Manager. The supporting staff includes Accountants and Assistant Accountant. The posts of Finance Controller, Finance Officer and Finance Manager are regular posts while the Accounts Assistants are recruited on contractual basis. The head of finance is a regular government employee from the state/centre cadre. Each SACS will require 3 to 4 posts for technically competent finance staff. In larger SACS, at least one chartered accountant/cost accountant is required in addition to the Finance Controller. Draft Terms of Reference for these posts will be prepared by NACO. SACS will have the autonomy to determine the size and structure of their finance departments and staffing needs.

In certain states, a District AIDS Coordination Committee (DACC) has been established by SACS. The District Magistrate (of the respective district) is the chairman of such DACC. The Chief Medical Officer (CMO) and the Deputy Chief Medical Officer of the Districts act as the District Nodal Officer and Programme Officer respectively.

NACP-III observed that some of the posts, particularly the financial management staff, at NACO and SACS have remained vacant. The work relating to these positions was appropriately delegated, but keeping in view the NACP-III requirements, as a result of up-scaling, the positions have been re-assessed and appropriate provision made. The revised organogram suggested for the Accounts and Finance Units at NACO/SACS has taken into account these aspects. NACP-III observes that these are likely to strengthen internal controls/checks. The personnel in Accounts and Finance unit would be strictly on deputation from the Central/ State Accounts department and only in case of non availability it would be filled through open advertisement. This would be done with the concurrence of NACO only. Director (Finance) or his representative would be a member of the selection committee. The main Finance Controller/ Finance Manager post in SACS will be on deputation from the Government service. Other posts may be filled from outside the government system. It will, however be difficult to attract suitably qualified staff from within the GoI system in many states. There is restricted scope to recruit salaried finance staff from outside the government system i.e. through the open market. GoI allows for open market recruitment of consultants for centrally sponsored schemes, but some states may not allow for this. In such case, NACO will follow a recruitment process similar to that of RCH-II.

It is also suggested that a support group of finance personnel be formed region-wise comprising one or two efficient FCs to help the weak SACS of the region. These groups can act as peer support group and alert NACO in case of special attention.

Field level observations suggest that SACS which employ professionals such as chartered accountants are comparatively better managed than those that are being headed by non-professionals. While recruiting these personnel, appropriate weightage should be given to persons having professional qualifications and the existing staff should be appropriately trained. It has been observed that pay-scales of contractual staff are same across all the offices in the country. Because of cost of living variations across country appropriate adjustments in remuneration packages would be made to account for these differences.

17.13.2 Training

The training of finance and accounts staff has not been adequate. NACP-III proposes to focus on training of these personnel, with special focus on operational and financial procedures, including CPFMS (Computerised Project Finance Management Systems).

At the beginning of project, NACO will prepare a yearly training calendar for accounts and finance staff. The training calendar will be prepared in such a way that all SACS and DACS are covered within a calendar year. Also the training calendar will be planned in such a manner that the training is provided at an appropriate time. For example, there will be training on the budgeting process much before the month of October (when the budgeting process starts).

The training programme will have the following components:

- CFMS training;
- Induction training for new recruits (to provide an overview of the finance processes and the NACP-III programme itself);
- Professional accounting training (for specified staff);
- Personal development training;
- Finance training for non finance staff (especially PDs); and
- Twice yearly conferences for all finance staff to share good practice and disseminate information from NACO to SACS, e.g. new initiatives.

At the beginning of NACP-III, NACO will organise an intensive orientation workshop (for 2-3 days) for AFU of all SACS on relevant financial management aspects such as (a) preparation of PIP and AWP, (b) performance based linking of budgets and activity based plans, (c) fund disbursement process, (d) preparation of SOEs and accounting and financial reporting, (e) MIS reporting and financial management indicators, and (f) auditing and internal control mechanism, etc. The orientation workshop will also cover intensive training on computerized system for budgeting, accounting and reporting (at present CPFMS is in use).

NACO will organise refresher training (at least once in a year during the project period) for the accounts and finance staff. The refresher training will also cover the relevant financial management aspects and the computerized system. NACO will prepare training kits as Videos/CDs containing training material, key features of financial management manual and computerized system. These training kits would help new persons joining the SACS/DACS understanding their job responsibilities.

17.14 NGO Financial Management

Generally, the funds are disbursed to the NGOs for TIs in two instalments. The first instalment is released on the approval of NGO budget by the Executive Committee and second is released on the basis of the utilisation of funds and submission of Statement of Expenditure by the NGO.

NACP-III will ensure that sufficient monitoring processes are in place to ensure that funds are used by NGOs as per the programme objectives. The NGO advisor at SACS is responsible for technical as well as financial monitoring of the NGOs. In addition, in certain states, PSUs are also responsible for assistance in selection of NGOs, monitoring of NGOs, project review and evaluation of NGOs based on process and outcome indicators, training of NGOs and support partnership and networking between SACS and NGOs.

Usually, the role of finance person in the NGO selection process was limited. To ensure effective assessment of the financial management system and procedures being followed in the NGO, the involvement of finance officials needs to increase. NACP-III places greater emphasis on training of these officials. Their role in NGO evaluation will be part of curriculum.

A large amount of funds was routed through the NGO sector in India. NACO will, therefore, collaborate with the Institute of Chartered Accountants of India to develop appropriate standard of accounting for NGOs working in the health sector. Such accounting standards would be developed in consultation with the Government Accounting Standards Board and the Controller General of Accounts. Once the standards are developed, these would be followed uniformly in all programmes Since large number of accounting professional and chartered accountants are going to be involved in auditing and monitoring, it is important to have accounting standards for the NGOs. Based on these standards, steps would be initiated to develop good accounting system manual and audit procedure for NGOs. This will reduce the lack of uniformity in financial reports submitted by NGOs. The accounting staff of NGOs will also be trained during NACP-III.

Guidelines for contract management with NGOs will be developed to include specific areas of internal control mechanism and delegation, funds management, maintenance of accounting records, accounting system and procedures, auditing and financial reporting.

The SOEs submitted by NGOs is not standardised and the frequency and periodicity also varies from state to state. The review and approval process also differs from state to state. In certain states, the auditor certification is required before submission of the SOE to SACS while in others, it is not. In NACP-III, steps would be initiated to standardise this. In certain states, the release of subsequent grant to an NGO is subject to the approval of SOE (submitted by NGOs) by the District Magistrate, while in others it is not. It should be noted that although the DM's approval helps in bringing a social responsibility element among the NGO partners, it results in substantial delays in the whole process of fund release and SOE approval.

NACP-III has noted the good practices of releasing funds to NGOs. For example, in Tamil Nadu, the contract with NGOs provides the following model: Disbursements to NGOs are made 3 times a year (month 1 – 25%, month 4 - 50%, month 10 - 25%); panel internal auditors perform audits every 6 months, de-linked to funding; and adequate training is provided to NGOs and auditors on panel.

This process ensures that a float of 1 to 2 months expenditure exists at the NGO level, addressing disbursement delays. NACP-III proposes to use these practices and incorporate the same in the manual. Accordingly, funding to NGOs will be de-linked from their reporting processes to ensure that NGOs are never without funds. This will also address the problem of disbursement delays.

NACP-III proposes to constitute PSUs in those states which are partnering with large number of NGOs. A dedicated Accounts Assistant would assist the NGO Advisor in key financial management aspects such as budgeting for NGOs, financial monitoring of NGOs, collection of reports and SOE from NGOs etc.

Chapter - 18

Programme Strategies - Financial Projections and Requirement

NACP-III envisages linking the financial requirements of the programme to targets set under targeted interventions (TIs) and package of services as discussed in "Targets for NACP-III" and "Package of Services" section. Unit cost has been worked out for most activities of NACP-III. Various consultations through workshops have helped in fine tuning the costs in the following manner:

- Clarity of activity and appropriate cost unit definition;
- Revision in monetary values of various cost units such as salary;
- Incorporating risk factors in each activity and suggesting preliminary requisites for carrying out that activity;
- Establishing criteria for need based support required;
- Estimating bulk cost for activities for which cost unit could not be clearly defined; and
- Sorting out duplication of efforts at various levels.

While estimating the financial requirements, NACO Costing Guidelines for estimating cost of targeted interventions were used. The following consultations and costing analysis were carried out to fine tune the costing estimates further:

- Workshops in West Bengal, Tamil Nadu, Gujarat and Haryana to discuss the costing;
- Costing study of selected interventions and services in Gujarat and using data from Kerala and Tamil Nadu;
- Developing a package of service model based on costing study of ART and ICTCT; and

- Two meetings convened by NACO of SACS Project Directors and agreement therein on utilisation and load linked estimation of financial requirements.

Following sections discuss the costing estimates of various components of the programme.

18.1 Costing of TIs for HRGs

The estimation of financial requirements for TIs is based on the desired number of TIs to saturate coverage of the high risk groups. While making the estimation, only three high risk groups have been taken into account. These are SWs, MSM and IDUs. The targets for these groups have also been specified.

As on 31 December 2005, 700 TIs covered about 659,213 persons belonging to the three high risk groups (see **Table 18.1**). The break-up is as follows.

Table 18.1: Costing of TIs for HRGs

Risk Groups	*Coverage*	*Per cent*	*Number of TI*	*Per cent*
CSWs	444,186	67 %	181	26 %
MSMs	126,833	19 %	30	4 %
IDUs	88,194	13 %	93	13 %
Composite TIs			396	56 %
Total	659,213	100 %	700	100 %

About 56 per cent of these interventions were composite in nature. Taking all the 700 TIs into account, the average coverage works out to be about 954 persons per TI.

NACP-III assumes that existing 700 TIs will continue with an average coverage of 954 persons. However, to achieve 80 per cent saturation, NACP-III proposes to increase TIs by three fold to 2100. NACP-III targets for HRGs are given in **Table 18.2**.

Table 18.2: NACP-III Targets for High Risk Group and proposed TIs

HRG	*Number*
SWs	1,000,000
MSM	1,150,000
IDUs	190,000
Total	2,340,000
Number of TIs (3 fold increase)	2100

NACP-III has prepared the costing templates based on current coverage. Targets for number of TIs and coverage of three HRGs have been set for the next 5 years. Year-wise targets used in estimation are as follows (**Table 18.3**).

Table 18.3: Targets to be achieved by intervention year

Target	*Current Coverage*	*Year 1*	*Year 2*	*Year 3*	*Year 4*	*Year 5*
SWs	44 %	60 %	80 %	100 %	100 %	100 %
MSM	11 %	30 %	60 %	100 %	100 %	100 %
IDUs	46 %	60 %	80 %	100 %	100 %	100 %
Target for CSWs	444,186	600,000	800,000	1,000,000	1,000,000	1,000,000
Target for MSM	126,833	345,000	690,000	1,150,000	1,150,000	1,150,000
Target for IDUs	88,194	114,000	152,000	190,000	190,000	190,000
Number of TIs	700	1,300	1,800	2,100	2,100	2,100

Through a rapid scale-up strategy, it is proposed to achieve the targets set for NACP-III by the end of the third year of the programme.

The cost of implementing TIs has been divided into the following three categories:

- One time cost to set-up TI. This cost has been budgeted for newly set-up TIs;
- Fixed recurring costs to implement TIs. These are fixed irrespective of the number of persons covered under each TI; and
- Variable recurring costs, linked to the number of persons covered in each TI.

In NACP-III, it is further proposed that 50 per cent of all TIs will be handed over to Community Based Organisations (CBOs). It is envisaged that while NGO TI will cover on an average 800 persons, CBO TI will cover on an average 1200 persons. In case of CBO TI, there will be an additional cost in term of contingency and enhanced amount for baseline survey considering that all CBOs will be newly set up and cover a wider population through intervention. NACP-III has used the guidelines developed by NACO for costing of NGO TIs with modification in certain items such as salary and provision of supplies in case of certain risk groups. These revisions are based on inputs received from the implementing agencies and SACS during the workshops. It is expected that while developing state-level budget for implementing TIs, the same principle will be applied. NACP-III has prepared costing templates for this purpose and these can be used by SACS for developing state level PIPs. The following implementation strategies would be taken into account at the time of implementing the programme.

(i) **Community based organisations and peer led interventions for saturating coverage of all HRGs in urban areas:** All town and cities (defined as per Census 2001) will be covered with high-intensity target interventions with outreach and service provisions for sex workers (female, male and Hijra populations) and their clients.

(ii) **NGO led intervention in rural areas with 5000+ population:** Given the large spread of villages, and the probability of there being more than 10 FSWs or more practising in villages, an outreach and service delivery plan to access these FSWs in line with the TI approach will be designed. This would include capacity building among smaller NGOs and subsequently linking them with the larger networks for long term sustainability.

(iii) **Mainstreaming interventions in rural areas with <5000 population**: In these villages, focus will be on creating general awareness about HIV/AIDS and STIs, and also providing referral services for STI treatment, VCTC/PPTCT, care and support. Such interventions will be done through a link worker model. This model implies having, for every 5000 population, 2 link workers (male and female), who will be trained in communication on HIV/AIDS and accessing referral services. The cost of the LW strategy would include monthly remuneration to LWs towards travel, supervision, training etc. In large districts, an estimated 400 link workers would be required. The actual numbers required will be based on the detailed risk assessment that will be undertaken in 50 districts in first year of implementation of the programme.

(iv) **Small, scattered villages**: In these villages, focus will be on environment building and integrating vulnerable persons with economic activities to provide livelihood opportunities and reduce the intensity of the circumstances that provide grounds for indulging in the sex trade.

The break-up of the costs involved in the implementation of TIs for HRG is given in **Table 18.4, 18.5, 18.6** and **18.7**.

Table 18.4: Management of TIs by NGOs

NGO TI	*Year 1*	*Year 2*	*Year 3*	*Year 4*	*Year 5*	*Total*
Unit	650	900	1,050	1,050	1,050	
						Rs. lakh
One-time Cost	553	213	128	0	[illegible]	893
Fixed Cost	4,246	5,880	6,860	6,860	6,860	30,705
Variable Cost	4,081	5,938	7,953	7,953	7,953	33,877
Total Cost	8,880	12,030	14,940	14,812	14,812	65,475
Unit Cost	13.66	13.37	14.23	14.11	14.11	

Table 18.5: Management of TIs by CBOs

CBO TI	*Year 1*	*Year 2*	*Year 3*	*Year 4*	*Year 5*	*Total*
Unit	173	383	663	840	1,050	
						Rs. lakh
One-time Cost	1,398	538	323	0	0	2,258
Fixed Cost	5,873	8,132	9,487	9,487	9,487	42,465
Variable Cost	7,655	11,174	15,086	15,086	15,086	64,088
Total Cost	14,925	19,843	24,895	24,573	24,573	108,810
Unit Cost	22.96	22.05	23.71	23.40	23.40	

Table 18.6: Cost for Link Workers

Link Worker	*Year 1*	*Year 2*	*Year 3*	*Year 4*	*Year 5*	*Total*
Districts covered	50	100	200	200	200	
Total Cost	3,951	7,903	15,806	13,440	13,440	54,540

In budgeting for link workers, the following assumptions were taken:

- Total work force of 200 link workers will be deployed in each district;
- Over the 5-year period, 200 districts will be covered in the programme; and
- There will be no training cost for these link workers from fourth year of the programme.

Table 18.7: Targeted Intervention Cost (Total)

(Rs. lakh)

TI	*Year 1*	*Year 2*	*Year 3*	*Year 4*	*Year 5*	*Total*
NGO TI	8,880	12,030	14,940	14,812	14,812	65,475
CBO TI	14,925	19,843	24,895	24,573	24,573	108,810
Link Worker	3,951	7,903	15,806	13,440	13,440	54,540
Total TI Cost	27,756	39,776	55,641	52,825	52,825	228,825

18.1.1 Financial Assumptions

NGO TI Cost:

- One time Cost: Rs. 85,000 per NGO-TI. The cost comprises recruitment, office infrastructure, computer peripherals, baseline need assessment.
- Fixed Cost: Rs. 653,300 per NGO-TI. This cost is incurred yearly and is based on the NGO TI costing guidelines.
- Variable Cost: This cost relates to salary of outreach workers, peer educators, counsellors, travel cost in programme, lubricants, detoxification, sub./detox, absess management, needles syringes, STD drugs. Cost has been calculated on the basis of the number of persons covered and type of TI.

CBO TI Cost:

- One time Cost: Rs. 215,000 per CBO-TI. The cost comprises recruitment, office infrastructure, computer peripherals, baseline need assessment.
- Fixed Cost: Rs. 903,500 per CBO-TI.
- Variable Cost: The cost relates to salary of outreach workers, peer educators, counsellors, travel cost in programme, lubricants, detoxification, sub./detox, absess management, needles syringes, STD drugs. Costs has been calculated on the basis of the number of persons covered and type of TI.

Link Workers:

- Incentives for link workers @ Rs. 1,500 per month per worker.
- Travelling allowance @ Rs. 500 per month (linked to number of villages).
- Supervisor's Incentive: 10% of link workers from each district @ Rs. 500 p.m. as an additional incentive.
- Two resource persons @ Rs. 10,000 p.m. each (support for first 3 years only).
- Training of resource persons @ Rs. 500 per day per person for 15 days (support for first 3 years only).
- Material for training of link workers @ Rs. 100 per link worker per annum (support for first 3 years only).
- Training of link workers @ Rs. 200 per day per link worker for 19 days (support for first 3 years only).
- Contingency and other incidental costs (support for first 3 years only).

18.2 Other Interventions focusing on Truckers, Prison Inmates, Migrants etc.

Physical targets to be covered under this component are relatively less known except in the case of truckers. According to estimates, there are 5-6 million truckers out of which 50 per cent are considered to be of high risk group. **Table 18.8** gives the budget estimates for truckers and other groups in this category.

Table 18.8: Budget Estimates for Truckers and Other groups

	Year 1	*Year 2*	*Year 3*	*Year 4*	*Year5*	*Total*
Coverage of truckers	40 %	60 %	80 %	100 %	100 %	
No. of Truckers (30 lakh)	12	18	24	30	30	
						(Rs. lakh)
Cost for truckers' interventions	456	684	912	1,140	1,140	4,332
NGO support/Access to STD/Treatment	456	684	912	1,140	1,140	4,332
Other group costs	500	500	500	500	500	2,500
Protocol development	460	660	560	260	110	2,050
Total Budget	1,872	2,528	2,884	3,040	2,890	13,214

18.3 Costing of Services

Financial requirements for services have been worked out on the basis of the targets specified, while the financial requirements for provision of services have been worked out on the following basis:

- Estimated capital expenditure and one-time cost required to implement the intervention of service provision;
- Estimated recurring fixed cost of intervention keeping in view the minimum scale of operations and mix of services in ICTC, and
- Estimated variable cost of each intervention by linking the requirements with the targets proposed in interventions as explained in "Targets for NACP-III" section.

While estimating financial requirements, costing of services has been worked out keeping in view the classification of districts in risk categories. For each category, NACP-III has developed service provision by focussing on PLHA, HRG and general population. Packages were defined at different levels to address prevention, care, support and treatment services. The four levels of service delivery worked out for defining provision of service are: State, District, Block/Sub-division and Village/Community. This approach is likely to ensure better economies of scale and bring more efficiency by avoiding duplication of services and by ensuring minimum threshold level of activities. It also helps in developing need based services, ensuring quality of activities and effective monitoring of services and activities. Since the financial requirements are linked to targets, setting the processes and benchmarks for monitoring are possible to implement.

NACP-III also proposes to develop implementation plan based on (i) integration of service delivery package, (ii) greater involvement of non-governmental agencies through effective public private partnership, (iii) differential service package based on prevalence and vulnerability, (iv) increasing access up to PHC level and focusing on community level identification of PLHA and HRG and referral, PHC for STD service, CHC for ICTC & PPTCT, District/Tertiary levels for ART, (v) demand generation activities through IEC, (vi) ensuring quality of service, (vi) enhanced institutional arrangements for coordination, (vii) ensuring regular supply of drugs and consumables – IT linked monitoring, and (viii) building capacity of infrastructure, training and equipment.

Targets specified for the package of services, their phasing and the spread of financial requirements are given in the **Tables 18.9** and **18.10**.

Table 18.9: Target for Package of Services

Target	*Year 1*	*Year 2*	*Year 3*	*Year 4*	*Year 5*
Target for ART	33 %	50 %	66 %	83 %	100 %
Target for ICTC	40 %	60 %	80 %	90 %	100 %
Target for PPTCT	30 %	50 %	60 %	70 %	80 %
Target for ART	100,000	150,000	200,000	250,000	300,000
Target for ICTC	6,500,000	12,000,000	15,000,000	18,000,000	22,000,000
Target for PPTCT	6,750,000	8,100,000	9,450,000	10,125,000	10,800,000

Table 18.10: Financial requirements for services (Rs. lakh)

Services	*Year 1*	*Year 2*	*Year 3*	*Year 4*	*Year 5*	*Total*
STD Services	1,549	2,382	2,938	3,419	4,485	14,774
ICTC Services	14,195	16,744	16,967	17,507	18,227	83,639
PPTCT	2,335	2,579	2,824	2,946	3,068	13,752
Palliative Drugs	112	135	169	202	225	843
OI Drugs	1,661	2,203	2,583	2,907	3,581	12,935
PEP	444	684	844	982	1,291	4,244
Safety Measures	988	1,468	1,816	2,120	2,717	9,109
Total	21,284	26,195	28,141	30,083	33,594	139,296

18.3.1 Financial Assumptions

Integrated Counselling and Testing Centre:

- Three types of ICTC are proposed in NACP-III:
  - General ICTC: existing 777, new centres in year 1: 1518, year 2: 622
  - General and PPTCT: existing 1378, no new centres envisaged
  - HIV/TB: existing 158, no new centres envisaged
- Minor modifications and civil works: Rs. 30,000, Equipment: Rs. 21,000.
- Salary: Rs. 24,500 p.m.
- Test cost: 100 % cases @ Rs. 13 per case, 10 % cases @ Rs. 40 per case and 1% case @ Rs. 100 per case.

Prevention of Parent to Child Transmission:

- 502 existing centres to continue through the project period.
- Salary @ Rs. 16,000 pm.
- Consumables @ Rs. 30,000.
- Test cost: 100 % cases @ Rs. 13 per cases, 10 % cases @ Rs. 40 per case and 1% case @ Rs. 100 per case.
- Drugs: Nevirapine tablets @ Rs. 10 per case, Nevirapine syrup @ Rs. 95 per case.

Provision for STD, palliative and OI drugs, post-exposure prophylaxis and safety measures are made at a defined rate per institution.

18.4 Blood Safety (including mobile blood banks)

The success of blood safety programme critically depends on the setting-up of blood storage units and augmenting the supply of fresh blood backed up by blood separation component units. NACP-III proposes to set up 3,222 blood storage units (BSUs) covering all CHCs over the next 5 years. The programme also proposes to set up additional 80 Blood Component Separation Units (BCSUs) and additional 22 mobile blood units. The existing number of BCSUs is 82. Financial requirements estimated here also take into account the support required to maintain the existing facilities at various levels. Since RCH-II also proposes to support safe blood initiatives through strengthening of blood storage units at first referral units, NACP-III seeks to achieve convergence with the RCH-II programme and hence, the estimates do not include creating blood facility at FRU level. Other efforts in this area will focus on promoting voluntary blood donation, monitoring and quality assurance. Public private partnerships will focus on developing effective linkages with agencies such as Indian Red Cross Society (IRCS). Targets under various components of the blood safety programme are given in **Table 18.11**.

Table 18.11: Blood Safety Programme: Targets

Programme Component	*Target*	*Existing*	*New*
Model Blood Banks	32	10	22
Blood Component Separation Unit (BCSU)	162	82	80
Blood Banks	1,177	1,138	39
Blood Storage Units (BSU)	3,222		3,222
Blood Mobiles	32		32
Refrigeration Vans	500		500
Plasma Units	2	1	1
Metro Blood Banks	4	–	4

For computing financial requirements of blood safety programme, following assumptions are made:

- The support to blood safety component is provided on the assumption that additional 80 units of BCSU would be in place by the middle of the programme. Capital and recurring cost for setting up BCSU are Rs. 40 lakh and Rs. 16 lakh p.a. respectively.
- Capital and recurring cost for setting up Model Blood Banks are Rs. 60 lakh and Rs. 25 lakh p.a. respectively.
- Capital and recurring cost for setting up district Blood Banks are Rs. 11 lakh and Rs. 4 lakh p. a. respectively.
- Capital and recurring cost for setting up Blood Storage Units are Rs. 0.75 lakh and Rs. 0.11 lakh p.a. respectively.
- Capital and recurring cost for setting up Blood Mobiles are Rs. 75 lakh and Rs. 6 lakh p.a. respectively.
- Capital and recurring cost for setting up Refrigeration Vans are Rs. 9 lakh and Rs. 2 lakh p.a. respectively.
- Capital costs for setting up Plasma Units are Rs. 3500 lakh.
- Capital and recurring cost for setting up Metro Blood Banks are Rs. 2000 lakh and Rs. 800 lakh p.a. respectively.
- Support to existing blood banks including state-of-the-art blood banks in some states would be continued (technical support to blood storage units would be provided in collaboration with RCH). NACP-III envisages to set-up one additional plasma unit and 4 metro blood banks.

- By year 3, new units would be in place and there would be no need for equipment purchase in subsequent years except for the replenishment of old equipments.

Based on these assumptions, the following financial requirements given in the **Table 18.12**, are proposed for this component:

Table 18.12: Financial Requirement for Blood Safety

						(Rs. crore)
Costs	***Year 1***	***Year 2***	***Year 3***	***Year 4***	***Year 5***	***Total***
Capital Cost	103	52	103	0	0	258
• Equipment purchase for blood bank	85	43	85	0	0	213
• Vehicle for Mobile blood banks	18	9	18	0	0	45
Recurring Cost	139	139	139	139	139	697
• Salary of Technical Assistant/ LabTech.	25	25	25	25	25	126
• Consumables	86	86	86	86	86	432
• Contingency	28	28	28	28	28	139
Total Cost	243	191	243	139	139	955

18.5 Communication, Advocacy and Social Mobilisation (CASM)

NACP-III proposes to develop a financial requirement plan for communication, advocacy and social mobilisation (CASM) component based on state-specific requirements. However, these requirements are not available in detail. NACP-III uses broad indicators and key strategies in estimating financial requirements:

As part of the process, the first step towards developing the strategic plan is completing the need assessment studies which would be done twice during the five-year period. For most of the activities carried out under this component, the expenditures should come down in the last two years of the programme period.

Significant work has already been done in NACP-II and awareness about modes of transmission and prevention methods is quite high. NACP-III needs to focus more on interventions which are community based and focus specifically on behaviour change. It will also sustain the awareness already created under NACP-II. Focused efforts on women, children and youth would be an integral part of the NACP-III communication strategy. Mass awareness programmes through the print and electronic media would be used for sustaining the efforts.

Most of the costs here are estimated as bulk costs except for the needs assessment studies and training of ASHA which have been worked out on the basis of districts and CHCs covered. NACP-III also proposes to keep some provision for innovative approaches in developing implementation strategies. **Table 18.13** gives broad financial requirements for communication, advocacy and social mobilization.

The activities proposed under various other components under NACP-III also involve a number of interventions which focus on social mobilisation and behaviour change. The CASM activities, therefore, constitute an integral part of all other components in NACP-III and budget allocations here do not reflect the total amount spent on this component.

Table 18.13: Financial Requirement for Communication, Advocacy and Social Mobilisation

						(Rs. lakh)
Activity	***Year 1***	***Year 2***	***Year 3***	***Year 4***	***Year 5***	***Total***
Media (Mass media, special events etc)	12,500	12,500	12,500	12,500	12,500	62,500
Need Assessment	1,000	0	1,000	0	0	2,000
Advocacy	1,000	1,000	1,000	500	500	4,000
Blood Safety promotion	1,000	1,000	1,000	600	500	4,100
Social Mobilisation – RRC, NYK, YFC	3,200	3200	3,200	3,200	3,200	16,000
IEC for Tribal	200	200	200	200	200	1,000
Support for state level resource centre	200	200	200	200	200	1,000
Special Events	400	900	900	900	400	3,500
PLHA support	200	300	500	200	200	1,400
Interpersonnel Training (ASHA)	200	200	200	200	200	1,000
Production of Materials	1,200	1,200	1,000	700	200	4,300
Innovative Approach	200	200	200	200	200	1,000
	21,300	20,900	21,900	19,400	18,300	101,800

18.6 Condom Promotion

Over the years the supply of condoms has increased from 1.4 billion pieces in 1999 to 2.3 billion in 2005. NACP-III proposes to increase the supply of condoms further with effective back-up strategy to improve access and social marketing initiatives. It envisages increasing the supply of condoms to 3.5 billion pieces per annum by 2011. Of this, one billion pieces will form part of free distribution, two billion through social marketing initiatives and 0.5 billion pieces through commercial marketing. The support to condom programme is primarily for purchase of condoms for free and social marketing. The commercial marketing support will be from private out-of-pocket expenditure. The purchase of special condoms like female condoms and dotted and thicker condoms for MSM population is also separately taken into account while estimating the requirements. The demand generation activities for condom have not been budgeted here as they are likely to be part of Communication, Advocacy and Social Mobilisation. Social marketing organisations and logistic management at district level have been budgeted. Establishment of non-conventional outlets for condoms and condom vending machines are to be taken up as part of public-private partnerships. Financial requirements for this component are given in **Table 18.14**.

Table 18.14: Condom Promotion Budget

(Rs. lakh)

Activity	*Year 1*	*Year 2*	*Year 3*	*Year 4*	*Year 5*	*Total*
Condom Procurement	21,350	26,090	33,000	34,400	34,900	1,49,740
Female Condom Procurement	400	600	800	1,000	1,000	3,800
Social Marketing Programmes	4,000	4,700	4,100	4,050	3,900	20,750
Generic Promotion	3,000	3,300	2,600	2,100	1,600	12,600
IT Enabled Logistic Management	3,000	300	300	500	500	4,600
Innovations in Programming	1,000	1,000	1,000	2,000	2,500	7,500
Technical Support Group	200	211	230	200	200	1,041
Total	32,950	36,201	42,030	44,250	44,600	2,00,031

18.6.1 Financial Assumption

Condom programme costing is done in four parts viz., (a) social marketing programme, (b) generic promotion, (c) commodity procurement, and (d) others

Social marketing programme is based on classification of four categories of states:

States with population over 100 million – 1 @ Rs. 3 cr. pa.

States with population 50-100 million – 6 @ Rs. 3 cr. pa.

States with population 25-50 million – 5 @ Rs. 1.5 cr. pa.

States of population below 25 million – 13 @ Rs. 0.5 cr. pa.

Generic Promotion (bulk provision)

Generic promotion comprises two elements: Generic Promotion Campaign and Designing Condom Promotion Package

Condom Marketing

Male condoms – 3.5 billion pieces (1.75, 2.25, 3.00, 3.25 and 3.5 billion pieces in five years)

Year 1: 20% SM and 80% Free Supply. Total Condoms 1.75 bn
Year 2: 35% SM and 65% Free Supply. Total Condoms 2.25 bn

Year 3: 50% SM and 50% Free Supply. Total Condoms 3.00 bn

Year 4: 60% SM and 40% Free Supply. Total Condoms 3.25 bn

Year 5: 75% SM and 25% Free Supply Total Condoms: 3.50 bn

Female condoms: 5 million pieces

Others (Bulk provision)

Others comprise of three elements, namely, IT enabled logistics management, innovations in programming and technical support group.

18.7 ART Costing

Calculations for ART are given in Table 18.15.

Table 18.15: Financial Requirement for ART

	Year 1	*Year 2*	*Year 3*	*Year 4*	*Year 5*	*Total*
Target	100,000	150,000	200,000	250,000	300,000	
			(Rs. lakh)			
Capital Cost	2,018	569	81	0	0	2,668
Fixed Cost	2,170	3,295	3,438	3,438	3,438	15,779
Variable Cost						
Drugs	8,000	12,000	16,000	20,000	24,000	80,000
CD4/8 test	1,000	1,500	2,000	2,500	3,000	10,000
Viral Load test	2,500	3,750	5,000	6,250	7,500	25,000
Total Cost	15,688	21,114	26,519	32,188	37,938	133,447

Financial requirements, exclusively for ART, work out to be Rs. 1334 crore which is about 11.4 per cent of the total budget.

18.7.1 Financial Assumptions

- Based on patient load, 4 categories of ART centres are proposed. These centres will have different staff supplement to cater to the demand for patients.
- Number of centres
  - Category 1: existing – 0, new in year 1 – 57, year 2 – 63
  - Category 2: existing – 77, new in year 1 – 10, year 2 – 13

  - Category 3: existing – 0, new in year 1 – 0, year 2 – 59
  - Category 4: existing – 2, new in year 1 – 12, year 2 – 14
- Minor civil works and necessary modifications
  - Category 1: Rs. 30 lakh, Category 2: Rs. 20 lakh, Category 3: Rs. 10 lakh, Category 4: Rs. 5 lakh.
- Equipment: Rs. 75,000
- Human Resource: Category 1: Rs. 1.39 lakhs p.m, Category 2: Rs. 1.03 lakh p.m, Category 3: Rs. 0.95 lakhs pm, Category 4: Rs. 0.75 lakh p.m.
- Consumables: Rs. 50,000 per centre p.a.
- ART drugs @ Rs. 8,000 per patient p.a.
- CD4 tests @ Rs. 1,000 per patient p.a.
- Viral load test @ Rs. 2,500 per patient p.a.

18.8 Paediatric ART

NACP-III plans to provide paediatric ART to 40,000 cases over a period of five years through 10 centres in the country. The total cost of the programme comes to Rs. 111 crore, as given in **Table 18.16**.

Table 18.16: Target and Budget for Paediatric ART

	Year 1	*Year 2*	*Year 3*	*Year 4*	*Year 5*	*Total*
Target	10,000	15,000	20,000	30,000	40,000	
No. of Centre	10	10	10	10	10	
						Rs. lakh
Cost of Personnel	60	60	60	60	60	300
DNA PCR Testing	90	90	90	90	90	450
Paediatric ART drug cost	900	1,350	1,800	2,700	3,600	10,350
Total Cost	1,050	1,500	1,950	2,850	3,750	11,100

18.9 Cost of Creating Centres of Excellence

NACP-III proposes to create 5 adult and 5 paediatric centres of excellence. Construction for 10 centres at the rate of Rs. 20 lakh per centre will be carried out during the second year of the programme. Salary cost for 10 research fellowships at the rate of Rs. 15,000 per month and training centres staff (5-8 people) will be provided at the rate of Rs. 50,000 per month. Research cost at the rate of Rs. 10 lakh per centre per year will be provided (see **Table 18.17**).

Table 18.17: Budget for Centres of Excellence

	Year 1	*Year 2*	*Year 3*	*Year 4*	*Year 5*	*Total (Rs. lakh)*
Construction Cost	0	200	0	0	0	200
Human Resource Cost	0	240	240	240	240	960
Research Cost	0	100	100	100	100	400
Total Cost	0	540	340	340	340	1,560

18.10 Care and Support (Community Care Centres, OIs and Impact Mitigation)

NACP-III proposes to set up 350 Community Care Centres. This will be done in partnership with PLHA networks and other CBOs. Financial plan is based on setting up 190 centres in the first year, going up to 310 in the second year and finally 350 in the third year. Other activities under this component include PLHA training, OI intervention, ART follow-up and drop-in-centres managed by PLHA networks. These drop-in-centres will provide positive living support and treatment counselling. NACP-III has also estimated capital expenditure requirement for viral load equipments to be set up in five regions. The proposed budget for this component is Rs. 493 crore for five years as per details given in **Table 18.18**.

Table 18.18: Budget Estimates for Care and Support

Component	*Year 1*	*Year 2*	*Year 3*	*Year 4*	*Year 5*	*Total*
Community Support Centres (Numbers)	190	310	350	350	350	
						(Rs. lakh)
Community Support Centres	3,301	5,410	5,816	5,694	5,694	25,917
Support to NGO for ART	1,200	2,400	2,400	2,400	2,400	10,800
ART Material	152	152	152	152	152	760
PLHA Training	190	190	190	190	190	950
Drop-in-Centres	750	750	750	750	750	3,750
Impact Mitigation	720	720	720	720	720	3,600
Opportunistic Infections	606	606	606	606	606	3,030
Regional Centres	58	58	58	58	58	288
PCR	125	0	0	0	0	125
Viral Load machines	100	0	0	0	0	100
Total	7,202	10,286	10,692	10,570	10,570	49,320

18.11 Establishment Support and Capacity Strengthening

It is estimated that in NACP-III, each SACS in 7 high prevalence states will get 2 vehicles, which SACS in 31 other states will get one vehicle each. The cost of each vehicle is estimated at Rs. 6 lakh each (see **Table 18.19**).

Table 18.19: Budget Estimates for Establishment Support and Capacity Strengthening

						(Rs. lakh)
Component	***Year 1***	***Year 2***	***Year 3***	***Year 4***	***Year 5***	***Total***
Salary	2,000	2,500	3,000	3,500	3,800	14,800
Infrastructure, office Equipment	500	500	1,000	1,000	500	3,500
Other establishment expenses	630	1,500	2,000	2,500	2,500	9,130
Vehicles	270	0	0	0	0	270
Total	3,400	4,500	6,000	7,000	6,800	27,700

18.12 Training in NACP-III

NACP-III proposes to earmark Rs. 220 crore (see **Table 18.20**) for training of different categories of staff. Training for Medical Officers in various government medical institutions is supposed to be carried out under RCH programme. It is estimated that NACP-III will train around 3.8 lakh personnel of different categories.

Table 18.20: Budget Estimates for Training

								(Rs. lakh)
Activity	*No. of Person*	*No. of Days*	*Year 1*	*Year 2*	*Year 3*	*Year 4*	*Year 5*	*Total*
NACO/ SACS Staff	500	3	65		65			130
DAPU	3,200	10	503		503			1,007
Targeted Intervention	2,100	3	436	502	554	554	554	2,600
Civil Society (600 districts)	15,000	2	98		98			195
25 heads of department at district level	15,000	2	68		68			135
25 block level officials	15,000	2	68		68			135
IEC training	Bulk		500		500			1,000
ART training	Bulk		600		600			1,200
Blood safety	Bulk		800		800			1,600
Surveillance & M&E	Bulk		500		500			1,000
ICTC	Bulk		4,400		4,400			8,800
Private Providers - RMP in A & B Districts	125,000	5	1,688		1,688			3,375
Private GPs for STD & OI Management	5,000	2	38		38			75
Public Health Functionaries including AYUSH	200,000		300		300			600
Training Module Development			150					150
Training Budget (Rs. lakh)			10,212	502	10.180	554	554	22,002

18.13 Mainstreaming/Private Sector Partnerships

NACP-III recognises that HIV/AIDS has to be on the agenda of development and regulatory agencies belonging to all sectors. It proposes to achieve this through mainstreaming and partnerships with government departments, the civil society and the private sector. NACO, under the guidance of National Council on AIDS, has already initiated steps to draw up department/sector specific plans of action on HIV/AIDS.

Financial requirements for this activity are based on mapping exercise to be carried out by holding sensitization and advocacy meetings with various departments, agencies and focusing on RCH convergence. Similar steps would also be followed with national/state level business trusts to mainstream HIV within the Corporate Social Responsibility Strategy of the private sector. Individual corporate entities or consortia would be provided with technical support for mainstreaming. The expenditure on mainstreaming, other than technical support, will be met from the budgets of the private sector.

Based on this, the budget estimates for mainstreaming and public-private partnerships are given in **Table 18.21**.

Table 18.21: Budget Estimates for Mainstreaming

(Rs. lakh)

Activity	*Year 1*	*Year 2*	*Year 3*	*Year 4*	*Year 5*	*Total*
Mapping	95	0	95	0	0	190
Advocacy Meeting	76	76	76	76	76	380
Sensitisation	76	76	76	76	76	380
Follow-up	100	100	100	100	100	500
Skill Building	152	152	152	152	152	760
Orientation of Staffs	95	95	0	0	0	190
Advocacy: Departmental agencies	1,520	1,520	1,520	1,520	1,520	7,600
Bi-annual Review	114	114	114	114	114	570
RCH Convergence	380	380	380	380	380	1,900
Total	2,608	2,513	2,513	2,418	2,418	12,470

18.14 Strategic Information Management

A nation-wide Strategic Information Management System (SIMS) would be developed and implemented for effective monitoring and evaluation of the programme. The establishment and maintenance of SIMS will include dedicated units with sufficient personnel and support systems for management etc. Following **tables (18.22, 18.23)** indicate budget requirements for SIMS and its subcomponents.

Table 18.22: Budget Estimate for SIMS

(Rs. lakh)						
Activity	***Year 1***	***Year2***	***Year3***	***Year4***	***Year5***	***Total***
SIMU	3,000	3,000	4,500	4,500	4,500	19,500
Surveillance	1,000	1,500	1,500	2,000	2,000	8,000
Research	1,000	1,500	2,000	2,000	2,000	8,500
Total	5,000	6,000	8,000	8,500	8,500	36,000

Table 18.23: Budget Estimate for SIM Unit

(Rs. lakh)						
Cost heads	***Year 1***	***Year 2***	***Year 3***	***Year 4***	***Year 5***	***Total***
Personnel	100	200	300	300	300	1,200
Str. Systems	800	600	700	700	700	3,500
Hardware/software/supplies	1,400	600	900	900	900	4,700
Technical assistance	300	800	1,200	1,000	900	4,200
Data generation/dissemination	200	400	700	800	800	2,900
Maintenance of systems	200	400	700	800	900	3,000
Total	3,000	3,000	4,500	4,500	4,500	19,500

18.15 Surveillance

Surveillance related activity-wise break-up and financial requirements are given in **Table 18.24**.

Table 18.24: Budget Estimate for Surveillance

(Rs. lakh)						
Cost Heads	***Year 1***	***Year 2***	***Year 3***	***Year 4***	***Year 5***	***Total***
Sentinel survey	300	300	300	400	400	1,700
STI survey	400	400	400	400	400	2,000
Annual risk assessment	150	150	150	200	200	850
BSS	0	400	0	400	400	1,200
Drug resistance surveillance	50	100	100	400	400	1,050
Evaluation	100	150	150	200	200	800
National family health survey	0	0	400	0	0	400
Total	1,000	1,500	1,500	2 000	2,000	8,000

18.16 Research

Bulk provision for identification of institutes, operational research, and national level research has been estimated according to programme objectives (see **Table 18.25**).

Table 18.25: Budget Estimate for Research

(Rs. lakh)						
Activity	***Year 1***	***Year 2***	***Year 3***	***Year 4***	***Year 5***	***Total***
Research	1,000	1,500	2,000	2,000	2,000	8,500

18.17 Managing Programme Implementation and Contracts

Most of the activities under the objectives of NACP-III are implemented by agencies outside of NACO and SACS. This can be seen as contracting out services by NACO and SACS. The effectiveness of programme implementation critically hinges on the performance of these contracts. NACP-III programme implementation plan can, therefore, be viewed as a series of contracts issued to various agencies who will be involved in ensuring that programme activities are implemented effectively.

It is envisaged that the number of such contracts will be in the range of 1,700 to 3,000 each year. Assuming that each renewed contract is treated as a fresh one, NACP-III will be handling nearly 12,620 contracts during the five year period. This includes the contracts issued to various NGOs, CBOs, research institutions, social marketing institutions and project support units etc.

NACP-III considers that the actual number of contracts is going to be much larger than the above number as there would be multi-tiered contracts and contracting agencies managing the sub-contracts. For example, if social marketing agencies are to be hired in every state, they can neither be managed by one national agency nor by SACS. Therefore, NACP-III proposes to set up five regional agencies to manage the SM contracts in their respective region. Broadly, these contracts can be seen as emanating from (a) NACO to national SM management agency, (b) from national SM agency to regional agencies, and (c) from regional agencies to individual marketing agencies. Similar arrangements would be needed in other areas which, among other things, would include:

- Procurement and Logistics;
- Strategic Information Management (for surveillance and behavioural surveillance);
- Research and Knowledge Management;
- External Quality Assurance;
- Migrant Support; and
- Technical Support Units for TIs.

Managing such large number of contracts is a major challenge for NACP-III. A key issue in contracting for services is the design of contracts which ensures quality of services at the lowest cost. Thus, NACP-III proposes to allocate specific budgets for managing the implementation process of such large number of contracts. It envisages that these contracts will be issued at the level of SACS and NACO. There will also be private agencies that are involved in implementing the programme through public-private partnerships and will also be issuing contracts directly.

It is proposed that while attempting to develop these contracts, performance and effectiveness should be integrated as part of the contract and stated in an explicit manner. In most performance contracts in the health sectors, it is sometimes difficult to verify various attributes of performance and quality. Therefore, contracts would necessarily be designed in such a manner that these provide appropriate and adequate incentives to implementing agencies to meet the objectives and ensuring that they are effective.

NACP-III proposes to use the second approach of developing incentives. It recognises the role of "implicit incentives" that may emerge from long-term relationships between the principal and the contract implementing agencies based on an informal understanding that as long as the agency performs at some satisfactory level (i.e. meeting benchmarks), it will be retained by the principal in the future. Sometimes, these implicit incentives are strong enough to maintain long-term relationships.

NACP-III has already defined the targets and package of services and benchmarks will be developed based on these, and accordingly the contracts will be implemented. It must also be recognised that NACP-III retains all risks related to supplies and availability of financial resources. These risks in some sense are insured and implementing agency would not have any financial risks. This would have implications for minimising the cost of contracts.

It is estimated that the total cost of managing these contracts would be Rs. 288 crore for five years. In addition, other monitoring costs would include: writing of contracts, search and bargaining costs and the thinking-through process provisions in contracts, besides various coordination issues. Most of the contracts envisaged in NACP are short-duration contracts and generally of one year duration. NACP-III proposes to limit the duration of these contracts to one/one and half-year so that appropriate feedback can be given to the providers of services at regular intervals. This will ensure that standards of quality of service are maintained.

18.18 Contracting for TA Contracts

NACO will develop appropriate contracting out procedure. This will focus on ensuring that most credible firms participate in the process. Conditions for selection will be laid down to ensure that the firms providing these services have adequate capacities and competencies. Adequate weightages would be given to these competencies and capabilities in selection process. The prospective firms would be invited to apply trough an advertisement. A meeting of top officials of NACO would be scheduled before the process is launched to sensitize the prospective providers about the contract requirements and provide them adequate information on various areas of contract. Based on the extent to which the firms demonstrate their understanding of the context, NACO's specific requirements, the firms' experience in assisting other organizations in similar requirements and the costs and time frames mentioned in the proposals, the most eligible firm will be short listed and invited to provide the required assistance and making available specialist services. The short listed firms must have adequate experience in providing services (see **Table 18.26**).

NACO will develop detailed guidelines for award of contracts and monitoring performance. These will include the following:

Objective Identification: Contracting arrangements can not be seen as ad hoc solutions to various problems. In order to have an objective identification of services to be contracted, NACO will carry out an economic analysis of in-house costs of carrying out the services. It must be ensured that there is no unfair distribution of risk to government.

Incentive System: There are three approaches which could guide the programme in developing incentive systems. These are: (a) payment, based on performance, (b) granting complete autonomy to implementing agency but monitoring the process of implementation and setting benchmarks and making payments based on compliance with the benchmarks, and (c) residual claims where the programme generates revenue. NACP-III proposes to use the second approach of developing incentives. NACP-III has already defined the targets for package of services. These targets define various requirements of services. Benchmarks will be developed based on these, and accordingly the contracts will be implemented. Since these contracts would be coming up for renewal, it provides a strong incentive to the provider to adhere to standards of quality and also gives flexibility to NACO/SACS.

Managing Conflicts: NACO will prepare appropriate guidelines to resolve issues and any conflicts which may arise while implementing contracts. NACO will strengthen the capacity to handle the contractual relationships. These include financial, negotiation and conflict resolution and legal skills. It is also evident that basic administrative systems such as financial, accounting and filing systems need to be in place for contracting out services.

Table 18.26: Technical Support Needs

	Purpose of the TA	*How/Mechanisms*	*No of Contracts*	*Who will do / Budget*	*(Rs. lakhs)*
Objective 1 Prevention					
Targeted Interventions among HRGs (FSW, MSM, IDU)	Provide TA to SACS to increase TIs from 700 to 2100	Contract one national level institution to support NACO	1	Partner agencies such as DFID	125
		Contract TSUs to assist SACS in identifying implementation agencies and managing the implementation of TIs through NGOs and CBOs s	20	DFID/Other Partners	9214
Other Interventions (truckers, street children, migrants etc.)	Provide technical support to NHAI, State agencies to set up and manage truckers interventions	Contract a national and five regional institutions	1+5	DFI / Other partners	1700
	Provide TA to NACO and SACS to manage migrant interventions	Contract a national and two regional institutions	1+2	DFI / Other partners	
Package of Services all districts (in PPTCT, ICTC, STI, Safety measures, OI & PEP)	Build the capacity of support institutions to facilitate expansion of preventive services up to PHC level	Contract regional institutions at and attach state training institutions to them for training and mentoring	10	Partner Partner agencies such asDFID	2500
Blood Safety (state + national level)	Provide technical support to NACO/ SACS in promoting voluntary blood donation, rational use of blood and logistics	Collaboration with Indian Red Cross	1	Partner agencies such as DFID	250
	Technical support to NACO for quality control, safety issues and other bio medical issues	Contract a national institution	1	Partner agencies such as DFID	250

	Purpose of the TA	*How/Mechanisms*	*No of Contracts*	*Who will do / Budget*	*(Rs. lakhs)*
Communication, Advocacy and Social Mobilisation (CASM)	Technical support to NACO to develop communication strategies and implementation guidelines	Contract a national agency/institution	1	UNICEF	250
	Technical support to SACS to design communication campaigns	Contract regional institutions and link states to them	6	Partner agencies such as DFID	1500
Condom Promotion (state + national level)	Manage social marketing	Contracting social marketing agencies	5	NACO, Private Sector	1250
ART	Train service providers to scale up treatment services up to district level and delivery of drugs up to CHC	Contract institutions with sufficient case load and experienced persons	10	WHO	1000
Care and Support	Technical support to NACO to develop protocols and standard operating manuals	Contract a national institutions	1		3000
Objective 3 Capacity Building					
Establishment Support and Capacity strengthening of SACS/NACO/DAPCUs	Provide support to NACO/ SACS for strengthening HR, decision making, finance and other management systems	Contract institutions at national and regional levels	1+4	Partner agencies such as DFID	500
	Support procurement units of NACO/ MoHFW / Procurement Agent for developing Technical Specifications, TORs, contract compliance and evaluation	Contract a national institution	1 + 4		500

	Purpose of the TA	How/Mechanisms	No of Contracts	Who will do / Budget	(Rs. lakhs)
Managing contract	Support NACO/SACS to contract other service providers and ensure contract compliance	Contract a national institution	1	Partner agencies such as DFID	100
Mainstreaming/Private Sector partnerships	Technical support to participating ministries to conduct risk and vulnerability analysis and mainstream prevention strategies	Contract institutions at national and regional level	2+4		1500
Objective 4 Strategic Information Management					
Strategic Information Management	Support to NACO/ SACS for use of Strategic information for programme planning and management	Contract institutions at national and regional level	1+4	AVAHAN/CDC/UNAIDS	625
Surveillance	Technical support to NACO/SACS to strengthen surveillance	Contract one epidemiologist for NACO and each state	1+ 38	AVAHAN	2000
Research	Technical support to NACO to facilitate identification of research priorities and manage research programmes and dissemination	Contract one national institution and consortium of institutions (10 institutions)	1+10		2500

Assumptions

- For TIs ,one contract will handle about 14 TIs and each contract will cost Rs10 lakhs. This includes the salary of resource persons to monitor these TIs
- For other interventions one contract will handle 5 interventions and each contract will cost Rs10 lakhs
- Monitoring each Community care centre would cost rs 10 lakhs and a national institution to oversee the whole activities
- TSU cost would cost Rs 25 lakhs
- Other contracts are also major contracts and each contract would cost Rs 20 lakhs

In addition to strengthening basic administrative systems, NACP-III should consider the following measures in order to strengthen its capacity to contract out services:

- Strengthen information systems to monitor contractor performance;
- Ensure a clear definition of roles between various members of stakeholders;
- Strengthen capacity at various levels to handle contracts;
- Ensure clear lines of communication between various stakeholders;
- Define clearly the performance of contracts;
- Ensure that NACO has direct control over the contract during contract negotiation and throughout the life of the contract;
- Ensure capacities are in place to directly negotiate the contract itself;
- Make available clear guidelines to guide the contracting process;
- Ensure that the guidelines incorporate measures (such as clear criteria for selecting the contract winner, requirements for numbers of bids) to ensure transparency;
- Build evaluations of previous contracts into the contracting process so that NACO can expect better performance from contracts in future;
- Draw upon contracting experience and skills acquired in other sectors and other countries.

The summary of financial requirements for NACP-III is given in the Table 18.27

Table 18.27: Financial Requirement of NACP-III

(Rs. crore)

Programme Components	*Total*	*per cent*
Objective 1: Prevention		
1. Targeted Interventions among HRGs (FSW, MSM and IDUs)	2288	19.7%
2. Other interventions (Truckers, Prison inmates, Migrants etc.)	132	1.1%
3. Package of Services	1393	12.0%
4. Blood Safety (including mobile blood banks)	955	8.2%
5. Communication, Advocacy and Social Mobilisation	1018	8.8%
6. Condom Promotion	2000	17.3%
Sub-total	**7786**	**67.2%**
Objective 2: Care, Support and Treatment		
7. ART	1334	11.5%
7.1 Paediatric ART	111	1.0%

(Contd...)

7.2 Centre of Excellence	15	0.1%
8. Care and Support (Community Care Centres and Impact Mitigation)	493	4.3%
Sub-total	**1953**	**16.9%**
Objective 3: Capacity Building		
9. Establishment Support and Capacity Strengthening	277	2.4%
10. Training	220	1.9%
11. Mainstreaming/Private Sector Partnerships	125	1.1%
12. Managing Programme Implementation and Contracts	288	2.5%
Sub-total	**910**	**7.9%**
Objective 4: Strategic Information Management		
13. Monitoring and Evaluation	195	1.7%
14. Surveillance	80	0.7%
15. Research	85	0.7%
Sub-total	**360**	**3.1%**
16. Contingency @ 5%	576	5.0%
Grand Total	**11,585**	**100.0%**

Summary of year-wise financial requirements are given in the Table 18.28.

Table 18.28: Year-wise Financial Requirement of NACP – III

(Rs. crore)

Programme Components	***Year 1***	***Year 2***	***Year 3***	***Year 4***	***Year 5***	***Total***	***per cent***
Objective 1: Prevention							
1. Targeted Interventions among HRGs (FSW, MSM and IDUs)	278	398	556	528	528	2288	19.7%
2. Other interventions (Truckers, Prison inmates, Migrants etc.)	19	25	29	30	29	132	1.1%
3. Package of Services	213	262	281	301	336	1393	12.0%
4. Blood Safety (including mobile blood banks)	243	191	243	139	139	955	8.2%
5. Communication, Advocacy and Social Mobilisation	213	209	219	194	183	1018	8.8%
6. Condom Promotion	329	362	420	443	446	2000	17.3%
Sub-total	1,295	1,447	1,748	1,635	1,661	7,786	67.2%
Objective 2: Care, Support and Treatment							
7. ART	157	211	265	322	379	1334	11.5%
7.1 Paediatric ART	11	15	19	28	38	111	1.0%
7.2 Centre of Excellence	0	5	4	3	3	15	0.1%
8. Care and support (Community Care Centres and Impact Mitigation)	72	103	107	106	105	493	4.3%
Sub-total	240	334	395	459	525	1953	16.9%
Objective 3: Capacity Building							
9. Establishment Support and Capacity strengthening	34	45	60	70	68	277	2.4%
10. Training	102	5	102	6	5	220	1.9%

(Contd...)

11. Mainstreaming/Private Sector Partnerships	26	25	25	24	24	125	1.1%
12. Managing Programme Implementation and Contracts	44	53	60	66	66	288	2.5%
Sub-total	206	128	246	166	163	910	7.9%
Objective 4: Strategic Information Management							
13. Strategic Information Management	30	30	45	45	45	195	1.7%
14. Surveillance	10	15	15	20	20	80	0.7%
15. Research	10	15	20	20	20	85	0.7%
Sub-total	50	60	80	85	85	360	3.1%
16. Contingency @ 5%	92	102	130	123	130	576	5.0%
Grand Total	1,882	2,071	2,599	2,469	2,564	11,585	100.0%
	16%	18%	23%	21%	22%	100%	

Chapter - 19

Programme Strategies - Outcome, Challenges and Risks

This section discusses objective-wise programme implementation outcome and risks.

Strategic Objective 1: Prevention

NACP-III proposes to spend approximately 67.2 per cent of the total budget on prevention. This includes targeted interventions and package of services (excluding ART). Financial requirements for TIs and package of services have been arrived at after taking into account the district classification based on risks and targets set for NACP-III.

The key risk factors and implementation issues include developing effective partnerships, networking of workplace interventions and clarity of state governments' policies to promote NGO/CBO partnerships. NACP-III proposes to link the performance of TIs and package of services with the targets set for the programme. Considerable capacity strengthening at various levels will be required as the programme performance hinges on availability of good counsellors, availability and involvement of resource persons, and development of IEC strategy. To reduce the risk factors, NACP-III proposes to set benchmarks for performance indicators for package of services which will focus on utilisation of services, referrals and counselling etc. Demand generation will be the key focus of IEC strategies. The success of TIs will also depend on how fast the ownership is transferred to CBOs. The risk factors are acceptability of support and facilitative supervision by CBOs.

Strategic Objective 2: Care, Support and Treatment

NACP-III proposes to invest 16.9 per cent of the total budget on this component. This includes ART services. The financial requirements for ART have been worked out on the basis of package of services, discussed earlier.

Key risk factors and implementation issues include the change in treatment protocol of ART. Involvement of NGOs and CBOs in care and support is critical. Since this component of activities will involve considerable amount of contracting out of services, the capacity to handle these contracts and the policy of state governments assume critical significance. Quality indicators and composite benchmark will be set accordingly. Networking strategies and involvement of PLHA will also be crucial to the success of CST implementation strategies.

Strategic Objective 3: Strengthening Capacities

Approximately 7.9 per cent of the total budget has been earmarked for strengthening of capacities and meeting administrative costs of implementing agencies at national, state, and district levels. This component also includes mainstreaming activities. The budgets indicated are based on preliminary estimates of total requirements and need to be revised as per institutional framework and training needs. Most of the budgets under this component are discretionary in nature. Therefore, for this component, an appropriate strategic plan will be required. It would be important to discuss the broad objectives and strategy for convergence of each activity and indicate means to verify how the activity has been carried out and develop benchmarks to measure the effectiveness of such activities.

Risk factors and implementation issues include assessment of training needs, competency of training institutions and benchmarks to assess the process and training outcome. The mainstreaming activities will need clear statement of goals and clear identification of risk factors. It would be critical to discuss the strategy with all stakeholders and include their perspective in implementation. Availability of high level resource persons who can handle the tasks of networking and developing collaborative strategies is another critical risk factor.

Strategic Objective 4: Strategic Information Management System

NACP-III proposes to allocate 3.1 per cent of the total budget for this component. Risk factors and implementation issues include availability of good research institutions to carry out surveillance and develop knowledge base. Concept of knowledge management will be introduced in the programme. Given the constraints on availability of good resource persons, NACP-III proposes to identify academic institutions of excellence to carry out various research tasks.

Challenges and Risks

Some programmes, particularly those which have discretionary expenditure components, face challenge of ensuring that money spent is as per the objective of the programme. Fiduciary risks arise when funds are not spent as per the objectives of the programme or do not deliver the results or organisation does not have adequate system to properly account for these funds. Proper implementation and management of NACP-III will address the fiduciary risk in the programme implementation.

In order to address this risk, the following has been envisaged in the proposed programme:

- Linking performance of high value interventions like targeted intervention and package of services with the targets set for the programme;
- Create benchmarks of performance indicators for package of services which with a focus on utilisation of services, referrals and counselling etc;
- Make performance and effectiveness an integral part of the contract and state it in an explicit manner;
- Grant complete autonomy to implementing agency for ensuring quality and achieving the desired outcome, but monitor the process of implementation and setting benchmarks and making payments, based on compliance with the benchmarks; and
- Adequately address fiduciary risks and draw clear guidelines for utilisation of funds and audit requirements.

Chapter - 20

Programme Strategies – Targets for NACP Implementation

Sl. No.	*Description*	*Programme Targets (units)*	*Year-end Targets*						
			2005	**2006**	**2007**	**2008**	**2009**	**2010**	**2011**
1-A	**Prevention Package in High Risk Population**								
1	Number of sex workers and their clients reached by intervention per year	1 million	0.44	0.55	0.65	0.80	1.00	1.00	1.00
2	Number of MSM reached by intervention per year	1.15 million	0.12	0.46	0.69	0.92	1.15	1.15	1.15
3	Number of IDUs accessing needle exchange	0.19 million	0.087	0.114	0.133	0.152	0.19	0.19	0.19
4	Number of TI for CSW, MSM, IDUs	2100	691	700	1300	1800	2100	2100	2100
	Prevention Package for Bridge Population								
5	Number of Truckers reached by intervention per year	3 million	1.5	1.8	2.1	2.4	3.00	3.00	3.00
6	Number of migrants covered through migrant support programmes	150 million	15	22.5	30	37.5	45	60	50
1-B	**Prevention in General Population**								
7	Rural population (15-45 yrs) reached through mass media and local activities	280 million	154	168	196	224	252	280	280
8	Number of schools with Adolescent Education Programme	144409	72205	86645	101086	115527	129968	144409	100

(*Contd...*)

9	Number of students covered under Adolescent Education Programme	25 million	8	10	12.5	15	17.5	17.5	70
10	Number of non-student youth reached	70 million	3.5	7	7	10.5	10.5	14	20
	Condom Promotion								
11	Number of condoms distributed	3500 million/year	1050	1400	1750	2450	2800	3150	100
12	Number condoms distributed by social marketing programmes	2000 million /year	600	600	700	800	900	1000	1200
13	Number of sex acts by HRG in which condoms are used	1200 million /year	600	660	720	840	960	1080	1080
14	Number of SM condoms utilized in TI	1000 million /year	100	300	500	700	800	900	1000
15	Number of commercial condoms	500 million/year	150	275	300	325	350	350	350
16	Number of free condoms	1000 million/year	500	450	400	350	300	280	280
	Improving STI Management								
17	Number of adults with STI symptoms accessing syndromic management	30 million	1	5	10	15	20	25	30
18	Number of STI accessing laboratory services	2 million	0.1	0.6.	0.8	1.0	1.4	1.6	2.0
	Voluntary Counselling and Testing								
19	Number of vulnerable population and clients of sex workers accessing ICTC services	22 million/year	1	3	6.5	12	15	18	22
	Blood Safety Measures								
20	Number of units of blood for transfusion	8.5 million	4.4	6.0	7.0	8.0	9.0	10	10
21	Number of Blood Component Separation Units established (cumulative)	162 units	82	100	130	162	162	162	162
22	Percentage of voluntary blood donation	90%	52	55	60	70	80	80	90
23	Number of plasma Fractionation Units established (cumulative)	2 units	1	1	2	2	2	2	2
	PPTCT Interventions								
24	Number of PPTCT centres established	4955	1508	2815	4333	4955	4955	4955	4955

(Contd...)

25	Number of pregnant women covered through PPTCT Counselling	7.5 million	0.64	2.0	2.02	3.78	4.9	6.5	7.5
26	Number of HIV infected mother baby pairs receiving prophylaxis ART	75600	16800	47250	56700	66150	70875	75600	75600
27	Number of Community Care Centres established and functioning well	350	50	121	69	120	40	350	350
28	Number of CHC, District & Tertiary Hospitals (PH) having access to PEP	3000	1200	1500	1800	2100	2400	27000	100
29	Safety Measures and Infection Control								
30	Number of Public health institutions supported for safety measures	3000	150	450	900	1500	1800	24000	90
II	**Care, Support and Treatment**								
31	Total Number of HIV +ve People in millions	5.21 million	5.206	5.082	5.018	4.933	4.846	4.780	5.21
32	Number of PLHA with AIDS	0.38 million	0.411	0.407	0.401	0.395	0.388	0.382	0.379
33	Number of OI episodes treated in public sector	0.33 million OI episodes	0.329	0.325	0.321	0.316	0.310	0.306	0.303
34	Number of AIDS patients needing TB referral	2.8 million per year	0.5	1.0	1.5	2.0	2.8	2.8	2.8
35	Number of ART centres established	250	54	100	125	150	200	225	250
36	Number of PLHA provided ART in the programme under public sector	0.3 million	0.035	0.100	0.150	0.200	0.250	0.300	0.300
37	Total number of children with HIV 0-14 Years	0.170 million	0.170	0.1696	0.1649	0.159	0.152	0.1462	0.140 1
38	Number of children requiring ART	0.04 million	5000	10000	15000	20000	30000	40000	40000
III	**Capacity Building**								
39	Number of Sero-Surveillance sites established	1200	600	600	1200	1200	1200	1200	1200
40	District level risk assessment studies	606 per year		154	465	606	606	606	606
41	Number of National BSS rounds completed	1 every 3 years		1				1	
42	Number of district units established	606 DAPCU	0	154	465	606	606	606	606
IV	**Monitoring and Evaluation**								
43	Number of research institutions supported	25		10	20	25	25	25	25
44	Number of research projects completed at the national/regional level	15 per year		5	10	15	15	15	15

Table 20.2: Basis for arriving at NACP-III Targets

Description	*Programme Targets*	*Rationale*
Prevention Package in High Risk Population		
Number of female sex workers reached by intervention per year	1 million	80% of 1.25 million Female Sex Workers estimated by expert group
Number of MSM reached by intervention per year	1.15 million	2.3 million MSM > 5 partners- HRG estimation by Expert Group. The programme will cover 50%
Number of IDUs accessing needle exchange	0.19 million	Expert group has estimated 1.8 +0.33 IDUs in the country. Programme will cover 90%.
Number of TI for CSW, MSM, IDUs	2100	Expert Group estimation
Number of truckers reached by intervention per year	3 million	Expert Group estimation of long distance truckers
Number of migrants covered through migrant support programmes	150 million	314 million migrants: Census India 2001 (221 million women and 93 million men) – 50% covered under programme
Prevention in General Population		
Number of rural population (15-45 yrs) reached through mass media and local activities	280 million	1 billion 70% in rural area. 60% of this population in the age group of 15-45 will be 420 million. The programme will target 66% of this population.
Number of schools with Adolescent Education Programme	144409	144409 Government Schools in the country
Number of students covered under school AIDS programme	25 million	Children in class 9th -11th grade in school
Number of non-student youth reached	70 million	400 million Youth – School /college /university about 50 million – 20% of out of school youth will be reached.
Number of workforce covered through interventions in the world of work	30 million	20 million workers in public sector and 10 million in private sector

(Contd...)

Number of sex acts by HRG in which condoms are used	1.2 billion/year	1.2 billion per year -50% condom covered from free 25% Social Marketing (SM), 25% Commercial Condom
Number of SM condoms utilized	1000 million /year	Expert Group estimation
Number of condoms distributed	3500 million /year	Expert Group
Number of condoms distributed by social marketing programmes	2000 million /year	
Number of commercial condoms	500 million/year	
Number of free condoms	1000 million/ year	
Number of adults with STI symptoms accessing syndromic management	30 million	5% of 600 million adults in India have STD symptoms. The programme will cover 50% (UNGAS) of those with symptoms totalling 15 million. 50% will be covered through Private Providers and will be the target for NACP-III (600 D + 3000 CHC + 22000 PHC + 22000 PP @ 2 cases per day
Number of persons with STI accessing laboratory services in public sector	2 million	Estimated that 2% of those provided syndromic management would need laboratory investigations
Number of vulnerable population and clients of sex workers accessing ICTC services	22 million/year	There are 60 million adults indulging in high risk behaviour (10% of adult population) and 3 million HRG group will have at least one test per year. The programme will progressively target to deliver ICTC services to 22 million/year of this vulnerable population
Number of units of blood for transfusion	8.5 million	Population standard for requirement of blood
Percentage of voluntary blood donation	90%	Currently 52% . estimated increase to 90%
Number of Blood Component Separation Units established (cumulative)	162 units	Currently available 82. Additional 80 new units will be supported
Number of plasma Fractionation Units established (cumulative)	2 units	Existing one; New one will be added.

(Contd...)

Number of pregnant women covered through PPTCT counselling & testing	7.5 million	27 million deliveries, 60% institutional. Six high prevalence states: 6.3 million (24% of pregnancies and 59% of all HIV+ve pregnant women), Epidemiologically vulnerable states 13.1 million (47% of pregnant women and 27% of HIV+ve), Other low prevalence and low vulnerable states: 8 million (29% and 12% of HIV+ve). Total of 7.5 million pregnant women
Number of HIV infected mother baby pairs receiving prophylaxis ART	75600	59% of HIV positives women in high prevalence states, 27% in vulnerable states and 12% in other states.
Number of CHC, District & Tertiary Hospitals (PH) having access to PEP	3000	All public sector units
Public Sector Institutions to be strengthened for infection control/safety measures including contruction	3000	
Number of PLHA with AIDS reached through the programme	0.38 million	It is estimated that 10% of 5.134 million PLHA (estimated in 2004) will be immuno-compromised. Currently only 10% of them know their HIV status. Currently 15%: increase to 80% by 2011 through effective outreach of services under NACP-III. It is envisaged that the programme will reach a target of 3.8 million by end of 5 years.
Number of people needing care with access to OI treatment	0.33 million OI episodes	10% of PLHA are immuno-compromised and prone to have Opportunistic Infections. 4 OI episodes per year reported (Tambaram). ART likely to reduce the OI incidence by 60%. The estimate of total number of OI episodes in 80% of identified AIDS patients will be 0.66 million (5.134 m x 0.8 x 0.1 x 4 x 0.4). Programme will target 50% of OI episodes under NACP-III resulting in an estimated 0.33 million OI episodes per year.

(*Contd...*)

Number of AIDS patients needing TB referral	2.8 million	Tuberculosis is the most common and serious OI seen in PLHA with a reported incidence of nearly 15% per year among AIDS patients. However to identify 15% of active TB in PLHA, nearly 5 times that number of suspected patients will need to be referred from ICTC and other service units to DOTS/Microscopic centres. This will amount to nearly 2.8 million referrals per year.
Number of PLHA provided ART in the programme	0.3 million	This is a national commitment made by the government and the rationale has been provided in the document itself under treatment section.
Number of children receiving ART	40,000	Expert Group estimate
Capacity Building		
Number of Sero-Surveillance sites established	1200	Expert Group estimate
Risk assessment studies	606 per year	
Number of National BSS rounds completed	1 every 3 years	
Number of district units established	611	
Monitoring and Evaluation		
Number of research institutions supported	25	
Number of research projects completed at the national/regional level	5-15 per year	

References

1. Andrews M. 2008. The good governance agenda: beyond indicators without theory. *Oxford Development Studies* 36: 379–407.
2. Bennett S, Hanson K, Kadama P, Montagu D. 2005. *Working with the Non-state Sector to Achieve Public Health Goals. Making Health Systems Work: Working Paper No. 2*. Geneva: World Health Organization, WHO/EIP/healthsystems/2005.2, accessed 3 December 2011.
3. Berry C, Igboemeka A. 2004. *Service Provision in Difficult Environments: Issues Arising from DFID Support to Health Sector Interventions in Burma, Afghanistan, and Nepal*. London: Department for International Development, www.gsdrc.org/docs/open/SD27.pdf (Accessed 3 December 2011).
4. Bossert T, Brune N, Bowser D, Solis F. 2003. *Social Capital and Health in Nicaraguan Communities: Final Report*. Boston: Harvard School of Public Health, Management and Leadership Project.
5. Bossert TJ. 2008. *Decentralization and Governance in Health*. Washington, DC: U.S. Agency for International Development, Health Systems 20/20, Policy Brief, June.
6. Brinkerhoff DW. 2004. Accountability and health systems: toward conceptual clarity and policy relevance. *Health Policy and Planning*19:371–9.
7. Brinkerhoff DW, Bossert TJ. 2008. *Health Governance: Concepts, Experience, and Programming Options*. Washington, DC: U.S. Agency for International Development, Health Systems 20/20, Policy Brief, February.
8. Brinkerhoff DW, Goldsmith A. 2004. Good governance, clientelism and patrimonialism: new perspectives on old problems. *International Public Management Journal* 7: 163–85.
9. Brinkerhoff DW, Morgan PJ. 2010. Capacity and capacity development: coping with complexity. *Public Administration and Development* 30: 2–11.

10. Cornwall A, Lucas H, Pasteur K (eds). 2000. Accountability through participation: developing workable partnership models in the health sector. *IDS Bulletin* 31.

11. Davis JH, Donaldson L, Schoorman FD. 1997. Toward a stewardship theory of management. *Academy of Management Review* 22: 20–47.

12. Eldridge C, Palmer N. 2009. Performance-based payment: some reflec- tions on the discourse, evidence and unanswered questions. *Health Policy and Planning* 24: 160–6.

13. Elgie R (ed.). 2001. *Divided Government in Comparative Perspective.* Oxford, UK: Oxford University Press.

14. Fox AM, Reich MR. 2011. Political economy of health reform: art of the feasible. In: Preker AS, Lindner MM, Cherchosky D *et al.* (eds). *Scaling Up Affordable Health Insurance: Staying the Course*. Washington, DC: World Bank.

15. Frenk J. 1994. Dimensions of health system reform. *Health Policy* 27: 19–34.

16. George A. 2009. 'By papers and pens, you can only do so much': views about accountability and human resource management from Indian government health administrators and workers. *International Journal of Health Planning and Management* 24: 205–24.

17. Go´mez E. 2006a. *A Political Science Perspective on Civil Society and AIDS: A Note on the Domestic and International Challenges to Successful Mobili- zation*. New York: Open Society Institute, George Soros Foundation.

18. Grindle MS (ed.). 1997. *Getting Good Government: Capacity Building in the Public Sector in Developing Countries*. Cambridge, MA: Harvard Institute for International Development.

19. Grindle MS. 2007. Good enough governance revisited. *Development Policy Review* 25: 553–74.

20. Grindle MS. 2011. Governance reform: the new analytics of next steps. *Governance: An International Journal of Policy, Administration, and Institutions* 24: 415–8.

21. Harpham T, Grant E, Thomas E. 2002. Measuring social capital within health surveys: key issues. *Health Policy and Planning* 17: 106–11.

22. Israr SM. 2006. Good governance and sustainability: a case study from Pakistan. *International Journal of Health Planning and Management* 21: 313–25.

23. Kettl D. 2000. The transformation of governance: globalization, devolution, and the role of government. *Public Administration Review* 60: 488–97.

24. Downloaded from http://heapol.oxfordjournals.org/ at George Washington University on September 22, 2014 Pratt JW, Zeckhauser RJ (eds). 1991. Principals and agents: an overview. *Principals and Agents: The Structure of Business*. Boston, MA: Harvard Business School Press, pp. 1–37.

25. Reich MR. 2002. The politics of reforming health policies. *Promotion and Education* 9: 138–42.

26. Ridde V. 2005. Performance-based Partnership Agreements for the reconstruction of the health system in Afghanistan. *Development in Practice* 15: 4–15.

27. Roberts MJ, Hsiao W, Berman P, Reich MR. 2004. *Getting Health Reforms Right: A Guide to Improving Performance and Equity*. London and New York: Oxford University Press.

28. Saltman R, Ferroussier-Davis O. 2000. The concept of stewardship in health policy. *Bulletin of the World Health Organization* 78: 732–9.

29. Savedoff WD. 2011. *Governance in the Health Sector: A Strategy for Measuring Determinants and Performance*. Washington, DC: World Bank, Policy Research Working Paper No. 5655, May.

30. Siddiqi S, Masud TI, Nishtar S *et al.* 2009. Framework for assessing governance of the health system in developing countries: gateway to good governance. *Health Policy* 90: 13–25.

31. Tantivess S, Walt G. 2008. The role of state and non-state actors in the policy process: the contribution of policy networks to the scale-up of antiretroviral therapy in Thailand. *Health Policy and Planning* 23: 328–38.

32. Tendler J, Freedheim S. 1995. Trust in a rent-seeking world: health and government transformed in Northeast Brazil. *World Development* 22: 1771–9.

33. Travis P, Egger D, Davies P, Mechbal A. 2002. *Towards Better Stewardship: Concepts and Critical Issues*. Geneva: World Health Organization, WHO/EIP/DP 02.48.

34. UNDP (United Nations Development Program). 1997. *Governance for Sustainable Human Development*. New York: UNDP.

35. Van Slyke DM. 2007. Agents or stewards: using theory to under- stand the government-nonprofit social service contracting rela- tionship. *Journal of Public Administration Research and Theory* 17: 157–87.

36. Waterman RW, Meier KJ. 1998. Principal-agent models: an expansion? *Journal of Public Administration Research and Theory* 8: 173–202.
37. WHO (World Health Organization). 2000. *World Health Report 2000*. Geneva: WHO.
38. WHO. 2007. *Everybody's Business: Strengthening Health Systems to Improve Health Outcomes*. Geneva: WHO.
39. World Bank. 2004. *Making Services Work for Poor People. World Development Report 2004*. Washington, DC: World Bank.
40. World Bank. 2007. *Healthy Development: The World Bank Strategy for Health, Nutrition, and Population Results*. Washington, DC: World Bank, April 24.
41. Systems Thinking for Health Systems Strengthening, WHO 2008.
42. MOHFW, GOI, Annual Report, 2007 to 2010.
43. MOHFW, GOI, National Strategic Plan, NACP-I, II, III: 2007-2011. and NACP IV National Implementation Strategy, 2017, NACO.
44. Paving Way for an AIDS Free India, 2017, NACO, MOHFW, GOI.
45. ***'Governance of HIV/AIDS: Implication for Health Sector Response'***– International Journal of Health Policy and Management, 2014 – Also published in Social Science Research Network e-library, 2014 (https://hq.ssrn.com)
46. UNDP Millennium Development Goal, Goal-6. Available from: http://www.undp.org/mdg/goal6.shtml
47. India: National AIDS Control Organization, Ministry of Health and Family Welfare, Government of India; 2008. Oct, HIV Sentinel Surveillance and HIV Estimation in India 2007 - A Technical Brief. [Google Scholar]
48. Technical Report, India HIV estimates year 2006, National AIDS Control Organization, Ministry of Health and Family Welfare, Government of India and National Institute of Medical Research, Indian Council of Medical Research, New Delhi [Google Scholar]
49. India: National AIDS Control Organization, Ministry of Health and Family Welfare, Government of India; 1999. Country Scenario 1998-99. [Google Scholar]
50. India: Ministry of Health and Family Welfare, Government of India; Annual Report 2009-2010, Department of AIDS Control. [Google Scholar]
51. Annual Report 2002-2003, 2003-2004 (up to 31 July 2004), National AIDS Control Organization, Ministry of Health and Family Welfare, Government of India [Google Scholar]

52. India: National AIDS Control Organization, Ministry of Health and Family Welfare, Government of India; 2006. Strategic and Implementation Plan, National AIDS Control Program, Phase III (2006-2011) [Google Scholar]
53. Annual Report 2008-2009, Department of AIDS Control, Ministry of Health and Family Welfare, Government of India [Google Scholar]
54. India: National AIDS Control Organization, Ministry of Health and Family Welfare, Government of India; 2008. NACP III to Halt and Reverse HIV in India. [Google Scholar]
55. New Delhi, India: National AIDS Control Organization, Ministry of Health and Family Welfare, Government of India; 2008. NACO. Office Communication, A11011/69/2007- NACO (A) [Google Scholar]
56. New Delhi, India: National AIDS Control Organization, Ministry of Health and Family Welfare, Government of India; 2008. NACO. Office Communication, T-11011/08/NACO/BSD (ICTC) [Google Scholar]
57. National AIDS Control Organization , Ministry of Health and Family Welfare, Government of India. India HIV Estimates 2015: Technical Report Available at: www.naco.gov.in/sites/default/files/India%20HIV%20Estimations%202015.pdf
58. Godbole S, Mehendale S. HIV/AIDS epidemic in India: risk factors, risk behavior and strategies for prevention and control. Indian J Med Res 2005; 121: 356– 368. [PubMed] [Google Scholar]
59. Ministry of Health and Family Welfare, Government of India About NACO. Available at: www.indiahivinfo.naco.gov.in/naco/content/national-aids-control-organisation-naco
60. National AIDS Control Organization , Ministry of Health and Family Welfare, Government of India. Annual Report 2014–2015. New Delhi: National AIDS Control Organization; 2015. Available at: www.naco.gov.in/sites/default/files/annual_report%20_NACO_2014-15_0.pdf
61. National AIDS Control Organization , Ministry of Health and Family Welfare, Government of India. National AIDS Control Programme Phase- IV (2012–2017) Strategy Document Available at: www.naco.gov.in/nacp-iv-components
62. National AIDS Control Organization, Ministry of Health and Family Welfare, Government of India. National Integrated Biological and Behavioural Surveillance (IBBS). 2014–2015. New Delhi. 2015

Available at: www.aidsdatahub.org/sites/default/files/highlight-reference/document/India_IBBS_report_2014-15.pdf

63. Thomas B, Mimiaga MJ, Mayer KH et al. The influence of stigma on HIV risk behavior among men who have sex with men in Chennai, India. AIDS Care 2012; 24: 1401– 1406. [PMC free article] [PubMed] [Google Scholar]
64. Chakrapani V, Velayudham J, Shunmugam M et al. Barriers to antiretroviral treatment access for injecting drug users living with HIV in Chennai, South India. AIDS Care 2014; 26: 835– 841. [PMC free article] [PubMed] [Google Scholar]
65. Global Fund The Global Fund's New Funding Model. The Global Fund to Fight AIDS, Tuberculosis and Malaria, Fourth Replenishment (2014–2016). April 2013 Available at: www.theglobalfund.org/en/fundingmodel/
66. WHO World Health Organization Global Strategy for the Surveillance and Monitoring of HIV Drug Resistance 2012. Geneva: World Health Organization; 2012. Available at: http://apps.who.int/iris/bitstream/10665/77349/1/9789241504768_eng.pdf
67. UNAIDS Fast-track. Ending the AIDS Epidemic by 2030. Geneva: UNAIDS; 2014. Available at: www.unaids.org/sites/default/files/media_asset/JC2686_WAD2014report_en.pdf

Annexures

Annexure - 1

District Classification

List of 611 Districts and their Classification Based on Epidemiology Risk and Vulnerability

	Name of State/UT	*Name of District*	*Classififaction*
1.	A & N ISLANDS (Censu	Andamans	D
2.	A & N ISLANDS	Nicobars	C
3.	ANDHRA PRADESH (Cens	Adilabad	C
4.	ANDHRA PRADESH	Anantapur	A
5.	ANDHRA PRADESH	Chittoor	A
6.	ANDHRA PRADESH	Cuddapah	A
7.	ANDHRA PRADESH	East_Godavari	A
8.	ANDHRA PRADESH	Guntur	A
9.	ANDHRA PRADESH	Hyderabad	A
10.	ANDHRA PRADESH	Karimnagar	A
11.	ANDHRA PRADESH	Khammam	A
12.	ANDHRA PRADESH	Krishna	A
13.	ANDHRA PRADESH	Kurnool	A
14.	ANDHRA PRADESH	Mahbubnagar	C
15.	ANDHRA PRADESH	Medak	A
16.	ANDHRA PRADESH	Nalgonda	A
17.	ANDHRA PRADESH	Nellore	A
18.	ANDHRA PRADESH	Nizamabad	A
19.	ANDHRA PRADESH	Prakasam	A
20.	ANDHRA PRADESH	Rangareddi	A
21.	ANDHRA PRADESH	Srikakulam	A
22.	ANDHRA PRADESH	Visakhapatnam	A
23.	ANDHRA PRADESH	Vizianagaram	A
24.	ANDHRA PRADESH	Warangal	A
25.	ANDHRA PRADESH	West_Godavari	A
26.	ARUNACHAL PRADESH (C	Anjaw	C
27.	ARUNACHAL PRADESH	Changlang	C

28.	ARUNACHAL PRADESH	Dibang_Valley	D
29.	ARUNACHAL PRADESH	East_Kameng	D
30.	ARUNACHAL PRADESH	East_Siang	C
31.	ARUNACHAL PRADESH	Kurung kurney	D
32.	ARUNACHAL PRADESH	Lohit	C
33.	ARUNACHAL PRADESH	Lowe Debang valley	D
34.	ARUNACHAL PRADESH	Lower_Subansiri	D
35.	ARUNACHAL PRADESH	Papum_Pare	C
36.	ARUNACHAL PRADESH	Tawang	D
37.	ARUNACHAL PRADESH	Tirap	C
38.	ARUNACHAL PRADESH	Upper_Siang	D
39.	ARUNACHAL PRADESH	Upper_Subansiri	D
40.	ARUNACHAL PRADESH	West_Kameng	C
41.	ARUNACHAL PRADESH	West_Siang_(Along)	C
42.	ASSAM (Census 23)	Barpeta	C
43.	ASSAM	Bongaigaon	C
44.	ASSAM	Cachar	C
45.	ASSAM	Darrang	D
46.	ASSAM	Dhemaji	C
47.	ASSAM	Dhubri	C
48.	ASSAM	Dibrugarh	D
49.	ASSAM	Goalpara	C
50.	ASSAM	Golaghat	C
51.	ASSAM	Hailakandi	D
52.	ASSAM	Jorhat	C
53.	ASSAM	Kamrup	B
54.	ASSAM	Karbi_Anglong	C
55.	ASSAM	Karimganj	D
56.	ASSAM	Kokrajhar	C
57.	ASSAM	Lakhimpur	C
58.	ASSAM	Marigaon	D
59.	ASSAM	Nagaon	D
60.	ASSAM	Nalbari	D
61.	ASSAM	North_Cachar_Hills	D
62.	ASSAM	Sibsagar	C
63.	ASSAM	Sonitpur	D
64.	ASSAM	Tinsukia	D
65.	BIHAR (Census 38)	Araria	C
66.	BIHAR	Arval	C
67.	BIHAR	Aurangabad-BI	D
68.	BIHAR	Banka	C
69.	BIHAR	Begusarai	C
70.	BIHAR	Bhagalpur	D
71.	BIHAR	Bhojpur	C
72.	BIHAR	Buxar	D

73.	BIHAR	Darbhanga	C
74.	BIHAR	Gaya	C
75.	BIHAR	Gopalganj	C
76.	BIHAR	Jamui	C
77.	BIHAR	Jehanabad	C
78.	BIHAR	Kaimur	B
79.	BIHAR	Katihar	C
80.	BIHAR	Khagaria	A
81.	BIHAR	Kishanganj	A
82.	BIHAR	Lakhisarai	C
83.	BIHAR	Madhepura	C
84.	BIHAR	Madhubani	A
85.	BIHAR	Munger	C
86.	BIHAR	Muzaffarpur	A
87.	BIHAR	Nalanda	D
88.	BIHAR	Nawada	C
89.	BIHAR	Pashchim_Champaran	A
90.	BIHAR	Patna	B
91.	BIHAR	Purba_Champaran	A
92.	BIHAR	Purnia	A
93.	BIHAR	Rohtas	C
94.	BIHAR	Saharsa	C
95.	BIHAR	Samastipur	C
96.	BIHAR	Saran	C
97.	BIHAR	Sheikhpura	C
98.	BIHAR	Sheohar	C
99.	BIHAR	Sitamarhi	A
100.	BIHAR	Siwan	D
101.	BIHAR	Supaul	C
102.	BIHAR	Vaishali	C
103.	CHANDIGARH (Census 1	Chandigarh	A
104.	CHHATISGARH (Census	Bastar	A
105.	CHATTISGARH	Bilaspur_CG	D
106.	CHATTISGARH	Dantewada	C
107.	CHATTISGARH	Dhamtari	C
108.	CHATTISGARH	Durg	D
109.	CHATTISGARH	Janjgir	D
110.	CHATTISGARH	Jashpur	C
111.	CHATTISGARH	Kanker	D
112.	CHATTISGARH	Kawardha	C
113.	CHATTISGARH	Korba	C
114.	CHATTISGARH	Koriya	D
115.	CHATTISGARH	Mahasamund	A
116.	CHATTISGARH	Raigarh_CG	C
117.	CHATTISGARH	Raipur	C
118.	CHATTISGARH	Rajnandgaon	D

119.	CHATTISGARH	Surguja	C
120.	D & N HAVELI (Census	Dadra_&_Nagar_Haveli	C
121.	DAMAN & DIU (Census	Daman	C
122.	DAMAN & DIU	Diu	B
123.	DELHI (Census 9)	Delhi_Central	B
124.	DELHI	Delhi_East	B
125.	DELHI	Delhi_North	B
126.	DELHI	Delhi_North_East	B
127.	DELHI	Delhi_North_West	C
128.	DELHI	Delhi_South	C
129.	DELHI	Delhi_South_West	C
130.	DELHI	Delhi_West	C
131.	DELHI	New Delhi	A
132.	GOA (Census 2)	North_Goa	A
133.	GOA	South_Goa	A
134.	GUJARAT (Census 25)	Ahmadabad	B
135.	GUJRAT	Amreli	B
136.	GUJRAT	Anand	B
137.	GUJRAT	Banas_Kantha	A
138.	GUJRAT	Bharuch	B
139.	GUJRAT	Bhavnagar	B
140.	GUJRAT	Dahod	B
141.	GUJRAT	Gandhinagar	B
142.	GUJRAT	Jamnagar	B
143.	GUJRAT	Junagadh	B
144.	GUJRAT	Kachchh	C
145.	GUJRAT	Kheda	B
146.	GUJRAT	Mahesana	A
147.	GUJRAT	Narmada	B
148.	GUJRAT	Navsari	A
149.	GUJRAT	Panch_Mahals	B
150.	GUJRAT	Patan	A
151.	GUJRAT	Porbandar	B
152.	GUJRAT	Rajkot	B
153.	GUJRAT	Sabar_Kantha	B
154.	GUJRAT	Surat	A
155.	GUJRAT	Surendranagar	A
156.	GUJRAT	Dang	A
157.	GUJRAT	Valsad	A
158.	GUJRAT	Boroda	B
159.	HARYANA (Census 19)	Ambala	C
160.	HARYANA	Bhiwani	C
161.	HARYANA	Faridabad	C
162.	HARYANA	Fatehabad	C
163.	HARYANA	Gurgaon	C

164.	HARYANA	Hisar	C
165.	HARYANA	Jhajjar	A
166.	HARYANA	Jind	C
167.	HARYANA	Kaithal	C
168.	HARYANA	Karnal	C
169.	HARYANA	Kurukshetra	C
170.	HARYANA	Mahendragarh	C
171.	HARYANA	Panchkula	C
172.	HARYANA	Panipat	C
173.	HARYANA	Rewari	C
174.	HARYANA	Rohtak	C
175.	HARYANA	Sirsa	C
176.	HARYANA	Sonipat	C
177.	HARYANA	Yamunanagar	C
178.	HIMACHAL PRADESH (Ce	Bilaspur-HP	D
179.	HIMACHAL PRADESH	Chamba	C
180.	HIMACHAL PRADESH	Hamirpur_HP	D
181.	HIMACHAL PRADESH	Kangra	D
182.	HIMACHAL PRADESH	Kinnaur	C
183.	HIMACHAL PRADESH	Kullu	C
184.	HIMACHAL PRADESH	Lahul_&_Spiti	D
185.	HIMACHAL PRADESH	Mandi	C
186.	HIMACHAL PRADESH	Shimla	C
187.	HIMACHAL PRADESH	Siramur	D
188.	HIMACHAL PRADESH	Solan	D
189.	HIMACHAL PRADESH	Una	C
190.	JAMMU & KASHMIR (Cen	Anantanag	C
191.	JAMMU & KASHMIR	Badgam	D
192.	JAMMU & KASHMIR	Baramula	D
193.	JAMMU & KASHMIR	Chilas (Gilgit)	C
194.	JAMMU & KASHMIR	Doda	B
195.	JAMMU & KASHMIR	Jammu	C
196.	JAMMU & KASHMIR	Kargil	C
197.	JAMMU & KASHMIR	Kathua	D
198.	JAMMU & KASHMIR	Kupwara	C
199.	JAMMU & KASHMIR	Leh(Ladakh)	D
200.	JAMMU & KASHMIR	Pulwama	D
201.	JAMMU & KASHMIR	Punch	D
202.	JAMMU & KASHMIR	Rajauri	C
203.	JAMMU & KASHMIR	Srinagar	C
204.	JAMMU & KASHMIR	Udhampur	D
205.	JHARKHAND (Census 22	Bokaro	C
206.	JHARKAND	Chatra	C
207.	JHARKAND	Deoghar	D
208.	JHARKAND	Dhanbad	C

209.	JHARKHAND	Dumka	D
210.	JHARKHAND	Garhwa	D
211.	JHARKHAND	Giridih	C
212.	JHARKHAND	Godda	C
213.	JHARKHAND	Gumla	D
214.	JHARKHAND	Hazaribagh	D
215.	JHARKHAND	Jamtara	D
216.	JHARKHAND	Kodarma	D
217.	JHARKHAND	Lohardaga	D
218.	JHARKHAND	Pakur	C
219.	JHARKHAND	Latehar	D
220.	JHARKHAND	Palamu	D
221.	JHARKHAND	Pashchimi_Singhbhum	C
222.	JHARKHAND	Purbi_Singhbhum	D
223.	JHARKHAND	Ranchi	C
224.	JHARKHAND	Sahibganj	D
225.	JHARKHAND	Saraikela	D
226.	JHARKHAND	Simdega	D
227.	KARNATAKA (Census: 2	Bagalkot	A
228.	KARNATAKA	Bangalore_City	A
229.	KARNATAKA	Bangalore_Rural	A
230.	KARNATAKA	Belgaum	A
231.	KARNATAKA	Bellary	A
232.	KARNATAKA	Bidar	A
233.	KARNATAKA	Bijapur	A
234.	KARNATAKA	Chamarajanagar	A
235.	KARNATAKA	Chikmagalur	C
236.	KARNATAKA	Chitradurga	A
237.	KARNATAKA	Dakshina_Kannada	A
238.	KARNATAKA	Davanagere	A
239.	KARNATAKA	Dharwad	A
240.	KARNATAKA	Gadag	A
241.	KARNATAKA	Gulbarga	A
242.	KARNATAKA	Hassan	A
243.	KARNATAKA	Haveri	A
244.	KARNATAKA	Kodagu	A
245.	KARNATAKA	Kolar	A
246.	KARNATAKA	Koppal	A
247.	KARNATAKA	Mandya	A
248.	KARNATAKA	Mysore	A
249.	KARNATAKA	Raichur	A
250.	KARNATAKA	Shimoga	C
251.	KARNATAKA	Tumkur	A
252.	KARNATAKA	Udupi	A
253.	KARNATAKA	Uttara_Kannada	A

254.	KERALA (Census: 14)	Alappuzha	B
255.	KERALA	Ernakulam	A
256.	KERALA	Idukki	C
257.	KERALA	Kannur	C
258.	KERALA	Kasaragod	C
259.	KERALA	Kollam	C
260.	KERALA	Kottayam	B
261.	KERALA	Kozhikode	B
262.	KERALA	Malappuram	C
263.	KERALA	Palakkad	C
264.	KERALA	Pathanamthitta	B
265.	KERALA	Thiruvananthapuram	B
266.	KERALA	Thrissur	B
267.	KERALA	Wayanad	C
268.	LAKSHADWEEP (Census:	Lakshadweep	C
269.	MADHYA PRADESH (Cens	Anuppur	D
270.	MADHYA PRADESH	Ashoknagar	D
271.	MADHYA PRADESH	Balaghat	D
272.	MADHYA PRADESH	Barwani	C
273.	MADHYA PRADESH	Betul	C
274.	MADHYA PRADESH	Bhind	C
275.	MADHYA PRADESH	Bhopal	A
276.	MADHYA PRADESH	Burhanpur	D
277.	MADHYA PRADESH	Chhatarpur	D
278.	MADHYA PRADESH	Chhindwara	C
279.	MADHYA PRADESH	Damoh	D
280.	MADHYA PRADESH	Datia	D
281.	MADHYA PRADESH	Dewas	C
282.	MADHYA PRADESH	Dhar	C
283.	MADHYA PRADESH	Dindori	D
284.	MADHYA PRADESH	Guna	D
285.	MADHYA PRADESH	Gwalior	C
286.	MADHYA PRADESH	Harda	C
287.	MADHYA PRADESH	Hoshangabad	C
288.	MADHYA PRADESH	Indore	A
289.	MADHYA PRADESH	Jabalpur	A
290.	MADHYA PRADESH	Jhabua	D
291.	MADHYA PRADESH	Katni	C
292.	MADHYA PRADESH	Khandwa	C
293.	MADHYA PRADESH	Khargone	B
294.	MADHYA PRADESH	Mandla	D
295.	MADHYA PRADESH	Mandsaur	A
296.	MADHYA PRADESH	Morena	C
297.	MADHYA PRADESH	Narasighpur	D
298.	MADHYA PRADESH	Neemuch	B

299.	MADHYA PRADESH	Panna	D
300.	MADHYA PRADESH	Raisen	D
301.	MADHYA PRADESH	Rajgarh	C
302.	MADHYA PRADESH	Ratlam	C
303.	MADHYA PRADESH	Rewa	B
304.	MADHYA PRADESH	Sagar	C
305.	MADHYA PRADESH	Satna	C
306.	MADHYA PRADESH	Sehore	C
307.	MADHYA PRADESH	Seoni	C
308.	MADHYA PRADESH	Shahdol	C
309.	MADHYA PRADESH	Shajapur	C
310.	MADHYA PRADESH	Sheopur	D
311.	MADHYA PRADESH	Shivpuri	C
312.	MADHYA PRADESH	Sidhi	D
313.	MADHYA PRADESH	Tikamgarh	D
314.	MADHYA PRADESH	Ujjain	A
315.	MADHYA PRADESH	Umaria	D
316.	MADHYA PRADESH	Vidisha	D
317.	MAHARASHTRA (Census:	Ahmadnagar	A
318.	MAHARASHTRA	Akola	A
319.	MAHARASHTRA	Amravati_Rural	B
320.	MAHARASHTRA	Aurangabad_MH	A
321.	MAHARASHTRA	Bhandara	A
322.	MAHARASHTRA	Beed	A
323.	MAHARASHTRA	Buldana	B
324.	MAHARASHTRA	Chandrapur	A
325.	MAHARASHTRA	Dhule	A
326.	MAHARASHTRA	Gadchiroli	A
327.	MAHARASHTRA	Gondiya	B
328.	MAHARASHTRA	Hingoli	A
329.	MAHARASHTRA	Jalgaon	A
330.	MAHARASHTRA	Jalna	A
331.	MAHARASHTRA	Kolhapur	A
332.	MAHARASHTRA	Latur	A
333.	MAHARASHTRA	Mumbai	A
334.	MAHARASHTRA	Mumbai (Suburban)	A
335.	MAHARASHTRA	Nagpur_Rural	A
336.	MAHARASHTRA	Nanded	A
337.	MAHARASHTRA	Nandurbar	A
338.	MAHARASHTRA	Nashik	A
339.	MAHARASHTRA	Osmanabad	A
340.	MAHARASHTRA	Parbhani	A
341.	MAHARASHTRA	Pune	A
342.	MAHARASHTRA	Raigarh_MH	A
343.	MAHARASHTRA	Ratnagiri	A

344.	MAHARASHTRA	Sangli	A
345.	MAHARASHTRA	Satara	A
346.	MAHARASHTRA	Sindhudurg	B
347.	MAHARASHTRA	Solapur	A
348.	MAHARASHTRA	Thane	A
349.	MAHARASHTRA	Wardha	A
350.	MAHARASHTRA	Washim	B
351.	MAHARASHTRA	Yavatmal	A
352.	MANIPUR (Census: 9)	Bishnupur	A
353.	MANIPUR	Chandel	A
354.	MANIPUR	Churachandpur	A
355.	MANIPUR	Imphal	A
356.	MANIPUR	Senapati	A
357.	MANIPUR	Tamenglong	A
358.	MANIPUR	Thoubal	C
359.	MANIPUR	Ukhrul	D
360.	MANIPUR	Moreh	A
361.	MEGHALAYA (Census: 7	East_Garo_Hills	C
362.	MEGHALAYA	East_Khasi_Hills	C
363.	MEGHALAYA	Jaintia_Hills	C
364.	MEGHALAYA	Ri_Bhoi	C
365.	MEGHALAYA	South_Garo_Hills	C
366.	MEGHALAYA	West_Garo_Hills	C
367.	MEGHALAYA	West_Khasi_Hills	C
368.	MIZORAM (Census: 8)	Aizawl	A
369.	MIZORAM	Champhai	A
370.	MIZORAM	Kolasib	A
371.	MIZORAM	Lawngtlai	C
372.	MIZORAM	Lunglei	D
373.	MIZORAM	Mamit	C
374.	MIZORAM	Saiha	A
375.	MIZORAM	Serchhip	A
376.	NAGALAND (Census:11)	Dimapur	A
377.	NAGALAND	Kohima	A
378.	NAGALAND	Mokokchung	A
379.	NAGALAND	Mon	A
380.	NAGALAND	Phek	D
381.	NAGALAND	Tuensang	A
382.	NAGALAND	Wokha	C
383.	NAGALAND	Kiphera	A
384.	NAGALAND	Longleng	A
385.	NAGALAND	Peren	A
386.	NAGALAND	Zunheboto	A
387.	ORISSA (Census: 30)	Anugul	C
388.	ORISSA	Bolangir	C

389.	ORISSA	Baleswar	C
390.	ORISSA	Bargarh	D
391.	ORISSA	Baudh	C
392.	ORISSA	Bhadrak	C
393.	ORISSA	Cuttack	A
394.	ORISSA	Debagarh	C
395.	ORISSA	Dhenkanal	D
396.	ORISSA	Gajapati	D
397.	ORISSA	Ganjam	A
398.	ORISSA	Jagatsinghapur	C
399.	ORISSA	Jajapur	C
400.	ORISSA	Jharsuguda	D
401.	ORISSA	Kalahandi	C
402.	ORISSA	Kandhamal	D
403.	ORISSA	Kendrapara	C
404.	ORISSA	Keonjhar	C
405.	ORISSA	Khordha	B
406.	ORISSA	Koraput	C
407.	ORISSA	Malkangiri	C
408.	ORISSA	Mayurbhanj	C
409.	ORISSA	Nawarangpur	C
410.	ORISSA	Nayagarh	C
411.	ORISSA	Nuapada	C
412.	ORISSA	Puri	C
413.	ORISSA	Rayagada	C
414.	ORISSA	Sambalpur	A
415.	ORISSA	Sonapur	C
416.	ORISSA	Sundargarh	C
417.	PONDICHERRY (Census:	Karaikal	D
418.	PONDICHERRY	Mahe	B
419.	PONDICHERRY	Pondicherry	A
420.	PONDICHERRY	Yanam	D
421.	PUNJAB (Census: 17)	Amritsar	A
422.	PUNJAB	Bathinda	C
423.	PUNJAB	Faridkot	C
424.	PUNJAB	Fatehgarh_Sahib	C
425.	PUNJAB	Firozpur	C
426.	PUNJAB	Gurdaspur	C
427.	PUNJAB	Hoshiarpur	C
428.	PUNJAB	Jalandhar	C
429.	PUNJAB	Kapurthala	C
430.	PUNJAB	Ludhiana	A
431.	PUNJAB	Mansa-PU	C
432.	PUNJAB	Moga	C
433.	PUNJAB	Muktsar	C

434.	PUNJAB	Nawanshahr	C
435.	PUNJAB	Patiala	C
436.	PUNJAB	Rupnagar	B
437.	PUNJAB	Sangrur	C
438.	RAJASTHAN (32)	Ajmer	A
439.	RAJASTHAN	Alwar	B
440.	RAJASTHAN	Banswara	B
441.	RAJASTHAN	Baran	D
442.	RAJASTHAN	Barmer	B
443.	RAJASTHAN	Bharatpur	C
444.	RAJASTHAN	Bhilwara	C
445.	RAJASTHAN	Bikaner	D
446.	RAJASTHAN	Bundi	D
447.	RAJASTHAN	Chittaurgarh	D
448.	RAJASTHAN	Churu	D
449.	RAJASTHAN	Dausa	D
450.	RAJASTHAN	Dhaulpur	C
451.	RAJASTHAN	Dungarpur	D
452.	RAJASTHAN	Ganganagar	A
453.	RAJASTHAN	Hanumangarh	C
454.	RAJASTHAN	Jaipur	B
455.	RAJASTHAN	Jaisalmer	D
456.	RAJASTHAN	Jalore	D
457.	RAJASTHAN	Jhalawar	A
458.	RAJASTHAN	Jhunjhunun	D
459.	RAJASTHAN	Jodhpur	D
460.	RAJASTHAN	Karauli	C
461.	RAJASTHAN	Kota	D
462.	RAJASTHAN	Nagaur	D
463.	RAJASTHAN	Pali	D
464.	RAJASTHAN	Rajsamand	C
465.	RAJASTHAN	Sawai_Madhopur	D
466.	RAJASTHAN	Sikar	D
467.	RAJASTHAN	Sirohi	B
468.	RAJASTHAN	Tonk	B
469.	RAJASTHAN	Udaipur	C
470.	SIKKIM (Census: 4)	East_Sikkim	D
471.	SIKKIM	North_Sikkim	D
472.	SIKKIM	South_Sikkim	B
473.	SIKKIM	West_Sikkim	B
474.	TAMIL NADU (Census:	Chennai	A
475.	TAMIL NADU	Coimbatore	A
476.	TAMIL NADU	Cuddalore	A
477.	TAMIL NADU	Dharmapuri	A
478.	TAMIL NADU	Dindigul	B

479.	TAMIL NADU	Erode	D
480.	TAMIL NADU	Kancheepuram	A
481.	TAMIL NADU	Kanniyakumari	A
482.	TAMIL NADU	Karur	A
483.	TAMIL NADU	Krishnagiri	D
484.	TAMIL NADU	Madurai	A
485.	TAMIL NADU	Nagapattinam	A
486.	TAMIL NADU	Namakkal	A
487.	TAMIL NADU	Perambalur	A
488.	TAMIL NADU	Pudukkottai	A
489.	TAMIL NADU	Ramanathapuram	A
490.	TAMIL NADU	Salem	A
491.	TAMIL NADU	Sivaganga	C
492.	TAMIL NADU	Thanjavur	A
493.	TAMIL NADU	The_Nilgiris	D
494.	TAMIL NADU	Theni	A
495.	TAMIL NADU	Thiruvallur	B
496.	TAMIL NADU	Thiruvarur	A
497.	TAMIL NADU	Tiruchirappalli	A
498.	TAMIL NADU	Tirunelveli	A
499.	TAMIL NADU	Tiruvanamalai	A
500.	TAMIL NADU	Toothukudi	C
501.	TAMIL NADU	Vellore	C
502.	TAMIL NADU	Viluppuram	D
503.	TAMIL NADU	Virudhunagar	C
504.	TRIPURA (Census: 4)	Dhalai	D
505.	TRIPURA	North_Tripura	B
506.	TRIPURA	South_Tripura	C
507.	TRIPURA	West_Tripura	C
508.	UTTAR PRADESH (Censu	Agra	B
509.	UTTAR PRADESH	Aligarh	C
510.	UTTAR PRADESH	Allahabad	C
511.	UTTAR PRADESH	Ambedkar_Nagar	C
512.	UTTAR PRADESH	Auraiya	D
513.	UTTAR PRADESH	Azamgarh	C
514.	UTTAR PRADESH	Baghpat	C
515.	UTTAR PRADESH	Bahraich	C
516.	UTTAR PRADESH	Ballia	C
517.	UTTAR PRADESH	Balrampur	A
518.	UTTAR PRADESH	Banda	A
519.	UTTAR PRADESH	Barabanki	C
520.	UTTAR PRADESH	Bareilly	C
521.	UTTAR PRADESH	Basti	C
522.	UTTAR PRADESH	Bijnor	C
523.	UTTAR PRADESH	Budaun	C

524.	UTTAR PRADESH	Bulandshahar	C
525.	UTTAR PRADESH	Chandauli	C
526.	UTTAR PRADESH	Chitrakoot	C
527.	UTTAR PRADESH	Deoria	C
528.	UTTAR PRADESH	Etah	A
529.	UTTAR PRADESH	Etawah	A
530.	UTTAR PRADESH	Faizabad	C
531.	UTTAR PRADESH	Farrukhabad	C
532.	UTTAR PRADESH	Fatehpur	C
533.	UTTAR PRADESH	Firozabad	C
534.	UTTAR PRADESH	Gautam_Budh_Nagar	C
535.	UTTAR PRADESH	Ghaziabad	C
536.	UTTAR PRADESH	Ghazipur	B
537.	UTTAR PRADESH	Gonda	C
538.	UTTAR PRADESH	Gorakhpur	C
539.	UTTAR PRADESH	Haldwani	C
540.	UTTAR PRADESH	Hardoi	C
541.	UTTAR PRADESH	Hathras	D
542.	UTTAR PRADESH	Jalaun	C
543.	UTTAR PRADESH	Jaunpur	C
544.	UTTAR PRADESH	Jhansi	C
545.	UTTAR PRADESH	Jyotiba_Phule_Nagar	C
546.	UTTAR PRADESH	Kannauj	C
547.	UTTAR PRADESH	Kanpur_Dehat	C
548.	UTTAR PRADESH	Kanpur_Nagar	C
549.	UTTAR PRADESH	Kaushambi	C
550.	UTTAR PRADESH	Kheri	C
551.	UTTAR PRADESH	Kushinagar	C
552.	UTTAR PRADESH	Lalitpur	C
553.	UTTAR PRADESH	Latehar	A
554.	UTTAR PRADESH	Lucknow	C
555.	UTTAR PRADESH	Maharajganj	C
556.	UTTAR PRADESH	Mahoba	C
557.	UTTAR PRADESH	Mainpuri	C
558.	UTTAR PRADESH	Mathura	C
559.	UTTAR PRADESH	Mau	C
560.	UTTAR PRADESH	Meerut	C
561.	UTTAR PRADESH	Mirzapur	C
562.	UTTAR PRADESH	Moradabad	C
563.	UTTAR PRADESH	Muzaffarnagar	C
564.	UTTAR PRADESH	Pilibhit	C
565.	UTTAR PRADESH	Pratapgarh	C
566.	UTTAR PRADESH	Rae_Bareli	C
567.	UTTAR PRADESH	Rampur	C
568.	UTTAR PRADESH	Saharanpur	C

569.	UTTAR PRADESH	Sant_Kabir_Nagar	C
570.	UTTAR PRADESH	Sant_Ravidas_Nagar	C
571.	UTTAR PRADESH	Shahjahanpur	C
572.	UTTAR PRADESH	Shravasti	C
573.	UTTAR PRADESH	Siddharthnagar	C
574.	UTTAR PRADESH	Sitapur	C
575.	UTTAR PRADESH	Sonbhadra	C
576.	UTTAR PRADESH	Sultanpur	C
577.	UTTAR PRADESH	Unnao	C
578.	UTTAR PRADESH	Varanasi	C
579.	UTTARANCHAL (Census:	Almora	C
580.	UTTARANCHAL	Bageshwar	C
581.	UTTARANCHAL	Chamoli	C
582.	UTTARANCHAL	Champawat	C
583.	UTTARANCHAL	Dehradun	C
584.	UTTARANCHAL	Garhwal	C
585.	UTTARANCHAL	Hardwar	C
586.	UTTARANCHAL	Nainital	C
587.	UTTARANCHAL	Rudraprayag	C
588.	UTTARANCHAL	Tehri_Garhwal	C
589.	UTTARANCHAL	Uttarkashi	C
590.	UTTARANCHAL	Pithoragarh	C
591.	UTTARANCHAL	Udhamsingh_Nagar	C
592.	WEST BENGAL (Census:	Bankura	C
593.	WEST BENGAL	Barddhaman	B
594.	WEST BENGAL	Birbhum	C
595.	WEST BENGAL	Dakshin_Dinajpur	C
596.	WEST BENGAL	Darjeeling	C
597.	WEST BENGAL	Howrah	C
598.	WEST BENGAL	Hugli	A
599.	WEST BENGAL	Jalpaiguri	B
600.	WEST BENGAL	Koch_Bihar	C
601.	WEST BENGAL	Kolkata	A
602.	WEST BENGAL	Maldah	C
603.	WEST BENGAL	Medinipur_East	C
604.	WEST BENGAL	Medinipur_West	B
605.	WEST BENGAL	Murshidabad	B
606.	WEST BENGAL	Nadia	C
607.	WEST BENGAL	North_24_Parganas	C
608.	WEST BENGAL	Puruliya	C
609.	WEST BENGAL	South_24_Parganas	C
610.	WEST BENGAL	Uttar_Dinajpur	C
611.	WEST BENGAL	Durgapur	A

Annexure - 2
Assumptions in the Modeling

Parameter/ Meaning	Value	RelevantReferences
15 – 49 Population	269,965,931 (M) 251,431,886 (F)	Census India 2001
Marriage rates	80 (F), 60 (M)	Census India 2001
HIV Infected gender ratio	1 M : 0.6 F	Sentinel Surveillance 2004
CSW population	1,040,558	Expert Group NACO on HRG estimation 2006
MSM population	2,352,113	Expert Group NACO on HRG estimation 2006
IDUs	143,096 (M), 43,447 (F)	Expert Group NACO on HRG estimation 2006
Death rate	0.006 (per 1000)	SRS
Average time from HIV infection to AIDS	8 Years	UNAIDS
AIDS death rate	0.103 %	Projections Report NACP-III
15 – 49 STI prevalence	6 % (M), 5 % (F)	Community Study STI NACO
Blood transfusions	4.4 million	Status report Blood Bank (NACO)
IDUs transmission rate through injections	30 %	UNAIDS 2005
Prevalence of HIV in IDUs	16.3%	Weighted Average of Surveillance data
HIV transmission through blood	0.034 %	NACO
HIV prevalence in MSM	7.7 %	Weighted Average of Surveillance data
Condom usage in high risk behavior	50 %	BSS report 2001
Condom use with regular sexual partners	30%	BSS report 2001
Condom use in marriage	5 %	Rao et al Lancet 2004
Condom use in those receiving ART	Up to 50 % in NACP III	Assumption (No current positive prevention activity) i.e. same as general population

Annexure - 3

Estimates of TIs Needed in Each State

	FSWs	*MSM*	*IDUs*	*Compt*		
State	*No of exclusive TIs needed (800/TI) FSWs*	*No of exclusive TIs needed (600/TI) MSM*	*No of exclusive TIs needed (500/TI) IDUs*	*No of composite TIs needed (250SW/TI and 200MSM/TI)*	*State-wise No. of TIs*	
	G5			G6		
Uttar Pradesh	102	26	28	108	**264**	**Category I 2 states (>200)**
Maharashtra	85	16	12	88	**201**	
Bihar	62	19	12	66	**159**	**Category II 8 states(100-200 TIs)**
Andhra Pradesh	51	12	5	57	**125**	
Tamilnadu	41	10	12	45	**108**	
West Bengal	52	18	27	55	**152**	
Madhya Pradesh	48	14	7	51	**120**	
Karnataka	44	12	10	47	**112**	
Rajasthan	40	13	8	43	**104**	
Orissa	29	8	31	31	**100**	
Delhi	26	3	19	23	**72**	**Category III 23 staes (up to 100 TIs)+S16**
Assam	22	6	3	18	**49**	
Jharkhand	21	6	-	22	**49**	
Punjab	19	6	17	18	**60**	
Haryana	16	5	27	14	**63**	
Chhatisgarh	16	5	-	17	**37**	
Gujarat	15	12	23	16	**65**	
Jammu & Kashmir	9	2	1	9	**21**	
Uttaranchal	7	2	0	7	**16**	
Manipur	5	0	48	5	**59**	
Kerala	4	7	24	7	**42**	
Himachal Pradesh	4	1	2	4	**12**	
Nagaland	3	0	31	3	**37**	
Chandigarh	3	0	6	3	**11**	
Tripura	2	1	14	3	**20**	
Meghalaya	2	1	3	2	**7**	
Goa	1	0	2	1	**5**	
Pondicherry	1	0	2	1	**5**	
Mizoram	1	0	18	1	**20**	
Arunachal Pradesh	1	0	2	1	**3**	
Sikkim	0	0	1	1	**2**	
A & N Island	0	0		0	**0**	
Daman & Diu	0	0		0	**0**	
TOTAL	**732**	**207**	**394**	**767**	**2100**	

Annexure - 4

Red Ribbon Clubs Programme (RRCP) Operational Guidelines for RRC Functionaries

Introduction

In addition to YFIC, NACP–III will promote Red Ribbon Clubs to cover young persons who are at greater risk to HIV both in campuses as well as in community. The programme will address the knowledge, attitude and behavior of youth in the interrelated areas of both HIV/AIDS and sexuality, as demanded by their age, environment, and life style. Thus, Red Ribbon Clubs will serve as a complementary and comprehensive prevention intervention to support and reinforce similar youth led initiatives.

Objectives of RRC Programme

- To reduce new HIV infection among the youth by raising their risk perception through proper education on sex and sexuality and HIV/AIDS by imparting new skills on communication, self-protection, negotiation, care and support and effective group interaction; and
- To prepare the youth as peer educators and agents of change by developing their skills on leadership and team building.

Intersectoral Collaboration

- Department of Higher Education, Ministry of Human Resource Development; and
- Department of Youth Affairs and Sports, Ministry of Youth Affairs and Sports.

Four Key Areas of RRC

- Vibrancy of Youth;
- Sex and Sexuality;
- HIV/AIDS/STI; and
- Peer Education.

RRCs can make use of the following IEC/BCC materials and strategies and due recognition will be given to creative innovations.

IEC/BCC Materials (Select List)

- CDs
- Training Manuals

- Exposure visits
- Glow sign box, stickers
- Handbills
- Hoardings
- Poster messages
- Video-on-wheels
- Wall paintings & wall writings
- Songs and Jingles
- Teasers

Strategies

- Awareness campaigns
- Debates, Workshops, Seminars
- Leadership Training
- Public Meetings
- Intra- and Inter- University Competitions
- Cultural programmes (Folk art, street play, etc)
- Popular Personalities Involvement
- Positive Persons Presentation
- Exhibition
- Rallies
- Road shows
- Use of local cables (talk shows, phone-ins, etc.)
- Publicity in dailies, AIR, TV, etc.
- Counselling
- Intersectoral partnership
- Newsletters
- Leadership and Communication skill training

Functioning of RRCs

- From among the enrolled members of the club, Sub-Committees in terms of its total strength can be formed by grouping students according to their talents. For instance, those who have theatrical talents can form Theatre Committee; those who are good in writing as Writers Group; those who are good in speaking can form the Oratorical Group.

- Active RRC members can be selected as leaders and representatives for planning and implementing out-reach activities in their surroundings.

Broad areas of performance for evaluation of RRC functionaries will be as follows:

- Forming new RRCs
- Innovative Functioning
- Networking
- Reporting
- Advocacy
- Monitoring
- Documentation

Performance Indicators for Field Officers

1. Number of active RRCs (15 students and more. Meeting once in a month).
   (a) Number of new RRCs started (formally inaugurated) atleast with 15 students as voluntary members in a month (This is applicable in the formation stage).
2. Number of active members in the club (who participate in at least one meeting and one activity in a month).
3. Number of activities (meetings, seminars, workshops, rallies, exhibitions, sports events, cultural events, competitions, etc.) and number of estimated people participated/reached.
4. Number of blood donors registered.
5. Number of local organizations (Lion's Club, Rotary Club, Local cable TV channels, magazines etc.) engaged in RRC activities.
6. Number of new IEC materials generated (plays, songs, posters, slogans, etc.).
7. Regular feedback to RMs and SACS.
8. Number of organizations (Arivoli Iyakkam, NYK, YRC, NCC etc) collaborated for conducting community awareness programmes.
9. Number of micro level studies, researches done in a year.
10. Courses started in the school/college.
11. Number of advocacies (policy level changes in college/university) done.

12. Regularity in reporting and documenting the activities. (once a month).
13. Number of cases helped to go for counselling (ICTCs).
14. Number of material and human resources mobilized.
15. Extent of initiatives taken to update technical knowledge.
16. List of innovative activities carried out.

These indicators are contextualized and will be used to evaluate both the general and temporal specific needs.

1. **Contingency**

- **Field Officers:** will be paid towards their contingency expenditures such as stationery, mail, fax, telegram, etc.
- **RRC Coordinators:** will be paid towards contingency expenditures such as stationery, mail, fax, telegram, etc.

1. **Formation of the RRC in Institutions**: Each institution will be given one time grant to form RRCs.

   The Utilization Certificate will be signed by the Programme Officer and sent to the RRC Coordinator, who in turn will forward a consolidated Utilization Certificate and statement of expenditure to TANSACS. The institutions can retain original vouchers unless called for.

2. **IEC materials:** IEC materials, printed and electronic, will be prepared by NACO/SACS and sent to the Coordinator who will distribute the materials to programme officers as per the need.

   The Coordinator with the assistance of the Field Officer will maintain a stock register for the materials received and distributed. Receipts and distribution need to be duly authenticated.

   (a) Membership Register: Coordinators for the University Clubs and Programme Officers in colleges and Polytechnics.

   (b) Club Activities Register: Coordinators and Programme Officers with the assistance of the RRC members.

Annexure - 5
Tribal Strategy and Implementation Plan

1. Social Assessment and Consultations

The National AIDS Control Programme (NACP) is expected to provide indigenous (tribal) people with benefits within its ambit to expand HIV/AIDS prevention, treatment, care and support to vulnerable rural and tribal areas, and is not expected to have any negative impacts on them. To develop appropriate program strategies and an implementation plan for tribal areas, a social assessment (SA) was carried out by the National AIDS Control Organisation, Ministry of Health & Family Welfare, and GOI. The SA included primary and secondary data collection and analysis, a review of the social dimensions of other project preparation studies, and primary and secondary consultations with tribal stakeholders and other participating agencies (e.g., the Ministry of Tribal Affairs of GOI, and civil society organizations).

Important among tribal stakeholders are people who are infected or affected by HIV/AIDS, and those at risk of infection, especially migrant workers (and families) and IDUs. The Northeast region of the country, especially the states of Manipur, Nagaland and Mizoram have predominantly tribal populations, and high HIV prevalence, fueled significantly by high injected drug use. Tribal areas near cities such as Mumbai, and through which truck routes pass are also highly vulnerable. The SA consultants interacted with these groups (and especially with women among them), and with health and non-health organizations working with them, in several states and districts in different parts of the country. Secondary consultations were held at the national level. In addition, the NACP-III Planning Team, 14 Working Groups and 11 thematically designed Research & Assessments who prepared the NACP III, also interacted with tribal (and non-tribal) people across the country. The draft SA report and Tribal Action Plan (TAP) were disclosed in May 2006 on a widely-known and interactive 'UNAIDS Solution Exchange' website. The final SA report and TAP take into account the feedback received through this mechanism, as well as through the consultative workshops and formal reviewers. They were made available on the NACO website.

2. Key findings of the SA include

Low awareness and knowledge of HIV/AIDS and STIs among tribal people, except in the Northeast; wide variation in sexual and marital practices which have a bearing on partner infection; very low access to modern health facilities and high use of traditional healers or unqualified practitioners; and high vulnerability among youth and those who come into contact with non-tribal populations, including migrants and women who engage in sex work. The TAP aims to address these issues, involving and benefiting tribal communities, as an integral part of the NACP-III.

3. Tribal Action Plan

The implementation plan (see matrix below) is designed to improve the access of tribal people to information, prevention and comprehensive care and support under NACP-III, and is tailored to three types of tribal situations. First, in the predominantly tribal northeastern region, AIDS prevention and treatment services will be strengthened and scaled up state-wide through NGOs and CBOs and government health facilities, under plans prepared and monitored by the SACS and DAPCUs. Second, in states with designated tribal sub-plan areas which have concentrated tribal populations (i.e., about 195 sub-district areas), the SACS and DAPCUs will map the vulnerable tribal groups and collaborate with officials of the Integrated Tribal Development Authorities (ITDAs) to improve prevention and treatment services. In both these sets of states, IEC materials will be translated (with the help of the local Tribal Research Institutes), and local communication channels would be used to promote safe behavior, increase access to condoms, and provide referrals to ICTC and ART services. NACO and the SACS will cooperate with the Health departments of all states to strengthen ICTC and ART services. These services will be provided free of charge to poor tribal people. Patients and attendants who travel to health centers for diagnostic or treatment services will be compensated for travel and related expenses. Districts have been categorized according to HIV prevalence and different packages of services (requiring difference resource allocations) will be made available for each category. Third, tribal people who are dispersed among non-tribal populations will be reached through mainstreaming efforts, particularly IEC, interventions for migrant workers, and other local initiatives. In all three situations, NGOs/CBOs (especially but not only those involved in tribal development activities, such as residential schools and producer cooperatives) will collaborate in prevention and referral activities, and those with hospitals and mobile dispensaries will also support treatment and care. Within all three situations, districts in the High and Moderate Prevalence categories will be given priority attention.

The TAP includes activities to (a) systematize information about HIV/AIDS in tribal areas/populations; (b) increase the access of tribal people to the range of services provided under NACP (including by improving cultural appropriateness); and (c) integrate HIV/AIDS prevention efforts in the work of other relevant government departments, local development agencies (NGOs/CBOs), and public and private health providers to expand reach to tribal people. The activities include: mapping of risk and vulnerability to HIV among tribal people; increasing awareness campaigns and condom distribution in tribal areas, with communication in tribal languages; increasing referrals of tribal people to ICTCs, STI/OI clinics, ART and other health programs; increasing ICTCs and other ART facilities in tribal areas; and training/sensitizing personnel of other departments so that they can promote HIV/AIDS prevention and care.

4. Implementation Capacity

As the NACP-III is expected to expand significantly in rural and tribal areas to scale-up HIV/AIDS prevention, treatment, and care and support activities, increasing implementation capacity is a central feature. The TAP includes: establishment of a Technical Resource Group on Tribal issues at the national level, and a regional office of NACO in the Northeast; contracting of NGOs and CBOs that are familiar with tribal culture and social development work to implement action plans in the districts as well as to carry out broader activities such as training at district and state levels; and increasing the capacities of other government agencies – from state-level tribal councils to field staff - to implement and monitor HIV/AIDS activities for tribal people. In all states the SACS will ensure that tribal people receive due attention and benefits from the program as well as other marginalized groups. The TAP also aims to sensitize health staff to cultural differences and train them to reach out and provide services to tribal people, and to involve traditional health practitioners in the program.

As the SA found that there are few NGOs in tribal areas, the program will build on other existing initiatives for social mobilization and community involvement, notably those of the Health and Tribal Affairs departments, particularly the ITDAs. The ITDAs have Tribal Facilitators who carry out IEC activities. The NACP will collaborate with these departments as well as with private health service providers and institutions, and civil society organizations engaged in tribal development programs.

5. Monitoring and Evaluation

Implementation of the TAP will be monitored quarterly at the district, state and national levels on the basis of mandatory reports filed by the implementing agencies. These reports will be made available to the Bank and other Development Partners during bi-annual review missions. The following key indicators will be used to assess progress in implementation of the program for tribal people:

- NACO policies and program documents specifically mention and plan to address socio-economically vulnerable groups including tribal people.
- Guidelines to integrate HIV/AIDS services with NRHM in tribal areas are available.

- Advocacy and intervention strategies are developed for vulnerable including tribal groups and implemented.
- NACO completes a comprehensive review to identify critical gaps in knowledge including gaps in behavioral and social information, including of/on tribal people.
- Number of districts preparing Tribal Action Plans (as a percentage of priority districts with tribal populations).
- Number of TIs implemented in tribal areas.
- Number of districts implementing TIs in tribal areas (as a percentage of priority districts with tribal populations).
- Number of NGOs/CBOs in tribal areas trained in HIV/AIDS prevention, care, support and treatment.
- Number of rural Private Practitioners and traditional healers in tribal areas sensitized to HIV/AIDS prevention, care, support and treatment.
- Submission to the SACS and NACO of acceptable MIS reports on program activities for tribal people.
- Numbers of diagnostic and treatment facilities established in tribal areas and numbers of people accessing services at these facilities.
- Numbers of facilities functioning effectively under PPPs in tribal areas.
- Numbers of people in tribal areas accessing services at Mobile facilities.
- Number of people in tribal areas utilizing Referral services effectively.

6. Budget

The Northeast Region will get 10 percent of the total budget for program implementation, which is 'earmarked' and 'non lapseable'. This would cover all six prevention components, treatment, care and support. Costing has been done with the special characteristics of the Northeast in mind. In other tribal areas, the ITDAs (which are 'single-window' authorities in which all departments report to a Project Officer) have a health budget for primary health care, mobile units, referrals to city hospitals, etc. The NACP-III will make an additional grant of a minimum of Rs. 5 lakh to each ITDA through the SACS to raise awareness and mainstream HIV into all programs being implemented by the ITDAs. Further funds will be provided through the micro-plans prepared by the SACS and DAPCUs, and hence cannot be computed at this time.

Tribal Action Plan

Activities	Responsibility	Implementation Mechanism	Schedule (see Note 1)				
			Year I Q 1 2 3 4	*Year II*	*Year III*	*Year IV*	*Year V*
For Entire Program							
Set up Tribal Technical Resource Group (TRG) at NACO	NACO (with MOTA)		x				
Hold quarterly meetings of TRGs	NACO		x x x	x	x	x	x
Prepare guidelines for mapping of risk and vulnerability among tribal groups	NACO (with MOTA)		x				
Translation of Training tools, protocols, IEC/BCC and advocacy materials	NACO through MOTA	Tribal Research Institutes (TRI)	x x x	x	x	x	x
Monitoring of tribal interventions	NACO	Consultants	x x x	x	x	x	x
Preparation of Quarterly reports on activities for tribal people	DAPCUs, SACs and NACO		x x x x	x	x	x	x
Evaluation of tribal interventions	NACO	Consultants	x	x	x	x	x
Northeast States							
Scaling up of interventions among HRGs (see note 2)	SACS and DAPCUs	Contracts with NGOs and CBOs					
(a) Map hotspots and vulnerable groups			x				
(b) Select NGOs and CBOs for TIs			x x x	x	x	x	x
(c) Continue support to on-going projects			x x x x	x	x	x	x
Advocate, facilitate, coordinate and support mainstream capacity building programs for IEC and Behavior Change, and training of departmental officers to mainstream HIV in their work	RACU and SACS	Coordinate with state Tribal Departments, Councils, etc. Contract with NGOs or others to conduct training.	x x x x	x	x	x	x
Increase numbers of ICTC and ART facilities at government Health Centers	NACO and SACS	State Health departments	x x x x	x	x	x	x
Monitoring of Activities	NACO	Consultants	x x x	x	x	x	x
Evaluation	NACO	Consultants	x	x	x	x	x

For Tribal Sub-Plan Areas and Concentrated Populations in other States							
Map hotspots and vulnerable groups	SACS and DAPCUs	TRIs and Consultants	x x				
Map health care facilities and providers	SACS and DAPCUs	TRIs and Consultants	x x				
Prepare Specific Tribal Action Plans within District AIDS Control Plans	SACS	DAPCUs (with help as needed)	x	x	x	x	x
Increase access to prevention and treatment services	SACS	DAPCUs					
a. Sensitize/Train ITDA staff and partner NGOs/CBOs	SACS and DAPCUs (with ITDAs)	Consultants/NGOs	x x x x	x	x	x	x
b. Include HIV/AIDS prevention, care, support and treatment activities in the health activities of ITDA projects	SACS and DAPCUs (with ITDAs)	ITDAs	x x x x	x	x	x	x
c. Implement HIV/AIDS awareness campaigns	SACS and DAPCUs (with ITDAs)	Links with other agencies and contracts with NGOs	x x x x	x	x	x	x
d. Expand prevention, treatment, and care services through hospitals, girls' complexes and residential schools in tribal areas	SACS and DAPCUs	Contracts with NGOs and CBOs; links with ITDAs and related state departments	x x x x	x	x	x	x
e. Build capacities of health care providers incl. traditional healers	SACS and DAPCUs	Contracts with NGOs and CBOs	x x x x	x	x	x	x
f. Support mobile dispensaries	SACS and DAPCUs	Contracts with NGOs	x x x x	x	x	x	x
g. Health check-ups and condom promotion at weekly markets	SACS and DAPCUs	Contracts with NGOs	x x x x	x	x	x	x
h. Establish referral services for STI and OI treatment and ART	SACS and DAPCUs	Contracts with local hospitals/NGOs	x x x x	x	x	x	x
i. Ensure coverage of contiguous tribal areas	SACS	DAPCUs to coordinate with each other	x x x x	x	x	x	x
Increase ICTC and ART facilities at govt. Health Centers in these areas	NACO and SACS	State Health departments	x x x x	x	x	x	x

(Contd...)

Reimburse cost of travel and expenses to ICTC facility for patient and attendant and waive CD4 and ART costs for tribal people	DAPCUs and SACS	State Health departments	x x x x	x	x	x	x
Translate IEC/BCC materials into local dialects; make them culture sensitive	SACS (with State Tribal Departments)	TRIs and contracts with NGOs	x x x x	x	x	x	x
Conduct training programs on HIV prevention (using trained trainers)	SACS and DAPCUs	TRIs and contracts with NGOs	x x x x	x	x	x	x
Monitoring of activities	SACS	Consultants	x x x x	x	x	x	x
Evaluation	SACS	Consultants	x	x	x	x	x
For Tribal People living among Mixed Populations							
Promotion of HIV/AIDS awareness and condom use	SACS and DAPCUs	Contracts with NGOs	x x x x	x	x	x	x
Increase referrals to ICTCs, and STI/OI treatment and ART for tribal migrant workers, slum dwellers, etc.	SACS and DAPCUs	Contracts with NGOs	x x x x	x	x	x	x
Baseline values and numerical targets for the above activities will be finalized along with those for the program at large by the end of the first quarter of project implementation (expected June 2007) and included in the overall M&E Plan for NACP-III.							

Notes: (1) In Years II to V, activities will be carried out continuously and reported and monitored every quarter. (2) Interventions to (a) increase access to (i) BCC (ii) condom promotion services, (iii) STI services (iv) referrals to ICTCs, (v) referrals to care, support and treatment facilities, (vi) mobile dispensaries and (vii) health check-ups and condom promotion through weekly markets; and (b) build the capacities of private practitioners (including traditional healers) in tribal areas to manage STIs, OIs, condom promotion, and referrals to ICTCs. The number and quality of these interventions would be reported and monitored separately.

Annexure - 6
Communication Strategy

Annexure - 6.1

Messages and Material for Various Target Audience

Priority One

A. Messages and Materials - Target Audience: HRG

- o Broad-based Information Education and Communication (IEC) through Mass Media Campaign in Print, TV and Radio – as well as Back-up Reminder Media such as Hoardings, Wall Paintings and Glow-Signs
- o Inter-Personal Communication (IPC) through One-to-One Counselling, Group Meetings and Discussions, Public Meetings, Peer Group Meetings
- o Supported by Communication Materials that are customized for the Target Audience - Support Materials such as Posters, Leaflets, Flip Charts, Games, Films, etc.

CSW

- CSW Approach for Behaviour Change will be to leverage the Mass Media Campaign – and the IPC will be through the NGO Partners working through the TIs.
- In this, the NACO and SACS IEC Divisions will work closely with the NGOs to understand the specific communication needs required by CSW be it in the form of Advocacy, Social Mobilization, or Communication Materials.
- Help and resources will be provided by the Technical Services Group. Training and Capacity Building will be given to the NGOs in better utilization of IPC activities.
- Additional forms of communication such as Folk Media, Role Play, Street Theatre will be used to support IPC
- Group Discussions and Personal Interactions in IPC will focus on Behaviour Change
- Communication on Trafficking will need to have some synergy with the NACP III Communication Strategy for CSW - as the selling of minors into the prostitution chain has to be addressed

Special Communication Activities will be directed towards creating an enabling and supportive environment:

- Pimps and Madams need to be brought into the fold of "Need To Use Condoms" Advocacy
- Police Advocacy Efforts will start to stop "harassment" and violence
- Healthcare Providers and Staff will need to be sensitized for an Attitude towards the CSW as "customers" of their services

IDU

- IDU Approach for Behaviour Change will be to leverage the Mass Media Campaign – and the IPC will be through the NGO Partners working through the TIs.
- In this, the NACO and SACS IEC Divisions will work closely with the NGOs to understand the specific communication needs required by IDU be it in the form of Advocacy, Social Mobilization, or Communication Materials.
- Help and resources will be provided by the Technical Services Group. Training and Capacity Building will be given to the NGOs in better utilization of IPC activities.
- Additional forms of communication such as Folk Media, Role Play, Street Theatre will be used to support IPC
- Group Discussions and Personal Interactions in IPC will focus on Behaviour Change
- Special Communication dealing with Drug Substitution, Rehabilitation Programmes, and Clean Needles needs to be created.

Special communication efforts will be directed towards:

- Social Advocacy Efforts need to be started through the NGOs with Parents and PTA in schools – since young people are particularly vulnerable to drugs because of a desire to experiment, "friends are doing it" creates peer pressure
- Youth Pressure groups can be started to talk about drugs in schools and colleges
- Youth Advocacy will support the campaign of "Say No to Drugs."
- Police will be sensitized not to brutalize drug addicts and be more sensitive about offering help, directing them to the NGOs in TIs
- Healthcare Providers and Staff will need to be sensitized for an Attitude towards the IDU as "customers" of their services

MSM

Approach through communication will need to be through the SACS and Districts interacting closely with the NGO Partners.

MSM are still a largely "hidden" population because of social pressures and approaching them will be easier through those groups with whom they feel safe and comfortable. These offer venues for meeting and interaction in privacy.

- This is an opportunity for use of communication materials in the form of Films and Posters created in the different languages for visual communication
- Books and pamphlets will depend upon specific target audience needs of those who are literate
- These will be the support materials for the IPC done by the Peer Educators, Counsellors and Outreach Workers
- Specific Condom Promotion Posters for Male/Male use of condoms will be helpful as a source of information
- Special meetings and discussions to motivate MSM to be more aware of the need for regular STD check-ups, clinical treatment for tears and abrasions, requirement for VCT

Special communication efforts will be directed towards:

- Social Advocacy Efforts need to be done through these NGOs in public so that there is a wider social acceptance of MSM
- The Media can be involved in printing stories on Gay Rights and similar activism /movements
- Police need to be sensitized not harass
- Hospital Staff need to be sensitized not to "condemn"

Priority One:

Messages and Materials - Target Audience: Bridge Populations

- Information Education and Communication (IEC) through a Mass Media Campaign in Print, TV and Radio
- Supported by Materials such as Posters, Leaflets, Flip Charts, Games, Comics
- Outdoor Reminder Media – Hoarding, Wall Paintings and Glo Signs
- Inter-Personal Communication (IPC) through One-to-One Counselling, Group Meetings and Discussions, Public Meetings, Peer Group Meetings

The Mass Media Campaign will be a General Campaign and its support materials will be of a general nature - but all other communication will Target Audience-specific and sensitive to local situations, needs, context and culture.

Clients of CSW

There are differentials among the Clients of CSW:

- Regulars: Shopkeepers, Office-goers, Single Workers Away from Families in poor and middle-class sections, Police, etc
- Impulse-based: Youth and young working men experimenting with sex from all sections of society

All of this Target Audience will be influenced by the Mass Media Campaign for Behaviour Change and appreciation of the need to use condoms. In addition:

- The CSW themselves should be empowered to exert pressure and negotiating power through IPC to convert them to use condoms and to check for STD and if necessary, opt for VCT as well
- This Target Audience can be influenced by the Mass Media Condom Campaigns of commercial and social marketing companies

  (eg – Discussions with NGOs in Migrant Labour Interventions under the purview of the Ahmedabad Municipal Corporation AIDS Control Society revealed that these 'Clients of CSW' prefer to use the condoms which are 'imported' because of the "suggestive photographs on the packet" and the pleasure connotations of "colours and spots, dots, ribs" etc.)
- This Target Audience can be influenced by Community Advocacy and Social Mobilization efforts

Truck Drivers

All of this Target Audience will be influenced by the Mass Media Campaign for Behaviour Change and understand the need to use condoms. In addition:

- The CSW themselves must be empowered to exert pressure and negotiate through IPC to convert them (as Clients) to use condoms and to check for STD. In addition, if necessary - opt for VCT.
- This Target Audience can be influenced by the Mass Media Condom Campaigns of commercial and social marketing companies

- There is an opportunity for a Multi-sectoral Approach here through the Fleet Owner and Transport/Logistic Companies, the Transport Departments of Companies which use a lot of Trucks and Haulage for goods movement, the Oil Companies which [a] Use transport and [b] Operate Petrol Pumps which are frequented by truck drivers
- Communication efforts may be started by this sector with the help of NACO – workshops and interactions will help the relevant companies understand HIV, the objectives of NACP III and how they can contribute to the programmatic interventions through Target-specific communication campaigns and materials
- The Dhaba owners may be inducted into Advocacy efforts to support the Behaviour Change in both condom use and the need to follow the A and B (of ABC). They must also speak about the need to treat STDs and opt for VCT
- The Dhabas and Petrol Pumps can stock condoms

Migrant Labour

There are different kinds of Migrant Populations:

Category 1: Casual Migrant Labour is most vulnerable to HIV infection because of the nomadic lifestyle, long periods away from home and low literacy levels, low awareness about HIV/AIDS – and they are the people targeted by the TI – brick kiln workers, construction site workers, casual field labour, rickshaw pullers, dock labour, coolies and porters, etc

This Target Audience needs to be primarily approached through IPC (although some spin-off effect will be derived from the Mass Media Campaign)

- o Communication materials in support of the IPC will be Playing Cards, Flip Charts, Audio Cassettes, Video shows (where possible) through a TV booth or through Van publicity.
- o Since most of this population lives in slums and shanty towns – Street Theatre, Folk Genre Communication like *Nukkad,* Mime, Puppets – can be used for "enter-educate'.
- o After the entertainment – there is scope for Group Discussions and IPC on safe sex, need to use condoms, need to check for STD, opt for VCT, etc

Category 2: The second category of migrant populations who are not necessarily in the 'labour class' but work away from home because of economic compulsions, can be *zari* and gold workers, diamond cutters, milk vendors, shop-keepers, tailors, cooks and caterers, and young men working in hotels and holiday resorts. They are extremely vulnerable to HIV infection because they visit CSW and also engage in sex with casual partners, not necessarily with any "commercial" purpose.

All of this Target Audience will be influenced by the Mass Media Campaign for Behaviour Change and appreciation of the need to use condoms. In addition:

- o Since they are Clients of Sex Workers - the CSW will be able to exert pressure and negotiating power through IPC to convert them to use condoms, to seek treatment for STD and if necessary, opt for VCT as well
- o This Target Audience can be influenced by the Mass Media Condom Campaigns of commercial and social marketing companies
- o Where some of these communities form "residential groupings", the NGOs engaged in TI can make use of communication through Street Theatre, Folk Genre like *Nukkad,* Mime, Puppets, etc. After the entertainment – there is scope for Group Discussions and IPC on safe sex, need to use condoms, need to seek treatment for STD and opt for VCT
- o This Target Audience can also be influenced by Advocacy and Social Mobilization efforts by the general public

Priorities Two - Four

A. Messages and Materials - Target Audience: Youth and Women

- o Information Education and Communication (IEC) through a Mass Media Campaign in Print, TV and Radio
- o Supported by Materials such as Posters, Leaflets, Flip Charts, Games, Comics
- o Outdoor Reminder Media – Hoarding, Wall Paintings and Glo Signs
- o Inter-Personal Communication (IPC) through One-to-One Counselling, Group Meetings and Discussions, Public Meetings, Peer Group Meetings

The Mass Media Campaign will be a General Campaign and its support materials will be of a general nature - but all other communication will Target Audience-specific and sensitive to local situations, needs, context and culture.

Youth

All of this Target Audience will be influenced by the Mass Media Campaign for Behaviour Change and appreciation of the need to use condoms. In addition:

- o Youth can be motivated to be the drivers of Advocacy Efforts themselves while being participants in similar initiatives
- o Schools (Classes 9 – 12), Local Community centres, and Youth political Cadres can start their own Advocacy efforts
- o Schools and Colleges can start youth engagement initiatives with the public in the context of HIV/AIDS
- o Schools and Colleges can have internal "Socially Useful Projects" where students volunteer with PLHA groups or move into "media dark areas" to extend the campaign – this can be done through the Link Workers
- o Workplaces must evolve a clearly defined HIV/AIDS policy that is visible, documented and explained to workers by HR personnel
- o Medical Officers at workplaces can encourage the use of condoms, check-ups for STD and counsel for VCT if they feel that behaviour patterns warrant such action
- o Young working men and women can start their own Advocacy efforts to encourage Behaviour Change.
- o The Mass Media Campaign will Help create an enabling environment for Behaviour Change
- o Government and Private Sector Hospitals "sensitized" under the Attitude Change initiative in service providers will also help create an enabling environment for young people who approach them with questions on sexuality or a need for check-ups, STD Treatment – a Special Media Kit for Youth can be prepared for this Target Audience

Women

All of this Target Audience will be influenced by the Mass Media Campaign for Behaviour Change. They will be exposed to Male and Female Celebrities endorsing the need to use Condoms/Partner Fidelity, etc They will also be a Target Audience under the Convergence with RCH Programme and communication channels may be opened through Anganwadi, ASHA workers.

In tandem with widespread Advocacy Efforts, this will help create an enabling environment where women can broach the topic of condoms in relation to 'sex without the context of family planning) with partners and husbands.

- o Women may be motivated to be the drivers of Advocacy Efforts themselves for women's groups in both urban and rural settings (eg: Under the Convergence suggested with RCH – is there scope for the Janani "Titli Centres" where a local couple in a rural setting (traditional health practitioner, school teacher and his wife) advises couples on Family Planning also raises awareness levels on HIV/AIDS?)
- o Similarly, Mahila Mandals and Samities, and Women's Self Help Groups may be supported by communication materials which are customized with "gender-sensitive messages." The Link Workers can even work with craft producer organizations *(such as SEWA)*, which can also be conduits for spreading "gender-sensitive communication messages" through Advocacy and with a supply of communication materials
- o The Public Sector Banks with Micro Lending Schemes *(eg State Bank Stree Shakti Yojana)* can create a special set of communication materials raising Awareness levels which can be given to women who approach them for loans. This will be an off-shoot of "Mainstreaming and Mutli-sectoral Partnerships."

Priority Two

Messages and Materials - Target Audience: PLHA

Background

NACP-II established that People Living with HIV and AIDS (PLHA) are a critical resource for appropriate and effective response to the epidemic. A significant development during NACP-II has been a shift in the role of PLHA from being beneficiaries of services to becoming important partners of NACO, SACS, Civil Society Organizations and service providers.

NACO has established clear guidelines for mobilization and networking among PLHA and utilizing them as advocates for prevention as well as care, support and treatment programmes - including setting up of Drop-in centres. PLHA have now organized themselves into networks/ formal and informal organizations/groups at the National and State Level and in some cases - District and Sub-District levels. Till December 2005, two national level networks, 25 state networks and 65 district networks were funded under NACP II. Concurrently, a number of initiatives taken at the national and state levels have led to substantial capacity building amongst PLHA –

both men and women. Organised groups of PLHA along with NGOs/CBOs and development organisations are now engaged in treatment education, positive living counselling, psychosocial support and positive prevention programmes.

Despite the steps taken to implement GIPA, there are gaps in the desired response. Effective partnership with PLHA at all levels has not yet been achieved and there is inadequate understanding of GIPA principles and implementation. Further, there are problems in systematic referrals from the VCT, PPTCT and ART to district level PLHA support groups/ structures. The necessary institutional mechanisms to support the implementation of PLHA and GIPA are still to be evolved. There is absence of clear organizational policies on hiring people living with or affected by HIV and AIDS.

NACP-III will build on the experience already gained by strengthening the organisations of PLHA at national/state/district level; promoting GIPA through sensitizing implementing agencies (Government, Private Sector and Civil Society) and creating an enabling environment for enhanced involvement of PLHA and affected people.

This Target Audience will be the beneficiary of Advocacy Campaigns which exhort the acceptance of HIV as a "manageable disease and therefore, not to marginalize those who are HIV-Positive."

- o Communication Materials must inform the general public about being sensitive to PLHA – through Films, *(eg Films like My Brother Nikhil, etc)*
- o Special Posters. Advocacy Campaigns can be supported by TV appearances of PLHA
- o PLHA Groups which are Networking need to have special Materials which explain HIV/AIDS to the Public – Routes of Transmission, VCT, etc
- o Type of Advocacy Efforts Suggetsed: Social leaders and influencers, as well as religious leaders must campaign on behalf of non-discriminatory practices towards PLHA.

Priority Two

Messages and Materials - Target Audience: Children

The members of this Target Audience will be exposed to the Mass Media Campaign, but will be outside its ambit of influence because they are not able to exercise any control over their life situation and environment.

The situations of abusive and exploitative child labour; the vulnerability of being a rag picker or in child labour, or being a homeless child on the streets leave this group the most difficult to access and help. Materials will be Films and Videos, Comic Books – largely pictorial (keeping in mind literacy levels). IPC Interaction will be required.

- More NGOs will need to work with this Target Audience to make sure that children are not sexually abused, trafficked by their own parents, and forced into prostitution in order to make a living.
- Where parents can be accessed – the NGOs can counsel them on the need to protect the children and educate them about safe sex
- For children who are orphans, homeless beggars, runaways and live on the streets – SACS can link with NGOs which offer Night Shelters, Safe Houses, Drop-in Centres, General Healthcare Centres.
- Similar NGOs may be approached which offer access to opportunities for education for such children
- NGOs working independently and with the SACS can persuade the employers of children in labour situations about the need to protect them from sexual abuse
- This Target Audience needs IPC, Group Meetings and Discussions and will be supported by communication materials. There will be a supply of the communication materials at Drop-in Centres – (Films, Flip Charts, Comics and Cartoons, Audio Cassettes).
- Major Advocacy efforts can be started with foundations like the Ram Krishna Mission, Birla Education Trust and others who work in the field of education and have special programmes for marginalized children

Priority Two

Messages and Materials - Target Audience: Tribal Populations

Background

Under NACP-II, there were no specific interventions among tribal populations except in the North East. In Andhra Pradesh and Rajasthan, these populations were covered under the interventions designed for the HRG. Very few NGOs were reported to be working specifically with tribal population on HIV/AIDS.

The tribal population is estimated to be 8.2 percent of nation's total population. Seven states account for more than 75 percent of the tribal population: the main concentration of tribals is in Central India and in the North-Eastern States: Arunachal Pradesh, Meghalaya, Mizoram, Nagaland. Prominent tribal areas constitute about 15 percent of the total geographical area of the country and correspond largely to the underdeveloped areas of the country (IDSP 2003).

A social assessment conducted during the NACP–III preparatory phase has identified factors of tribal vulnerability to sexual networking patterns, migratory status and exposure to tourists and external influences. The study has referred to a number of states where tribal women/girls are now being increasingly lured into commercial sex and trafficking.

Knowledge and awareness about HIV/AIDS/STI is low among the tribals. In the matter of treatment-seeking behaviour, gender differences exist among these groups across all states except Manipur. Overall, however, non-availability and/or lack of access to health care facilities has been the main factor inhibiting health seeking on the part of the tribals. Trust in faith healers and non-qualified private practitioners was identified as another area of challenge.

During NACP-III, the capacity building of such providers and their role in referrals will be very important. Collaboration with the Ministries of SJE and Tourism will be the main vehicles for reducing the vulnerability of tribal people to HIV/AIDS. Establishing linkages with the Departments of Tribal Welfare and the Department of Health and Family Welfare at the state levels to mainstream HIV AIDS prevention education and access to services through their ongoing district health plans will be stressed. NACO activities will be fully converged with RCH II and NRHM.

Communication

- Increase Awareness through Target-Specific Messages and through Films, Posters, Flip Charts IEC.
- IPC will play a major component of the engagement for sensitizing and involving traditional healers and private practitioners in tribal areas in management of STIs and OIs and encourage referrals to ICTCs: to Focus on issues of migration and developing special programmes for migrant workers on lines discussed in earlier paragraphs.

Priority Three

Messages and Materials - Target Audience:

Service + Service Delivery

Healthcare Staff in Hospitals and PHCs

Staff and Counsellors of VCT and PPTCT

RCH and RNTCP Staff

NRHM Staff

The Healthcare Service Provider will need training and capacity building to support the Behaviour Change of the Target Audience, and in order to provide better and more sensitive care and treatment, advice and counselling

- o Communication will be implemented through Training and Capacity Building, supported by customized materials.
- o Location and Programme-specific materials in the form of Films, Posters, Flip Charts will need to be created (e.g. – integrating RCH Message to include message for HIV/AIDS)
- o This Target Audience will benefit from the Mass Media Campaign and Advocacy/Mainstreaming Efforts

The Convergence Element of NACP III envisages integration with other national disease control programmes as crucial. Government of India has launched the National Rural Health Mission (NRHM) to coordinate the delivery of services under different disease control programmes.

NACP III will synergise all its services with the NRHM, especially with the Reproductive and Child Health (RCH) programme and the Revised National TB Control Programme (RNTCP) in the light of the recommendations of the Tasks Forces constituted for the purpose. Action Plans prepared by the State Health Society set up under NRHM and the State AIDS Control Society and their M&E systems will be dovetailed into each other for more effective implementation.

The components of RTI/STI, blood safety, condom promotion, sentinel surveillance and PPTCT have close links with RCH and NACP. This will be reflected in the training and implementation arrangements including procurement and logistics. Collaboration is also feasible with such other programmes as CGHS, Drug De-addiction, Hospital Waste management and Integrated Disease Surveillance Programme. NACP-III will utilise the expertise available in research institutions under the ICMR and Health Ministry.

- o Communication will be implemented through Training and Capacity Building, supported by customized materials.
- o Location and Programme-specific materials in the form of Films, Posters, Flip Charts will need to be created *(e.g. – integrating RCH Message to include message for HIV/AIDS)*
- o This Target Audience will benefit from the Mass Media Campaign and Advocacy/Mainstreaming Efforts

Messages and Materials - Target Audience:

Staff of Blood Banks

The broad objective of the blood safety programme under NACP-III is to ensure provision of safe and quality blood within one hour of requirement through a well-coordinated national blood transfusion service. The specific objective is to ensure reduction in the transfusion associated HIV transmission to 0.5 per cent.

There is a serious mismatch between demand and supply of blood in the country. Another issue of concern is that the proportion of voluntary blood donation is to the tune of 52 per cent only which is grossly inadequate. Several activities to promote public awareness of the need for voluntary blood donation have been undertaken in collaboration with NGOs. These will be strengthened.

In addition, through collaboration with the Indian Red Cross Society, voluntary blood donation camps and other activities will be regularly undertaken to increase blood collection in the country. The target is to raise voluntary blood donation to 90 per cent by end of the programme.

Communication:

- Training and Support Materials
- Events around Blood Safety and Voluntary Blood Donation

Special Campaigns around:

- Observance of Voluntary Blood donation Day on 1 October
- IEC materials for Blood Safety and voluntary blood donation
- Promotional schemes for increasing VBD
- Capacity Building among the personnel in Blood Banks
- Voluntary Blood Donation Media Campaign in Print, TV and Radio with supportive Posters and Hoardings
- Advocacy Efforts in Colleges ands Corporate Workplaces to motivate Blood Donation drives
- Youth "Safe Health Awareness Clubs" to be drivers for "Blood Donation Camps

Priority Four:

Messages and Materials - Target Audience

Mainstreaming and Multi-sectoral Partnerships

National Level interactions will motivate these Target Audiences to join the "Advocacy Movement"

Communication will be through Workshops, Seminars, Consultations–with support materials

Subsequently – The Mainstreaming and Multi-sectoral Partners can develop their own Communication Materials and Campaigns and design their own events for enlarging the scope of creating an atmosphere supportive to raising awareness levels about HIV/AIDS, inculcating Behaviour Change and creating an enabling environment

Messages and Materials – Target Audience

Social and Community Organizations

Influencers, Public Persona

Media

Background

Under NACP II, efforts to involve religious leaders, youth forums, District and Rural bodies were started. But they were neither sustained nor sufficient in numbers to achieve critical mass – and the result of the inadequate advocacy efforts has been:

- Prevailing environment of discrimination for PLHA
- Feeling of insecurity for people at risk who may be aware that they need to have a Test, but are frightened to come forward
- This points to fear of social marginalization, loss of jobs
- Lack of community involvement to reduce gender inequality, which makes women more vulnerable to HIV infection
- Lack of community mobilization to educate youth on safe sexual behaviour, which makes youth more vulnerable to the infection
- No safety net/community care for orphans and vulnerable children – which makes them vulnerable to HIV infection, trafficking, sexual abuse

The NACP III Communication Strategy and Implementation Plan has an in-built Road-Map for Advocacy Efforts and Programmes, along with Social Mobilization Initiatives.

There is a Campaign within a Campaign:

- The Mass Media campaign creates opportunities for programmes and events around it on a sustained, long-term basis
- At the other end of the spectrum, Advocacy and Social Mobilization initiatives will have the permanent and visible support of the Mass Media campaign

- They will also have the leverage of AIDS Celebrity Endorsements which can generate " Baby Kissing" and "Shaking Hands" opportunities and lead to Guest Appearances at entertainment programmes, public meetings, political rallies, etc

Annexure 6.2

Media Planning and Buying – The Mechanics of Implementation

Coordination on Mass Media buying between NACO and SACS

The media environment has changed tremendously between NACP II and NACP III and continues to do so. New media are continuously being added and older ones such as radio evolving. In this complex and dynamic environment it is important to be able to plan and buy media in a way that optimizes expenditures, through professional agencies who have the expertise as well as the databases form syndicated research such as NRS and IRS. This is essential for ensuring that NACO gets the best value for the money spent on mass media.

- It is proposed that mass media be bought centrally by NACO on behalf of all SACS so that the best rates can be negotiated and bulk discounts availed of.
- Media which can only be bought locally and for which centralised buying is not possible will be bought be SACS.
- For this the mass media requirements of all the SACS need to be available to NACO in a timely fashion each year, so that they can feed into a coordinated media buying plan.
- It is proposed that the SACS who will be using mass media in a major way will have professional advertising agencies contracted to work with them.

Components of the Mass Media Campaign

- Majority media buying will be done at the National level to achieve cost effectiveness and it will be shared with the SACS who may also buy media space in case of local needs.
- NACO will take the leadership for building communities around local radio and work for convergence and partnering with RCH, RD, WCD, SACS, and relevant NGO/CBO/any academia available for concurrent research/programme coordination. This could be done through developing core listener groups, their leaders, through intermediate agencies like NGO etc. and facilitate formation of discussion forum. This allows "last mile" linkage of programmes.

- Majority media buying will be done at the national level to achieve cost effectiveness and it will be shared with the SACS who may also buy media space in case of local needs.
- Strategic partnerships will be developed with Prasar Bharati and other electronic media organizations for carrying informative programmes on HIV/ AIDS as part of regular health and information related programmes of these channels.
- Potential of news channels and print media will be fully utilized for augmenting coverage of news on HIV/ AIDS.
- NACO will develop and produce mass media materials through selected professional media and advertising agencies with common branding using a common logo. States will adapt the materials produced nationally.
- The process will be managed through a Technical Resource Group (TRG) for communication. TRG will also be available to SACS if any specific state level requirements need to be met.

Implementing Local Level Activities

- Locations will be identified in collaboration with other departments and hoardings will be erected at these locations in partnerships. Some of the suggested locations are petrol pumps, toll plazas on the highways and state roads, Sulabh toilets, tourist points, localities inhabited by High Risk Groups and Highly Vulnerable populations. Similarly, message panels will also be installed in government departments, industrial establishments, hospitals, ICTCs, PPTCT centres etc. and also at schools, colleges and universities with appropriate messages for specific target and age groups.
- There will also be a large number of other local activities (e.g. exhibitions, caravans, rallies, street plays, song and drama performances etc.). Identification and planning for the activities would be done at state and district levels.
- One of the key operational modes proposed in NACP-III is the setting up of Red Ribbon clubs and branding of the communication outlets at various levels. Red Ribbon Clubs would be community-led initiatives that will become the catalysts for communication and link to services.
- Optimal use will be made of the available civil society networks and organisations like SHGs, NYKS, NSS, PRIs, Red Ribbon Clubs, youth clubs, literacy mission clubs, mahila mandals, water

user associations / cooperatives and new ones created for social mobilization. RCH-II, Rural Development, and workers like ANMs, AWWS, ASHA will also be put into service for awareness and BCC. Prominent role would be given to HIV positive networks and TI partners.

- Over 10,000 service delivery points including blood banks, ART centres, PPTCT centres, ICTC/ VCTCs, STI clinics, district nodal offices, community care centres, District Information Centres, and condom outlets will be developed as communication hubs by placing IEC materials and propagating the messages through service providers.
- Media dark areas would be reached through a special strategy of mobile vans, outreach and community radio activities. About 100 mobile vans equipped with services and IEC materials for A and B districts will be deployed. Community radio stations in these areas will also be set up on an experimental basis, if clearances are obtained.

Annexure - 6.3

Suggested Media Mix For Mass Media

Media	*Channels*	*Frequency of Spots/Advertisements*	*Programme Selection*	*Media buying*
Radio	AIR: FM, Vividh Bharati, Primary (National as well as regional), pvt. FM channels	Major spots at prime times with reminder spots of 10" – 20" at different time intervals. "time checks" messages	Entertainment, youth, women, rural, health, news etc. also depending on ratings and target audience	i. Majority of media buying to be done at the national level and to be shared with SACS keeping the factor of cost effectiveness and bonus time under consideration. There may be spikes of activities during the period coinciding with events such as VBDD, WAD etc. ii. NACO and SACS to identify Radio/ TV programmes where HIV messages/themes can be incorporated as part of CSR iii. Close interaction with media persons for broadcasting / publishing news on HIV/AIDS issues
TV	Doordarshan, C&S channels (national as well as regional)	Major spots at prime times with reminder spots of 10" – 20" at different time intervals.	Same as above	
Print	National English, Hindi and vernacular language newspapers and magazines	Advertisements on special days such as VBDD, WAD, Int. Women's Day, Int. Day Against Drug Abuse etc. and for special campaigns launched from time to time.	Same as above	

Annexure - 6.4

Optimal Media Mix for Outdoors – Hoardings, Mobile Vans, Signages

Sl.No.	*Media*	*Locations*	*Implementing Agency*
1.	Hoardings	Hospitals, Railway Stations, Post Offices, Municipal compounds, Petrol Pumps, Toll Plazas etc. on Highways and state roads, Tourist spots, Sulabh Toilets, areas inhabited by high risk and highly vulnerable populations, SACS may identify more locations depending on availability of space	NACO and SACS. Primarily free space should be identified as partnership effort for erecting permanent hoardings.
2.	Information Panels	Hospitals, ICTCs/ VCTCs, PPTCT centres, Art centres, Schools, Colleges, University campuses, Govt. ministries/departments, other mainstreaming partners	NACO and SACS to develop information panels on different themes such as generic information, condoms, gender, youth, stigma and discrimination, myths and misconceptions on sun board/vinyl boards etc.
3.	IPC Activities	i. Nukkad Nataks, Folk Shows, village meetings etc.	At least 1-2 events covering a cluster of 5-6 villages particularly high prevalence, medium prevalence and highly vulnerable states. The vulnerability factor to decide the number of events / shows in the area
		ii. Through AWWs, ANMs, SHGs, NYKs, NSS, RCH, RD and by forming RRCs	SACS to integrate HIV/AIDS programme with other health, social and development programmes by sensitizing officials/ workers of these programmes.
4.	Services Delivery Points as Communication Hubs	Hospitals, ICTCs / VCTCs, ART centres, STI clinics, condom outlets to function as information providers on HIV/AIDS	SACS to coordinate
5.	Mobile Vans	Media dark areas/low media reach areas of A&B districts	To be run under supervision of SACS. The vans will provide services as well as function as communication hubs.
6.	Community Radio	Same as above	To be run by local institutions under overall supervision of SACS

Annexure - 6.5

Advocacy Interventions in NACP-III

Community in need	*Need*	*General barrier to need*	*Specific barrier*	*Intervention*	*Indicators*
People with HIV	Enabling environment	Stigma and discrimination	Community attitudes	Positive media initiatives	1 No of Media clips on major channels with positive initiatives 2 Prashar Bharti and I& B ministry have an advocacy policy on HIV/AIDS
				Policy champions	Nos of policy champions
				Laws to protect PLHA	
				Government statements in support of PLHA	
			Discriminatory health care services	Reviews of services/Rights-based approaches to service delivery	1Rights based approach as a policy is adopted by the NHRC and NACO
				Laws to protect PLHA	Legal Cell under NACO is formulated and active.
			Lack of awareness of rights	Rights awareness campaigns	
				Media initiatives	
				Better resourced PLHA groups	
		Unhelpful legal environment	Discriminatory laws	Review and amendment of laws	Legislative reform bill is tabled in the parliament.
				Support for Lawyers' Collective etc.	

(Contd...)

				More functional Government advisory bodies	
			Laws applied in discriminatory way	Police sensitivity training	
				PLHA groups better resourced	
				Support for groups defending PLHA rights	
				Judicial training	
	Participation in HIV decision-making forums	Exclusion/non-involvement	Lack of PLHA capacity	Improved funding	1 Funding for HIV /AIDS increases 2 Increased Govt resource allocation 3 Improved mechanisms for budget utilization
				Technical assistance	
				Improved access to government information regarding HIV surveillance data etc.	
			Absence of consultative forums	Establishment of consultative fora	
				Inclusion of PLHA in existing fora	
			Commitment to GIPA	Promotion of successful partnership approaches	
			Lack of understanding of value of advocacy	Measurement and promotion of advocacy successes	Advocacy as a consultative process is recognized & implemented by the Govt. and involves all stake holders.

(*Contd...*)

Key communities	Enabling environment	Stigma and discrimination	Police harassment	Police/NGO collaborations	1Top Level body for Advocacy formed 2 NGOS involved in police trg
				Documenting police practices	1 Best practices documented & Disseminated
				Government leadership	
				Police sensitivity training	Harm reduction is the core of all police trg manuals.
			Community attitudes	Positive media initiatives	1Nos of positive speakers
				Policy champions	
				Laws to protect key communities	
				Government statements in support of key communities	
			Discriminatory health care services	Reviews of services/Rights-based approaches to service delivery	1Health sector Policy on stigma and discrimination is formulated 2 Nos of reported cases of stigma & discrimination go down
				Laws to protect key communities	
			Lack of awareness of rights	Rights awareness campaigns	
				Media initiatives	
				Better resourced representative groups	

(*Contd...*)

Unhelpful legal environment	Discriminatory laws	Review and amendment of laws	Laws are reviewed and advocacy for change in the legal environ is taken up by the forum.
		Support for Lawyers' Collective etc.	
		More functional Government advisory bodies	
	Laws applied in discriminatory way	Police sensitivity training	
		Key community groups better resourced	
		Support for groups defending key community rights	
		Judicial training	1 Nos of Judges sensitized 2 Judiciary talks about discriminatory laws 3 Key cases study
Exclusion/non-involvement	Lack of capacity	Improved funding	
	Lack of commitment to involvement	Promotion of successful partnership approaches	
Inadequate information about HIV	Poor media coverage of HIV issues	Support for positive voices	
		Positive media initiatives	
		Policy champions	
	Lack of Government support for awareness	Government leadership	1 Nos of studies carried out by the Parliamentary forum on HIV response in various countries. 2 Political champions are identified
		Effective Government advisory structures	1 Evidence based data is generated on the epidemic scenario 2 Data is analyzed and advocacy is based on the data
Inadequate testing	Poorly trained and discriminatory testing services	Service reviews and improvements	1 VCCTC services improve 2 Nos of individuals wanting to know their status increases 3 No Mandatory testing is done
		Better funding	

(*Contd*...)

Fear of testing	Media scare mongering	Media initiatives	1 Reduced negative reporting by media 2 Positive images are produced regarding HIV + persons
		Visibility of positive people	
		Positive images of PLHA	
	Inadequate access to/understanding of treatment	Improved treatments access	1 Role out of HAART improves 2 Nos of physicians trained in HAART 3 A public Health Approach is adopted for role out of HAART
		Treatments awareness	
Inadequate surveillance and other data	Poor data collection	Improved research	Data generated is validated, representative of the epidemic
	Poor data dissemination	Consultative foras	
Inadequate information about HIV	Poor media coverage of HIV issues	Media initiatives	
		Policy champions	1 Bollywood feels responsible as key stake holder in the response 2 The nos of policy champions are better informed
	Need for increased Government support for awareness	Government leadership	1 Nos of IAS, IPS officers sensitized 2 The IAS, IPS officers have a raised KAP level in studies conducted scientifically.
		Effective Government advisory structures	
Inadequate consultative forums	Absence of forums	Government leadership	
	Non-inclusive forums	Community involvement in forums	INP+ and KP are involved in the planning, implementation and evaluation.

Annexure - 7

Infection Control and Waste Management Plan & Construction Guidelines

Annexure - 7.1

Infection Control and Waste Management Plan

The **IC-WM Plan** (Plan) provides a consolidated, reference material on IC-WM good practices that may be further tailored to suit the facility's needs. The Plan is build on the following framework:

- Section I: Infection Control and Waste Management
- Section II: Capacity Building
- Section III: Institutional Framework
- Section IV: Monitoring and Evaluation
- Section V: Implementation Schedule

Section I: Infection Control and Waste Management

Healthcare workers involved in the NACP face the highest occupational risk due to the nature of their work dealing with testing and treatment of HIV/AIDS cases. Infectious waste from AIDS related activities include primarily: needles and sharps, blood and blood bags, used test kits, culture samples and slides and other related infectious waste such as swabs, gloves, bandages, sputum cups etc. Thus it is imperative that good IC-WM practices are implemented. This activity should not be restricted only to certain sections of the healthcare facility like VCTC, PPTCT, etc. but as mentioned clearly in section.....above, the coordination of such integrated approach to IC-WM should be undertaken at the state level with DOHFW taking the lead.

1. Waste Segregation and On-site Storage

Segregation at source is the most critical step towards a well-functioning waste management system. Separation of infectious and non-infectious waste becomes impossible once mixed, resulting in greater risk to all concerned. Additionally infectious waste, when segregated is a minor part of total waste generated, amounting to about 20-25% and can be easily managed.

The Biomedical Rules provides color coding for waste segregation and their respective treatment options, as listed below:

WASTE SEGREGATION AND COLOR CODING[1]		
Colour Coding	***Waste Category***	***Treatment option as per Schedule I***
Yellow	Plastic bag Cat. 1, Cat. 2, and Cat. 3, Cat. 6.	Incineration / deep burial
Red	Disinfected container/plastic bag Cat. 3, Cat. 6, Cat.7	Autoclaving / Microwaving / Chemical Treatment
Blue / White Translucent	Plastic bag/puncture proof Cat. 4, Cat. 7. Container	Autoclaving / Microwaving / Chemical Treatment and Destruction / shredding
Black	Plastic bag Cat. 5 and Cat. 9 and Cat. 10. (solid)	Disposal in secured landfill

The facility should ensure that there are designated segregation points, as close to the generation points as possible. Segregation requires appropriate consumables, such as good quality and adequately sized containers, non-chlorinated plastic bags, needle cutters and safety boxes. The specifications and colour-coding provided in the BioMedical Rules need to be strictly followed. NACP III needs to ensure that all these tools needed are provided to all their facilities which are involved in HIV/AIDS related testing and treatment activities.

2. Collection and Transportation of Biomedical Wastes

Transportation of biomedical wastes, within and outside the healthcare facility needs to be secure and well-managed. Spills and leakages can be risky for patients and the community, but can also result in pilferage and reuse of potentially infectious items such as syringes etc.

Specific steps to be taken by each facility include:

- Waste should be collected from various sources and transported to a central location.
- Within the facility, special waste routes should be designated to avoid patient care areas.
- Special timing should be identified for transportation of biomedical waste to the central point.
- Dedicated wheeled containers, trolleys or carts should be used to transport the waste to the collection/treatment site. These should be such that the waste can be easily loaded and emptied and remain secured during transportation. They should not have any sharp edges and be easy to clean and disinfect.

- If disposal is done within the premises of the healthcare facility, care should be taken that different categories of waste are disposed of accurately (sharps in sharps pit, anatomical waste in deep burial pits etc) as designated in the BioMedical Rules.
- Waste handlers should be properly trained and should use barrier protection duringtransportation.

Whilst transporting infectious waste outside the facility, dedicated vehicles with Cytotoxic/biohazard waste symbols should be used. This responsibility however, is usually that of the Centralized Biomedical Waste Treatment Facility, which are contracted for treatment and disposal of biomedical waste.

3. Treatment and Disposal of Biomedical Wastes

This section details the various waste treatment and disposal practices in the absence of a Centralized Biomedical Waste Treatment Facility, drawing primarily from the Biomedical Rules.

- Used sharps (needles, slides, scalpels etc), blood bags, syringes and other infectious plastic and liquid wastes (Categories 4, 7, 8, and 10 of the BioMed Rules) need to be disinfected by immersion in 1% hypochlorite solution or any other equivalent chemical reagent. It must be ensured that chemical treatment ensures disinfection.
- Waste containers should contain freshly prepared disinfectant solution and be kept closed all the time. At all times, the waste container should not be more than 3/4th full.
- The waste containers should be emptied at least once everyday.
- Infected linen in the hospital should be carefully packed in plastic bags, and disinfected before being sent for washing. Personnel involved in laundering infected linen should take adequate precautions to prevent the exposure to infections.
- A log of quantity of waste generated by type, name of waste handler, time of emptying waste container, time of cleaning container and pouring disinfectant should be maintained.
- Disposal as recommended in the Rules, should be as follows:
  - **Sharps** in their puncture proof containers should be drained of the disinfectant and disposed in the sharps pit, constructed within the premises.
  - **Infected organic waste** should be disposed of in the deep burial pits also constructed within the facility and covered with a layer of lime and soil.

- **Infected recyclables** such as plastics and metals, can be sent for recycling but only after disinfection and/or autoclaving.

All equipment used for bio-medical waste treatment should be periodically subjected to maintenance checks to ensure its functioning. Both preventive and corrective maintenance schedules and records should be retained in the facility.

As a general practice of maintaining good hygiene, the floors of the facility should be first swabbed with a wet cloth, then swept to remove grits to avoid dust carrying pathogens from rising into the air and, finally, swabbed with a disinfectant solution. The swab cloth should be washed with detergent after every use. The housekeeping personnel should employ use of protective barriers to prevent exposure to infection.

4. Sharps Management

Given the high risk of infection from infected sharps, a separate section on the safe use and disposal of sharps is being detailed. Sharps are anything that may cause puncture and cuts. Sharps include needles, scalpels, blades, broken glass, slides, lancets, sutures, and IV catheters. Infected needles, sharps and blood, if improperly handled, can be a source of infection for the HCWs.

Chances of infection to a HCW from an infected syringe have been estimated are as follows: Hepatitis B: 30%; Hepatitis C: 3-5%; HIV: 0.3%[2].

The following is the estimated risk per contaminated sharp, depending upon the source[3]:

HbeAg positive	30-40%
HCV PCR positive	10%
HBsAg positive	2-6%
HCV positive (PCR negative) 1%	
HIV positive	0.3%

It should be noted that these statistics come from Western countries with both comparatively low prevalence rates and well developed reporting and surveillance systems.

Higher prevalence rates in countries like India with inadequate IC-WM practices could entail a greater order of risk for exposed HCW.

Although the risk of infection from contaminated sharps is high for all categories of HCW, those most at risk of exposures are nurses, medical staff and clinical laboratory staff (blood collectors). Physicians are at some risk, but surgical and dental staff, although at high risk of injury, have a lower risk of infection. It must be remembered that all health care personnel (including cleaners, laundry staff and waste contractors) may be exposed to inappropriately discarded sharps. While emergency rooms and operating theatres pose high risk for HCW, it has been found that (a) the majority of exposures have occurred in general ward areas and (b) a larger number of exposures which would be classified as high risk have occurred in medical wards.

The following measures must be taken to ensure sharps safety in the work-place:

- Barrier protection must always be used when handling sharps.
- Sharps must be segregated and stored in puncture-proof containers at the point of generation.
- Sharps must be mutilated before treatment and disposal. Used disposable or Autodisable (AD) syringes should be mutilated by using needle cutters/ destroyers and hub-pullers and dropped into a puncture-proof container. Clipping, bending or breaking of needles by hand or re-capping should be avoided as this may cause accidental injuries.
- Used sharps should not be left untreated or carelessly on counter tops, food trays, or beds, as this can pose a risk to all concerned.
- Mutilated sharps should be immersed in 1% hypochlorite solution or any other equivalent chemical reagent for disinfection. Treatment by autoclaving / microwaving is also approved.
- Final disposal should be in a secured landfill. Wherever this is not available everywhere, sharps pits or encapsulation should be used.
    - o A sharps pit is a circular or rectangular pit, where sharp wastes are disposed. These pits are lined with brick, masonry or concrete rings. The pit should be covered with a concrete slab. When the pit is full, it should be sealed completely and another pit is prepared.
    - o Encapsulation is another method. When a container (puncture & leak proof containers) is three-quarter full, material such as cement mortar, bituminous sand, plastic foam or clay is poured until the container is completely filled. After the medium has dried, the containers are sealed and disposed in landfill sites.

- All the employees must be vaccinated, at a minimum, against Hepatitis B.

GUIDELINES FOR DISPOSAL OF USED DISPOSABLE SYRINGES[4]	
No.	**Steps / Stages**
1.	Severe needles from disposable syringe immediately after administering injection using a needle cutter/hub-cutter that removes the needle from disposable syringes or cuts plastic hub of syringe from AD syringes.
2.	The cut needles get collected in the puncture proof container of the needle-cutter/hub-cutter. The container should contain an appropriate disinfectant and the cut needles should be completely immersed in the disinfectant
3.	Segregate and store syringes and unbroken (but discarded) vials in a red bag or container.
4.	Send the collected materials to the Common bio-medical waste treatment facilities. If such facilities do not exist, then go to the next step.
5.	Treat the collected material in an autoclave. If this is unavailable, treat the waste in 1% hypochlorite solution or boil in water for at least 10 minutes. It shall be ensured that these treatments ensure disinfection.
6.	Dispose the autoclaved waste as follows: (i) Dispose the needles and broken vials in a pit / tank, (ii) Send the syringes and unbroken vials for recycling or landfill.
7.	Wash the containers properly for reuse.
8.	Make a proper record of generation, treatment and disposal of waste.

5. Blood safety in Laboratory

Blood is the single most important source of HIV, HIB and other blood borne infections for HCWs. The legal framework with regard to blood safety has been adequately outlined in the Drugs and Cosmetics Act/Rules (Schedule XII B), which makes mandatory the universal screening of blood units for five transmissible infections: Hepatitis B, Hepatitis C, HIV, syphilis and malaria. The rules also provide for adequate testing procedures, quality control, standard qualifications, and experience for blood bank personnel, maintenance of complete and accurate records, strict guidelines for holding of blood donation camps etc.

Careful donor screening, discouraging use of paid donors, stringent screening of donated units of blood and licensing of blood banks has become mandatory in India to prevent HIV transmission through blood and blood products. Another important action taken by NACO has been to modernize 815 blood banks (282 major blood banks, and 533 district level blood banks). HIV testing facilities were identified in 154 Zonal Blood Testing Centres with functional linkages to blood banks that did not have the facilities to screen blood for HIV [5]. A significant portion of the blood banking activity is now also being carried out in the non-government sector for instance, through the Indian Red Cross (IRCS), other NGOs, and private hospitals.

Risk of infection varies with a number of factors, including type and number of exposures, amount of blood involved in the exposure, amount of virus in the patients' blood etc. Modes of exposure to blood borne pathogens in a laboratory have been defined as below[6]:

Procedure	*HCW at risk*	*Source/Modes of Transmission*
Collection of blood/body fluid	Laboratory technician	▪ Needle stick injury ▪ Broken specimen container ▪ Blood contamination of hand with skin lesions/breach
Transfer of specimen	Laboratory technician and transport worker	▪ Contaminated exterior of container ▪ Broken specimen container ▪ Spills/splashes of specimen
Processing of specimen	Laboratory personnel	▪ Puncture of skin ▪ Contamination of skin from spills, splashes, glassware and work surface ▪ Faulty techniques ▪ Perforated gloves
Cleaning /Washing	Laboratory support staff	▪ Puncture of skin ▪ Contamination of skin from spills, splashes, glassware and work surface
Disposal of waste	Laboratory support staff	▪ Contact with infectious waste, specially sharps, broken containers
Specimen transportation/mailing	Transport/postal staff	▪Broken/leaking container or packaging

- As per the BioMedical Rules, infected blood and blood samples is characterized as liquid waste and should be disinfected with hypochlorite solution.
- Screened positive blood bags, contaminated test kits and items are categorized as infected solid waste and should be disinfected by chemical treatment / autoclave and mutilated before disposal.
- Transport of specimens should be done in a diligent manner. The sample should be kept first in primary container with enough absorbent material around it. The primary container should then be placed in secondary container.
- Staff should take care that the secondary container is also leak-proof, properly sealed and labeled. Upright position must be maintained at all times.

6. Infection Control

The four key areas of infection control for the NACP III are:

- o Immunization against nosocomial infections
- o Availability and use of barrier protection
- o Management of PEP
- o Awareness

NACO has developed Guidelines on Post Exposure Prophylaxis Guidelines for Occupational Exposure which provides instructions on prevention of occupational exposure and universal precautions.

- Activities of high risk include invasive diagnostic and therapeutic procedures, wound dressing, operation theatre procedures, handling of blood/serum/body fluids and tissues etc. and special attention should be paid to ensuring safety precautions during these activities.
- Barrier protection (gowns, masks, caps, gloves, shoes) should be maintained to prevent contact with contaminated blood/body fluids.
- HCW working in high risk areas should be immunized, at the minimum, against HBV.
- Daily cleaning of facility premises with appropriate disinfection should be done.
- Spills are an important source of infection and should be cleaned up immediately. The spill should be covered with absorbent material, disinfectant poured around the spill and over the absorbent material. The surface should be wiped again with disinfectant. HCW must utilize barrier protection, specially gloves, when managing spills.
- General observance of personal hygiene is important. All staff must be neat and clean always, with clean uniforms, nails, short or tied-up hair, etc.
- PEP is required when there has been contact with known HIV/HBV infected material resulting from:
  - o Percutaneous inoculation (needle stick, cut with a sharp, etc.)
  - o Contamination of an open wound
  - o Contamination of breached skin (chapped, abraded, dermatitis)
  - o Contamination of a mucous membrane including conjunctiva
- In all such instances immediate post-exposure management is crucial to reducing the risk of acquiring infection. This should be

done in the manner prescribed by the above mentioned guidelines disseminated by NACO.

- All accidents whether needle stick injuries or spills should be reported in the Accident Reporting Format, i.e. Form III of Biomedical Rules.

Section II: Capacity Building and Awareness

Training and sensitization of various HCWs and functionaries within and outside the health care systems is vital for the successful implementation of any IC-WM Plan. The training should focus on Universal Precautions, principles of waste management, identification of roles and responsibilities for implementation, monitoring and reporting. IEC material on Universal Precautions have also been disseminated across the states and union territories.

As defined in Section 3.3 above, institutional coordination between DOHFW/centrally funded programs such as RCH, TB etc and NACP III for capacity building programs should be considered to optimize resources and provide a coordinated and integrated approach to IC-WM practices in the entire healthcare facility. All awareness, training and communication initiatives should be oriented towards providing knowledge / information, building skills & competencies and bringing about a fundamental, mindset change in the attitudes of staff & personnel.

Most of the initiatives detailed below have to be done at the state level and be coordinated by the SACS, with technical and financial support from the national level. The Training Plan and budget should be included into the State PIP and into NACO's PIP and program budget.

The following steps should be followed for implementing training:

- SACS Joint Director (Training) should conduct baseline assessment of training needs for HCWs involved in the NACP III.
- A Training Plan needs to be developed, based upon existing capacity and training needs. At the outset, this plan should distinguish between trainers and non-trainers and elaborate the criteria for identifying trainers and their requirement for training.
- Training should be provided to all HCWs, including doctors, nurses, ward boys, paramedics, laboratory technicians, and Class IV and/or housekeeping staff.
- Training should be imparted through:
  - o Dissemination of Information, Education and Communication (IEC) material that will sensitize HCWs and create general awareness on importance of IC-WM.

  - o Technical training for HCWs with specific responsibilities for discrete activities related to IC-WM.

- Training in Infection Control and in Waste Management should be a comprehensive package as the two are closely inter-twined.
- The Train the trainer program will have to be undertaken at two levels – state and district levels. Training should be provided on an annual basis, with refresher courses annually or biannually.
- In addition to classroom type training, IEC material and awareness-creating activities also need to employed for training the HCW. Training should preferably be provided on site.
- Each facility should keep records of training provided to employees, by category of employee.
- The IEC material must be prepared in the local language on both IC and WM and should be prominently displayed at various places. It should serve as a reminder for all the trained employees as well as sensitize patients visiting the facility. JD (IEC) should be responsible for this activity.

Section III: **Institutional Framework**

Effective implementation of the IC-WM Plan necessitates a strong institutional framework:

- A JD or APD and one Nodal officer should be identified and given the overall responsibility for IC-WM planning and implementation. The JD/APD will coordinate with other JDs for IEC, Surveillance and Training and interlink requirements and activities of the IC-WM plan with their respective activities. e.g. Coordination with JD-IEC to develop IEC material for IC-WM; with JD-Blood Safety to include IC-WM in guidelines for blood safety; with JD-Training for dissemination of IC-WM plan and related technical training; with JD-Surveillance to ensure monitoring, evaluation and reporting of IC-WM plan.
- Whilst the JD/APD shall provide oversight, the Nodal Officer will be responsible for monitoring, reporting and follow-up at all facilities being operated by SACS.

Cross-cutting issues such as infection control and waste management need a coordinated and integrated approach for the entire healthcare sector. Therefore, while this IC-WM plan is restricted to the NACP-III and its institutional framework, closer linkages and working relationships need to be developed with the DOHFW/centrally funded programs to.

This IC-WM Plan recommends that a three-tier IC-WM Task Force should be instituted with the following as Chair and Member Secretary respectively:

- At the **state level**, Principal Secretary and PD SACS
- At the **district level** DM/Collector and District Nodal Officer/Chief Medical Officer/District Medical & Health Officer
- At the **facility level** the Medical Superintendent (MS) or Resident Medical Officer (RMO)
- Representatives of the State Pollution Control Board and its district level offices should be included in the Task Force

The Task Force shall ensure implementation of the Plan at all departments of the hospitals within the legal framework of Biomedical Rules. It shall ensure that similar IC-WM guidelines and instructions are provided under the different programs and the overall health care sector. To avoid duplication and for optimization of resources, integrated training modules and programs can be designed along with designated trainers for SACS and the host facilities. Utilization of common resources such as treatment and disposal facilities can be monitored and maintained as a shared responsibility.

Section IV: Reporting, Monitoring and Evaluation

Monitoring & evaluation will be done through a mix of internal and external approaches. The internal reporting and evaluation mechanism on the IC-WM implementation should be integrated with overall NACP-III reporting. Management Information Systems (MIS) indicators pertaining to the IC-WM will be developed during implementation. External monitoring in the form of IC-WM implementation audits is also being recommended.

(i) Quarterly monitoring

Each facility must establish a robust system of monitoring through regular documentation and assessments. Ideally, each facility should designate one senior employee responsible for documentation and another for internal evaluation. In the case of VCTC, PPTCT and Blood banks, the laboratory technician should maintain records of waste sharps, gloves, etc. and infectious waste. The records must be maintained on a daily basis and internal assessments should be conducted on a monthly basis. Examples of reporting formats are provided in tables 2, 3 and 4 in the Annex 4:

The monthly monitoring reports from SACS shall be complied and sent to the district and state IC–WM task forces every quarter. The SACS PD should then forward the report to NACO with his comments on the success of implementation of the Plan and follow-up actions required along with budgetary requirements, if necessary.

The monthly monitoring reports from SACS shall be sent to the district and state IC–WM task forces. The SACS PD should then forward the report to NACO with his comments on the success of implementation of the Plan and follow-up actions required along with budgetary requirements, if necessary.

(ii) Periodic Implementation Review

Periodic implementation review of the IC-WM should be undertaken, and as far as possible, this review should be inbuilt into the regular review process of the NACP-III. This review should focus on consolidated information and reporting from individual facility and district levels. To facilitate regular and sustained monitoring, each SACS should develop annual Action Plans specifically for IC-WM, which should be included into the State PIPs.

- **State-level**

The IC-WM Task Force should review overall implementation of the IC-WM Plan on an annual basis. This review should cover the following:

- Positive outcomes of IC-WM implementation and how these can be enhanced.
- Major deviations from IC-WM implementation, if any.
- Training implementation and its effectiveness.
- Outcomes of monitoring & evaluation such as periodic progress reports or audit reports.

Some generic Performance Indicators of the IC-WM Plan have been recommended below, which can be easily monitored at the state level.

- Availability an use of equipment and consumables for IC-WM (syringes, gloves, soaps, disinfectants, PEP, etc);
- Compliance of facility with BioMedical Rules (accident reporting and waste segregation, disinfection, colour-coding etc);
- Annual training hours for trainers, HCWs and refresher training;
- Behavourial practices of HCWs and employment of IC-WM practices

- Adequacy and completeness of reporting
- Issues relating to inadequacy in host facility, which will hinder effective waste management at the SACS level.
- National-level

The Review should be done on an annual basis and the national level IC-WM review committee should be chaired by the PD, NACO. It is recommended that key management of NACO, MOHFW, CPCB, RCH and RNTCP programs also be members of the review process. The timing of this review should be concurrent with the NACP-III programmatic evaluation.

At the National level, this Review should cover the following:

- Positive outcomes of IC-WM implementation and how these can be enhanced.
- Major deviations from IC-WM implementation, such as:
- Training implementation and its effectiveness
- Poor implementation practices and inadequate use of equipment and consumables
- Irregular or incomplete documentation
- Outcomes of monitoring & evaluation such as periodic progress reports or audit reports.
- Issues that have been raised by the IC-WM Task forces during monthly and state level reviews.
- Need for modifications to existing operational guidelines or introduction of new guidelines.

(iii) Performance Indicators

NACP-III envisages a robust nationwide Strategic Information Management System (SIMS) with focus on implementation, monitoring, evaluation and strategic surveillance, appropriate standards for measuring performance, analyzing variances, identifying bottlenecks, alerting program managers and facilitating corrective measures. Some generic Performance Indicators of the IC-WM Plan have been recommended below, which should be integrated into the NACP-III SMIS.

- Implementation of all components of the IC-WM Plan
- Timely procurement and distribution of IC-WM consumables and equipment
- Regular and timely training programs undertaken

- Regular evaluation of training effectiveness and assessment of employee behavioural practices
- Timely interventions and coordination with host facility on significant issues which could hinder effective implementation of IC-WM Plan
- Timely and regular reporting and evaluation undertaken, with corrective measures when necessary.

(iv) External Implementation Audits

The SACS will be responsible for hiring of an external technical consultant/firm to undertake an independent evaluation of the program and its implementation. The agency to conduct this technical review should be chosen on the basis of their technical expertise and established experience in BioMedical waste management and environmental auditing. Such an independent audit review will be undertaken once during the life of the program, preferably before a mi-term evaluation is conducted.

Section V: Implementation Schedule

A generic Implementation Schedule for the IC-WM for a 12 month period is detailed below. It is recommended that the IC-WM activities get incorporated into each state level PIPs and into the national PIP.

Activities	*Q1*	*Q 2*	*Q 3*	*Q 4*
Resource Identification for implementation of IC-WM Plan				
Inclusion of IC-WM Plan activities into PIP				
Establishment of Task Force				
Preparation of Training Plan				
Finalization of Training modules and schedules				
Implementation of Training Plan				
Procurement of consumables and equipment				
Monitoring and Evaluation				
Monthly monitoring of activities				
Annual Monitoring of activities				
External Evaluation*				

Cost Estimates for Recommended Infection Control and Waste Management Plan

Cost estimation for implementation of the IC-WM plan has been done for SACS level, with the recommendation that this will be included into the state budget and into NACO's the national budget for the NACP-III.

Since SACS facilities are hosted by large healthcare facilities, it is reiterated that there is coordination with DOHFW and the host facilities to ensure that IC-WM practices are observed in the entire healthcare facility.

Annual Cost Estimates for SACS Facility (With 10 health care workers)

	Quantity	*Unit cost (INR)*	*Total (INR)*
Personal protective equipment			
Gloves – Disposable	4000	2.5	10000
Industrial	2	50	100
Aprons	30	300	9000
Face masks	4000	1.5	6000
Hand-washing soap	15	10	150
Needle cutter	5	1600	8500
Waste buckets /baskets (with lids)	5	80	400
Bins/Drums (with lids)	2	400	800
Puncture proof plastic bags	400	3	1200
Hypochlorite solution	50lt	50/lt	2500
Mops	2	250	500
TOTAL			**29,050**

Notes

1. Categories 8 and 10 (liquid) do not require containers/bag and Cat 3 if disinfected locally need not be put in containers/bags.
2. Source: OR-OSHA 216 Exposure Control/Blood Borne Pathogens.
3. Guidance Note on Health Care Worker Safety from HIV and other Blood Borne Infections- HNP Discussion Note, The World Bank, May 2004.
4. Adapted from GoI Guidelines for AD Syringes.
5. An Action Plan for blood Safety, NACO 2003.
6. Manual on Quality Assurance Practices in HIV Testing Laboratories: published by NICD and NACO.

Annexure - 7.2

Environmental Management for Construction Activities

I. Background

On the eve of the World AIDS Day, 2003, the Government of India announced a program for free distribution of Antiretroviral (ARV) drugs in selected states. The roll out started in April 2004, and covered three groups: women covered under 'Prevention of Parents To Child Transmission' (PPTCT) program, children below 15 year of age, and AIDS cases that seek treatment in public sector hospitals. The program was started in the six high prevalence states of Tamil Nadu, Andhra Pradesh, Maharashtra, Karnataka, Manipur and Nagaland, and in Delhi, with the objective of providing free anti-retroviral treatment to 100,000 people living with HIV/ AIDS by the end of 2005, and to provide treatment to an additional 15-20 percent of AIDS cases each year, thereafter, for a period of five years.

According to NACO, currently, there are about 39,000 patients on Anti-Retroviral Treatment (ART), of which more than 76 percent access ART from NACO-supported ART centres. These ART centres are physically adjunct to government (district) hospitals/medical colleges and provide counselling, adherence monitoring and treatment. For in-patient treatment existing facilities in the medical colleges or district hospitals are used. There are other sites where ART is offered for free are covered by the NGO sector (about 10%) and 6% by the private sector. In all, there are currently 54 NACO supported ART sites all over the country, of which 39 are in GFATM (high prevalence) states and 15 are in medium/low prevalence states.

Under the NACP-III, NACO is planning to build additional ART facilities in 250 high priority districts, including upgradation and/or expansion of the existing 54 centres. Each of these ART facilities will be attached to medical colleges/district hospitals and will require an area of about 2,000-3,000 sq ft (300 sq.m). While there is a model design available, it is expected that this will be customized for different locations, depending upon the space (built space) and facilities extended by the host building. Additional space, facilities, renovations (and therefore civil works and interiors) will be needed if there is a requirement to create the required ambience for specialized treatment (including confidentiality).

The NACP-III also proposes to build 10 Centres of Excellence to provide training to district staff, undertake drug resistance monitoring, and periodic reviews and oversight. These COEs will require additional area of about 250 sq.m, to accommodate conference rooms, stores and offices. 5 of these COEs are proposed to become treatment hubs.

Overall, the total built space requirement is around 78,750 sq.m (80,000 sq.m) and estimated budget is about $14 million, less than 1% of the overall program cost. Under the National Plan, there is a provision of Rs. 75crore ($16 million) for contingency and innovation, which can be accessed for improving site environmental conditions, if required. An additional amount of Rs. 25 crore ($8 million) is available for community and social mobilization.

II. Environmental impacts related to civil works

Construction activities generate varied kinds of waste which have the potential of polluting the neighbouring air, water and land. The neighbourhood and surrounding areas of any construction can be adversely affected by the huge amounts of construction materials, waste and large number of temporary construction workers, if they are not managed properly. Health, safety and sanitation of these temporary workers is an added concern which needs to be addressed during the course of the construction activity.

NACO and the SACS will ensure that all these new constructions and upgradations/extensions are being done on land which is belongs to the Government and/or is free of any occupation or "encroachment". If there is any issue related to relocation of encroachers, the Bank should be informed accordingly. During the course of the program, if NACO decides to undertake a major construction, (such as a complete building, treatment and in-patient centres and/or which require land acquisition etc, the Bank will need to be informed well in advance and the appropriate environmental plan will need to be developed.

III. Construction Guidelines

The design and construction of the planned facilities under the NACP-III should comply with the existing set of codes, regulatory guidelines and manuals of the Government of India, as listed below:

- National Building Code of India
- IS 1172-1983: Code of basic requirements for Water Supply, drainage and Sanitation
- IS 2065-1983: Code of practice for water supply in buildings
- IS 1742-1983: Code of practice for building drainage
- IS 1200: Code of practice for water supply and drains

- Central Public Health and Environmental Engineering Organization (CPHEEO) manual on Water Supply & Water Treatment
- CPHEEO manual on Sewerage & Waste Treatment
- CPHEEO manual on Solid Waste Management.
- Tariff Advisory Committee (TAC) manual on Fire Protection System

The construction practices shall also comply with the national standards and code of practices established by the Ministry of Environment and Forests and other environmental agencies.

The following construction guidelines will be followed during the implementation of NACP-III for renovation, up-gradation of health care and laboratory facilities. NACO and SACS should ensure that the requirements defined in the Addendum are included into the bid documents with civil works contractors. Additionally, experts in environmental planning and designing should review and approve all designs before construction. NACO and SACS should undertake periodic reviews of construction practices and ensure these guidelines are being adhered to.

III(a). Site selection

When a health care facility renovation /up-gradation is planned, site selection is an important consideration. A site wrongly chosen can result in environmental problems that will persist throughout the operation of the health care facility. This should be avoided. In this section, guidelines for selecting a suitable site are given.

The following points should be given due consideration prior to the selection of the upgradation/renovation of site for a health care facility:

- The chosen site should have adequate water supply, both for washing / cleaning and drinking purposes. In particular, the quality of water should be tested, as poor quality of drinking water could be a health hazard.
- Prior land use of the proposed site should be determined, as the facility should necessarily be built only on non-hazardous land.
- The drainage pattern of the site and the region should be studied to determine whether the site would be subject to flooding and stagnant water. The chosen site should be free from water logging problems.
- The setting of the upgraded/renovated facility should not harm natural habitats or biodiversity of the region, e.g. forest areas, wet lands, historic, archaeological or religious sites.

- The setting of the upgraded/renovated facility should not be in close proximity to areas susceptible to health or other hazards (such as slow-moving or stagnant water bodies, industrial waste disposal sites, municipal landfills and/or any other probable source of infectious diseases).

III(b). Guidelines for design

Designing a layout of a facility or up-gradation of a building is important as any deficiency can result in health and environmental issues during its operation. In this section, some guidelines for design have been included.

General

- The facility should be large enough to provide service delivery for target populations. Coherent and responsive planning should be included based upon present and projected needs.
- Facility design features must ensure adequate space and equipment for health service delivery.

Equipment-related Specifications

- Appropriate standards for non-medical equipment (solar hot water, pumping systems, sanitary equipment, etc) are to be in compliance with Bureau of Indian Standards, if available.
- Specifications for medical equipment should be in compliance with applicable norms.

Bio-medical Waste Management Facilities

- Medical waste segregation, collection, storage, treatment and disposal are to be practised or outsourced as per the Bio-Medical Waste (Management & Handling) (2000) Rules.
- In designing the layout of a facility, proper waste movement should be planned.
- Storage bins and collection equipment for different categories of waste should be provided.
- Lockable storage space should be provided for segregated infectious waste prior to disposal or transport to other facilities for disposal.
- Areas should be earmarked for sharps pit and deep burial pits, if there isn't any access to centralized bio-medical waste treatment facilities.

Building-related Specifications

- Proper ventilation and natural lighting should be provided so that there are no adverse health impacts. Lighting and ventilation standards should be in compliance with Indian norms.

- Good indoor air quality and ventilation should be ensured in the building design.
- The flooring design should be such that it does not lead to falls, slippage and retention of infectious material.
- Good construction practices should be planned. This should include the usage of environment friendly construction products such as fly ash.
- Building materials should be fire resistant and there should be provision for evacuation in the event of fire.

Water Supply and Quality

- Adequate provision for storage of sufficient volumes of water should be provided to ensure continuous availability of water to all designated locations within the building during any period and when water supply is interrupted.
- Water supply must be assured on a regular basis. A fallback mechanism should be made, if the water supply fails.
- Water supply and distribution standards should be in compliance with Indian norms.
- Water supply should be planned to all required points of use in the facility in sufficient volumes and pressure to satisfy needs.
- Wherever possible the facility should get the water supply from the water board and adequately treat it and make it potable.
- Water quality must meet acceptable norms. If not, provisions for clean drinking water in sufficient quantities should be made. Specific plans to address any particular issues of water quality, such as arsenic and fluoride contamination, should be made if that is required.
- Water quality should be monitored and controlled periodically.
- Rainwater harvesting systems should be planned in all the buildings in the facility.

Wastewater and Sanitation

- Sanitary standards for waste water treatment storage and disposal should be in compliance with Indian norms
- Possible improper and indiscriminate disposal of solid waste, garbage, blocked drains, stagnant water within and outside the health care facilities needs to be addressed at the planning stage itself.

- Sufficient number of toilets should be provided.
- Wastewater and effluents should be treated and recycled wherever feasible.
- Provisions should be made for septic tanks and soak pits in all Health care facilities.
- Adequate drainage and evacuation arrangements should be made at all points where water is available.

General / Communal Solid Waste

- Sufficient number of bins should be provided to collect general solid waste
- Wherever the collection of garbage/municipal solid waste is not streamlined by the municipality/panchayat, a pit to decompose organic waste should be provided for.
- For recyclables, storage locations should be planned.

Miscellaneous

- The facility / building should have an emergency egress.
- Easy access for the physically challenged should be provided.
- Unsafe building materials such as asbestos should be avoided
- Low-cost lead-based paints, anti-termite chemicals and other pest management using chemical pesticides should be avoided.

III(c). Construction Management Guidelines

Any upgradation/renovation of a building creates environmental impacts, which can be minimized through good construction management practices. This section includes some guidelines on how these impacts can be mitigated or reduced.

- *Generation of dust* is common in a construction site. In order to reduce dust emissions, periodic watering should be done. In addition, temporary fencing should be provided along the boundary so that the emissions do not affect the immediate neighbours.
- *Noise pollution* due to operation of different types of equipment and machinery during construction activities may disturb the surrounding premises, including residential dwellings, schools, hospitals etc. Construction should be carried out only during the daytime and as per permitted timings. If there is an educational institution in the neighbourhood, proper temporary noise barriers should be erected to reduce construction-related noise impacts.

- Labour camps on site should be as per Indian norms. Clean and well-maintained toilets should be made available at the construction site.
- If there is any eco-sensitive habitat in the vicinity of the construction site, care should be taken to ensure that there are no adverse impacts on the habitat. Any existing streams and drains within, and adjacent to the site should be kept safe and free from any debris and any excavated materials arising from the works.
- *Construction waste* generated should be properly stored on site and disposed by filling low-lying areas after obtaining the required local permissions.
- *Liquid spills* of lubricant, fuel and oil within the site should be attended at the earliest in order to minimize land & groundwater contamination.
- Temporary fencing around the project site should be provided to regulate the entry and exit of material, personnel and equipment.
- Construction workers, managers and visitors to the site should use personnel protective equipment such as helmets, gloves, safety boots and goggles.
- *Waste water* generated from wash-pits, wheel washing, equipment cleaning, etc can be a source of water pollution if the drainage system is ineffective. Additionally sanitary waste generated by the temporary construction workers can pollute the surface/underground water. There is the added risk of mosquito breeding, if water around the construction site is allowed to stagnate. Temporary drainage works should be constructed and maintained.

Annexure - 8

A Capacity Development (Training Need, Strategy) Plan

1. Goal

3.1 To ensure that all personnel and stakeholders in HIV prevention and control programme have capacities needed for performing their roles.

2. The Need

2.1. Fulfillment of human resource needs in terms of number alone would not help the programme without provision of appropriate **training to develop capacity** among all constituencies involved in NACP implementation. There is a direct correlation between training and quality of performance/delivery.

2.2. The fluid and dynamic HIV/AIDS scenario under which NACP–III is to be implemented would require **regular updating of job skills, competencies and knowledge**. NACO, SACS and the newly created DAPCUs would need efficient and committed working teams who should function proactively as cohesive groups with clarity, motivation and passion.

2.3. To achieve this, people who lead the organisation and its various units should have **positive leadership** qualities to inspire the work teams for optimal utilization of their potential. This would require continuous training and retraining in human resource development in order to promote professional, attitudinal and behavioural changes in the organizational culture.

2.4. Training will be imparted at **various levels/tiers** for senior managers, regular and contractual staff, technical/clinical personnel, NGOs/CBOs and PLHA networks implementing the programme, public and private sector partners, care providers in health and non-health sectors at the grass root level, stakeholders and gate keepers etc.

3. Objective & Approaches

3.1. **Service providers and stakeholders at all levels** in both public and private sector would be the target group for capacity building.

3.2. A cohesive **capacity development strategy** will be adopted to translate the overall objectives of HIV/AIDS prevention and control into reality, with capacity building as the **guiding principle**.

3.3. All capacity development programmes will be **need based** with focus on **knowledge management, skill enhancement** and **up-gradation**. Technical support would be provided through the already created national resource pool.

3.4. **Capacity development approaches** would include:

- o Training, orientation , refresher courses and workshops
- o On-site technical support and experiential learning
- o Mentoring, exchange of visits and exposure to best practices
- o Sensitising District AIDS Control & Prevention Units

3.5. To ensure development of **managerial as well as technical capacity**, NACO would identify and develop a pool of institutions including centres of excellence, academia, health training institutions, national/regional training organizations and reputed civil society organizations including selected PLHA/GIPA networks for long term collaboration.

3.6. The faculty of such training institutions/orgns. will also undergo induction to be facilitated by NACO to gain first hand experience and an understanding of NACO/SACS/ DAPCU, expectations including current policy, strategy, programme and action plans.

4. Training: Goals and Focus

4.1. Each programme will have a **training goal**, a **learning goal** and an **action goal**.

4.2. Training will aim at creating a **critical mass/ cadre of key trainers** on issues and concerns related to HIV/AIDS in different parts of the country based on felt needs and specific requirements.

4.3. It would also ensure that a set of master trainers and consultants, at the country and state level, whose capacity has been built, are available to provide **field support** to SACS, DAPCUs, and community based organizations implementing NACO - III.

4.4. In addition, a **pool of mentors** will be developed who will provide **handholding** and support function to various intervention programmes of the SACS.

4.5. Because of the interconnected and overlapping responsibilities in NACO, SACS and DAPCU during NACP-III, the **focus of training** would be on promoting **creative collaboration** and integration of knowledge and skills, so that the **combined expertise** of the personnel could be used to achieve the common goals of HIV prevention and control.

5. Training: Strategy

5.1. People dealing with complex HIV/AIDS issues cannot work in silos and have to partner each other. Training should always lead to knowledge based action and interventions. Towards this end, NACO would develop **cross-functional teams** who could work beyond their **functional corridors** making innovative and dynamic contributions

5.2. For other in-house professional and management staff in NACO and SACS, **periodic training will be mandatory**. All programme staff will undergo a short induction training at the entry level. All new programmes and interventions are to be preceded by an induction training so that the key stakeholders are fully conversant with the programme and its objectives.

5.3. Stand alone modules for skill up-gradation, orientation and refresher courses would be developed on **emerging issues** that would require new approach and interventions strategies whereas composite modules will be developed on interconnected themes.

5.4. A **one-stop training institution** in each region will be preferable to several training institutions imparting trainings in individual thematic areas. A **joint task team** in NACO and SACS will ensure that the training components are not repeated for the same trainee.

5.5. **Networking with model projects** for exposure and demos: The SACS technical staff and their implementing NGO teams will be provided opportunity to visit effective ongoing projects to get a clear understanding of the needs, strategies, implementation, monitoring and the outcome as part of the CB in technical areas wherever possible.

5.6. Region-wise/language-wise models will be developed for thematic training. A set of experts could **visit regional programmes and document the experiences** for developing model programmes as demonstration centres of learning. Staff of these programmes would be helped to develop the capacity to explain and demonstrate the components of their intervention.

5.7. Enhancing the attention towards **special groups and special situations**: NACP–III training efforts will need to pay special attention to some of the populations where the epidemic is taking serious roots and have not been addressed during the course of the NACP–II in a strong and sustained manner. These groups are (a) Men who have sex with men (b) injecting drug users and (c) population in rural areas and migrant people (d) youth, adolescents and women.

5.8. **Retraining** and regular refreshers are essential to make up the deficiencies, **maintain the skill level** and cover all those who have not been trained due to various reasons including those who missed out the first round.

5.9. It would be ensured that all staff and health care workers are trained on patients'/ PLHAs rights to equal care and confidentiality, principles and procedures of voluntary testing and counseling. Clinical staff are regularly trained and re-trained in case management of HIV/AIDS.

5.10. There are 750,000 practicing doctors (modern medicine) in the country out of which only 180,000 are registered with Indian Medical Association. For training purpose they can be divided into three categories: (1) family physicians, (2) specialists co-managing HIV/AIDS cases and (3) physicians practicing treatment of PLHAs.

6. Duration, Methods, Evaluation and Follow-up

6.1. The **duration** of **an induction** training may vary from 1 to 3 days, a subject and **skill oriented** training between 7 to 10 days and a **refresher** between 2 to 4 days. For specialized and advanced courses a selected number of professionals may be sponsored for 4 to 6 weeks training in a centre of excellence on the subject. For senior managers at policy/planning level **1 day workshops** can be organized.

6.2. For senior and middle level programme managers, the organization must **commit atleast ten days** in a year for training purpose. For junior level staff atleast seven days should be committed for training. A separate budget head at NACO and SACS should be opened to meet the expenditure on training.

6.3. The **training methods** should be participatory in nature with focus on cognitive and competency building and should include, icebreaking, group discussion, brainstorming, subject lectures, small group discussion, role-playing/exercises/games, cases studies/ site visits.

6.4. Each training programme should include an **evaluation and follow-up plan** to assess the impact of the training and the way the training will be used as the basis for a follow-up plan. The training agencies should have a plan to check whether the training has led to results and also to find out what further training is required.

7. Coordination Arrangements/ Responsibility

7.1. A senior manager at NACO and SACS will be incharge of HRD to ensure that appropriate trainings are organized for various types of personnel in time, its **impact is evaluated** and corrective measures taken. It must be ensured that everybody in the organization undergoes **atleast one training and one refresher** during a three year tenure.

7.2. It will be the **responsibility** of NACO to facilitate training programmes for its senior programme managers as well as those of the SACS, whereas it will be the responsibility of SACS to ensure training for its own personnel and district level programme staff as well as NGOs/CBOs working in the field of HIV/AIDS.

7.3. The training coordination units in NACO and SACS will work out how many will be trained, what experience they have, what their professional/occupational needs are, what potential role (in decision making, programme development for programme management) they will play after the training. They will have regular interactions with the training institutions to ensure that the **quality and relevance** of the training is maintained.

8. Curriculum and Materials Development

8.1. The current training syllabi, manuals/operational manuals and modules **will be reviewed, updated and improved** if necessary. A list of core competencies for different types of training will be prepared.

8.2. Special training modules for **front line health care and treatment providers**, social mobilisers, community based organizations engaged in targeted interventions and prevention services, private health sector personnel, peer-leaders, youth volunteers, and outreach workers, have to be developed. For supervisors, on-site, function-specific and workplace oriented training designs are to be developed.

8.3. Similarly training materials will be developed for existing and new staff involved in VCT and YFIC, modified TIs and any innovative interventions including **age and gender specific materials** on prevention as well as on life after infection. **Special capsule courses** for senior level managers working on AIDS will be prepared.

8.4. **Interactive self-learning resource materials**: Sets of self-learning material will be developed to help different levels of workers. These may be printed manuals, (if possible with a lot of graphics), comic, cartoons, picture book type material, interactive CDs, audiovisual materials etc.

8.5. To further enhance this process it would be necessary **to set up a help line** which answers the questions through e-mail, phone/fax etc. in the local languages. A toll-free line may be of great help. This is particularly of importance at the SACS level.

8.6. Rapid turnover among the staff and the need to start performing immediately would necessitate a comprehensive and timely orientation package. However, a **self-learning orientation package** can be a useful primer.

8.7. It is important to develop materials that are informative, interactive and accepted by the community, with components of pre and post testing for assessing its effectiveness.

All activities under this head will be completed within the first six months of the launch of NACP-III. Expert agencies to carry out these functions will be identified by NACO and the SACS.

9. Training Guide

9.1. To ensure uniformity in message transmission in all states, a comprehensive Training Guide will be developed detailing the overall training policy and implementation approaches including outsourcing, networking, supporting training initiatives and training modules, duration etc.

9.2. The training guide would also include information on training facilities, and their capacities, availability of institutions in different States whose services can be tapped fruitfully by the implementing agencies. The process will be completed within six months of the launch of the NACP-III.

10. Outsourcing

10.1. **Outsourcing** needs to be in-built in the training strategy since it may not be possible to have, or develop in a short period, all the required facilities and faculty skills. Available expertise in different fields, may be identified in each state and neighbouring areas.

10.2. NACO will **outsource an expert agency** as soon as the NACP to launched to complete the initial processes like review and update of material and modules, curriculum development, designing a training guide etc.

10.3. **Technical institutions** for training and capacity development will be engaged based on the qualification and experience of their professional staff and infrastructure. Initially their services will be outsourced for a period of two years.

10.4. These institutions are expected to have the needed **skill base and expertise** in areas of social mobilization, counselling, communication, rights issues, gender, youth & children, programme management, clinical and diagnostic services, treatment & support, monitoring and evaluation.

11. Training Plan: Key Areas

Broadly the **key areas** and action steps of the training plan will be:

- o **Identification** of the trainees' universe and their needs through TNA
- o **Review** of existing training manuals, modules, and development of learning materials to meet emerging training needs
- o **Estimating** the training load
- o Identifying **centres of excellence**/institutions with suitable training facilities
- o **Strengthening infrastructure** and faculty at such facilities
- o Arrangements for infrastructure and **faculty outsourcing**
- o **Networking** with available training and capacities in different sectors
- o Technical assistance and support to institutions already engaged in HIV training activities
- o Preparation of **training calendar,** time-line and load
- o Identification of **resource persons**, subject specialists and trainers at various levels
- o Organisation of **trainers' training** programmes
- o **Evaluation** of impact of the training including concurrent evaluation

The key activities and initiatives under the training plan will be completed **within the first four months** of NACP – III.

12. The Trainee Universe

12.1. NACO Programme Managers, officials & professional staff

12.2. SACS Programme Managers, officials & professional staff

12.3. District Porgramme Managers & programme staff

12.4. Legislators, heads of PRIs

12.5. Front line Care & Treatment Providers -

12.6. Nodal officers from PSUs

12.7. Personnel working for VCTC, PPTCT, TIs, STI clinics, blood banks

12.8. Senior Treatment Supervisors & Senior Laboratory Supervisors (TB/HIV)

12.9. Diagnostic Service Providers

12.10. Health care providers including private sector

12.11. ART management personnel

12.12. NGOs, CBOs, Social Mobilisers working on AIDS

12.13. PLHA network managers

12.14. Wardens, extension workers in Prisons

12.15. Youth friendly info. centre / Youth Clinic personnel including YDCs, Univ. youth centre, NLM Centre staff,

12.16. Youth Volunteers & Peer Educators-Scouts & Guides, NSS, NYKS, NCC, Youth, Red-cross/Red Crescent Reps.,

12.17. Key personnel of industry, workers' orgnisations, TUs

12.18. Orgnisations working for migrants & OVC and street children, mobile population

12.19. Personnel working on HIV among uniformed forces

12.20. Voluntary Blood Donation orgns.

12.21. Managers of Community Care Centres

12.22. Personnel of Drug De-addiction Centres

12.23. Highway Transport Agencies Reps/Key Personnels.

12.24. Nodal officials, technical staff of Line Ministries with HIV Control plans

12.25. Private Medical Practitioners (STI/RTI/HIV/TB)

12.26. Personnel of Research Institutions & Collaborating Centers

13. Who will train

13.1. National and Regional Resource Centers, Collaborating Partner Institutions

13.2. Centres of Excellence on HIV/AIDS/STI/RTI related Training

13.3. Reputed Institutions providing Training on Health and HR Management

13.4. SCERT, DIETs of Ministry of HRD and similar training institutions of line ministries

13.5. Departments of Social Work in the universities

13.6. TOC, TORC, IDARAS, RGNIYD, Sports Training Institutions of Ministry of Youth Affairs & Sports

13.7. International Agencies with training expertise on health issues

13.8. MOHF sponsored Training Institutions

13.9. State Academies of Administration

13.10. Training Institutions/ Networks of PLHA

13.11. NGO/CBO based Training Institutions

14. Components of Training

14.1. Induction Training – Familiarization with policy, plans and programmes, strategic information management, and introduce new activities and initiatives to be undertaken.

14.2. Sensitization of policy makers and planners at various levels including PRIs

14.3. Training of States & District level program managers

14.4. Training on mainstreaming & convergence with health and other sectors.

14.5. Surveillance, Epidemiology, Mapping of HRGs

14.6. Training on Management of Targeted Interventions, including clinical issues, harm reduction, substitution therapy etc.

14.7. Training on counseling VCTC, PPTCTs

14.8. Communication (BCC, IPC), Social Mobilization & Advocacy

14.9. Condom Programming & Social Marketing

14.10. HIV, Gender & Equity, Stigma, Discrimination, Human Rights, Work Place Intervention

14.11. Youth Friendly Information Services/ Youth Clinics

14.12. Training of non-health sector functionaries

14A.

- Modular training of Doctors on Care, Support and Treatment
- Modular Training on OI Management
- Special Training Programme on ART
- Diagnostic and syndromic management of RTI/STI for health functionaries at various level
- Training on blood safety, transfusion services, PEP, hospital infection control, waste management

14B.

- Financial Management, Procurement management
- Strategic Information Management and Planning, Performance Appraisal
- Research, development and knowledge management

- Developing capacities at states and national level to use evaluation results for redesign of programmes

14C.

The NACO and SACS would strengthen and support the training efforts of institutions and programmes which are already engaged in HIV/AIDS prevention and control activities i.e.:

- Training support to Adolescents Education Programme
- Training support to College/university AIDS Education Programme
- Training support to Village Talk AIDS Programmes for rural youth and adolescents
- Training support to PLHA networks
- Training support to organisations engaged in Research, Development & Knowledge Management
- Training support to RCH, DOTS programme etc.
- NACO will also support **online Training & Resource Centres** with components of E-Forum, E-Library, E-Support and E-Training to promote ICT based awareness, training programmes on HIV/AIDS, STI and life skills.

15. Other Training Components/ New Training Activities

15.1. Identify & establish/ support regional resource/ training centres
15.2. Distance Training through Edusat
15.3. Online Training,
15.4. E-Forum
15.5. E-Learning
15.6. E-Training
15.7. Need based manuals, modules review & updating
15.8. Appropriate age & issue specific syllabi
15.9. Curriculum support to RCH, ARSH, ANM/ ASHA, training Programme
15.10. Training protocols for first line ART referral
15.11. Refresher & capsule courses, repeat training
15.12. Maintaining Training roaster
15.13. Identification of field training sites
15.14. Exposure visits to successful interventions
15.15. Clinical attachment to institutions with adequate case load
15.16. Workshops, capsule courses on new challenges

Training/CB Plan: NACO, SACS and DAPCU

Sl. No.	*Personnel whose capacities are to be built*	*Competence/skill sets to be covered*	*Implementing agency*	*2006*	
				No of Persons	*No of sessions*
1.	DG, Addl.DGs, Directors	Epidemiology of AIDS, Developments in AIDS Programming, Programme management including personnel, systems, strategies and structures, Decentralization, use of SIM for programme management, learning systems.	Technical support unit for programme management at national level		
2.	Programme Directors of State AIDS Control Societies	Epidemiology of AIDS, Developments in AIDS Programming, Programme management including personnel, systems, strategies and structures, Decentralization, use of SIM for programme management, learning systems.	Technical support unit for programme management at national level	38	
3.	Addl. Programme Directors and Joint Directors of State AIDS Control Societies (Programmes and services)	Public health and social aspects of AIDS, Management of programme components, Integration with health services, RCH, HIV/TB co-infections, Integration of prevention and treatment.	Technical support unit for programme management at national level in collaboration with other national institutions for technical support	32	
4.	Addl. Project Directors and Asst. Directors of SACS (Fin, Admn, HR, Coordination)	Programme management including personnel, systems, strategies, finances and structures, decentralization, use of SIM, mainstreaming and partnerships.	Technical support institution for programme management at national level	10	
5.	Joint Director & Deputy Director (Prevention and clinical services)	Protocols, capacity needs, implementation arrangements and integration of STI/RTI, VCTC, Blood Safety. PPTCT services.	National technical support institution for medical services	32	
6.	Asst. Director (Prevention and medical services)	Protocols, capacity needs, implementation arrangements and integration of STI/RTI, VCTC, Blood Safety. PPTCT services.	National technical support institution for medical services	32	

(*Contd...*)

7.	Asst. Dir (Blood Safety)	Protocols, capacity needs, implementation arrangements of blood banking, rational use of blood, promotion of voluntary blood banking and hospital safety.	National technical support institution for medical services	24	
8.	Asst. Dir (Condom Programming)	Management of free supply, social marketing of condoms for HRG and general population.	Agency for condom programming	24	
9.	Deputy Director/ Asst. Director (CST) (CST)	Management of opportunistic infections, ART, Linkages between prevention and treatment, social and psychological support to infected persons, support to PLHA networks, impact mitigation.	National technical support institution for medical services	36	
10.	GIPA Coordinator	Capacity building of PLHA to participate in management, formation and support of networks, advocacy for GIPA.	INP+	24	
11.	JD/AD (IEC)/ AD (IEC and condoms)	Communication (Strategy, campaigns, capacity building, media planning, monitoring and impact assessment)-, Behaviour change communication/IPC, demand generation for services.	National technical support institution for communication	62	
12.	JD/DD(NGO)	Developing and managing Targeted interventions, Leadership development and mobilisation of vulnerable, migrant populations.	National technical support institution for social support	32	
13.	JD /AD (SIM & Plg)	Management of Surveillance, M&E, interpretation of data, Learning systems, Research and knowledge management Implementation tracking and resource tracking.	M&E training agency/institution to be identified	36	
14.	AD (Surveillance)	Management of behavioural and sero-surveillance.	M&E training agency/institution to be identified	24	
15.	Statistical officer cum Data processing	Data analysis and interpretation, use of data in HIV programming.	M&E training agency/institution to be identified	32	
16.	JD/ Asst. Dir (Admn., HR, Fin)	Programme management including personnel, systems, strategies, Finances and structures, decentralization, use of SIM for programme management, Mainstreaming and partnerships.	Technical support institution for programme management at national level	32	

(Contd...)

17.	DD (Mainstreaming)			28	
18.	AD (Procurement)			32	
19.	AD (Audit)			24	
20.	AD (Admn., Fin)			42	
21.	Joint training of all programme officers	Basic strategies of components of NACP-III, roles of different functionaries, team building, integration of management practices of different programmes.			

Capacity Building needs of Targeted Interventions

Sl. No.	*Personnel whose capacities are to be built*	*Competence/skill sets o be covered*	*Implementing agency*	*Total Number*	*2006*	
					No. of Persons	*No. of Sessions*
1.	Director/Trustee of the NGO	Concept and components of TIs, basics of HIV prevention and programme, Financial and programme components, advocacy, sustainability, networking, mainstreaming.	Technical support unit/ training units of DPs working	2500		
2.	Project Managers of targeted interventions	planning, programme and financial management, power dynamics, gender issues, components of TI viz: STD, condom,, BCC, enabling environment & community mobilization & participatory mapping of HRGs, Linking prevention and care, Documentation and reporting, Proposal writing, M&E, advocacy.		2500		
3.	Accountant	Planning, programme and financial management, maintenance of books of accounts, preparation of reports, programme components of TI.		2500		
4.	Counsellor	Basics of HIV transmission and management, Behaviour and attitudes of HRG, their Psycho social needs, support for infected persons, referral linkages, community dynamics and organisation of HRG and barriers to access, communication and documentation skills.		2500		

(Contd...)

5.	Outreach workers	Basics of HIV transmission and management, behaviour and attitudes of HRG, community dynamics and mobilisation of HRG and barriers to access, communication skills, needs of infected HRG, M&E.		17500		
6.	Leadership training for CBO potential leaders	Social basis of vulnerability, power dynamics, skills in communication, mobilisation, organisaiton management, advocacy, formal systems for participation in decision making.				
7.	Training of CBO leaders on programme management	Community mobilisation for HIV prevention, management structures and systems, conducting meetings, conflict resolution, leadership strategies, advocacy.				
8.	Training CBO members and programme managers on participative mapping	Techniques of mapping, community validation of results, data management, implications of data for programme management.				
9.	Nurses in IDU Unit					
10.	Doctors in IDU unit					
11.	Peer educators					
12.	PLHA representative from HRG population					
13.	Providers of STI care					
14.	Staff of project support units					

Capacity Building of Civil Society Representatives

Sl. No.	*Personnel whose capacities are to be built*	*Topics to be covered in all trainings*	*Implementing agency*	*2006*	
				No. of Persons	*No. of Sessions*
1.		Basics of HIV/AIDS, social and political factors that impact on HIV prevention and management, impact of HIV on individuals, families and community, socio-economic impact of HIV on the nation. Support to people living with HIV, Impact mitigation.			

(*Contd...*)

		Competence/skill sets to be covered in specific groups			
2.	District heads of SHG organisations	Vulnerability of women and strategies for prevention with focus on women, equitable access to prevention and treatment services, managing the impact of infection on individuals and families, social support structures, role SHGs can play in AIDS prevention and mitigation of impact.			
3.	Heads of urban local bodies	Role of local bodies in identifying and working with vulnerable groups, in supporting infected and affected persons, mainstreaming HIV prevention and mitigation of impact into development work of local bodies.			
4.	Zilla Panchayat Presidents	Do			
5.	Block Panchayat Presidents	Do			
6.	Grama Panchayat Presidents	Do			
7.	Office bearers of civil society partners forum at state, district and national level	Role of civil society organizations in HIV prevention, their participation in national programme, monitoring programme implementation, participation in decision making structures of national programme, advocacy, mainstreaming in work of CSOs.			
8.	Office bearers of PLHA networks at district, state and national level	Role of PLHA in prevention and treatment programmes, GIPA principles and practice, community mobilisaiton, management of organisation, advocacy, impact mitigation strategies, linking up with national and state programmes.			
9.	Nehru Yuvak Kendra regional and district Coordinator	The role of youth organizations in HIV prevention and management, information related to HIV/AIDS, reproductive and sexual health, prevention and treatment, peer education, outreach skills, leadership programmes, reinforcement of positive social & cultural values, campaign strategies for social mobilization, partnership development with stakeholders.			
10.	Trade and industry associations	Mainstreaming HIV into HR policies, prevention and treatment of HIV for employees and associates, CSR in HIV, networking with other organizations.			

Capacity Building needs of Service delivery

Sl. No.	Personnel whose capacities are to be built	Competence/skill sets to be covered	Implementing agency	Total number	2006	
					No. of Persons	No. of Sessions
1.	Counsellors	Basics of HIV prevention, confidentiality, pre-test, post test counselling, counselling for prevention, psycho social needs of HRG, of young people about their reproductive health, life styles, substance abuse, tobacco, STI and unsafe sexual practice, anxiety, stress, frustrations and insecurity, understanding issues affecting PLHA, counselling people living with HIV/AIDS, PPTCT.	Regional/State institution for counselling training. Trainers would be trained at national institution of excellence.	4137		
2.	Lab Technicians	Basic biology of HIV, practical training on different methods of testing, quality assurance, sentinel surveillance, inventory management.	Regional/State institution for counselling training.	2401		
3.	Medical Officers in charge of VCTCs	Management of voluntary counselling and testing, testing protocol, quality assurance, logistics and inventory management, referrals, reporting.				
4.	Ob & Gyne, Paediatric Medical Officers	Clinical manifestation of HIV in children, perinatal transmission of HIV, Chemoprohylaxis for PMTCT, care of new born of mother living with HIV, Pediatric HIV, PEP.	Regional/State institution for counselling training.	3342		
5.	RNTCP Medical Officers	Management of HIV/TB co-infection.				
6.	Medical Officers in ART clinics	Natural history of HIV, Management of opportunistic infections, management of ART, Pharmacology, resistance monitoring, record keeping.		503		
7.	Nurses	Natural history of HIV, taking care of persons with HIV, persons on ART, Drug combinations and reactions, record keeping.		657		
8.	Pharmacists	Pharmacology of OIs and ART, Patterns of ART management, adherence counselling, inventory management.		219		
9.	Record Keepers	Use of data for ART management, recording and verifying data.		219		
10.	Lab Technicians	Testing for OIs, CD4 testing, resistance monitoring, quality assurance.		438		

(Contd...)

11.	PHC and CHC Medical Officers	Basics of HIV transmission and prevention, Management of OIs, HIV/TB, PPTCT, Basics of ART, VCT, PEP, Universal precautions.		26.475		
12.	Medical Officers in government hospitals	Do				
13.	Private practitioners	Do				
14.	Nurses	Do				
15.	Para medical staff	Do				
16.	Lab Technicians	Do				
17.	Medical Officer in charge of blood bank	Safe transfusion and management plans, rational use of blood, voluntary blood donation on External Quality Assurance Scheme (EQAS).		1C30		
18.	Blood Bank Technicians	Safe transfusion, techniques of cross matching.		1030		
19.	Technical Assistants in Component Separation Units			82		
20.	Managers of community care centres	Natural history of HIV infection, common Ois and their management, counselling PLHA and families, Psycho social needs of infected and affected persons, legal and social support, preventing burnout among staff.		152		
21.	Outreach volunteers for treatment adherence	Basics of ART, Functions of different drugs, need for adherence, psycho social needs of PLHA, their family and community, communication for treatment literacy and adherence, common barriers to adherence, social structures to support PLHA.		C		
22.	Orientation of Labour Welfare Officers on interventions in the place of work					
23.	Orientation of Programme Managers of NGOs on migrant support					
24.	STI specialists					
25.	Lab Technicians in district and medical college hospitals					
26.	Programme Managers of social management organisations					

Annexure - 9

Technical Support for NACP – III

Compared to the second phase of NACP, the third phase will require additional capacity in the existing interventions, skills needed for new interventions and capacity built at additional levels. The core technical skills must be available or developed in implementing agencies. But given the complexity and diversity of the skills involved it is unlikely that entire capacity needed for programme implementation would be available or built in implementing agencies at the beginning of the programme. These would have to be sourced from external units as technical support. This is distinguished from training where the technical capacities are available within the system but has to be passed on to other members in the system that do not have access to such capacity. Therefore, technical capacity is to be made available in two ways: through technical support, and capacity building.

Technical Support

Technical support may be described as effort to increase the knowledge and skills of the individuals and the organization involved to achieve an output. This can be provided by other individuals/institutions/organizations, which have access to such knowledge and skills. Technical support is useful only if it helps improve the structures, systems, capabilities and capacities of organizations to achieve their objectives efficiently.

Checklist of Technical Support Activities

- Identify the technical knowledge and skills needed for each area. This has been done as part of the working group recommendations in most of the programme delivery components and institutional arrangements, procurement, financial management and monitoring and evaluation;
- At each level of implementing agencies, identify the key persons involved in programme delivery and support functions;
- Identify and engage the technical support provider (TSP). In case the needed expertise is not available a consortium will be engaged. If needed expertise is not available nationally the identified institution will team up with an external institution that can build capacity of the local TSP;

- Assess the knowledge and skill levels of key persons involved and determine areas where they have to be supported;
- Put together a facilitation team with the right mix of knowledge, skills and experience. Prepare the training materials modulated to the identified needs and guidelines on how the learnings will be transferred to the institutions/agencies work to achieve the outputs planned for; and
- Document and evaluate the technical support content, systems and effectiveness for mid-course correction.

These need a combination of traditional and innovative techniques of technical support. Technical support will be provided by:

- Identified institutions with expertise in the field;
- Agencies which have implemented successful interventions;
- Community based organisations or NGOs with close links in the community; and
- Individual consultants.

They will be engaged based on TORs developed from tasks identified above. The criterion will be expertise of key personnel and past work done in the area.

Facilitation of Technical Support

Institutions and agencies that need technical support the most are often the ones least likely to accept it. Generating demand for and facilitating provision of technical support is the task of NACO and SACS. This will be done by NACO and SACS. The steps involved are:

- Participative identification of technical support needs for each component;
- Assisting the agency/organisation being supported to identify the technical support provider (TSP), contracting and orienting the TSP;
- Working with the TSP in assessing the current capacities and technical support needs of the organisation and preparing a costed workplan;
- Timely approval of the workplan;
- Facilitating and monitoring implementation of the work plan and trouble shooting; and
- Participative evaluation of technical support.

Financing of Technical Support

During NACP-III, all development partners working in HIV/AIDS have agreed to contribute to the national response based on the national PIP. Development partners will be persuaded to move from direct implementation to facilitation of implementation by NACO, SACS, NGOs and CBOs. Main component of this facilitation will be providing technical support to implementing partners. It is expected that most of the technical support needs will be met by funding from development partners. Should such support not be forthcoming TSPs will be funded from the budget.

Operational Plan for Technical Support

Component - I

No.	*Component*	*Technical competency needed*	*Agency to be provided TA*	*No. of mandays of TA anticipated yearly*	*Year*				
I.	**Saturation of Coverage of HRGs through Targeted Interventions**				2006	2007	2008	2009	2010
1.i	Participatory Mapping	Skills for involving HRG members in mapping	NACO	30	30				
			SACS	32 *15		24*15	8*15		
		Skills in participatory mapping	NGOs/ CBOs	200*6		150*6	50*6		
1.ii	Components of Targeted Interventions and Prioritization	Innovative strategies for working with HRG population	NACO	60	15	30	30		
1.iii	Creating an Enabling Environment	Advocacy skills	NACO	60	30		30		
			SACS	32*30	8*15	24*15	16*15	16*15	
		Empowering communities for advocacy	SACS	32*30		8*15	30*15	16*15	10*15
1.iv	Increased Ownership of Civil Society (NGOs, CBOs, PLHA Networks)	Policy and programme changes in developing community ownership	NACO	15	15				
			SACS	32* 10		24*10	8*10		
		Handholding of CBOs	CBOs	125* 5		50*5	50*5	25*5	

(Contd...)

1.1	**Scaling up of Interventions among General Population**								
1.i	Increasing Awareness through Communication, Community Mobilization and Advocacy	Communication needs assessment and development of communications strategy	NACO	75	30	15	15	15	
			SACS	32*45		32*15	32*15	32*15	
		Evaluation of communication efforts	NACO	30			15		15
			SACS	32*30			31*15		32*15
1..ii	Assured Safe Blood and Blood Products	Developing district level packages for safe transfusion	NACO	10	10				
			SACS	32*10	24*10	8*10			
			DPCU	600*5		100*5	300*5	200*5	
1..iii	Improved Access to Quality Condoms	Social marketing of condoms	NACO	60	30	10	10	10	
			SACS	32*30	32*15	32*10	30*5		
1..iv	Expanding HIV/AIDS Response in the World of Work	Designing and managing interventions in place of work	NACO	15	15				
			CII/FICCI/ASSOCHAM	3*5*30		3*5*15	3*5*10	3*25	
1.v	Focused Efforts on Migrants, Mobile Populations and Populations in Cross-border Areas	Designing and building capacities to manage source to destination projects	NACO	60	30	15	15		
			Agency for managing migrant support	240		120	60	60	

Component - 2

No.	*Component*	*Technical competency needed*	*Agency to be provided TA*	*Number of mandays of TA - anticipated yearly*	*2006*	*2007*	*2008*	*2009*	*2010*
2	**Improved treatment access for Opportunistic Infections and continuum of care**								
2.i	Quality of ART Services	Developing ART protocols	NACO	60	60				
		Evaluation and revision of protocols	NACO	30			30		
		Evaluating impact of patents and preparation of advocacy packages	NACO	60	30		30		
2.ii	Establishing Paediatric ART services	Developing ART protocols	NACO	30	30				
			National technical support agency	30	30				
2.iii		Evaluation and revision of protocols	NACO	30			30		
			National technical support institute	60			60		
2.iv	Strategy for management of ART drug resistance	Protocols for drug resistance surveillance	National reference laboratory	60	30		30		
			Regional reference laboratory	4*30	4*15		4*15		
		Laboratory analysis of drug resistance	National reference laboratory	120	60	30	30		

(*Contd...*)

2.v	Financing of ART drugs	Alternate financing strategies for second line ART	NACO	30		30			
		Advocacy package for inclusion of ART in current financing strategies	NACO	20			20		
2.vi	Integration of Prevention with Care, Support and treatment								
2.vii	Greater focus on women, children	Strategies to integrate AIDS prevention and management in SHG functioning	SACS	16* 30		6*30	10*30		
2.viii	Children Infected and Affected by HIV/AIDS	Developing strategies and advocacy packages to support children orphaned and affected by AIDS	NACO	30		30			
			SACS	12*30			8* 30	4*30	
			NGOs	60*15			40*15	20*15	
2.ix	Community care and support programme	Developing strategies for community and home based care	NACO	60		30	30		
			SACS	12* 30		8*30	4*30		
			PLHA/ NGOs	150* 10		25*10	100*10	25*10	
2.x	Collaboration with PLHA networks	Capacity building of PLHA networks at state and district level	INP+	30		30			
			State networks	15* 30		10*30	5*30		
2.xi	Improving the quality of life of PLHA by reducing stigma and discrimination	Developing strategies for reduction of stigma and discrimination	NACO	30	30				
			SACS	15* 30		10*30	5*30		
			PLHA networks	15*10		5*10	10*10		
2.xii	Impact mitigation and linking livelihood support	Strategies for livelihood support for HIV infected and affected families	NACO	30					
			SACS	12*15		6*15	6*15		

Component – 3

No.	*Component*	*Technical competency needed*	*Agency to be provided TA*	*Number of mandays of TA - anticipated yearly*	*2006*	*2007*	*2008*	*2009*	*2010*
3.i	Capacity Development of NACO, SACS, District AIDS Control Units	Management issues of NACP III	NACO	500	150	100	100	100	50
			SACS	38* 300	38* 100	38*50	38* 50	38*50	38*50
			DAPCU	200*250	200* 100	200*50	200*40	200*40	200*20
3.ii	Mainstreaming (Government Departments/Agencies and other public sector institutions)	Strategies for mainstreaming in 15 government departments	NACO	15 * 10* 2	15*10		15*10		
			SACS	32* 15 * 10		16*15*10			
3.iii	Coordination and partnerships with donors, stakeholders and interest groups (private sector, voluntary & faith based groups, CBOs, professional bodies & other civil society	Developing strategies for incorporating HIV prevention and control into corporate and private sector	NACO	30		30			
			SACS	32* 15		8*15	24*15		
			Industry associations	4*30		2*15	2*15		

Component 4:

No.	*Component*	*Technical competency needed*	*Agency to be provided TA*	*Number of mandays of TA - anticipated yearly*	*2006*	*2007*	*2008*	*2009*	*2010*
4	**One Nationwide Strategic Information Management System (SIMS), monitoring and evaluation system**								
4.i	Sero-Surveillance	Developing and revamping sero-surveillance system	NACO	75	30	15	15	15	
		Quality control of sero surveillance	NACO	450	100	100	50	50	50
4.ii	Behavioural surveillance survey	Designing the BSS	NACO	180			100		80
		Support to states for conduct of BSS	SACS	32*30			32*15		32*15
		Analysis of BSS data	SACS	32 * 30			32*15		32*15
			NACO	60			30		30
4.iii	Improving Evidence Based Strategic Planning, Program Management Capabilities (District, State and National Levels)	Developing a national strategic information system	NACO	120	60	20	20	20	
		Redesigning the software for support to MIS	NACO	180	100	20	20	20	20
		Developing software for generating management reports from MIS	NACO	140	60	20	20	20	20
4.iv	Evaluations	Methodologies for impact evaluation	NACO	280	160		80		40
4.v	Research and Development, Knowledge Management and Dissemination	Biomedical and clinical research on HIV/AIDS	NACO	60	20	20	20		
		Epidemiology of HIV/AIDS	NACO	60	20	20	20		
		Economics of HIV/AIDS	NACO	60	20	20	20		
		Social and behavioral research on HIV/AIDS	NACO	60	20	20	20		

Annexure - 10

Role & Function of NACO, SACS & District Unit

	Thematic component	*NACO*	*SACS*	*DAPCU*
1	Targeted Interventions	▪ Develop protocols for identification of groups at risk, prioritising of interventions, interventions modalities ▪ Advocacy for supportive legal and policy regime for TIs ▪ Identify national and regional institutions for technical support and capacity building ▪ Monitor performance of states on TIs ▪ Conduct impact assessment	▪ Map the number and locations of at-risk population and prioritise sub populations and sites for interventions ▪ Identify NGOs to manage the interventions ▪ Contract a project management unit ▪ Build the capacity of NGOs to manage the project and provide facilitative supervision ▪ Conduct annual evaluations of TIs ▪ State level advocacy for supportive environment ▪ Handhold the creation of CBOs and facilitate their gradual take over of interventions	▪ Facilitate access to AIDS prevention and treatment services, general health services and other entitlements ▪ Create a supportive environment for TIs to function
2	Women, Children and young adults	▪ Develop protocols for integrating HIV prevention and care interventions to existing programme for women, children and young adults ▪ Advocacy with national departments and development partners to integrate HIV programmes into their work	▪ State level advocacy with departments and organisations dealing with women, children and adolescents	▪ Working with district level departments for prevention, treatment and impact mitigation on women, children and adolescents

(Contd...)

3	Migrants, Trafficked Persons & Populations in Cross-border areas	▪ Develop guidelines on working with the population groups ▪ Commission studies to identify source and destination sites of migrants and trafficked persons ▪ Assist and provide linkages between SACS/DAPCU in source and destination areas to develop source to destination migrant projects ▪ Interact with neighbouring nations to check trafficking and to deal with vulnerabilities of cross border migration	▪ Develop source to destination interventions, in partnership with other SACS ▪ Take measures to prevent trafficking into and out of their areas	▪ Provide pre departure guidance to migrants and provide linkages to organisations in destination areas
4	HIV/AIDS Response in the World of Work	▪ Develop protocols on HIV Intervention in the place of work ▪ Advocate with ministries, industry associations and national trade unions for support to work place interventions ▪ Identify national and regional institutions for capacity building and technical support	▪ Identify industries or clusters where interventions in work place can be initiated ▪ Persuade employers to adopt the place of work interventions ▪ Train resource persons ▪ Monitor implementation of the programme	▪ Facilitate access to treatment and prevention services for referrals from interventions
	Package of Services	▪ Develop protocols and guidelines for each ingredient of the package of services ▪ Identify national and regional institutions for capacity building and technical support ▪ Procure the drugs, consumables and equipments that fall into national procurement ▪ Set up and monitor the EQAS ▪ Evaluate impact of interventions	▪ Identify institutions and services providers to locate each component of package of services ▪ Build capacity of service providers ▪ Procure items not made available by NACO and manage supply chain of all items ▪ Monitor offtake of services and take remedial action	▪ Monitor the delivery of services ▪ Manage the integration of services with the general health system and other non health interventions ▪ Collect and forward samples for EQAS

(Contd...)

5	Assured Safe Blood and Blood Products	▪ Develop national standards for blood banking and prevention of hospital acquired infections ▪ National level procurement of equipments and test kits ▪ Identify national and regional institutions for technical support ▪ Monitor the availability of blood in states	▪ Assess the need for blood and blood components in the state and plan for the needed blood banks, component separation units and storage centres ▪ Create infrastructure needed for new centres ▪ Manage procurement and supply chain ▪ Build capacity of blood bank medical officers and technicians ▪ Train providers on rational use of blood ▪ Provide technical support to states to develop district system to ensure availability of blood.	▪ Develop a district wise information and transportation scheme to provide blood and blood components to Blood Storage Centres ▪ Systematise voluntary blood donation ▪ Deal with infrastructure issues of new blood banks ▪ Monitor disposal of hospital waste
6	Condom Programming	▪ Identify national and regional social marketing agencies ▪ Develop strategies on social marketing including pricing and subsidies ▪ Procure condoms for free supply and social marketing ▪ Track the off take of condoms	▪ Management of the supply chain of condoms ▪ Integration of service providers with social marketing agencies ▪ Tracking of condom use and preventing wastage ▪ Quality control of condoms	▪ Monitor availability of condoms at service provision point
7	Communication and Social Mobilization	▪ Identify national and regional institutions for capacity building and technical support ▪ Develop generic messages ▪ Monitor the quality of messaging in states ▪ Manage national IEC and mobilisation campaigns	▪ Conduct Communication needs assessment and develop state level communication strategies ▪ Plan and manage state level IEC campaigns ▪ Coordinate with service providers for demand generation for services	▪ Conduct district level IEC campaign ▪ Use local channels for demand generation ▪ Work with PRI institutions and local CSOs for social mobilisation for HIV prevention and management

(Contd...)

8	Mainstreaming with Public and Private Sector	▪ Advocacy and technical support to mainstreaming HIV in central departments ▪ Advocating with national level organisations of private sector	▪ Advocacy and technical support to mainstreaming HIV in state level departments	▪ Technical support to district level organisations to integrate HIV in their functions ▪ Provide linkages to HIV services in to district departments and organisations
9	Convergence with RCH, TB and other MOHFW	▪ Devise common operational guidelines with concerned divisions	▪ Issue guidelines and orders on convergence	▪ Work with concerned programme officers to effectively integrate their functions
8	Mainstreaming with Public and Private Sector	▪ Advocacy and technical support to mainstreaming HIV in central departments ▪ Advocating with national level organisations of private sector	▪ Advocacy and technical support to mainstreaming HIV in state level departments	▪ Technical support to district level organisations to integrate HIV in their functions ▪ Provide linkages to HIV services in to district departments and organisations
10	Civil Society Partnership forum at National, State and District levels	▪ Develop guidelines on institutional arrangements for civil society partnership forum and their participation in decision making bodies ▪ Support the formation and functioning of national civil society forum ▪ Build the capacity of office bearers of state and national civil society forum ▪ Provide national civil society partners forum with plans and progress reports	▪ Support the formation and functioning of state level partners forum ▪ Build the capacity of office bearers of district civil society partners forum	▪ Support the formation and functioning of district civil society partners forum
11	Improved access to treatment for opportunistic infections and continuum	▪ Develop ▪ protocols on management of OIs ▪ Identify institutions for capacity building and technical support ▪ Develop protocols for EQAS for OI laboratory diagnosis ▪ Track the pattern of OIs	▪ Procure drugs for management of OIs ▪ Build capacity of service providers	▪ Monitor the management of OIs

(Contd...)

12	Increasing the number of PLHA on anti-retroviral drugs	▪ Procure drugs and diagnostic equipments and consumable needed for ART ▪ Train PLHA networks on demand generation for VCTC and ART services ▪ Mobilise resources and negotiate with government departments and pharma companies for price reduction	▪ Manage the logistics of drug supply chain ▪ Train PLHA on assisting others on accessing treatment	
13	Providing care support and treatment for children infected and affected with HIV/AIDS	▪ Develop national protocols for treatment of Paediatric ART ▪ Set up diagnostic facilities to support paediatric ART ▪ Negotiate with ministries and pharma companies to reduce the prices of paediatric formulations ▪ Procure paediatric formulations ▪ Identify and train national and regional institutions for capacity building and technical support ▪ Advocate with ministries and other organisation working on child entitlements to protect the rights of HIV infected and affected child.	▪ Build the capacity of service providers to manage paediatric ART ▪ Put in place systems for forwarding samples to the diagnostic facilities ▪ Advocate with state departments and organisations dealing with child welfare to protect the interests of HIV infected and affected child ▪ Monitor instances of alienation of rights of HIV affected and infected children	▪ Monitor children born to sero positive mothers for early signs of the need for ART ▪ Monitor and investigate any instance of denial of rights to HIV infected and affected children ▪ Advocate with district authorities and organisations to protect the rights of children
14	Ensuring Quality of ART Services	▪ Develop protocols on treatment and laboratory services ▪ Develop training manuals ▪ Identify national and regional institutions for capacity building and technical support ▪ Identify and train National Reference Laboratories and regional reference laboratories for EQAS of ART lab services ▪ Develop systems for accreditation of ART providers	▪ Monitor the quality of ART services being provided by the public and private sector ▪ Train PLHA networks on monitoring of service quality of ART	
15	Management of ART drug resistance	▪ Develop protocols on drug resistance monitoring ▪ Contract national and regional institutions for resistance testing ▪ Train the trainers ▪ Organise training and modify guidelines on monitoring and ART practices	▪ Train practitioners on identifying, monitoring and managing drug resistance ▪ Develop systems for collection and transportation of samples for resistance monitoring ▪ Disseminate guidelines on resistance	▪ Arrange for transportation of samples

16	Innovative Financing of ART drugs	▪ Develop generic schemes for alternate financing of ART drugs ▪ Provide technical support to states to develop proposals ▪ Approve proposals ▪ Evaluate and arrange for dissemination of good practices	▪ Develop state specific proposals for alternative financing ▪ Develop linkages with organisations to support alternate financing mechanism ▪ Support PLHA networks or other decentralised bodies to manage financing mechanisms	
17	Strengthening community care and support programs	▪ Develop guidelines and protocols to management Community Care Centres ▪ Approve proposals for setting up new centres	▪ Identify new centres ▪ Assess project proposals ▪ Monitor and evaluate functioning of CCCs	▪ Establish referral linkages to service providers ▪ Monitor functioning of approved centres
18	Linking care, support and treatment with prevention	▪ Developing guideline on integrating prevention with care interventions and vice versa ▪ Develop training modules on integration ▪ Build capacity of state level programme managers for integration	▪ Monitor interventions on integration ▪ Incorporate integration into training of both prevention and treatment programme personnel	▪ Monitor integration
19	Impact mitigation	▪ Advocacy with national government, national and international organisations ▪ Support to national networks of infected and affected persons	▪ State level advocacy with government departments, social welfare organisations for support to affected families ▪ Capacity building of PLHA networks to access support for affected persons ▪ Redressal of complaints regarding denial of entitlements	▪ Set up linkages with district level organisations and departments for support to PLHA and their families ▪ Facilitate access of PLHAs to social support
20	Monitoring Systems	▪ Develop and review indicators ▪ Upgrade CMIS software to allow entry of data from all partners and newly developed programmes. ▪ Develop protocols to combine technical. logistic and financial program monitoring ▪ Create standardized reports ▪ Reviews the programme at state and national levels.		

(Contd...)

21	Evaluation	▪ Annual evaluation of inputs and processes at state and national level ▪ Mid term and end of project evaluation of outcomes ▪ Technical support to States ▪ Dissemination of results	▪ Input and process evaluation of implementing partners at state and district level	
22	Surveillance	▪ Develop protocols for HSS and BSS ▪ Procure test kits ▪ Train resource persons ▪ Ensure quality of collection and testing of samples ▪ Analyse data and disseminate results	▪ Identify state level institutions ▪ Procure consumables ▪ Train personnel ▪ Make arrangements for collection and forwarding of samples ▪ Analysis of state level data	▪ Oversee collection and forwarding of samples
23	Operations Research	▪ Approve OR proposals ▪ Contract agencies for conduct of OR ▪ Disseminate results ▪ Modify policy and programmes based on OR findings	▪ Identify areas for OR in the state ▪ Conduct OR approved by NACO	
24	Capacity building	▪ Identify and contract national and regional institutions for capacity building ▪ Develop training modules and materials ▪ Compile annual training calendar ▪ Conduct training effectiveness evaluation	▪ Arrange for training of resource persons for district level training ▪ Adapt and translate training materials ▪ Oversee state level trainings	▪ Conduct district level trainings

Key functions of NACO:

- *Technical:* Developing national protocols, capacity building and technical support to manage the protocols, and monitoring quality and compliance to the protocols.
- *Policy and Planning:* National strategic planning, response tracking, mainstreaming and partnerships, International collaborations and Global obligations, special initiatives, legislation, facilitation of decentralised response.
- *Strategic Information:* Sentinel Surveillance, Knowledge management, Research, Synthesis of data at national level.
- *Finance and Administration:* Resource Mobilisation and management, procurement, human resources, contract management, Secretariat to the apex level bodies.

Key functions of SACS:

- *Technical:* Capacity building, problem solving, technical support to implementing partners, quality assurance.
- *Policy and Planning:* Advocacy, strategic and implementation planning, state level initiatives, mainstreaming and partnerships.
- *Monitoring and Evaluation:* Analysis of data and application to programme management, state level studies, impact evaluation.
- *Finance and Administration:* Management of finances, state level resource mobilisation, logistics, local procurement, recruitment, infrastructure, coordination with implementing partners.

Key functions of DAPCUs:

- Developing district implementation plans, implementing and monitoring components of implementation plans, partnership with civil society and facilitating creation of enabling environment.

Annexure - 11

List of Indicators

KEY PROGRAMME INDICATORS

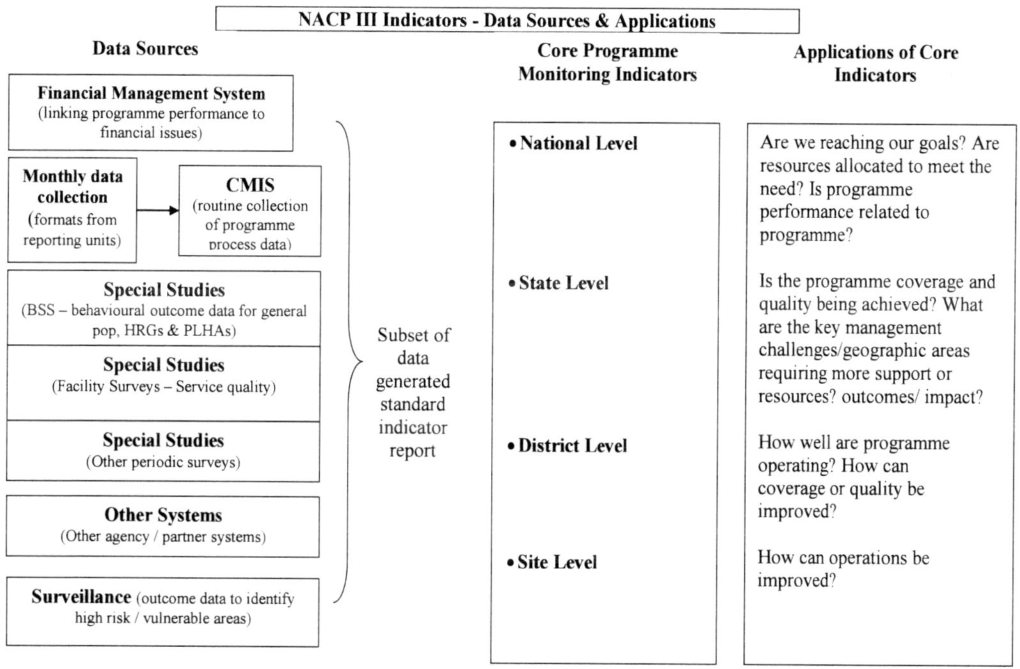

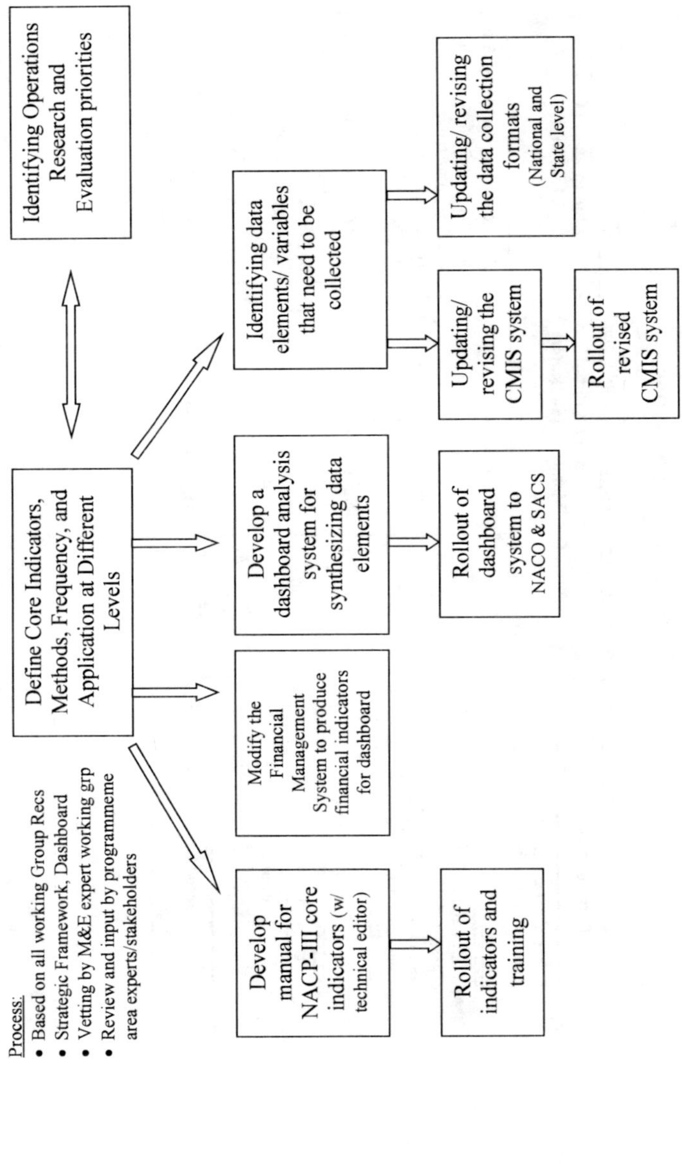
Process:
Based on all working Group Recs
Strategic Framework, Dashboard
Vetting by M&E expert working grp
Review and input by programmeme area experts/stakeholders
Define Core Indicators, Methods, Frequency, and Application at Different Levels
Identifying Operations Research and Evaluation priorities
Develop manual for NACP-III core indicators (w/ technical editor)
Rollout of indicators and training
Modify the Financial Management System to produce financial indicators for dashboard
Develop a dashboard analysis system for synthesizing data elements
Rollout of dashboard system to NACO & SACS
Identifying data elements/ variables that need to be collected
Updating/ revising the CMIS system
Rollout of revised CMIS system
Updating/ revising the data collection formats (National and State level)

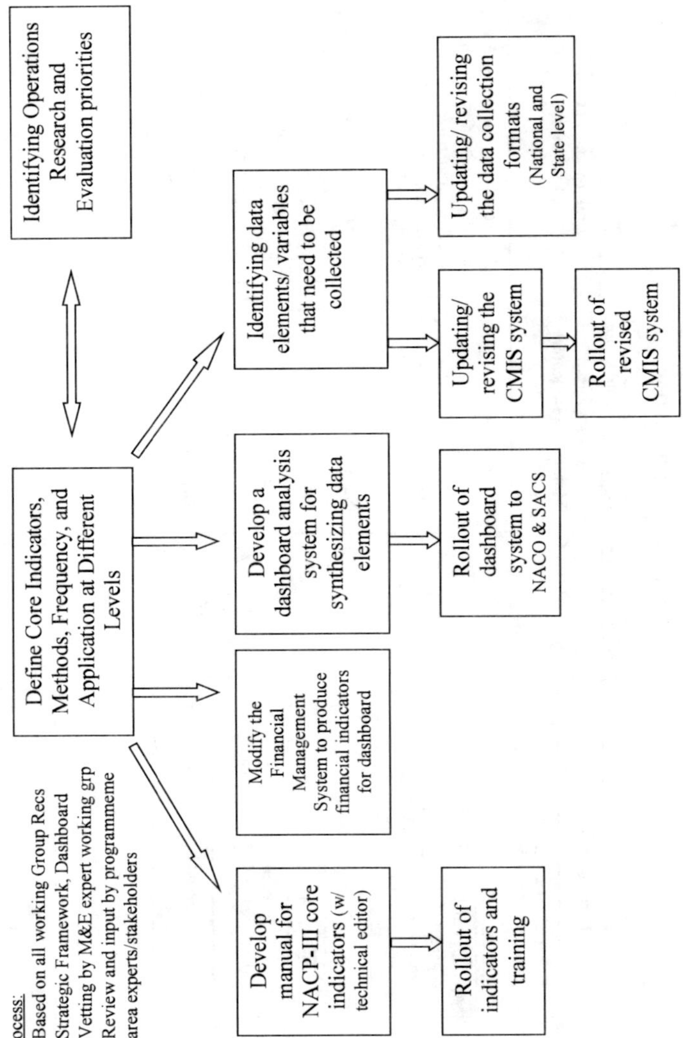

Sl. No.	List of Indicators – by components (Note: phased achievements are relative to targets set)	Programme Targets (NACP-III)	Level of Analysis: N- National S - State D - District	Data Source for Indicator Information	Frequency of Indicator Generation	Current status of indicator Y – being generated N- not being generated	Comments
1	**Prevention and Enabling Environment**						
1.1	**Preventive interventions for HRG (Targeted Interventions)**						
1.	Percentage of districts which have updated HRG mapping data.		S	CMIS	Annually	N	
2.	No. & Percentage of specific HRG population reached by intervention. **FSW**: 45% in 2005 to 100% in 2011 **MSW**: 10% in 2005 to 100% in 2011 **IDU** (needle exchange): 40% in 2005to 100% in 2011 **MSM**: 10 % in 2005 to 100% in 2011.	Sex workers: 1 million (=80% of estimated FSW) MSM: 0.235 million (=80% of estimated high risk MSM) IDU (needle exchange): 1.9 lakhs (=80% of estimated IDU)	N / S / D	CMIS	Quarterly	Y	
3.	Percentage of IDU population reporting use of safe equipment in the last month (clean needles – UNGASS(C) 8.		N/S	BSS for HRG	Once in 3 years	Y	
4.	Percentage of IDU reporting use of condoms at last sex – UNGASS(C) 8.		N/S	BSS for HRG	Once in 3 years	Y	
5.	Percentage of female and male sex workers reporting use of condoms with their most recent client – UNGASS (C) 6.		N / S	BSS for HRG	Once in 3 years	Y	
6.	Percentage of men reporting use of condoms in the last time they had anal sex with a male partner – UNGASS (C) 7.		N / S	BSS for HRG	Once in 3 years	Y	
7.	Percentage of truckers reporting use of condoms with last non-regular partner.		N/S	BSS for truckers	Once in 3 years	Y	
8.	Percentage of FSW, MSM, general pop men with STI symptoms seeking services from qualified medical providers.	80% among those with STI symptoms	N / S	BSS of HRG and general pop men	Once in 3 years	N	
9.	percentage of NGOs engaged in TIs providing or linking to basic AIDS care and support		N / S / D	CMIS	Quarterly	N	NEW Programme issue. Indicator may require adjustment.

10.	Numbers of needles and syringes distributed to IDUs.		S / D	CMIS	Monthly	N	
11.	Percentage of TIs implementing quality interventions (as defined by standard service quality assessment tool).		S / D	SS	Annual		
12.	Percentage of TI projects reporting no interference from local power structures in this month.		S / D	CMIS	Monthly	Y	
13.	Proportion of high risk groups and bridge populations reached through BCC activities during the reporting period*.		S / D	CMIS	Quarterl y	Y	
14.	Percentage/List of STI clinics for high risk groups reporting stock out of essential STI drugs.		S / D	CMIS	Monthly	N	
15.	Number of HRG PLHA in TIs who receive ARV treatment.		S	CMIS ART center	Quarterl y	N	
16.	Number of targeted interventions where CBOs are formed.		S / D	OR	Annual	N	Model of transferring ownership to be evaluated through OR.
17.	Number of SACS, DACS and NGOs who have members of HRGs on their decision making bodies.		S / D	SS	Annual	N	
1.2	**Interventions for Vulnerable Populations (women, children, adolescents, migrants, trafficked persons, and workers.**						
	a) Women						
18.	Increase in the number of women who access HIV services (VCT/STI/PPTCT/ART).		Refer to previous indicators				
19.	Budget amount for HIV programmes for vulnerable populations by women, children, adolescents, migrants, and workplace.		N/S	Budget Review / PFMIS	Annual	N	New Programme area. May be difficult to separate funding.
20.	Percentage of women's self help groups/ women's org who have trained peer educators on HIV.		S/D	SS	Annual	N	New Programme area, indicator may be modified.

	b) Youth						
21.	Percentage of youth with accurate knowledge of HIV/AIDS (who recall 3 modes of transmission, 2 modes of prevention and who reject major misconceptions about HIV transmission) – UNGASS(G) 10.		N/S	BSS among Youth	Once in 3 years	N	
22.	Median age at first sex among young men and women.		N/S	BSS among Youth 15-24	Once in 3 years	N	New programme area. Need to ask among 15-20 for current status.
23.	Percentage of youth in high prevalence/ high priority districts using youth friendly information centres/ youth-friendly. health services in their town/district		S/D	SS	Monthly	N	Explore MIS of Dept. of Youth
	c) Workers						
24.	Percentage of workers who have access to information and services on HIV/AIDS at their work place (by formal and informal sectors). from 5% in 2005 to 100% in 2011.	30 million workers with access to information/ services at work	N/S	BSS in Gen Pop	Once in 3 years	N	New programme area. Indicator may be modified
25.	Percentage of formal employers who have HIV workplace policy and provide HIV prevention and care services to their employees.		S	SS by CII	Once in 2-3 years	N	Industrial Partners
	d) Migrants						
26.	No. & Percentage of High risk men reached by intervention. **Truckers:** 50% in 2005 to 100% in 2011.	Truckers: 3 million (=100% of estimated truckers)	N/S/ D	CMIS	Quarterl y	Y	
27.	No. of migrants covered through migrant vulnerability reduction programmes from 10% in 2005 to 100% in 2011.	150 million	N/S	CMIS	Quarterl y	N	New Programme area, indicators to be modified according to programme.
28.	Key information on migrants and migration included in existing survey/surveillance systems.		N/S	Compilation from NFHS; NSS; Census		N	New Programme area.
29	% of migrants with accurate knowledge of HIV/AIDS (who recall 3 modes of transmission, 2 modes of prevention and who reject major misconceptions about HIV transmission).		N/S	BSS of migrants	Once in 3 years	N	

30.	Identification of priority in and out migrant districts/villages (criteria for prioritization to be proposed by experts).		S/D	SS	Annual	N	Census; ANM records;
1.3	**Package of Services**						
(a)	**STI**						
31.	Percentage of general population males with STI seeking treatment from qualified personnel.		(See TI section)				
32.	Percentage/List of STI Clinics providing good quality services (as defined by standard service quality assessment tool).		S/D	SS	Annually	Y	Health Facility Survey
33.	Percentage/List of clinics reporting a stock out of essential STI drugs.		S/D	CMIS	Monthly	Y	
34.	Percentage/List of clinics reporting stock out of condoms.		S/D	CMIS	Monthly	N	
35.	Percentage of STI clinic patients receiving laboratory services. From 5% in 2005 to 100% in 2011.	2 million (= number of STI cases w/ lab tests)	S/D	CMIS	Quarterly	Y	
36.	Percentage of partner referrals- refers to any sexual partners of STI patients attending clinics.		S/D	CMIS	Monthly		
37.	Reduction in prevalence of most common STIs (Syphilis, Gonococci, Chlamydia, HSV, Candida and Bacterial Vaginosis) by 30% of the baseline by 2011.		S/D	CMIS	Annual	Y	
(b)	**VCTC**						
38	No. of service outlets providing VCTC.		N/S/D	CMIS	Annually	Y	
39.	No & % of persons receiving pre and post test counseling by age and gender, HRG member.		N/S	CMIS	Monthly	Y	
40.	No. of persons who got tested at VCTC by age, gender, and HRG member.		N/S	CMIS	Monthly	Y	
41.	No. of persons who return for test report at VCTC- by age, gender, HRG member, and by HIV status.		N/S	CMIS	Monthly	Y	

42.	No. and % of persons who test positive by age, gender, and HRG member.		N/S	CMIS	Monthly	Y	
43.	No. of persons seeking VCTC who are referrals from DOTS centers.		N/S/D	CMIS	Monthly	Y	
44.	Percentage of FSW, MSM, and IDU who received HIV testing in the last 12 months and who know their results – UNGASS (C) 3.		N/S	BSS among HRGs	Once in 3 yrs	N	
45.	Percentage of FSW, MSM, IDU who are HIV infected – UNGASS (C) 9.		N/S	AHSS	Annually	N	
46.	% of Community Health Centres & PHCs with both PPTCT and VCTC facilities.		S/D	CMIS	Annually	N	
47.	% of VCT reporting inadequate quantities of HIV test kits.		S/D	CMIS	Monthly	Y	
48.	No. of HIV positive persons referred to ART centre		S/D	CMIS	Monthly	N	-
49.	Percentage testing positive getting their partner for testing.		S/D	CMIS	Monthly	N	
(c)	**PPTCT**						
50.	Percentage districts providing PPTCT services		N/S	CMIS	Annually	Y	
51.	No. of service outlets providing PPTCT services.		N/S/D	CMIS	Annually	Y	
52.	Percentage of pregnant women receiving HIV counseling from 11% in 2005 to 100% in2011	22 million	N/S	CMIS	Monthly	Y	
53.	Percentage of pregnant women being tested for HIV and collecting test results (each is separate indicator)		N/S	CMIS	Monthly	Y	
54.	% of women in PPTCT/ANC who are HIV positive		N/S	CMIS	Monthly	Y	
55.	No. & % of HIV infected women receiving a complete course of ARV prophylaxis. From 20% in 2005 to 100% in 2011.	80000	N/S	CMIS	Monthly	Y	Modified from "infected mother baby pairs"
56.	No. & % of infants of HIV + mothers knowing their status by 18 months.		N/S	CMIS	Monthly	N	New programme area. Indicator may be modified.

57.	% of infants born to HIV infected mothers who are infected.		N/S	SS as done for ART	Annually		New programme area. Indicator may be modified.
58.	Number of HIV positive mothers referred to ART center.		S/D	CMIS	Monthly	N	-
59.	Percentage of women in PPTCT/ANC referring their partners for testing.		S/D	CMIS	Monthly		
(d)	**Post Exposure Prophylaxis**						
60.	Percentage of health providers who access PEP within 24 hours of exposure.		S/D	SS	Quarterly	N	
1.4	**Condoms**						
61.	Percentage of persons reporting consistent use of condoms with non regular partners in the last 12 months – (last time - UNGASS (G) 13.		N/S	BSS of Gen Pop	Once in 3 years	Y	
62.	Number of condoms distributed by social marketing programmes.	2 billion per year	N/S	NIHFW	Annually		
63.	Number of commercial condoms (fully priced) sold.		N/S	Retail Audit	Annually	N	Need to define commercial condoms.
64.	No. of free condoms distributed through TI – VCT – STD Clinics – From 10% in 2005 to 100%.	1 billion per year	N/S	CMIS	Monthly	partly	
65.	No. of female condoms socially marketed and distributed free.		N/S	Retail Audit	Annual	N	
66.	Percentage of persons reporting availability of condoms within 15 minutes of walking distance.	To 95% in urban and 80% in rural areas from the existing levels of 78% and 41% respectively (of home / sex)	S	BSS	Once in 3 years	Y	New programme area, indicator may be modified.
67.	Percentage increase in the number of non traditional outlets for condoms (75% of all non traditional).		S	Retail Audit	Annual	N	
1.5	**Blood Safety**						
68.	Percentage of HIV transmission through blood transfusion. target: <0.5%.		N/S	SS	Monthly	Y	New indicator. Indicator may be modified.

69.	Proportion of blood units collected through voluntary blood donation. From 52% in 2005 to 100% in 2011.	90% of all blood units	N/S	CMIS	Monthly	Y	
70.	Percentage of blood being processed into components.		N/S	CMIS	Quarterly	N	Formats need some modification
71.	No. of Blood Component Separation Units established (total).	244	N	CMIS	Annual	Y	Formats need some modification
72.	No. of Plasma Fractionation units established (total). From 1 in 2005 to 4 in 2011.	4	N	CMIS	Annual	N	Formats need some modification
73.	Percentage of health providers who access PEP within 24 hours of exposure.		S/D	SS	Quarterly	N	
1.6	**Communication and Social Mobilization**						
74.	Percentage of general pop with accurate knowledge of HIV/AIDS (who recall 3 modes of transmission and 2 methods of prevention and who reject major misconceptions about HIV transmission) by urban vs. rural.		N/S	BSS of Gen Pop	Once in 3years	Y	
75.	Percentage of schools with Adolescent Education Programme w/ teachers trained and who have used the curriculum in the last academic year. – UNGASS(G) 3. From 50% in 2005 to 100% in 2011	150,000	N/S	Ministry of Education	Quarterly	Y	
76.	Percentage of students covered under School AIDS programme. From 30% in 2005 to 100% in 2011	25 million	N/S	CMIS	Quarterly	Y	
77.	Percentage of out of school youth reached by HIV awareness programme From 10% in 2005 to 100% in 2011	70 million	N/S	BSS among out of school youth	Once in 3 years	N	
78.	Percentage of village health committees/ panchayats engaged in TI programmes		S/D	SS	Annually	N	
79.	Percentage increase in media coverage on HIV/AIDS issues (sexuality/legal issues).		S	Press & TV Audits	Annually	N	

2	**Care, Support and Treatment**						
80.	Total No. of HIV+ people in million.	4.735 million	N/S/D	AHSS and modeling	Annual	Y	May not be possible in all districts
81.	Total no. of children (0-14 years) with HIV. From 1.7 lakh in 2005 to 1.4 lakh in 2011.	1.7 lakhs	N/S/D	SS	Annual	N	
82.	No. of HIV+ diagnosed as immune compromised. From 0.411 million in 2005 to 0.379 million in 2011.	0.38 million	N/S	AHSS, modeling, SS	Monthly	Y	
2.1	**Improved treatment access for OIs & continuum care**						
83.	No. of service outlets providing treatment for OI.		N/S/D	CMIS	Annual	Y	
84.	Number of PLHA access OI treatment at PHC/CHC/ District hospital/ CCC/Medical college by gender.		S/D	CMIS	Monthly	N	
85.	Number of PLHA (in VCT or ART) who were (a) referred to DOTS; (b) positive for TB; (c) are on TB treatment.	Referred from ART: 30 lakhs	N/S/D	CMIS	M	N	
86.	Number of doctors trained in OI management – as a separate course or as part of other training programmes.		N/S	CMIS	Quarterly	Y	
2.2	**Increased no. of PLHA on ART**						
87.	No. of service outlets providing ART services by public/private.		N/S	CMIS	Annually	Y	
88.	No. & % of eligible PLHA (by CD4 count) currently receiving ART – by age (including children), gender, and public/private centers – UNGASS (G) 7.		N/S	CMIS	Monthly	Y	
89.	% of persons put on ART who report (95%) adherence at the end of 12, 24, 36 months (by age including children and gender).		N/S	CMIS	Monthly	Y	
90.	No. & % of persons still alive and on ART at 12, 24 and 36 months after initiation of ART (by age including children and sex).		N/S	SS	Monthly	Y	

91.	Number of doctors trained in ART management – as a separate course or as part of other training programmes.		N/S	CMIS	Quarterly	Y	
2.3	**Establishing Pediatric ART services**						
92.	No. & % of children eligible (by CD4 count) receiving ART – by age and gender.		N/S	CMIS	Monthly	Y	
93.	Number of NGOs involved with provision of care and support to affected children. From 2 % in 2005 to 100% in 2011.	1.2 lakhs	N/S/D	CMIS	Quarterly	N	
94.	No. of children requiring ART. From 38.98 in 2005 to 33.57 in 2011.	39 thousand	N/S/D	SS	Quarterly	N	
2.3 .1	**Quality of ART Services**						Criteria developed based on accreditation standards
95.	No. & % of ART centres having linkages with NGOs/CBOs for community outreach and home based care.		N/S	CMIS	Annual	Y	
2.3 .2	**Surveillance of ARV drug resistance**						
	Initiation of at least 5 regional units for resistance monitoring by end of 2006.		N			N	
	No. of newly infected that have resistant strains.		N	SS			
2.3 .3	**Financing ART drugs**						
	Number of PLHA participating in saving schemes.		N/S	SS	Once in 2yrs	N	New Programme Area, indicator may be modified.
	Number of PLHA accessing ART with support from alternate financing systems.		N/S	SS	Once in 2 yrs	N	New Programme Area, indicator may be modified.
2.4	**Integration of Prevention with Care, Support and Treatment**						
96.	No. of New Life Centres established.		N/S	CMIS	Annual	N	Will need to add PLHA networks to CMIS

97.	No. of 'Sathi' clinics and CHCs linked with 'New Life centres' supporting positive living.		N/S				
98.	No. of PLHA enrolled in a district network. From 10% in 2005 to 100% in 2011.	2.8 lakhs	S/D	CMIS	Quarterly	N	
99.	No. of districts with a network for positive people by new and old registrants.		S/D		Annual		
2.5.1	**Children Infected and Affected by HIV/AIDS**						
100.	No. of infected and affected children linked to child welfare scheme.	1.2 lakhs	S/D	CMIS	Monthly	N	Through NGOs
2.6	**Community care and support programmes**						
101.	No. of service outlets providing community care. From 90 CCCs in 2005 to 500 CCCs in 2011.	500 CCCs	N/S/D	CMIS	Quarterly	N	
102.	Number of PLHAs (and their family members) receiving services from NGOs/CBOs –excludes CCC by gender and age.		S/D				
2.7	**GIPA**						
103.	Number of decision making bodies at national, state, and district levels and NGOs working in the field of HIV having PLHA representatives.		N/S	SS	Twice in 5 yrs	N	
2.8	**Stigma and Discrimination**						
104.	Increase in the number of reporting of instances of stigma and discrimination.		N/S	Press/ TV Audit	Monthly	N	
105.	Percentage increase in PLHA accessing social and community services and educational services without discrimination.		N/S	SS	Twice in 5 years	N	
2.9	**Human Rights, Legal and Ethical Issues**						
106.	AIDS legislation adopted and ratified by 2007		N	Review		N	
107.	Amendment of laws such as NDPS Act, ITPA and Section 377 of the IPC by 2007		N	Review			
108.	Reduction in number of reported cases of police harassment of TI outreach workers.		N/S/D	CMIS	Monthly	N	

2.10	**Laboratories**						
109.	No. of labs participating in EQAS in a year.		N/S	CMIS	Annual	N	New Programme Area, indicator may be modified.
3.0	**Programmme Management**						
110.	No. of district units established. From 0 in 2005 to 606 in 2011.	606 DAPCU	S/D	CMIS	Annual	N	
3.1	**Capacity Strengthening**						
111.	No. and proportion imparted induction and refresher training – for blood banks, labs, facilitators for workplace interventions, counselors, doctors, technicians and nurses in VCTC and PPTCT centres and PHCs/CHCs trained , SIM staff, and ART staff.		N/S/D	CMIS	Monthly	N	
3.2	**Mainstreaming**						
112.	No. of Ministries with a budget line on HIV prevention and control.		N/S	SS	Annual	N	New Programme Area, indicator may be modified.
113.	Number of states having a donor coordinating committee.		N/S	SS	Annual	N	New Programme Area, indicator may be modified.
4.0	**Strategic Information Management Systems**						
114.	Percentage of reporting units (75%) reporting timely. Timely: refers to receipt of reports within 3 months of due date.		N/S/D	CMIS	Quarterly	Y	
115.	No. of states with 70% completion of district data analysis sheets.		S/D	CMIS	6 monthly	N	
116.	No. of SACS generating a report every quarter which includes (i) monitoring indicators (ii) findings of the ongoing evaluation.		N	CMIS	Quarterly	N	
117.	Number of States conducting at least two key intervention evaluations per year.		N/S	SS	Annual	N	
118.	NACO conducting one participatory programmematic and one scientific/analytical evaluation every three years.		N	SS	Annual	N	

119.	No. of states with timely annual ANC HIV reporting according to standard protocol		N	AHSS	Annual	N	
120.	No. of sero-surveillance sites established. From 600 in 2005 to 1200 in 2011.	1200	N/S	AHSS	Annual	Y	
121.	Number & proportion of all sentinel sites meeting the minimum quality standards i.e 70% usable samples of their quota.		N/S	AHSS	Annual	Y	
122.	Proportion of districts with M&E staff in place.		S/D	CMIS	Annual	N	
123.	Percentage of budget spent for M&E at national, state and district level.		N/S/D	FMIS	Quarterly	N	
124.	No. of State PDs conducting: a) quarterly review meetings including a review of M&E information; b) engaging partners in the review meeting; c) providing feedback on performance and reporting.		N/S	SS	Annual	N	Based on review of minutes of meeting
125.	Number and proportion of partners sharing information with SACS.		N/S	CMIS	Annual	N	Includes info for CMIS plus others like BSS
126.	Availability of M&E guidelines and tools* (CMIS manual, CMIS software, Sentinel Surveillance Guidelines) at all levels, of at least 70% levels. **Tools, at various levels to be defined, indicator has to be refined.*		N/S/D	CMIS	Annual	N	
127.	Number of districts/SACS using programme data to develop annual action plan.		N/S	SS	Annual	N	Scrutiny of the annual action plan
4.1	**Research**						
128.	Increased allocation of funds for research in NACP - III as compared to NACP – II.		N/S	SS	Annual	N	
129.	NACO website created for online sharing and disseminating research data and reports.		N	Review of website	Annual	N	

130.	No. of research conferences organized for knowledge sharing, dissemination and programme development.		N/S	SS	Annual	N	
131.	Number of research agencies collaborating with NACO/ SACS.	25	N/S	SS	Annual	N	
132.	Number of papers based on NACO programme data or NACO sponsored research published in peer reviewed journals.		N	SS	Annual	N	
133.	No. of research projects completed at the national/regional level. From 5 in 2005 to 15 in 2011	15 per annum	N/S	SS	Annual	N	
134.	No. of district level risk assessment studies. From 0 in 2005 to 606 in 2011	606 per annum	S/D	CMIS	Annual	N	

Programme Indicators for each type of Facility e.g. VCTCs, ART Centres, blood banks etc.

In addition to the above indicators, following programme indicators will be generated for each type of facility

- Proportion of the facilities that have the sanction for the requisite staff (e.g whether VCTCs have the sanction of counsellors, etc.).
- Proportion of key sanctioned positions filled (e.g doctors, nurses, counselors, etc.).
- Proportion of key staff having received relevant training in the past 3 years.
- Aspects related to infrastructure and equipment viz. functional status of key. equipments, availability of essential space for counseling, etc.
- Proportion of facilities with critical level of stocks of key drugs and kits.
- Turnaround time for test results.
- Extent of optimal resource utilization i.e doctors vs patient ratio, machine vs. test ratio, etc.

Annexure - 12.1

Procurement Plan

PROCUREMENT PROPOSALS (Out side the Pool)														
														Annex 12.12
				Year Wise Procurement (value in Lakhs of Rs.)										
Sl. No.	*ITEM CATEGORY*	*Total Qty.*	*Unit Cost*	*18 Months*		*6 Months*		*Year 3*		*Year 4*		*Year 5*		*Grand Total*
		(Nos.)	*(Rs.)*	*Qty*	*Value*	*Qty*	*Value*	*Qty*	*Value*	*Qty*	*Value*	*Qty*	*Value*	
	DRUGS													
1	ARV Drugs			16500		6000		13500		15000		16500		67500.00
	infection (as per **Annex 12.3)**													
	SUPPLIES													
2	CONDOMS													
	Male (Qty in Billions)	13.75	1.3	1.75	22750	2.25	29250	3	39000	3.25	42250	3.5	45500	178750
	Female (Qty in Millions)	18	43	1	430	3	1290	4	1720	5	2150	5	2150	7740
									Grant Total					**253990.00**

Annexure - 12.2

Governance and Accountability Action Plan (GAAP) for NACP-III

Introduction

NACO, Ministry of Health and Family Welfare (MOHFW) is fully committed for ensuring better competition and transparency in procurement and supply of health sector goods and services required for delivery of quality services in all its programs. An Empowered Procurement Wing (EPW) has been established in MOHFW to support this process. To strengthen the capacities of the EPW in all aspects of procurement, the Department for International Development (DFID) is funding Technical Assistance.

Scope and Purpose

NACO, MOHFW has developed this Governance and Accountability Action Plan (GAAP), in consultation with the pooling partners (the Bank, DFID and UNFPA), to address critical operational concerns in Bank and pooled partner funded procurement of health sector goods and services. The key issues and actions to address these concerns are included in the matrix below.

The GAAP applies to NACP Phase–III supported by the Bank and other pooling partners, articulating the specific roles and responsibilities of different stakeholders (public, private and civil society institutions) in ensuring timely supply of quality commodities at a competitive price.

The GAAP will be strengthened, as necessary, based on risks identified and the recommendations of the RCH I investigations, the DIR, the procurement review by the EPW consultant, and the report on the quality and quantity of pharmaceuticals and medical goods.

The Bank financed "Food and Drugs Capacity Building project (Credit No. 37770)" would also support some of the broader issues related to strengthening of regulatory institutions especially effective implementation of GMP in the pharmaceutical sector as envisaged under the GAAP.

Issue	***Agreed actions***	***By when***	***Person/agency responsible for implementation***
I. Improving quality assurance mechanism	• Implement the quality assurance mechanism agreed to by MOHFW (listed below) *i) Making WHO GMP (TRS 863) certification mandatory for ICB* *ii) Pending new certification procedures (see next bullet) ensuring 100% post certification of all successful bidders recommended for award of the contract on the basis of existing WHO GMP certificates.* *iii) Agreeing on actions for GMP certification process and implementation arrangements satisfactory for pooling partners for non-ICB procurement of pharmaceuticals and medical supplies under pooled financing.*	• Agreed, to begin from project effectiveness • Agreed, to begin from project effectiveness • *Implementation will start from first Bank financed project after the date of this plan* • Completing the agreed actions and incorporating recommendations from the detailed implementation review in the GAAP will make non-ICB procurement eligible for pooled financing.	• NACO, MOHFW (to co-ordinate for SACS and act as nodal point)

Issue	*Agreed actions*	*Implementation Status*	*Person/agency responsible for implementation*
II. Increasing competition and mitigating collusion	• Finalizing future lot size, estimated prices and qualification criteria for procurement of pharmaceuticals and medical supplies based on market surveys about availability of products, prices and production capacities of manufactures.	• Agreed and to begin from project effectiveness. • Based on toolkit developed by the Bank, DFID has awarded the contract for market surveys for pharmaceuticals and the results from first round are expected by August, 2006.	1.NACO & MOHFW (to co-ordinate for SACS and act as nodal point)
	• Including a qualification requirement of minimum share of at least 20% revenue to be derived from non-Bank financed contracts in bid documents.	• Agreed and to begin from project effectiveness.	
	• Seeking "list of references" in the form of an affidavit in case of supplies made to public sector in past contracts. In the case of supplies made to private sector in the past, affidavit as well as supporting evidence will be sought. However, no bid would be rejected on the basis of non submission of documents on past performance above referred to.	• Agreed and to begin from project effectiveness. • NACO/SACS will verify the authenticity of referred documents on past performance only for the successful bidder.	
	• Including "independent experts" in the bid evaluation process.	• Agreed and to begin from project effectiveness.	
	• Sharing record of public opening of bids for all contracts with the Pooling Partners within 2 working days.	• Agreed and to begin from project effectiveness.	
	• Ensuring payment within 30 working days of receiving the bill with supporting documents from the suppliers or communicating deficiency in the Bill within 15 working days.	• Agreed and to begin from project effectiveness.	
	• Establishing clear and concise bid evaluation criteria.	• Agreed and to begin from project effectiveness.	

Issue	*Agreed actions*	*Implementation Status*	*Person/agency responsible for implementation*
III. Strengthening procurement implementation and contract monitoring	• Strengthening procurement capacity at NACO and SACS, including engagement of an external consultants, if necessary, for capacity building and development of procurement monitoring and complaints database.	• The procurement capacity at NACO to be strengthened for more effective monitoring of procurement and supply chain management, before loan negotiations • Procurement arrangements at SACS to be reviewed and strengthened suitably before NCB procurement is commenced by SACS	• NACO & MOHFW (to co-ordinate for SACS and act as nodal point)
	• Establishing a "procurement monitoring and complaints" database* to monitor adherence to the standards listed in Procurement Manual. This database would be online with restricted access.	• Manual database established in MOHFW and computerized database is expected by March, 2007. • NACO/SACS to follow the same format.	
	• Developing and deploying a software for the early identification of indicators of fraudulent or corrupt practices	• Software at MOHFW to be developed by July 1, 2008. • NACO/SACS to use the same software.	

* The database should specifically allow: (i) complete and adequate record keeping and retrieval of all documents supporting each bid including unit prices quoted and prices at which contracts are awarded; (ii) Quantities and dates of supply as per the contract and actual; (iii) Rejection of supplies, if any, with reasons; (iv) Date bill received, value, and date of payment and (v) complaints received, responses sent and actions taken by dates.

Issue	*Agreed actions*	*Implementation Status*	*Person/agency responsible for implementation*
IV. Handling procurement complaints	a) Updating the "Procurement monitoring and complaints" database on a monthly basis.	• Manual database established in MOHFW and computerized database to be operational by March, 2007 • NACO/SACS to follow the same database format	• NACO & MOHFW (to co-ordinate for SACS and act as nodal point).
	b) Listing and discussing all complaints received and actions taken in the bid evaluation report.	• Agreed and to begin from project effectiveness.	
	c) Providing details of the administrative process for the disqualification of bidders who engage in misrepresentation in the bid process or in contract execution	• Agreed and to begin from project effectiveness.	
	d) Reporting the status of investigation of complaints and measures taken in monthly progress reports to the Sercertary (Health & Family Welfare)	• Agreed and to begin from project effectiveness.	
	e) Sharing complaints status with the pooling partners once every quarter	• Agreed and to begin from project effectiveness.	

Issue	*Agreed actions*	*Implementation Status*	*Person/agency responsible for implementation*
V. Disclosing Information and promoting oversight by the civil society	a) Making publicly available all annual procurement schedules for ICB and NCB promptly after finalization on the NACO website.	• Agreed and to begin from project effectiveness.	• NACO & MOHFW (to co-ordinate for SACS and act as nodal point).
	b) Posting all bidding documents and requests for proposals (RFP) for all procurements above US $ 100 000 on the NACO website.	• Agreed and to begin from project effectiveness.	
	c) Making available to any member of the public promptly upon request all shortlist of consultants and in case of pre-qualification, list of pre-qualified contractors and suppliers.	• Agreed and to begin from project effectiveness.	
	d) Disclosing information on prequalification, all bids received reasons for rejections, and award of contracts at the NACO website and sharing the same with the pooling partners to disclose at their preferred Websites.	• Agreed and to begin from project effectiveness.	
	e) Posting annual progress and Mid Term Review reports of the program on the NACO website.	• Agreed and to begin from project effectiveness.	
	f) Moving to e-procurement	• Will be developed under the Bank supported E-Bharat project.	

Annexure - 12.3

List of Std Drugs

Essential STI Drugs	*Primary Indication*	*No. of tablets per course*	*Alternative STI Drugs*
Acyclovir 400 mg tablets	Genital herpes (HSV-2)	21 for first episode 15 for recurrent infection	
Azithromycin 1 gram tablets	GUD (chancroid) Ureathal Dischage, cervicitis (chlamydia)	1 tablet	Doxycycline 100 mg tablets or Erythromycin 500 mg tablets
Benzathine penicillin 2.4 million IU intramuscular injection	GUD (syphilis) Reactive syphilis test	1 vial	Doxycycline 100 mg tablets or Erythromycin 500 mg tablets
Benzyl benzoate 25% lotion or Gamma benzene hexachloride 1% lotion or cream	Scabies, pubic lice	100 ml pack	Permethrin 5% cream
Cefixime 400 mg tablets	Ureathal Discharge, cervicitis-gonorrhea lower abd. pain Scrotal swelling	1, [exception lower abdominal pain & scrotal swelling(14)}	Ceftriaxone 250 mg intramuscular injection
Clotrimazole 500 mg vaginal pessaries or Fluconazole 150 mg tablets	Vaginal candidiasis (fluconozole is also recommended treatment for oral and esophageal candidiasis)	1	Clotrimazole 1% cream or Miconazole 2% cream Miconazole 100 mg vaginal pessaries Nystatin 100,000 IU vaginal supp.
Doxycycline 100 mg tablets	Alternative treatment for chlamydial infection or syphilis	14 to 30 (42 in scrotal swelling syndrome)	
Erythromycin 500 mg tablets	Alternative treatment for chlamydial infection or syphilis (pregnant women)	20 to 56	
Metronidazole 400 mg tablets	Bacterial vaginosis, trichomoniasis	5	Tinidazole 500 mg tablets (optional)
Podophyllin tincture 20%	Genital warts (*Condylomata acuminata*)	Local applicant to be applied under supervision	Trichloroacetic acid 80 to 90%